Black Nationalism

A Search for an Identity in America

Black Nationalism

A Search for an Identity in America

E. U. ESSIEN-UDOM

THE UNIVERSITY OF CHICAGO PRESS

Chicago & London

The University of Chicago Press, Chicago 60637
The University of Chicago Press, Ltd., London

© 1962 by The University of Chicago. All rights reserved. Published 1962
Sixth Impression 1971. First Phoenix Edition 1971
Printed in the United States of America

ISBN: 0-226-21851-1 (clothbound); 0-226-21853-8 (paperbound)
LIBRARY OF CONGRESS CATALOG CARD NUMBER: 62–12632

TO My Parents
and to Gil, Ruby,
and Windom

There is no sense in hate; it comes back to you; therefore, make your history so laudable, magnificent and untarnished, that another generation will not seek to repay your seeds for the sins inflicted upon their fathers. The bones of injustice have a peculiar way of rising from the tombs to plague and mock the iniquitous.

MARCUS GARVEY

Preface

The tragedy of the Negro in America is that he has rejected his origins — the essentially human meaning implicit in the heritage of slavery, prolonged suffering, and social rejection. By rejecting this unique group experience and favoring assimilation and even biological amalgamation, he thus denies himself the creative possibilities inherent in it and in his folk culture. This "dilemma" is fundamental; it severely limits his ability to evolve a new identity or a meaningful synthesis, capable of endowing his life with meaning and purpose.

This book is about the phenomenon of black nationalism in the United States — the effort of thousands of American Negroes to resolve for themselves this fundamental problem of identity and to provide a context for their moral, cultural, and material advancement within the limits set by the American scene. The book describes the ideology of black nationalism, its organizations, leaders, and programs, focusing on the Nation of Islam — a Muslim movement led by Elijah Muhammad. It attempts to explain not only the behavior of the black nationalists, but also the meaning and significance of the movement for the participants and for the society as a whole.

The study was made over a period of two years during which the writer participated continuously in the religious, social, and, to a limited extent, business activities of the Muslims in Chicago. He attended two Muslim Annual Conventions in Chicago and interviewed ministers and lay Muslims from other cities on many occasions. He observed the meetings of other black nationalist organizations in Chicago and New York City, and discussed their objectives and programs with members. He learned the "ways" of the Negro lower class in Chicago's Black Belt; in addition, he spent considerable time at many Negro civic, social, and religious activities in Chicago. Aside from these two years of formal and systematic study of black nationalism, his interest in the Negro problem in America extends from 1952 to the present. He lived in the Black Belt most of these years, as well as on the campuses of Oberlin College, Ohio, and the University of Chicago. Although these experiences by themselves are not sufficient reasons for broad generalizations about the Negro problem, they gave a sense of the general mood of the northern Negro community. Consequently, aside from the formal method of collecting data, the writer learnt a great deal which, here and there, accounts for, and to some extent justifies, his observations outside the scope of the present study.

The method of study consisted primarily of observation and informal discussions with Muhammad, his officers, and followers in Chicago. During this time, the writer kept an intensive file of notes taken during meetings and interviews and of newspaper clippings on the movement. He studied the publications of the movement, including some earlier literature which is kept under lock and key at the University of Islam or which was lent to him by the Muslims. In addition, he had access to some publications and directives which are available only to "registered" Muslims. Minister Malcolm X of the New York Temple, who has been described as the "Nation's Ambassador at Large," proved to be of great assistance concerning the ideological questions and administrative problems posed by the movement.

Two separate attempts were made to secure personal data on the mobility and social aspirations of the Muslims in Chicago. The first was a carefully structured interview focused on the attitudes of the Muslims about their past and present condition and perspective. About sixteen Muslims were reached who had the time and the interest to subject themselves to such interviews in depth. Although the material obtained from so few persons was insufficient for evaluation of their newly acquired ethos, it is used in this study as illustrative material rather than as a basis for generalizations about the Muslims as a group. The second approach was a questionnaire aimed at securing personal data on members. The Muslims, apparently directed by the officers at the Temple, failed to respond. Consequently, five hundred copies of a twelve-page questionnaire prepared at considerable expense were utterly wasted. Only four Muslims returned them. The difficulty of studying the group lies partly in its lack of appreciation of the "scientific" value of the information they would provide. Partly, it lies in their deep-seated suspicion of the outsider. The Muslims' sense of persecution and fear of the so-called "enemy" thus makes their co-operation difficult to secure. Sometimes, they simply do not know what information is permissible from the point of view of those in authority. Suspicion, fear, and the apparent atmosphere of secrecy which surrounds the movement made it difficult for the writer to secure exact data on its membership and its finances. The figures reported in this study were obtained indirectly. The writer believes, however, that checking and cross-checking has made them reasonably accurate.

The first chapter is concerned with the cultural and psychological dilemmas of Negroes, the consequences of their caste status, and the developing class consciousness within the caste itself. Chapter II sketches briefly the tradition of Negro nationalism and the influences on Negro thought and social action which are not nationalistic in the narrow sense of the word, but which incorporate some elements of messianism. Chapter III is an account of the rise, growth, and leadership of the Nation of Islam and its expansion into a nation-wide movement. This is followed by a chapter which explores the reasons why Negroes join and remain in the movement, the meaning and significance of the movement for its members, and the patterns of behavior of the Muslims resulting from their commitment to the movement. The remaining chapters describe the ideology, organization, programs, and limitations of the Muslim movement. The conclusions follow.

* * * * *

The contribution of many persons to this book cannot be recorded fully. Since I can name only a few, I hope that others unnamed will not feel my gratitude toward them wanting. However, I am deeply indebted to my friend and teacher, Professor Edward C. Banfield, whose untiring guidance, encouragement, patience, and comprehension of my difficulties made this book possible. I profited immensely from the counsel and insights of Professors Charles M. Hardin, Edward A. Shils, and Myron Weiner, all of whom read the drafts of the manuscript at one stage or another. Gilbert F. Williams and Max Hall read the manuscript and offered valuble suggestions. Miss Alice M. Windom typed two drafts of the manuscript; I am deeply indebted to her. Others who assisted or gave me notable encouragement throughout the period of this study are: Messrs. E. Mungai Nduru and Evelyn O. Chiseley, Attorney W. Robert Ming, Jr., and Mr. and Mrs. Sidney Williams. The dedication is but a partial acknowledgment of the contribution made by my wife, Ruby. Needless to say, I am solely responsible for the views and shortcomings of the book.

It will become clear that I have drawn a great deal from published and unpublished works of other scholars. I have recorded my debt to them in both the text and the bibliography.

This book would have been much less than what it is without the active co-operation of the Honorable Elijah Muhammad and his followers. My association with them was very cordial and rewarding. Mr. Muhammad and his wife, Sister Clara Muhammad, were particularly courteous toward me. They invited me to dine with them on several occasions, and Mr. Muhammad made it possible for me to see him as frequently as his busy schedule permitted. Minister Wallace D. Muhammad and Mr. Akbar Muhammad, Mr. Muhammad's sons, were very helpful to me. Minister James 3X (Anderson), Mr. Muhammad's assistant in Chicago, gave me inestimable assistance and co-operation. I am especially grateful to the staff of the University of Islam, in Chicago, and recall with deep feelings of kinship and friendship their courtesies and regard for me. I should also express my thanks for the very significant help I received from Mr. Muhammad's chief lieutenants: Minister Malcolm X (Little), New York; Supreme Captain Raymond Shar-rieff; Brothers Charles Betha (and his wife), John W., Kwamenr, and Vernon; and Sisters Mildred, Margarett, Edith, June, Nellie, Susan, and Velora. I wish to thank all the Muslims whose names space does not permit me to list. Needless to say, they are absolved from any responsibility for my views or interpretations. I am also grateful to leaders and members of other black nationalist organizations in Chicago and New York for their co-operation.

E. U. Essien-Udom

Harvard University
Cambridge, Massachusetts

Contents

Illustrations

The Negro Dilemma

I.

> The question, then, is posed whether this unparalleled alienation and our partial entrance into what is termed the mainstream of American life precludes our exploration of our identity as a minority of African descent and our recourse to the African heritage as a fructifying source of our creative endeavor.
>
> SAMUEL W. ALLEN [*]

A CENTURY after the Emancipation, nineteen million black Americans, robbed of their traditions and of a pride in their past, are still seeking acceptance by the white majority but are continuing to live in semibondage on the fringes of American society. They are groping for a way out of this dilemma, but no way is clear, certain, or easy.

Few middle- and upper-class Negroes [1] have escaped the cultural subordination and degradation of the Negro masses. Some have striven to become "white middle class," believing and acting as if they were exempt from the open contempt in which whites hold their race. Their world view and philosophy is a naive individualism. The road to success for the majority of them lies in trying to escape psychologically from their identity as Negroes and in practicing an unmitigated opportunism.

[*] *The American Negro Writer and His Roots* (New York: American Society of African Culture, 1959), p. 14.

[1] For a most illuminating study of the Negro middle class, see E. Franklin Frazier, *Black Bourgeoisie* (Glencoe, Ill.: Free Press, 1957).

1

Until the early part of this century, most Negro leaders and many individuals among the first generation of educated Negroes proudly styled themselves "race men" who were above all concerned with reconstructing the economic, moral, and cultural life of their people. Today, however, such a reference is not only shunned but repudiated. The identification of middle-class Negro leaders with the masses of their race has grown increasingly tenuous and weak. They appear no longer to be seeking the dignity and the integrity of their race in America, but rather the political rights of Negroes as American citizens — a valuable goal but only one aspect of the Negro's experience and goals in American life.[2] The bonds of race which bind them to the masses are increasingly loose and involuntary. They are no longer the leaders of their race, for they have arrived, i.e., gained entrance into white middle-class society.[3] They cannot, however, take the millions of other Negroes along with them. They reject and despise the Negro masses, whom they deem responsible for what they know to be a continuing rejection by the whites, into whose society they are not really assimilated.[4]

White middle-class society, in reality, is not, and for a long time to come may not be, open to the millions of black Americans. But, in fact, neither is Negro middle-class society open to them. The inferior material and cultural standards of the Negro masses prevent them from entering either society. Their economic status, their moral habits, and the image they have been given of themselves, condemn them to live and die trapped in the Negro ghettos of the urban centers of America. In all probability, most will remain members of the lower class, despised by white and Negro middle-class

2. For a good discussion of "race values" and "race ends" among Negroes, see James Q. Wilson, *Negro Politics: The Search for Leadership* (Glencoe, Ill.: The Free Press, 1960), chap. XIII, "Goals of Negro Leaders." See also Gunnar Myrdal, *An American Dilemma* (New York: Harper, 1944) for the ambivalences in Negro behavior concerning "race ends"; Frazier, *op. cit.*, pp. 216 ff.; R. Kinzer and E. Sagarin, *The Negro in American Business: The Conflict Between Separation and Integration* (New York: Greenberg, 1952); St. Clair Drake and Horace Cayton, *Black Metropolis* (New York: Harper, 1945), pp. 716–54.

3. The term "white middle class" is used here as the norm of individual social attainment in the United States.

4. We do not deny that there is greater social mobility among Negroes at the present time than in any other time in their history. In fact, it is for this reason that class distinction within the Negro group is acquiring new social significance. It makes the disparity obvious between the "fortunes" of the lower classes and those of the middle and upper classes.

society alike. The overwhelming objective limitations placed on their cultural, economic, and political aspirations make it impossible for them to escape from their community; they cannot wish away their racial identity. Whether they view it positively or negatively, they cannot be indifferent to it. It is the stuff of their lives and an omnipresent, harsh reality. For this reason the Negro masses are instinctively "race men."[5]

This feeling of being "race men" as opposed to racists is an inarticulate but common one among the Negro masses. It was particularly exemplified in the lives and teachings of the Negro leaders of the nineteenth and early twentieth century, for these men identified themselves with, and were continuously involved in, the fate of the Negro masses without developing a racist ideology. The intelligentsia of the present, however, have lost touch with this concept in their concern over the legitimate importance of integration. In their anxiety not to appear racist in their thinking, they have repudiated all racially conscious movements and organizations, but at the same time, they find themselves, because of this repudiation, powerless to move the Negro masses toward their professed goals. Their attempt to be at once Negro and non-Negro is an insoluble dilemma. To some extent it accounts for their disdain and rejection of the black nationalist movements.[6] It also explains their failure to appreciate the as yet imprecise and conflicting yearnings of the Negro masses for racial definition and integrity.

The nationalist leaders contend that the Negroes must become consciously aware of their identity as a group in America; they must realize their degradation and strive by individual and collective effort to redeem their communities and regain their human dignity. The Negro masses, unlike the middle and upper class, are seeking a way out of a sociocultural environment, a spiritual and psychological impasse, fostered by the stubbornly lingering mores of slavery and complicated during the present century by the urban-

5. Cf. David Riesman, *Faces in the Crowd: Individual Studies in Character and Politics* (New Haven: Yale University Press, 1952), p. 91.

6. For attitudes of middle-class Negro leaders and intellectuals toward the Garvey movement, the only truly nationalist movement among American Negroes during the twenties, see Edmund D. Cronon, *Black Moses* (Madison, Wisc.; University of Wisconsin Press, 1957), pp. 113 ff.; Frazier, *op. cit.*, pp. 121–23.

ization of American society. The vast majority of black Americans, however, do not know how to liberate themselves. They look forward to that day when they will find themselves in the "promised land" without making any effort to bring it about.

This book attempts to record the striving of thousands, and perhaps unrecorded millions, of American Negroes to reclaim for themselves and their group the normal self-pride and confidence which their history in America has denied them. It is an account of their struggle to recover, even to reconstruct, a world in which they can enjoy an unashamed sense of identity and to vindicate their honor as black Americans.

The focus of the study is the Nation of Islam, a movement led by Georgia-born Elijah Muhammad, who is known to his followers as the Messenger of Allah and whom they believe to be divinely chosen and divinely inspired to unite American Negroes under the Crescent of Islam. In the early nineteen-thirties, the Nation of Islam was led by Prophet W. D. Fard, who is said to have come from Arabia. His organization first concentrated on Detroit Negroes and gained an estimated membership of perhaps 8,000 during the critical years of the depression. Late in 1933 he disappeared and Elijah Muhammad became the leader of the movement. Prophet Fard is acknowledged by Muhammad and his followers as the Mahdi. He is "Allah in the Person of Master Wallace Fard Muhammad."[7] (The Mahdi occupies the same position of Messiahship in Islam as the person of the Christ in Christianity.) Between 1934 and 1946 Elijah Muhammad also organized followers in Chicago, Milwaukee, and Washington, D. C. Prophet Fard's initial success in Detroit, however, was not matched at that time by comparable successes in any other large city. In fact, in 1942, when Muhammad and his followers were indicted and imprisoned for violations of the Selective Service Act, the total membership of the movement came to only a few hundred. Today, it is estimated at a quarter of a million, and followers are organized in twenty-one states and the District of Columbia.[8]

7. The title "Mr." preceding the present leader's name distinguishes him from "Allah in the Person of Wallace Fard Muhammad," for whom the title "Master" is reserved.

8. Membership has been estimated variously by the following publications: at 70,000 (*Time*, August 10, 1959, p. 25); at 200,000 (*Sepia*, November, 1959, p. 21).

The movement is organized about Temples, each known as "Muhammad's Temple of Islam."[9] By December, 1959, there were said to be fifty such Temples in various parts of the United States. Each Temple is under the direction of a minister who is directly responsible to Muhammad. The present study is based on an intensive examination of Muhammad's Temple No. 2, in Chicago, which was established in 1934 and now has a regular membership of nearly 1,000 adults. It functions also as the headquarters — "the Mecca" — of the movement.

For more than two decades the Nation of Islam was a small, highly secretive group known to few Negroes. Its activities and influence expanded immensely during the years 1954–61, however, and Muhammad now bids openly for the allegiance of the Negro masses of the country. His name is widely known among Negroes, not only because of the activities of the Muslims,[10] but also because of weekly columns which he writes for nationally circulated Negro newspapers; and he has also come to public notice through alarmist white newspaper, radio, and television publicity. The movement is under police surveillance in every city where there is a Temple, and the Federal Bureau of Investigation is said to have closely watched it for possible subversive tendencies. In 1959 the American white public became aware, to some extent, of this movement's existence and of the name of its spiritual leader. It can be asserted with some confidence that the Nation of Islam is now the most important black nationalist movement in the United States.

Elijah Muhammad claims that "Allah in the Person of Master Wallace Fard Muhammad," or Prophet Fard, confronted him in 1930 and for the following three years explained to him the history and significance of the "Black Nation." He taught Muhammad his beliefs concerning the Caucasian race, the religions of Islam and

Muhammad is quoted in *Time* as claiming a total membership of 250,000. *U.S. News and World Report* notes that "other sources place its size at anywhere from 10,000 to 70,000" (November 9, 1959, p. 112).

9. Renamed "Muhammad's Mosque" in 1960. However, they shall be designated as "Temples" throughout this study, the name by which these organizational units are widely known.

10. Followers of Muhammad profess faith in Islam as they understand it. They refer to themselves as "Muslims." In order to avoid confusion with other believers in Islam who go by the same name but whose creed is different, the English spelling "Moslem" is used to distinguish these other believers from Muhammad's followers.

Christianity, as well as the "truth" about the beginnings of creation, the "impending" destruction of the Caucasian race and its civilization, and the final overthrow of white rule over the black peoples. Furthermore, Allah revealed to him that the United States would be destroyed in 1970. After this apocalypse, the Black Nation — the entire world population of the "black, brown, yellow, and red" races — would emerge as the sole ruler of the world under Allah's benign and righteous guidance.

The Nation of Islam, however, is distinguished from the Black Nation in that it is a chosen people within the Black Nation, elected by Allah as His special instrument for the entire redemption of the Black Nation. In theory the Nation of Islam consists of the Negro population of the United States; but in practice and for the time being, it is confined to the followers of Elijah Muhammad. Muhammad proclaims that his mission on earth is to deliver this message to the "so-called American Negroes," who until the coming of Master W. F. Muhammad had no knowledge of themselves or of their enemy (the Caucasian race and its Christianity), their religion (Islam), or of their God (Allah). For the present he is concerned with organizing them so that they may return to their own religion and their own kind in fulfillment of the covenant which he believes Allah made with their "patriarch," Abraham of the Old Testament. But he is also bent on moral reform and dedicated to the cultural and economic advancement of his followers. Present membership in the Nation of Islam, which is strictly limited to non-whites, consists almost entirely of American Negroes. Belief in Allah and acceptance of Islam as taught by Muhammad are minimum requirements for membership.

The concept of nationalism, which is germane to this study, may be thought of as the belief of a group that it possesses, or ought to possess, a country; that it shares, or ought to share, a common heritage of language, culture, and religion; and that its heritage, way of life, and ethnic identity are distinct from those of other groups. Nationalists believe that they ought to rule themselves and shape their own destinies, and that they should therefore be in control of their social, economic, and political institutions. Such beliefs among American Negroes, particularly among the followers of Muhammad, are here called black nationalism.

It must be admitted at the outset that neither the Nation of Islam nor any other black nationalist organization wholly conforms to this definition. Nonetheless, it may be helpful, in comprehending certain patterns of behavior among the black nationalists, to observe the degree to which they incorporate nationalist symbols, and in remarking deviations from the ideal type. Although black nationalism shares some characteristics of all nationalisms, it must be considered a unique type of separatist nationalism seeking an actual physical and political withdrawal from existing society. Apart from the unifying symbols of race and religion, it employs the heritage of abuse and indignity to which the Negro people in the United States have been subjected and, perhaps more importantly, their common desire for self-improvement. Although most nationalisms involve the idea of race, they are able to develop historically within a definite geographical territory and can therefore easily evoke the common traditions and symbols of that region. The Nation of Islam, however, lacks both a territorial base and the symbolism drawn from either the Negro's past in the United States or from his African origins. This peculiar nationalism has placed its antecedents in what it believes to be "Arabian civilization," the highest development of which was reached in Egypt. It is also extraordinary that its belief in itself as a definite nation of people has produced absolutely no political program for the establishment of a national home. Rather, the final national homeland is guaranteed solely through eschatological beliefs taken from Old Testament prophecies.[11]

The ideas of an eventual return to a national homeland and of black redemption after the apocalypse (the latter a version of the Armageddon of the Book of Revelation) lend the movement two forceful ideological dynamics and inform it with an abstract world view. Both ideas have inspired religious zeal, loyalty to the move-

11. For an excellent discussion of eschatology, see Norman Cohn, *The Pursuit of the Millenium* (London: Secker and Warburg, 1957), p. xiii. In Christian doctrine, the final struggle is to be between the hosts of Christ and the hosts of anti-Christ. In Muhammad's teaching, the struggle is to be between the Black Nation and the Caucasian race — the world of Islam and the world of Christianity.

ment and its leader, and personal sacrifices for the common good. The Muslims' sense of expectancy aids them in persevering and in sustaining their hopes.

However, the religious teachings of Muhammad do not fully explain the behavior patterns of the Muslims. *Esoteric* in nature, centered upon eschatological and apocalyptic hopes, they are too removed from the present realities of the Muslims' lives to account for the sincerity of their daily practices, their ethical and cultural prescriptions. Although extremely important as a psychological factor of unity and hope, they must be distinguished from the *exoteric* teachings of Muhammad, with which they of course interact. The exoteric forms of the religion stem directly from Muhammad's attempt to cope with the social, cultural, and psychological environment in which the Negro finds himself. They offer the believer a set of incentives and a definite discipline which enable him to transcend the common plight and degradation of the Negro masses, and they impart to the movement an active, cohesive, and expanding existence. Foremost among these incentives is the belief that they, the Muslims, are laying the foundation for a nation, even though it is now only a "nation within a nation." Second, they believe that in Islam, and particularly in the Nation of Islam, they now enjoy freedom, fraternity, justice, and equality under their own government. Third, they affirm that their lives have been morally and materially bettered since they accepted Islam as a way of life. As shall be shown in later chapters, this last belief is an immeasurably strong motivation.

Muhammad's exoteric teachings emphasize the techniques for attaining the good life in the "sweet here and now" and not in the "sweet bye and bye." Heaven and hell are thought to be "two conditions on earth which reflect one's state of mind, his moral condition and actions." Knowledge of one's identity — one's self, nation, religion, and God — is considered the true meaning of the Resurrection, while ignorance of it is the meaning of hell. An interplay between the esoteric religious beliefs and the techniques for rising above the environment and attaining the good life has significantly limited the lack of discipline and the other-worldliness which the

Muslims deplore as characterizing the religious life of the Negro masses. Similarly, it serves as an antidote to the intense messianic expectancy which often informs chiliastic movements. The Muslims have gained an enthusiasm for acting together to achieve their ends without necessarily sacrificing the mood of "watchful waiting."

The history of the alienation of Africans from their homeland and of their subsequent subordination and humiliation in the New World for over two centuries is well known. Equally familiar is the contribution of slavery to family disintegration and to cultural disorientation.[12] The result is that Negroes have acquired what appears to be an appalling sense of inferiority and even of hatred for their "Negro-ness." This heritage of slavery, as well as their continuing subjection to abuse and indignity, must be fully recognized and appreciated before the problem which black nationalism seeks to resolve can be understood.

Elijah Muhammad makes his appeal primarily to the urban lower-class Negroes, who are for the most part migrants from southern rural sections where they had been accustomed to a way of life markedly different from that encountered in the city. In common with the white working class, they share the frustrations, anxieties, and disillusionments of contempory urban life; but the Negroes' experience in adjusting to city life is additionally complicated and aggravated by their special status in American society. Black nationalism has its roots in these urban tensions and in the hopeless frustration which the Negroes experience in trying to identify themselves and their aspirations with white society. Compelled by segregation, discrimination, poverty, and ignorance to remain on the periphery of white society and to live and die within the subculture of the Negro ghettos, the Negro masses have had to disassociate themselves from white society. At the same time, however, they are compulsively attracted to it, since power, status, security, even beauty remain white priorities, white possessions. This conflict in Negro thinking is further disturbed by the demand of white society that the Negroes conform to its material, cultural, and moral stand-

12. See E. Franklin Frazier, *The Negro Family in the United States* (Chicago: University of Chicago Press, 1939).

ards while denying them the economic and social resources for so doing. Thus, the burden of a final irony is added to the Negro's dilemma.

White society assumes that the Negro will almost always act in accordance with the stereotypes of Negro behavior which it has evolved. Thus, in its view, the Negro will always act as a paragon of almost supine patience and reasonableness; he will not be subject to the human emotions of hatred, anger, and love, nor of personal and group pride. He will be content with employment which does not challenge his intelligence and which pays him only a subsistence wage; he will be happy to live and raise his family in patently inadequate housing within a congested ghetto; and send his children to schools which add to confusion and frustrations rather than elevating human intelligence, talent, and dignity.[13]

Faced with these stereotypes and rebelling against them because of their untruth and hostile intent, the Negro also unconsciously rejects the standards of the ruling white society which has foisted them upon him. In doing so, he succeeds merely in perpetuating the stereotypes and in incurring the added opprobrium of white society, which sees in this rejection a confirmation of its unflattering views.

This dilemma, so fraught with paradox, is responsible for the attempt by middle-class Negroes to conform in detail to white standards and to separate themselves from the Negro masses. The black nationalists, however, though they too seek to differentiate themselves from the Negro subculture, have eschewed all *rapprochement* with white society.

However, the majority of Negroes accept their "place" in white society and in the Negro subculture as inescapable while at the same time unconsciously rejecting the subculture because of its low prestige, insecurity, and futility. Consequently, most Negroes live and die without ever achieving a unified consciousness of their membership in the Negro community or in the larger American society:

It is a peculiar sensation, this double-consciousness, this sense of always looking at one's self through the eyes of others, of measuring one's soul by

13. Cf. James B. Conant, *Slums And Suburbs: A Commentary on Schools in Metropolitan Areas* (New York: McGraw-Hill Book Company, 1961), pp. 2, 3, 18–27.

the tape of a world that looks on in amused contempt and pity. One ever feels his two-ness — an American, a Negro; two souls, two thoughts, two unreconciled strivings; two warring ideals in one dark body, whose dogged strength alone keeps it from being torn asunder.[14]

The Negro cannot choose both the dominant white culture and his own subculture. This sense of suspension between two societies and of dual membership presents enormous impediments to the process of adjustment. Negroes are involved, subconsciously though it may be, in assertion of membership in one and in denial of membership in the other, or in a feeble assertion of both, or in the denial of their affinity with both. In consequence no Negro "ethos" has developed, no ethnic and institutional loyalty aiding Negroes in pursuing common goals.[15] Involved only peripherally in the American ethos, they are thus only partially inspired by it.

Black nationalists have in general attempted to deal with the problem of the Negro's ethnic identity by insisting that "what the Negro needs" is complete separation from the white majority and the establishment of a national home. Unlike the vast majority of American Negroes, the nationalists maintain that a positive identification with their "Negro-ness," or with their ancestral homeland, is a prerequisite to both personal dignity and effective social action. There is, however, no agreement among them as to what their ethnicity is. They are not even agreed upon a name for themselves. Some prefer "Afro-Americans," others "Aframericans," "Africans Abroad," "Persons of African Descent," "Asiatics," or simply "black people."[16] Thus, when the word "Negro" is used by the Mus-

14. W. E. B. DuBois, *The Souls of Black Folk*, 7th ed. (Chicago: A. C. McClurg, 1907), pp. 3–4.

15. W. G. Sumner defines the word "ethos" as: "the sum of the characteristic usages, ideas, standards, and codes by which a group was differentiated and individualized in character from other groups." *Folkways* (Boston: The Athenaeum Press, Ginn and Co., 1906), p. 36. The writer is especially indebted to Professor Edward C. Banfield's application of this concept in his analysis of an Italian community. See *The Moral Basis of a Backward Society* (Glencoe, Ill.: Free Press, 1958).

16. Although the controversy over the use of the word "Negro" or "colored" is now less frequently voiced, the use of either word in addressing different Negro audiences continues to evoke a lively agreeable or disagreeable emotional reaction. The controversy finds guarded expression in print. See J. A. Rogers, *Africa's Gift to America* (New York: Futuro Press, Inc., 1959). Although Rogers prefers to use all the prevailing names, such as Negro, colored, black, African-American, he has suggested that the "correct" term would be "African-European-American-Indian."

lims, which is rarely, it is qualified by "so-called" or used contemp-tuously to differentiate Negroes not belonging to the movement from themselves. They are also careful about the word "race" because they believe themselves to constitute a "nation." It is the Cauca-sians, they believe, "racing with time," who form a "race."

This lack of consensus about the Negro's ethnicity appears also among non-nationalists. Although the majority of Negroes accept their American nationality and patiently and hopefully await the day when their citizenship will neither be qualified nor left in doubt, there is no consensus as to the terminology by which they wish to be known. They are still ambivalent toward the term "Negro," even though both "colored" and "Negro" are most widely used. The in-tellectuals as well as the ordinary Negroes frequently assert that since there is no complete biological unity within the group, the very term "Negro" is a social rather than a racial classification in the United States.[17]

Some emphasize the fact that historical circumstances have made Negroes a "nation within a nation," and have evolved an indige-nous "Negro culture" based upon their experiences in America or on their African origin, or on both.[18] Dr. W. E. B. Dubois has been foremost among those who emphasize this dualism (Negro-Ameri-canism) in Negro thought — a nation without a polity, nationals without citizenship. His writings, strongly tinctured with national-ism, represent the effort of a highly sophisticated man to resolve these dilemmas and, in effect, they parallel efforts of others who

17. James W. Ivy, "Le fait d'être Nègre dans les Amériques," *Présence Africaine* (Paris), No. 24–25, Fev.-mai, 1959, pp. 123–24; also E. Franklin Frazier, "What Can the American Negro Contribute to Africa?" in *Africa as seen by American Negroes*, Special Issue of *Présence Africaine*, ed. J. A Davis, August, 1959, pp. 275–76. Cf. W. E. B. DuBois, *An Appeal to the World* (New York: N.A.A.C.P., 1947) p. 1.

It is interesting to note that Dr. DuBois again discussed the problem of terminology for the Negro in a speech before the Seventh Annual Conference, the All-African Stu-dent Union of the Americas, Inc., held at the University of Chicago, June 18–21, 1958 (mimeographed), pp. 2–3. See also George S. Schuyler, "The Caucasian Problem," *What the Negro Wants*, ed. Rayford W. Logan (Chapel Hill: The University of North Carolina Press, 1944), p. 284: "The term Negro itself is as fictitious as the theory of white racial superiority on which Anglo-Saxon civilization is based, but it is never-theless one of the most effective smear devices developed since the Crusades. It totally disregards national, linguistic, cultural and physical differences between those unable to boast a porcine skin, and ignores the findings of advanced sociologists and ethnolo-gists. . . ."

18. Cf. *The American Negro Writer and His Roots* for this subject in general.

seek resolution in black nationalism. Negro fraternal, philanthropic, and business associations are practical responses to the dualism of loyalty arising from the tensions of black-white relationships.

Black nationalists insist that these dilemmas, confusions, and the absence of internal cohesion are largely responsible for the failure of Negroes to exert concerted pressure for the things that they demand from society.[19] They claim that the solution to the problem of the Negro's identity and to internal constraints which arise from it is a prerequisite of all other solutions. They seem to believe that these internal constraints are overlooked by many Negroes (especially the middle class) and, consequently, that most Negroes tend to perceive their problems as well as their communities *solely* as the creation of white society. They come to the inevitable conclusion that their efforts must be directed to making white society recognize and assume full responsibility for the solution of these problems. The nationalists admit that attitudes and actions of white society are powerful obstacles to their solution, but they point out that the level of community involvement among the urban Negro masses — other than for "funerals, food, and fun" — is either nonexistent or absolutely minimal.

The writer has been impressed by the absence of internal cohesion and the low level of community involvement among the urban Negro masses. These explain in part the inability of Negroes to have a significant say concerning the economic and political norms of their communities. Furthermore, the Negro community provides few or no criteria by which its members can meaningfully interpret and relate the dominant white culture and the realities of American society to their specific experiences. The Negro masses cannot participate fully and responsibly in their communities. Perhaps more than is

19. Aside from their antagonism toward the National Association for the Advancement of Colored People, the nationalists point out that it does not receive the support of the Negro masses. The NAACP, which is the most "militant" organization seeking full citizenship for Negroes, can only boast a total membership of 334,000 as of December 15, 1959. The increase over the previous year is said to be a little over nine per cent. Considering the importance of the objectives of the organization, this is a rather small number out of a total population of Negroes estimated at nearly 19 million. It should be added that the membership also includes whites. See the *Chicago Daily Defender*, January 11, 1960, p. 7, for membership figures.

generally admitted, the internal constraints account for the Negroes' general lack of a sense of common need.[20]

It is no wonder that so many Negroes resort to mere opportunism and become totally preoccupied with immediate survival values (shelter, clothing, food, and recreation) or that they are easily swayed to seek salvation in escapist or purely diversionary activities such as alcoholism, drug addiction, gambling, spiritualism, and conspicuous display. Many Negroes, however, hope that eventually the American Dream will be fulfilled for them as individuals, if not through their own efforts, then by "good luck."

Black nationalism has brought these problems into sharp focus, especially those internal constraints and divisions which prevent Negroes from acting in unison or even in seeking individual self-improvement. Although it would be hard to determine how much of Muhammad's effort is deliberate and how much is unconscious, the impression is given that he is trying to create a Negro ethos and hence a self-consciously unified Negro community. Examining his exoteric teachings reinforces this impression.

Because it symbolizes the oppression of the Negro, the white culture's political and religious basis is rejected: the Muslims do not vote in local or national elections; they resist induction into the United States military services; and they categorically reject Christianity as the "graveyard" of the Negro people. The Negro sub-culture is as well rejected as "uncivilized," and as impeding their material, cultural, and moral advancement.

In order to create, to fashion a unified community, Muhammad first directs his attack against those forces which have so disastrously atomized and weakened Negro society. He seeks to provide the Negro with a spiritual and moral context within which shaken pride and confidence may be restored and unused or abused energies directed toward an all-encompassing goal; to heal the wound of the Negro's dual membership in American society. Specifically, Muhammad denounces the matriarchal character of Negro society; the relative lack of masculine parental authority which makes the

20. Although this view does not deny the meagreness of material resources available within the Negro community, it emphasizes the absence of a psychological "leverage" necessary for mobilizing whatever resources there may be.

enforcement of discipline within the family difficult; the traditional lack of savings- and capital-accumulation habits; and the folk belief that "white is right," which leads to a dependence upon the initiative of the white man. Personal indolence and laziness are sternly deprecated. Habits of hard work and thrift are extolled.

The Muslims disapprove of the expression of undisciplined, spontaneous impulses. The pursuit of a "righteous" life as prescribed by the "Laws of Islam" and by Muhammad's directives is seen as the major purpose of existence. These laws and directives prohibit the following: extra-marital sexual relations, the use of alcohol, tobacco, and narcotics, indulging in gambling, dancing, movie-going, dating, sports, long vacations from work, sleeping more than is necessary to health, quarreling between husband and wife, lying, stealing, discourtesy (especially toward women), and insubordination to civil authority, except on the ground of religious obligation. Maintaining personal habits of cleanliness and keeping fastidious homes are moral duties. The eating of pork, cornbread, collard greens, and other foods traditional among southern Negroes is strictly proscribed. No one is permitted to straighten his hair. Women may not dye their hair or conspicuously use cosmetics. Intemperate singing, shouting, laughing loudly are forbidden. Violation of any of these or other rules is punished immediately by suspension from the movement for periods ranging from thirty days to a maximum of seven years, depending on the gravity of the offense. The most important sanctions which appear to regulate the behavior of Muslims are loss of membership in the movement and the chastisement from Allah.

Muhammad's effort to inculcate a sense of self-esteem in the Muslims by encouraging them to practice and assimilate habits that we associate with the middle class is obvious in his teachings. The quest for respectability within and without the Negro community is a primary goal. Their enthusiastic desire to be independent of white control is demonstrated partly by their willingness to overstretch their resources in order to maintain private elementary and high schools in Chicago and Detroit. The effort to strengthen the Muslims' sense of pride is apparent in Muhammad's emphasis on the "glorious" past of the Black Nation: the special relationship between the Muslims and Allah and their connection with "Arabian-Egyptian" civilization.

It should be stressed, however, that Islam is not offered to Negroes merely as a divisive symbol. To the believers it is a living faith and a positive way of life, enabling them, in unacknowledged ways, to follow with devotion moral values reminiscent of the New England Puritans and to aspire to a style of life usually associated with the middle class.[21] The Muslims, being the elect of God, are obligated to pursue a righteous life which would justify their special status in His sight. The pursuit of wealth is good only in so far as it enhances the common good — the elevation of the Nation of Islam and, in general, the masses of American Negroes. The Muslims are determined to rise on the social scale by their own efforts. Imbued with a common purpose, the Muslims appear to drown their fears, frustrations, anxieties, and doubts in the hope of attaining a national home and in the promise and assurance of redemption *now* in the "New World of Islam," purged of the suffering and corruption of the world about them. Such is the sense of "tragic optimism" which has characterized the organized effort of the Negro nationalists to assert their identity and to discover their human worth and dignity in American society.

21. Cf. Max Weber, *The Protestant Ethic and the Spirit of Capitalism*, trans. Talcott Parson (New York: Charles Scribner's Sons, 1958), chap. V, on the relationship between "Asceticism and the Spirit of Capitalism." Elsewhere (p. 39), Weber notes that "National or religious minorities which are in a position of subordination to a group of rulers are likely, through their voluntary or involuntary exclusion from positions of political influence, to be driven with peculiar force into economic activity." Although Negroes have not been able to make a serious inroad into the economy, a few Negro leaders from Frederick Douglass to Muhammad have urged economic independence as a means to their "salvation."

II. The Nationalist Tradition

> The reliance of our race upon the progress and achievements of others for a consideration in sympathy, justice and rights is like a dependence upon a broken stick, resting upon which will eventually consign you to the ground . . . .
>
> The Negro needs a Nation and a country of his own, where he can best show evidence of his own ability in the art of human progress. Scattered as an unmixed and unrecognized part of alien nations and civilizations is but to demonstrate his imbecility, and point him out as an unworthy derelict, fit neither for the society of Greek, Jew nor Gentile.
>
> MARCUS GARVEY

NATIONALIST GROUPS, separatist religious movements, and fraternal associations among American Negroes have had a long, related history. They have a common origin in the unresolved problem of the Negro's status as a second-class citizen in the United States, each developing as a necessary *ad hoc* response to this experience. The result of this experience is that Negroes have acquired a sense of ethnic identity imposed almost entirely from without. In time this negative sense of ethnic identification tended to acquire positive characteristics; concomitantly, Negroes have sought to strike out for themselves in those areas of activity in which the resistance of the white society is marginal.

Nationalist movements and organizations show these efforts in exaggerated terms. The Negro church, other religious bodies, and fraternal (to a lesser extent, business and labor) associations, in practice, have given some reality to these aspirations without commitment to a nationalist ideology. The Negro church and the other associations are not nationalist in the narrow sense of the word. Neither are they racially conscious. They differ from the nationalist organizations in that they seek their ends within the framework of existing society. However, the historical and social circumstances which have dictated their rise have given them some nationalist and racial characteristics. In a broad sense, they are the antecedents of black nationalism, although their contribution to its ideological development has been indirect and incidental.

Historically, the Nation of Islam has much in common with the separate Negro church and associations, and more directly with the nationalist movements led by Noble Drew Ali and Marcus Garvey, but it differs from the earlier traditions in that its ideology is intensely chiliastic and buttressed by racial doctrines.

This chapter shall examine these traditions as well as the cultural nationalism once advocated by Dr. W. E. B. DuBois in order to give a historical perspective to the narrower problem of black nationalism with which we are concerned.

The importance of the nationalist tradition among American Negroes may be exaggerated. It should be placed here in its proper social perspective, with all its weakness and restrictiveness. Its weakness stems from the destruction of the African social heritage and the interaction of Negroes with American society.[1] Also, the separatist religious movements have been inconsequential as centers of nationalistic agitation compared with similar movements and cults in Asia and Africa.[2] On the other hand, while the fraternal-co-operative organizations (including the Negro churches) have gained a strong following, they still represent the dominant accul-

1. E. Franklin Frazier has maintained that the Negro's African social heritage was completely destroyed in America and that the Negro's cultural patterns result from interaction with American society. See Frazier, *The Negro Family in the United States*, p. 21. His position has been challenged by Melville J. Herskovits, *The Myth of the Negro's Past* (New York: Harper, 1942). According to Herskovits, many social characteristics of Negroes in the United States are attributable to African survivals. He admits, however, that they are few and not easily recognizable.

2. See Georges Balandier, "Messianismes et nationalismes en Afrique Noire," *Cahiers internationaux de sociologie*, XIV (1953), 41–65; Justus M. van der Kroef, "The Messiah in Indonesia and Melanesia," *Scientific Monthly*, LXXXV (September, 1952), 161–65.

turation strand and an assimilationist ideology.[3] They offer no perspective on the basic Negro dilemma. The following account attempts to explain some of the fundamental issues raised by black nationalism, especially during this period of rapid change in the status of American Negroes, aside from their legal rights, the practice of discrimination, and the trend toward integration.

NEGRO NATIONALISM

"Negro nationalism" found expression during the nineteenth century in the Negro-sponsored emigration movement as well as in Negroes' response (though limited) to the emigration scheme of the American Colonization Society.[4] The leadership came mainly from a small but vocal minority of educated Negroes who felt that:

> The question is not whether our condition can be bettered by emigration, but whether it can be made worse. If not, then, there is no part of the widespread universe, where our social and political conditions are not better than here in our native country, and nowhere in the world as here, proscribed on account of color.[5]

Negro emigration from the United States was first sponsored in 1815 by Paul Cuffee, a New England Negro sailor who had attained some wealth. In that year he sent thirty-eight Negro colonists to Africa. His action is believed to have inspired the formation of the American Colonization Society in 1816.

However, the most important social movement among the free Negroes was the Negro Convention Movement, which met annually for three decades before the Civil War. Concerned primarily with

3. Compared with such organizations as the National Association for the Advancement of Colored People (founded in 1909 and concerned with securing first-class citizenship for Negroes) and the Urban League (concerned with Negro employment opportunities and other social welfare services), the nationalist tradition has been a failure. Although we shall not include these organizations in this discussion, their importance should be borne in mind.

4. Negro nationalism is distinguished from black nationalism in that its concern has been with the specific problem of the American Negroes, whereas the latter's concern has been with the universal redemption of the black race. Apparently, the problem of the Negro's identity, which is central in black nationalism, was not an issue prior to the present century. For an account of the leadership of the American Colonization Society, see P. J. Staudenraus, *The African Colonization Movement 1816–1865* (New York: Columbia University Press, 1961).

5. Martin R. Delany, *The Niger Valley Exploration Party* (New York: Thomas Hamilton, 1861), p. 6.

seeking ways to alleviate the Negro's plight in the United States, as a secondary interest it favored Negro emigration to Canada but not to "any part of the Eastern Hemisphere." The first of its conventions was local and held in Philadelphia in January, 1817, to protest against the American Colonization Society "that had been organized to remove systematically from this country all the free colored people in the United States."[6] On September 15, 1830, a more representative convention met in Philadelphia to combat the program of the American Colonization Society. The question of Negro emigration to Canada West was raised and fully discussed. The convention recommended the purchase of a colony in Canada.

During the Convention of 1832 at which Negroes from eight states (mostly northern) were represented, "the question exciting the greatest interest was one which proposed the purchase of other lands for settlement in Canada; for 800 acres of land had already been secured, two thousand individuals had left the soil of their birth, crossed the line and laid the foundation for a structure which promised an asylum for the colored population of the United States."[7] The convention rejected all colonization plans except the Canadian settlement and sent a strong protest to Congress against any appropriation for the American Colonization Society. The majority of the delegates expressed no interest in Africa. In fact, at the 1835 Convention, anti-African feelings were voiced by one William Whipper who advocated that the word or title "African" should be removed from the names of churches, lodges, societies, and other institutions. In their desire for acceptance by white Americans, articulate Negroes were already beginning to differentiate themselves from Africans. They were ashamed of their African origins. They, too, had come to accept uncritically the white man's caricature of Africa as populated by comic-opera savages. In time Negroes developed a deep aversion toward Africa and many rejected all affinity with its people.[8] Thus, not only did the majority

6. John W. Cromwell, "The Early Convention Movement," *American Negro Academy, Occasional Papers* No. 9 (Washington, D. C.: American Negro Academy, 1905), p. 8.

7. *Ibid.*, p. 5.

8. Harold R. Isaacs, "The American Negro and Africa, Some Notes," *The Phylon* (Atlanta University) XX, No. 3 (Fall, 1959), 232: ". . . Africa was the

of the leaders of the Negro Convention Movement oppose any consideration of emigration to Africa, but its dissident members also
did, who saw in emigration the solution to the evils with which they
were beset. The dissident faction of the Convention Movement called
another convention to consider and decide upon the issue.

. . . our object and determination are to consider our claims to the West
Indies, Central and South America, and the Canadas. This restriction has
no reference to *personal* preference, or *individual* enterprise; but to the great
question of national claims to come before the Convention.[9]

THE EMIGRATION CONVENTION OF 1854

The convention to consider and decide on emigration was finally
held in 1854. There were three factions at this convention, each
representing the foreign field to which its members preferred to
emigrate. Dr. Martin R. Delany, editor of *The Mystery*, a Pittsburgh
weekly newspaper, led the faction which advocated emigration to
the Niger Valley in West Africa. A contemporary described him as
"unadulterated in race, proud of his complexion and devotedly
attached to his fatherland."[10] James M. Whitfield of Buffalo, New
York, well known as a Negro poet, led the faction which preferred
colonization in Central America, and the Reverend James Theodore
Holly headed the party which preferred to go to Haiti. The convention authorized Dr. Delany to go to the Niger Valley and sent Whitfield to Central America and Holly to the Black Republic of Haiti.
Each was instructed to negotiate with the governing authorities

'darkness' they wanted to leave behind in order to rise to the 'light' of the white man's
world, his religions, philosophies, his ways of life. . . . Hence the pride in mixed forebears, the white, the Indian, the "Spanish," in anything but the African. Hence the
ambivalences and confusions at the margins of the dominant white society, the self-
hatred, the 'yearning after whiteness'. . . ."

However, Isaac's judgment is rather extreme. It leaves out of consideration substantial evidence of Negroes' interest and degree of identification with Africa from the
nineteenth century until the present. Aside from evidence of Negro missionaries in
Africa, George Shepperson recently has provided very revealing data on this subject.
See his "Notes On Negro American Influences on the Emergence of African Nationalism," *Journal of African History*, I, No. 2 (1960), 299–312.

9. Delany, *op. cit.*, p. 6. Invitations to the convention specifically stated: "No person
will be admitted to a seat in the Convention, who would introduce the subject of Emigration to the Eastern Hemisphere — either Asia, Africa, or Europe . . ." (*Ibid.*, p. 6).

10. William Wells Brown, *The Rising Son; Or, The Antecedents and Advancement
of the Colored Race* (Boston: A. G. Brown & Co., 1874), pp. 460–61.

of the various territories and report at future conventions. Reverend Holly was the first to execute his mission: he visited Haiti in 1855 and received a commission from the Haitian government, at one thousand dollars per annum and traveling expenses, to secure emigrants to Haiti. He reported at the next emigration convention, which met in 1856 at Chatham, Canada West. Dr. Delany sailed off to the Niger Valley in 1858. There he concluded a treaty, and "eight kings offered inducements for Negro emigrants to their territories." Whitfield went to California, intending to go from there to Central America, but died in San Francisco before he could do so.

Agitation for emigration was so intense in the eighteen-fifties that Frederick Douglass and other non-emigrationists were alarmed:

> I really fear that some whose presence in this country is necessary to the elevation of the Colored people will leave us — while the degraded and worthless will remain behind — to help bind us to our present debasement.[11]

The emigrationists replied that opposition was "for the purpose of keeping full churches and school-houses, a plenty of patients, waiters, and other assistants."[12] To counteract the growing interest in emigration, the conservative leaders unwittingly resorted to a sort of Negro nationalism by setting up in 1853 a Negro National Council having supervisory authority over a Negro National College, a Negro National Arbitration Committee, Consumers' Union, Trade and Labor Office, and a National Library and Propaganda Headquarters.[13] The emigrationists described this program as "an informal national organization of a denationalized people, whereby an organic, though premature and sickly birth was given to the idea of national independence."[14] The Pittsburgh *Daily Morning Post*, a white newspaper, described the emigration proposals as "a vast conception of impossible birth," arguing that the idea of Africanizing more than half of the Western Hemisphere "overlooked the strength of the 'powers on earth'" but recommended Liberia as a fitting home for the Negroes.[15]

11. Quoted in Howard H. Bell, "The Negro Emigration Movement, 1849–1854: A Phase of Negro Nationalism," *The Phylon*, XX, No. 2 (Summer, 1959), 135.
12. *Ibid.*, p. 136.
13. *Ibid.*, p. 140.
14. *Ibid.*, p. 140.
15. Quoted in Delany, *op. cit.*, p. 10.

Negro nationalism before the Civil War was led by a group of educated men and found expression in the emigration movement. However, emigration to Africa received little support from the articulate, freed Negroes. Although emigration to Canada was favored by the Convention Movement, it achieved little success because Canadians did not encourage further sale of land to the Negroes. The three schemes authorized by the Emigration Convention of 1854 failed for several reasons. In 1861, the first shipload of emigrants from Philadelphia sailed to Haiti. Of the nearly two thousand persons who emigrated, "not more than one third . . . permanently abided there":

They proved to be neither intellectually, industrially, nor financially prepared to wring from the soil the riches that it is ready to yield up to such as shall be thus prepared; nor are the government and influential individuals sufficiently instructed in social, industrial and financial problems which now govern the world, to turn to profitable use willing workers among the laboring class.[16]

The Civil War put a stop to emigration. Dr. Delany, leader of the faction which desired emigration to Africa, was commissioned a major by President Lincoln, and the Central American scheme died out upon the death of Whitfield:

The Civil War destroyed many landmarks. . . . Slavery was dead; the colonizationists to Canada, the West Indies and Africa abandoned the field of openly aiming to commit the policy of the race to what was considered expatriation.[17]

The period immediately following the Civil War ended all consideration of emigration as a possible solution to the problem of the freed Negroes. The most important reason was that emancipation meant citizenship. Many Negroes had a firm belief and hope in the eventual achievement of the rights of citizenship:

The chains of slavery had been severed; and although he had not been clothed with all the powers of the citizen, the black man was, nevertheless, sure of all his rights being granted, for revolutions seldom go backwards . . .[18]

16. Cromwell, *op. cit.*, p. 21.
17. *Ibid.*
18. Brown, *op. cit.*, p. 413.

THE NEGRO CHURCH AND FRATERNAL-
CO-OPERATIVE ASSOCIATIONS

Religious bodies and fraternal-co-operative associations were the major forms of deliberately organized Negro activities during the nineteenth century. The Negro church was the parent of both fraternal societies and schools. Until the founding of the separate Negro church, free Negroes worshiped in white churches in both the North and South. In the South, when Negroes were allowed to worship at all, segregation was enforced; they worshiped either at a different hour from the whites or were seated in a different section of the church. In the North, segregation was usually not so rigid. Consequently, the religious estrangement of the Negroes and the embarrassments they endured in white churches led to the founding in 1786 of the African Methodist Episcopal Church in Philadelphia by Richard Allen and his associates.

The relationship of the Negro church to black nationalism is four-fold. First, it is the best and most successfully organized Negro institution in the United States, and the Negro, like most Americans, values success. He also takes pride in the monumental edifices which the churches have erected throughout the country. Similarly, he admires a minister who has acquired money and face, even at his own expense. Invariably, such a minister becomes a "national" symbol of success for his congregation; and often the communicant, in spite of his lowly material condition, identifies his aspirations with the minister's achievements. He may even point with pride to a minister who owns "two Cadillacs" and who "recently spent $25,000 for the interior decoration of the home we bought for him." Identification of one's aspirations with the success of a leader is equally evident among the rank and file of the nationalist movements.

Second, the Negro church provides the widest community for the Negro's participation; it satisfies his need to belong. This is particularly so in the long-established denominations with a national organization and membership, which unite their members with the larger Christian community. In fact, the ability of Negroes to maintain foreign missions, particularly in Africa, has also given them a feeling of being the "chosen" — and hence a sense of superiority to the peoples in those lands. This sense of a "mission" to convert the non-Christian peoples in Africa parallels the fantasy of racial redemption held by the black nationalists. However, the Negro church may be regarded as the single institution which has uniquely given a sustained, positive sense of ethnic identity to American Negroes without beating the nationalists' drums. The retention of the word "African" in the titles of some of the large denominations, and interaction with Africa through the foreign missions, have perpetuated the Negro's identification with Africa more than is generally admitted.

Third, the Negro church embodies the race's desire for independence from white leadership and control and until the present century, it was an important vehicle for the evolution of Negro leadership and authority in the Negro community. The Negro's aspiration for status, thwarted in white society, found expression in the church organization. The church leaders became the earliest spokesmen for Negro advancement. They interpreted the norms and standards of white society to their communities.

Within the separate church, militant Negro ministers can castigate with complete freedom the injustices of white society and denounce with equal vehemence the evils of the Negro community. That the Negro minister does not depend on white support for his income has also been a great asset. Economic independence from white support is important for the style of leadership of black nationalists. The separate church enables the Negro minister to wash the dirty linen of the congregation in private, away from the view of white society. The secrecy of black nationalists' meetings may also be explained by the need for freedom for self-criticism as well as for castigation of the white society.

Lastly, the Negro church was once the most important center of social life for its members. The preacher, though he might be illiterate, was a man of authority and prestige in his community. He was the "counselor of the unwise, the friend of the unfortunate, the social welfare organizer, and the interpreter of the signs of the times."[19]

19. Carter G. Woodson, quoted in Richard Bardolph, *The Negro Vanguard* (New York: Rinehart & Co., 1959), p. 35.

The Negro church remains an important institution in Negro life. Although it has declined as a source of civic leadership, it continues to furnish a few nationally prominent leaders.[20] To a limited extent it shares with other agencies the burden of providing social services for its members. But its primary significance lies in the fact that it symbolizes the Negro's desire for independence; it is a citadel where he can withdraw from daily hardships and injustice. Here, at least once a week, he feels "at home" among friends and equals in the sight of God. Particularly in the South, the church is the "interpreter of the signs of the times" and the moulder of the Negro's world view.

The Negro church has been on the whole anti-nationalistic, partly because of its undisciplined "otherworldliness," and partly because it is split into numerous denominations. Black nationalists are in general opposed to the Negro church because they believe it impedes Negro advancement. Consequently, they tend to become anti-Christian or try to establish a "nationalist" church as an adjunct of the nationalist movement.

In the urban centers, the relative decline of the role of the Negro preacher as the interpreter of the realities of American society to the masses and the consequent loss of his prestige within the community, appear in part to account for the attractiveness of the "prophetic" role to Negro religious leaders of the present century. The nationalists now seek to assume this interpretive function.

The first Negro lodge, the Masons, received its charter from England in 1787, and African Lodge No. 459 was formally organized with its founder, Prince Hall, as the Master. Other fraternal societies were organized later in the nineteenth century, such as the Elks in 1898. Like the Negro church, the fraternal societies were organized because the free Negroes had been denied membership in the white lodges. The lodges appear to have been far more race-conscious than the Negro church. The secrecy, rituals, and the spirit of brotherliness and equality fostered by the lodge members are similar to

20. St. Clair Drake, "Churches and Voluntary Associations in the Chicago Negro Community" (University of Chicago, WPA Project, 1940, Mimeographed). Also, Benjamin E. Mays and Joseph Nicholson, *The Negro Church* (New York: Institute of Social and Religious Research, 1933).

some of the practices of the nationalist and separatist religious movements of the present century. The fraternal societies strengthened group solidarity, promoted a sense of belonging, and provided mutual assistance to their members. They were avenues for the recruitment of Negro leadership, and, like the church, allowed Negroes to act independently of white leadership and control. The influence of the fraternal-co-operative or mutual-aid societies seems noticeably on the decline, particularly in the urban areas.[21]

CULTURAL AND ECONOMIC NATIONALISM

Towards the turn of the present century, Booker T. Washington and W. E. B. DuBois emerged as important Negro leaders. Neither advocated nationalism in the sense in which it has been defined here. Both were "race" leaders within the framework of the prevailing society. Washington emphasized the uplifting of the Negro masses through economic self-sufficiency and the separation of the races except for "non-essential" social contacts. He was willing to forego full political participation (at least in the short run) as an instrument of Negro advancement. His lack of confidence in direct political action and acceptance of social separation as a means of accommodating the hostility of the dominant white society are important ingredients of the withdrawal tendency in Negro behavior, which is now dramatized in black nationalism.

DuBois advocated full political participation, and saw in racial unity and action the instrument of Negro advancement. Consequently, in 1897 DuBois argued that Negroes in the United States were not only American citizens, but also members of a historic race. Like Garvey, DuBois envisaged the role of the American Negro as forming the advanced guard of the black race.[22] DuBois

21. St. Clair Drake, *op. cit.*, pp. 107–209.
22. DuBois, "The Conservation of Race," *The American Negro Academy, Occasional Papers*, No. 2 (1897), p. 10: ". . . the advance guard of the Negro people — the 8,000,000 people of Negro blood in the United States of America — must soon come to realize that if they are to take their just place in the van of Pan-Negroism, then their destiny is *not* absorption by the white Americans. That if in America it is to be proven for the first time in the modern world that not only Negroes are capable of evolving individual men like Toussaint, the Saviour, but are a nation stored with wonderful possibilities of culture, then their destiny is not a servile imitation of Anglo-Saxon culture, but a stalwart originality which shall unswervingly follow Negro ideals."

said that the Negro people as "a race, have a contribution to make to civilization and humanity, which no other race can make." He believed it "the duty of the Americans of Negro descent, as a body, to maintain their race identity until this mission of the Negro people has become a practical possibility." He believed that "unless modern civilization is a failure, it is entirely feasible and practicable for two races in such essential political, economic and religious harmony as the white and colored people of America, to develop side by side in peace and mutual happiness, the peculiar contribution which each has to make to the culture of their common country."[23]

This cultural nationalism may be called Negro-Americanism. DuBois later advocated a type of pragmatic nationalism for the Negro's protection and for "inner development and growth in intelligence and social efficiency."[24] The international implications of Negro-Americanism led DuBois in 1897 to the idea of Pan-Negroism (a variation on the racial redemption theme of the black nationalists). In 1919 DuBois transformed this into Pan-Africanism, a movement seeking the political unification of Africa, which has since found adherents among leading African politicians and statesmen. Kwame Nkrumah, President of the Republic of Ghana, is its leading exponent. DuBois remains a staunch advocate of Pan-Africanism, and has organized and participated in five Pan-African Congresses held between 1919 and 1946. He has given a general indication of what Negro-Americanism entails:

It may, however, be objected here that the situation of our race in America renders this attitude impossible; that our sole hope of salvation lies in our being able to lose our race identity in the commingled blood of the nation; and that any other course would merely increase the friction of races which we call race prejudice, and against which we have so long and so earnestly fought. Here, then, is the dilemma, and it is a puzzling one, I admit. . . . We are Americans, not only by birth and by citizenship, but by our political ideals, our language, our religion. Farther than that, our Americanism does not go. At that point, we are Negroes, members of a vast historic race that from the very dawn of creation has slept, but half-awakening in the

23. *Ibid.*, pp. 10–14.
24. DuBois, *Dusk of Dawn: An Essay Toward an Autobiography of a Race Concept* (New York: Harcourt, Brace and Company, 1940), p. 306. Cf. Francis L. Broderick's discussion of this phase of DuBois' thinking, in *W. E. B. DuBois: Negro Leader in a Time of Crisis* (Stanford, Calif.: Stanford University Press, 1959), chap. VI.

dark forests of its African fatherland. We are the first fruits of this new nation, the harbinger of that black tomorrow which is yet destined to soften the whiteness of the Teutonic today. We are that people whose subtle sense of song has given America its only American music, its only American fairy tales, its only touch of pathos and humor amid its mad money-getting plutocracy. As such, it is our duty to conserve our physical powers, our intellectual endowments, our spiritual ideals; as a race we must strive by race organization, by race solidarity, by race unity to the realization of that broader humanity which freely recognizes differences in men, but sternly deprecates inequality in their opportunities of development.[25]

DuBois returned to this theme in 1935 when he wrote that if the economic and cultural salvation of the Negro means more prejudice and more segregation, the Negro must accept it and so plan his future that his survival as a people will be insured.

Negro-Americanism, however, has never become a cultural movement. Margaret Just Butcher observes that the "Negro has rarely set up separate cultural values or developed divergent institutional loyalties or political objectives." Actually, the contrary has been true.

In basic attitude and alliance with over-all American concepts and ideals, the Negro is a conformist. He believes implicitly in the promise and heritage of basic American documents, and he has applied the principles of self-reliance, personal dignity, and individual human worth to the long, rewarding fight to achieve full and unequivocal first-class citizenship. *The American Negro's values, ideals, and objectives are integrally and unreservedly American.*[26]

Although she finds the Negro conforming with American concepts and ideals, she notes that the Negro "may well have to take the lead in recasting universal social values."

The experience of the Negro in America has made him less susceptible to the pitfalls of nationalism, and this in itself may be one reason why the Negro may play a dramatic role in bringing about world democracy.

. . . .

If the only civilization that can survive is a civilization of humanity, the men and women who bring this civilization into being must be citizens of

25. DuBois, *The American Negro Academy, Occasional Papers*, No. 2, pp. 10–12. This most illuminating essay also deals with the fundamental ambivalences in the Negro's attitudes.

26. *The Negro in American Culture* (New York: New American Library, 1957), p. 221. (Emphasis added.)

the world. Curiously enough, it has been easier for Negro Americans to be full citizens of this world than to be full citizens of their native land. This is an unfortunate (but, happily, changing) circumstance, but it is also the basis for a brilliant opportunity for the American Negro to implement both cultural democracy and the concept of cultural pluralism.[27]

The problem of Negro-Americanism as well as its relationship to the Negro's African "roots" was the subject of a conference of Negro writers in 1959.[28] Guy B. Johnson, a white sociologist, regards it as mere fantasy:

Much has been said lately by Negroes about the possibility of their creating a unique type of culture in the United States. Some would base this culture on the peculiar experience of the Negro in America. In view of the ever increasing likeness of white and Negro culture, this goal must remain a mere fanciful dream. If Negroes were separated territorially from white people, they might, after several hundred years produce some unique cultural elements. Other advocates of the new culture would have the Negro reidentify himself with African heritages and forsake the ways of the white man.[29]

DuBois has maintained that divergent cultural tendencies among American Negroes can be explained by "outer compulsions" rather than "inner plan." "The Negro group has long been internally divided by dilemmas as to whether its striving upwards should be aimed at strengthening inner cultural and group bonds, both for intrinsic progress and for offensive power against caste; or whether it should seek escape wherever and however possible into the surrounding American culture. Decision in this matter has been largely determined by outer compulsions rather than inner plan; for prolonged policies of segregation and discrimination have involuntarily welded the mass almost into a nation within a nation with its own schools, churches, hospitals, newspapers and many business enterprises."[30]

In recent years, there seems to be a growing interest in a sort of cultural "restoration." Much of this interest has undoubtedly been spurred by developments in Africa within the last decade and, more

27. *Ibid.*, p. 227.
28. See *The American Negro Writer and His Roots.*
29. "The Development of Negro Social Institutions," *American Journal of Sociology,* XL, No. 3 (November, 1934), 337.
30. *Current History,* CVL (June, 1935), 265.

particularly, by increasing contacts between Africans and Negroes in the United States.[31]

It is difficult at this time to assess the implications and the possible direction of this interest, but:

> Surely it was no accident that the pull back to Africa expressed in the Garvey movement was also an aggressive pull back to blackness, or that the re-emergence of Africa now is having as one effect the re-establishment of some virtue, even beauty, in blackness; the Nkrumahs and the Tom Mboyas are knocking over more than the cruder old stereotypes. This is the root, I believe, for the Negro's rejection of Africa was, at bottom, his rejection of himself.
> Can we say, then, that this was the principal stuff of which the "aversion" to Africa was made? And can we say that in acquiring a new image of Africa now, the Negro American is really engaged in acquiring nothing less than a new image of himself? [32]

SEPARATIST RELIGIOUS MOVEMENTS

The Negro church previously described differs from the separatist religious movements in that it is patterned after and conforms doctrinally to the major white Christian denominations. The separatist religious movements do not adhere either to the doctrines or to the practices of the established churches. Some are Christian in outlook, and others deviate. They appeal mainly to the lower-class

31. One of the significant developments of this emergent interest is the response of some Negro intellectuals to the international movement "of men of culture of the Negro world." The formation of the American Society for African Culture, New York, is the result of the First International Congress of Negro Writers and Artists, held in Paris, September 19–22, 1956. The major objectives of the Congress were: ". . . to unite by bonds of solidarity and friendship the men of culture of the Negro world . . . conscious of their duty, the latter intend: (a) To cooperate in the development and improvement of world cultures: (b) To create or promote, during the present crisis, the conditions necessary for the full development of their cultures." The Congress presently publishes *Présence Africaine* in Paris, France. See Georges Balandier, "Negritude" in *Race — Individual and Collective Behavior*, eds. Edgar Thompson and Everett Hughes (Glencoe, Ill.: Free Press, 1958), pp. 364–70. In the United States the Society has held four annual conferences, in 1958, 1959, 1960, and 1961. It is interesting to note that the Society in the United States admits whites only as "associate" members but denies them (at least in theory) full participation in the formulation of policies. This is indicative of their desire (like the black nationalists) to be independent of white leadership and control. It is ironical, however, that while the Society seeks independence from white control it is supported financially almost wholly by whites. Of course, this interest is expressed in various other groups and organizations and for a variety of reasons. The Society is strictly a middle-class intellectual affair. In June, 1961, it had a total membership of three hundred and fifty.

32. Isaacs, *op. cit.*, p. 233.

Negroes; more often than not, they are led by a self-styled "Prophet," "God," or "Savior." Although these movements exhibit the withdrawal tendencies evident in black nationalism, they are not necessarily either nationalistic or racist.[33]

Father Divine's Peace Movement deserves brief mention here. Father Divine started his movement about 1915. During its early stages he styled himself the "Messenger," implying that he was the "Son" of God or a "Prophet" of God. At that time he taught his followers that God is in every person, but later he changed from this conception of God to the idea that God is in Father Divine. He directed his appeal to both Negroes and whites. His teachings, like those of the black nationalists, display the mood of alienation from existing society. As a leader he created a messianic image of himself and attempted to transcend his limitations by denying the relevance of "color" or "race," as well as the dominance of white society and the marginal character of Negro society. He was also attracted to white society, asserting that everyone can be part of it only if it is transformed into a colorless society. But this can be realized only in a government under God, and Father Divine is God:

> Out of all the higher education, it does not profit until you get away from racism. Until we get away from a race or color, our representatives need a higher degree! I desire to give our representatives in government a new birth of freedom, under God, so that they might represent one nation, indivisible with liberty and justice for all! That is my work and my mission.[34]

Sara Harris has said that his teaching to his early New York followers and friends was a "new kind of chauvinism":

> It was a new kind of chauvinism the Messenger preached to his early New York followers and friends. He went a step beyond what even Marcus Garvey, the most aggressive Negro chauvinist of recent years, had ever dared to say. Where Garvey had said that black was basically superior and white was basically inferior, the Messenger exemplified that statement. He said, I am a Negro and God dwells in me. You are a Negro and you are like unto me. Therefore, you are superior to white.[35]

33. A. H. Fauset, *Black Gods of the Metropolis: Negro Religious Cults in the Urban North* (Philadelphia: University of Pennsylvania Press, 1944).

34. Quoted by Sara Harris in *Father Divine: Holy Husband* (New York: Doubleday and Company, 1953), p. 27.

35. *Ibid.*, p. 21.

Father Divine had a very large number of followers in the nineteen-thirties. He provided much-needed services, material and otherwise, to many of the unemployed masses during the depression. He instituted a collectivist economy among his followers, demanded celibacy of them, and sought to exact total submission to his authority.

Independence of white control, rejection of the traditional Christian concept of God, denial of the power of the dominant society, and differentiation of his followers from the Negro subculture and society are policies which Father Divine shares with the black nationalists.

PIONEERS OF BLACK NATIONALISM

Noble Drew Ali and Marcus Garvey represent two traditions of black nationalism in the United States. Both men are now dead, but their teachings form the core of contemporary nationalist ideologies, and both continue to have adherents. Drew Ali was an American citizen. Marcus Garvey was a West Indian. Both began nationalist agitation during the decade of the first World War — a decade of unprecedented Negro migration from the southern rural areas to northern cities. The two leaders disappeared from the scene shortly before the depression. Garvey was deported from the United States in 1927 and Drew Ali died mysteriously in 1929.

THE MOORS

Noble Drew Ali, before becoming a "prophet" of Islam, was known as Timothy Drew. He was born in North Carolina in 1886 and at one time was an expressman in Newark, New Jersey. In 1913 he founded the first Moorish-American Science Temple, in Newark. Before he came to Chicago in 1925, he had established a Temple in Pittsburgh, Pennsylvania, and one in Detroit, Michigan. Although Drew Ali had little formal education, he had become acquainted with certain phases of Islamic teachings, and became convinced that Islam was the only instrument for Negro unity and advancement.[36]

36. Arna Bontemps and Jack Conroy, *They Seek a City* (Garden City, New York: Doubleday, Doran, 1945), pp. 174–77. Also cf. Fauset, *op. cit.*, pp. 41–51.

According to the legend, Drew Ali is said to have visited North Africa where he received a "commission" from the King of Morocco to teach Islam to the Negroes in the United States. He is also reputed to have met with the President of the United States (which President is not specified) in order to receive a "charter" for the propagation of Islam. The President is said to have told him that "it would be as difficult getting Negroes to accept Islam as trying to fit a horse with a pair of pants."[37]

Noble Drew Ali's teachings are embodied in a secret text known as the "Holy Koran."[38] Drew Ali taught that the people termed "Negroes" in the United States are "Asiatics" and, specifically, that they are Moors whose forebears inhabited Morocco before they were enslaved in North America. Thus he not only denied the affinity of Negroes to the white center of power, but he also attempted to differentiate them from their "Negro-ness" or from their subculture. He insisted that "for a people to amount to anything, it is necessary to have a name (nation) and a land." North America is the Negroes' land — it is only an "extension" of the African continent. He taught that the "so-called Negroes" must know their national origin and refuse to be called Negroes, black folk, colored people, or Ethiopians. They must call themselves Asiatics, Moors, or Moorish-Americans. He believed that before a people can have a God they must have a nationality, and the Moorish Nation is Morocco. The word "Ethiopian" signifies division, "Negro" (black) means death, and "colored" signifies something that is painted. He contended that the name is all-meaningful, for by stripping him of his Asiatic name and calling him Negro, black, colored, or Ethiopian, the European robbed the Moor of his power, his authority, his God, and every other worthwhile possession. Christianity, he said, is for the European (white), and Islam is for the Asiatics (olive-skinned persons).

37. Informant's account at Muhammad's Temple of Islam. However, the Moors believe that the "charter" or what is here referred to as "commission" came from "the great capital empire of Egypt." See Fauset, *op. cit.*, p. 47.

38. Bontemps and Conroy, *op. cit.*, p. 175: "Drew Ali had written and published his Koran, a slim pamphlet consisting of a curious mixture of the Mohammedan holy book of the same name, the Christian Bible, the words of Marcus Garvey, and anecdotes of the life of Jesus — the whole bound together with the prophet's own pronouncements and interpretations. Garvey was eulogized at every meeting as the John the Baptist of the Movement."

He believed that until each group has its own peculiar religion there will be no peace on this earth.[39]

In addition to his religious leadership, Drew Ali established a number of small businesses, collectively owned by his followers. When lack of formal education hampered his business affairs, he enlisted the aid of "several men who proved to be more cunning than scrupulous." By 1929 his leadership was contested by Sheik Claude Greene, "a small time politician and once butler of Julius Rosenwald, the philanthropist." The contest between them ended in Greene's death. He was shot and stabbed in his offices at the Unity Club in Chicago on the night of March 15, 1929. Drew Ali was arrested, and while in jail awaiting trial, he sent this last message to his followers:

TO THE HEADS OF ALL TEMPLES, ISLAM

I, your prophet, do hereby and now write you a letter as a warning and appeal to your good judgment for the present and the future. Though I am now in custody for you and the cause, it is all right and it is well for all who still believe in me and my father, God. I have redeemed all of you and you shall be saved, all of you, even me. I go to bat Monday, May 20, before the Grand Jury. If you are with me, be there. Hold on and keep faith, and great shall be your reward. Remember my laws and love ye one another. Prefer not a stranger to your brother. Love and truth and my peace I leave you all.

Peace from
Your Prophet
NOBLE DREW ALI [40]

He was eventually released on bond, but a few weeks later, he died under mysterious circumstances. Some people claim that he died from injuries inflicted by the police while he was in jail. Others, however, suggest that he was killed by Greene's partisans. For some time, one W. D. Fard assumed leadership of the Moorish movement. According to Bontemps and Conroy, Fard claimed that he was the reincarnation of Noble Drew Ali. By 1930 a permanent split developed in the movement. One faction, the Moors, remains faithful to Noble Drew Ali, and the other, which is now led by Elijah Muhammad, remains faithful to Prophet Fard (Master Wallace Fard Muhammad). However, Minister Malcolm X and other leaders of the Nation of Islam have emphatically denied any past con-

39. Fauset, *op. cit.*, chap. V.
40. Bontemps and Conroy, *op. cit.*, p. 177.

nection whatsoever of Elijah Muhammad, Master Wallace Fard Muhammad, or their movement with Nobel Drew Ali's Moorish-American Science Temple.

AFRICAN NATIONALISM: U.S.A.

Marcus Garvey, the "Black Moses," was born in Jamaica on August 17, 1887. As an African nationalist, he strongly differed from Noble Drew Ali. Garvey identified the problems of American Negroes with the problem of colonialism in Africa. He believed that until Africa was liberated, there was no hope for black people anywhere. He not only traveled extensively in the Latin American countries, but in 1912 he journeyed to London to learn what he could about the condition of Negroes in other parts of the British Empire. While in London he associated himself with an Egyptian author, Duse Mohammed Ali, publisher of the *Africa Times and Orient Review*. Through this association, meeting with African and West Indian students, African nationalists, sailors, and dock workers, and reading, he delved deeply into the condition of Africans under colonial rule. In addition, he developed an interest in the condition of Negroes in the United States. He was profoundly influenced by Booker T. Washington's autobiography, *Up From Slavery*:

I read *Up From Slavery* by Booker T. Washington, and then my doom — if I may so call it — of being a race leader dawned upon me. . . . I asked: 'Where is the black man's Government? Where is his King and his Kingdom? Where is his President, his country, and his ambassador, his army, his navy, his men of big affairs?' I could not find them, and then I declared, 'I will help to make them.'[41]

In the summer of 1914 Garvey returned to Jamaica with a vision of "uniting all the Negro peoples of the world into one great body to establish a country and Government absolutely their own." He envisaged the coming of "a new world of black men, not peons, serfs, dogs and slaves, but a nation of sturdy men making their impress upon civilization and causing a new light to dawn upon the human race."

On August 1, 1914, he established the Universal Negro Improvement Association and African Communities League, with the motto:

41. Cronon, *op. cit.*, p. 16. This account is based in part on Cronon's work.

"One God! One Aim! One Destiny!" In 1915 Garvey was in communication with Booker T. Washington, who agreed to confer with him, and on March 23, 1916, he arrived in New York's Harlem. Washington was dead by this time. A year later, Garvey established a branch of the Universal Negro Improvement Association (U.N.-I.A.) in Harlem. In two months he built up a new organization of about 1,500 members. Five years later the membership had increased to "several" million Negroes in the United States, the West Indies, Latin America, and Africa. No exact information on the total membership of the movement has been compiled, but figures ranging from one million to six million have been suggested by various writers. For 1923, during the Black Star Line trials in which Garvey was involved, the following figures for some divisions of the movement were revealed: New York City, 30,000; Chicago, 9,000; Philadelphia, 6,000; Cincinnati, 5,600-6,000; Detroit, 4,000; Washington, D.C., 700; Jamaica, 5,000; Guatemala, 3,000.[42]

Garvey's ideology was both nationalist and racial. His nationalist objective was the redemption of Africa for "Africans abroad and at home." He advocated racial purity, racial integrity, and racial hegemony. He sought to organize Negroes in the United States into a vanguard for Africa's redemption from colonialism and hoped eventually to lead them back to Africa. The major instrument for the achievement of these objectives was economic cooperation through racial solidarity. He believed that if the Negroes were economically strong in the United States, they would be able to redeem Africa and establish a world wide confraternity of black people. Above all, he believed that the Negroes of the world, united

42. *Ibid.*, p. 206.

43. The following excerpts give a general idea of Garvey's teachings: "We are too large and great in numbers not to be a great people, a great race and a great nation. I cannot recall one single race of people as strong numerically as we are who have remained so long under the tutelage of other races. The time has now come when we must seek our place in the sun. . . . Without Africa, the Negro is doomed even as without America the North American Indian was lost. We are not preaching any doctrines to ask all the Negroes of Harlem and of the United States to leave for Africa. The majority of us may remain here, but we must send our scientists, our mechanics, and our artizans, and let them build railroads, let them build the great educational and other institutions necessary, and, when they are constructed, the time will come for the command to be given, 'Come Home!' . . . Africa must be linked to the United States, to South and Central America, to the West Indies by vessels which will unite in fraternal ties the ebony-hued sons of Ethiopia in the Western Hemisphere with their brothers

together by the consciousness of race and nationality, could become a great and powerful people.[43]

The Universal Negro Improvement Association and African Communities League was the organization for the propagation of his teachings. On August 1, 1920, Garvey convened in New York an International Convention of the Negro People of the World at which he called upon the delegates "to work towards the one glorious end of a free, redeemed, and mighty nation. Let Africa be a bright star among the constellation of nations. . . ."

The Association stressed the "spirit of pride and love," raising the "fallen," the development of independent Negro nations and communities, a "pan-Negro Nation," and racial education and culture:

To establish a universal confraternity among the race; to promote the spirit of pride and love; to reclaim the fallen; to administer to and assist the needy; to assist in civilizing the backward tribes of Africa; to assist in the development of independent Negro nations and communities; to establish a central nation for the race; to establish commissaries or agencies in the principal countries and cities of the world for the representation of all Negroes; to promote a conscientious spirit of worship among the native tribes of Africa; to establish universities, colleges, academies and schools for the racial education and culture of the people; to work for better conditions among Negroes everywhere.[44]

The 1920 Convention was marked by pomp and fanfare. Garvey was elected the provisional president of Africa and also President-General and Administrator of the Universal Negro Improvement Association. As head of the African republic he envisaged, his of-

across the sea. . . . If you cannot live alongside the white man in peace, if you cannot get the same chance and opportunity alongside the white man, even tho you are his fellow citizen; if he claims that you are not entitled to this chance or opportunity because the country is his by force of numbers, then find a country of your own and rise to the highest position within that country. . . . The hour has come for the Negro to take his own initiative. . . . Any race that has lost hope, lost pride and self-respect, lost confidence in self in an age like this, such a race ought not to survive. Two hundred and fifty years we have been a race of slaves; for fifty years we have been a race of parasites. Now we propose to end all that. No more fear, no more cringing, no more sycophantic begging and pleading; the Negro must strike straight from the shoulder for manhood rights and for full liberty. Destiny leads us to liberty, to freedom; that freedom that Victoria of England never gave; that liberty that Lincoln never meant; that freedom, that liberty, that will see us men among men, that will make us a great and powerful people. . . . Race amalgamation must cease; any member of this organization who marries a white woman is summarily expelled." Quoted by Rollin L. Harttin, *The Independent* (New York), CV, No. 3760 (February 26, 1921), 206, 218–219.

44. George Padmore, *Pan-Africanism or Communism?* (New York: Roy Publishers, 1956), p. 93.

ficial title was "His Highness, the Potentate" and his honorarium $22,000 per year. The eighteen members of the "High Executive Council" were to receive from $3,000 to $10,000 per year. After the "Provisional Government" had been formed and sworn in, Garvey conferred peerages and knighthoods upon them.[45]

Garvey's economic program included the establishment of the Black Star Steamship Company[46] (which included four ill-fated ships) and the Negro Factory Corporation. He sent to the Republic of Liberia a commercial and industrial mission which consisted of fifteen technicians. These enterprises were complete failures because of incompetence, mismanagement, and other difficulties. The other auxiliaries of the movement were: African Orthodox Church, the Universal African Legion, the Universal Black Cross Nurses, the Universal African Motor Corps, the Juvenile, and the Black Flying Eagles, all equipped with officers and uniforms.[47] A weekly newspaper which Garvey edited, *The Negro World*, was the main propaganda organ.

The Negro Political Union was established in 1924 to "consolidate the political union of the Negro through which the race would express its political opinion." This was Garvey's latter-day adventure into the domestic politics of the United States. During the presidential election of 1924, Garvey issued a list of approved candidates and came out strongly in support of Calvin Coolidge, the Republican presidential nominee. In New York City, Garvey supported a white Tammany nominee against a Negro candidate for Congress from the Harlem district. In Chicago, the Union gave its support to the Negro candidate, who later admitted that the Garveyites had "worked like Trojans" and had been "a material factor" in his campaign.[48]

45. *Ibid.*
46. This title is echoed in Ghana's Black Star Line Company, initially a joint enterprise between the governments of Ghana and Israel.
47. There are still a number of African Orthodox Churches in the United States, in New York, Chicago, Cincinnati, and the writer knows of a branch in Nigeria. However, he does not know whether those in the United States and those in Africa are connected. Garvey grasped the importance of the Negro church and challenged it by creating his own. The church was an adjunct of the movement and not an integral part, as it is with the Nation of Islam.
48. Drake, *op. cit.*, pp. 238–39: "But the U.N.I.A. did help me. One of their leaders heard me speak. He was impressed with what I had to say and so he made it possible for me to speak before them. They liked my talk and they voted to support me. Some

Garvey combined business enterprises with nationalist agitation. It was in connection with his business activities that he got into difficulties with the United States government, which led to his imprisonment on February 8, 1925, after being convicted of using the mails to defraud. Garvey's followers to this day believe that he was framed by "Negro Uncle Toms" and whites who were threatened by his success in organizing the Negro masses. President Coolidge commuted the sentence late in 1927. In December of the same year, Garvey was deported as an undesirable alien. While in the federal penitentiary at Atlanta, Georgia, Garvey sent the following message to his followers:

If I die in Atlanta my work shall then only begin, but I shall live, in the physical or spiritual to see the day of Africa's glory. When I am dead wrap the mantle of the Red, Black, and Green around me, for in the new life I shall rise with God's grace and blessing to lead the millions up the heights of triumph with the colors that you well know. Look for me in the whirlwind or storm, look for me all around you, for, with God's grace, I shall come and bring with me countless millions of black slaves who have died in America and the West Indies and the millions in Africa to aid you in the fight for Liberty, Freedom and Life.[49]

The above passage indicates that the struggle between the oppressed and the oppressor is seen as between the forces of "good" and "evil" and redemption is promised after the apocalypse.

After deportation Garvey returned to Jamaica and then went to London, where he died in 1940. He tried to revive the movement but never again was the Universal Negro Improvement Association what it had been before 1925. Today Garvey is "Our Saint" to his strict followers. Garveyites are still active in Harlem, Chicago, and other cities, but the movement remains split, small in membership, and organizationally weak. In New York, the African Nationalist Pioneer Movement is one neo-Garvey group which continues to keep his memory alive on the streets of Harlem. The group, under the

people say that I bought them off. But, I didn't give them a cent and they didn't ask for a cent either. They were a material factor in my campaign. They worked like Trojans for me. They were bold and fearless. I don't know how many were in the organization but it was very powerful and I got every one of their votes. Five thousand is a very conservative estimate of their strength."

49. Marcus Garvey, *Philosophy and Opinions*, comp. Amy Jacques-Garvey (New York: The Universal Publishing House, 1925), II, 239.

leadership of Carlos A. Cooks, has been trying to raise money to build a hall in memory of Garvey. In 1959, this movement issued "A Call to Convention," which invited "All Nationalist, Fraternal, Benevolent, Civic, Social and Religious Organizations of the African ethnic group throughout the world" and urged "delegate representatives to attend and take part in a positive program of total unification of the African peoples of the world." The agenda was as follows:

No. 1. The complete abrogation of that ominous appelation "Negro," (a term that is closely connected with "Nigger"). It is derogatory, vulgar and offensive. It neither defines man, land of origin or heritage. Therefore, we submit that the members of the African racial group shall henceforth be addressed with the same dignity and respect extended to all other races and nationality groups. We demand to be called, when dealing with color, Black men and women: And when dealing with race, land and heritage, Africans.

No. 2. The total mobilization of all the material resources of the Black race in all areas of the world, binding them together into one grand racial hegemony, whose only purpose shall be the welfare and security of black people everywhere.

No. 3. The activation of African-Community Leagues in all communities where people of the African ethnic group are in the majority. The economy of all African communities must be marshalled, controlled, and channelled in a progressive direction, so that the commerce business life, and body politic of the community, be controlled totally by the resident majority.

No. 4. The synchronization of all organizations, regardless of religious passions, or sectional sentiment, to one overall aim and endeavor towards the complete freedom of Africa, for the benefit of the African peoples of the world. This should include moral, physical and material support to the needy cause of the valiant Africans at home who are fighting against tremendous odds.[50]

The Convention was scheduled for August 16, 1959, at the Williams Institutional C.M.E. Youth Center, 168 West 132nd Street, New York. The meeting was held but only a handful of other organizations were represented. Mr. Cooks has said that he is not a "Negro" because "Negroes" are people of no value to the black race.[51]

On May 29, 1960, The Committee To Present The Truth About The Name "Negro" met in New York City to discuss the "origin, purpose and evil use" of the name "Negro." It was an *ad hoc* meet-

50. *A Call to Convention* (African Nationalist Pioneer Movement, n.d.).
51. He and his followers seek to disassociate themselves from white stereotypes

ing of Harlemites presided over by an attorney, Horace I. Gordon. Among the discussants were Bishop Reginald Grant Barrow and Richard B. Moore.[52] There is a growing interest among American Negroes who wish to be called collectively Afro-Americans or African-Americans.

Liberty Hall, the Garveyites' center in Chicago in the twenties, no longer exists. But Garveyites still meet to discuss, among other things, the "redemption of Africa." There are at least four factions still in existence, each claiming to represent the purest of Garvey's teachings. At one meeting of the Garveyites in Chicago which was attended by only a handful of devotees, the president made the following declaration:

> We are not a social club. We must press the issue of nationalism. We have the right to resolve the universal conflict of the Negro people of the world. We've got to redeem Africa. We must be radical and nationalistic. We are hungry for freedom and liberty. This is not a private club, not a private society. It is a universal business. It is not a religious organization. It is a nationalist organization to stop everything that prevents black people everywhere from enjoying their freedom.

> Garvey was sent by God to tell the people what they needed. Ninety per cent of the Negroes do not want anything important. We have been praying too long. You've got to be hungry for freedom. . . .[53]

The meetings generally open with a prayer. The members face toward the East while praying. Other speakers at the meeting emphasized the points the president had made; all gave the very strong

about Negroes. He believes that anyone who fits into one or more of these categories is a "Negro":

> Niggers, Negroes
> Casteman — Colored People
> Integrationists Negroes
> Handpicked House Niggers
> Wouldbe Black
> People not Organized
> Brainwashed Negroes
> Uncle Tom Niggers
> Handkerchief Head Negroes
> Conked Head Negroes
> Other People Niggers — Stool Pigeons.

The writer copied this statement from a billboard displayed at a street meeting of the African Nationalist Pioneer Movement (Harlem, New York) in the summer of 1960.

52. See Richard B. Moore, *The Name "Negro" — Its Origin and Evil Use* (New York: Afroamerican Publishers, Inc., 1960).

53. From the writer's notes.

impression that they regard Garvey as one sent by God who is now one of the "saints" in His Kingdom. The chaplain stated in his speech that "every other race had a chance to redeem the world and now it is Africa's turn to do that job which they have so far failed to do."

NOBLE DREW ALI "REINCARNATED"

It has already been indicated that upon the death of Noble Drew Ali, one W. D. Fard claimed that he was Drew Ali reincarnated.[54] Fard founded a Temple in Detroit in 1930. He is said to have declared, "I am W. D. Fard, . . . and I came from the Holy City of Mecca. More about myself I will not tell you yet, for the time has not yet come. I am your brother. You have not yet seen me in my royal robes."[55] Master Fard proclaimed that his mission was to secure "freedom, justice and equality" for his "uncle" living in the "wilderness of North America, surrounded and robbed completely by the cave man." "The Uncle of W. D. Fard" became the symbolic term for all Negroes of North America. The white man was referred to as the "cave man," "satan," or the "Caucasian devil." According to this account, Fard maintained that he was racially identical with North American Negroes, "in spite of the fact that he is said to have been born in Mecca, the son of a wealthy member of the Koreish tribe of which the Prophet Mohammad was a member." He is reputed to have been educated in England and at the University of Southern California in Los Angeles and to have been trained for a diplomatic career in the service of the Kingdom of Hehaz. He has been described as "light color," with an "oriental cast of countenance."

54. Those who do not accept Fard's claim of "reincarnation" constitute the present-day Moors. Today Noble Drew Ali's corpse "lies in a stately mausoleum in Lincoln Cemetery. It can be viewed from windows from all sides and he looks exactly as though he will keep his promise to 'rise up and walk with my people again' sometime in the very near future. Fez-wearing Moors (and there are many of them still to be seen around the city) keep a vigil at the cemetery to be on hand when Noble Drew gets up from his death couch." Dan Burley, "Elijah Muhammad: Part II — Pomp, Mysticism Key to Power," *Chicago Defender*, August 22, 1959, p. 2.

55. Bontemps and Conroy, *op. cit.*, p. 178. What follows here is taken from the account of these authors. It is interesting to notice that Fard also sought to buttress his status by appealing to the educational institutions of the society against which he revolted.

Fard used various names: Walli Farrad, Professor Ford, Farrad Mohammed, F. Mohammed Ali, and even God, Allah. He is said to have peddled silks and raincoats from door to door in "Paradise Valley," the Negro neighborhood of Detroit.

> He came first to our houses selling raincoats, and then afterwards silks. In this way he could get into the people's houses, for every woman was eager to see the nice things the peddlars had for sale. He told us that the silks he carried were the same kind that our people used in their home country and that he had come from there. So we all asked him to tell us about our own country. . . .[56]

It has been estimated that between 1930 and 1934, Fard recruited eight thousand followers among Detroit Negroes. The rapid growth of the first Temple was accompanied by the establishment of various subsidiary organizations, among which was the University of Islam for the training of "Moslem" youth and families in the "knowledge of our own" as distinct from that of the "civilization of the Caucasian Devils."

Having thoroughly organized the Detroit Temple, W. D. Fard seems to have "receded into the background, appearing very seldom to his followers during his final months in Detroit," and this mysterious aloofness fostered the belief that he was indeed the "Supreme Ruler of the Universe" or as he called himself, the "God, Allah." Apparently, not all his followers believed in his divinity, and "controversy over this was one of the several causes of dissension in the movement." As a direct consequence of an internal dispute, the Chicago branch of the Nation of Islam was established in the latter part of 1933 or early 1934. W. D. Fard left Detroit in 1933, "disappearing altogether as far as any authoritative record is concerned."[57] Some of his Detroit followers immediately identified him with Allah and claimed that he had returned to the Holy City of Mecca. Others continued to regard him simply as the Prophet. A split occurred, and "that faction favorable to the deification of W. D. Fard assumed 'Temple People' as a name, severed all connec-

56. Erdmann D. Benyon, "The Voodoo Cult Among Negro Migrants in Detroit," *American Journal of Sociology*, XLIII, No. 6 (May, 1938), 895. Here, Benyon is quoting from an interview with a follower.

57. It has been suggested that Prophet Fard might have moved to Chicago but, as we shall see later, there is little evidence of his activities there.

tions with the parent group, and eventually set up its headquarters in Chicago under Elijah Mohammed whose original name had been 'Robert Poole.' "[58] The Detroit Temple is now called Muhammad's Temple of Islam, No. 1.

PROPHET FARD IN CHICAGO

Little is known of Fard's activities in Chicago. Police investigation of a courtroom riot in 1935, which involved members of the "Allah Temple of Islam," then located at 3643 South State Street, identified the leader of the "colored cult" as "W. D. Fard, or Fard Mohammed, or Elijah Mohammed":

> Among the 43 prisoners were King Shah, 38 years old, 3242 South State Street, and Allah Shah, 18 years old, 2556 Warren Boulevard, the two wounded cultists. Their "Moorish" names puzzled the police until King Shah disclosed that the prophet of their order, W. D. Fard, or Fard Mohammed, or Elijah Mohammed, had christened them thus last spring.
>
> A police search for Prophet Fard was started but he could not be found last night. He was described as one "born in the holy city of Mecca in 1877," who came to America on July 4, 1930.[59]

There is no certain knowledge as to the identity of Master Wallace Fard Muhammad.[60] An Arab was thought to be the founder and leader of the "Allah Temple of Islam" between 1930 and 1933 after the breach developed between the Moors and those who believed that "Prophet" Fard was Noble Drew Ali reincarnated. The second split, which came over the question of whether or not Prophet Fard was the "God, Allah," led to the rise and leadership of Elijah Muhammad. Bontemps and Conroy have indicated that there was a man by the name W. D. Fard. The Chicago police investigation of the courtroom incident suggests that Prophet Fard was also known as "Fard Muhammad or Elijah Muhammad." Muhammad claims that Master W. D. Fard or Wallace Fard Muhammad came from Mecca, Arabia, and that he was with the Mahdi at the airport when

58. End of Bontemps and Conroy's account, pp. 177–84.
59. *Chicago Daily Tribune*, March 6, 1935, p. 1. See chapter III for an account of this riot.
60. Benyon, *op. cit.*, p. 896: "Although the prophet lived in Detroit from July 4, 1930, until June 30, 1934, virtually nothing is known about him, save that he "came from the East and that he called the Negroes of North America to enter the Nation of Islam. His very name is uncertain. . . .""

he was deported. Aside from this account, there is no evidence of who Prophet Fard was, where he came from, or what happened to him. Muhammad's own account and those of others are examined in later chapters.

THE NATIONALIST TRADITION IN CHICAGO

During the first wave of intensive nationalist agitation — about 1915 to 1930 — the Garvey and Moorish movements gained a large number of adherents in Chicago. However, neither received the support of the majority of the people in the Chicago Negro community.[61] Aside from these, there were two or three other nationalist groups in Chicago. A group of Negroes who styled themselves "Abyssinians" seems significant among these minor associations.

The existence of the "Abyssinians" in Chicago drew public attention for the first time in a dramatic shooting and killing of two persons on Sunday afternoon, June 20, 1920. This incident followed a parade and a ceremony at which the Abyssinians deliberately burned two United States flags. A Negro patrolman was wounded and several other persons were injured. Grover C. Redding, who is reputed to have been the leader, and his colleague, Oscar McGavick, were indicted for murder by a grand jury.[62]

A study by the Chicago Commission on Race Relations describes the Abyssinian movement as "an illegitimate offspring" of the Garvey movement.[63] The *Chicago Tribune* sought to link the Abyssinian incident with "Racial 'reds' " and also with the writings of W. E. B. DuBois.[64]

61. Membership figures for the Garvey movement have been given. The Moorish movement, at the peak of its success, had about 2,000 to 3,000 followers in Chicago, according to a former follower of Drew Ali. The combined strength of all nationalist groups by 1925 seems to have been close to ten per cent of the total Chicago Negro population (109,458) in 1920.

62. Chicago Commission on Race Relations, *The Negro in Chicago: A Study of Race Relations and a Riot* (Chicago: University of Chicago Press, 1922), pp. 59–64, 480–81, 537–39.

63. *Ibid.*, p. 61.

64. *Ibid.*, pp. 538–39: "The agitators have used considerable skill in exploiting the Negroes by use of doctrines which they have taken from Dr. Du Bois, as expressed in *Darkwater*. Here are some of them: 'The world market most widely and desperately sought today is the market where labor is cheapest and most helpless and profit is most abundant. This labor is kept cheap and helpless because the white world despises

The back-to-Abyssinia movement was semireligious and nationalistic, and Redding was both a secular and religious leader. He claimed that he was a prophet and a native of Ethiopia. In addressing the court at his trial, Redding stated the following as his mission:

My mission is marked in the Bible. Even if they have captured me, some other leaders will rise up and lead the Ethiopian back to Africa. The Bible says, "So shall the King of Assyria lead away the Egyptian prisoners and the Ethiopian captives, young and old . . . to the shame of Egypt." The Ethiopians do not belong here and should be taken back to their own country. Their time was up in 1919. They came in 1619. The Bible has pointed out that they were to appear in three hundred years. The time is up. The burning of the flag last Sunday night by me was a symbol that Abyssinians are not wanted in this country. That was the sign the Bible spoke of.[65]

The prophetic role is particularly attractive to the leaders of the black masses. Lower-class Negroes are somewhat "superstitious" and the leaders can exploit their religious susceptibilities. However, most of these leaders have no significant social status and prestige which would lend credibility and legitimacy to their leadership. The other leaders of this movement included Joseph Fernon, known as the "Great Abyssinian," his son, "The Prince," and a "doctor," R. D. Jonas, a white man.

The belief of the Abyssinians that they are Ethiopians and not Negroes is an obvious device to avoid the label "Negro" with all its connotations of inferiority. To differentiate themselves from their "Negro-ness" became a means of escaping the abuse and insults of the whites. For a dollar, a member could purchase an Abyssinian flag, a small pamphlet containing a prophecy relating to the return of the dark-skinned people of Africa, a so-called treaty between the United States and Abyssinia, and a picture of the "Prince of Abyssinians." In addition, a member could sign up to return to Ethiopia in order that he might fill any one of forty-four

'darkies'. . . . But what of the dark world that watches? . . . Most men belong to this world. With Negro and Negroid, East Indian, Chinese, and Japanese they form two-thirds of the population of the world. A belief in humanity is a belief in colored men. If the uplift in mankind must be done by men, then the destinies of the world will rest ultimately in the hands of darker nations.'" The Commission notes: "It is doubtful whether the 'Abyssinian' leaders, who were ignorant fanatics little known within the Negro group, had read Du Bois' books."

65. Bontemps and Conroy, *op. cit.,* p. 174.

positions, such as chemist, civil engineer, mechanic, chicken farmer, teacher, cartoonist, etc.[66]

Aside from these pedestrian goals, concrete activities to realize the back-to-Abyssinia objective are not apparent. The esoteric teachings of the Abyssinians emphasized their connection with the "source" of civilization — curiously enough, Israel via Ethiopia — and the expectation of their redemption after the apocalypse when "God's chosen people will be alright." This assertion of a connection with the "sacred" as well as with the source of civilization were means of enhancing self-esteem and status. Perhaps the mainstay of the movement was its preachment of hatred for the white man and its rejection of the pejorative label "Negro."[67] The Abyssinian movement received little support from Negroes and now seems to have entirely disappeared, superseded by other organizations interested in Negro repatriation to Ethiopia.

BLACK NATIONALISM IN DECLINE: 1930–1945

The decline of black nationalist appeal began in the late nineteen-twenties and continued until the end of the second World War. The splits which occurred in both Marcus Garvey's and Noble Drew Ali's movements weakened the possibility of a "united nationalist front." Second, a number of separatist nationalist movements were begun but only one of them has, since the last war, been able to make an impression on the Negro community. The inception of the Nation of Islam belongs to this period.

The Peace Movement of Ethiopia, in the Garvey tradition, was founded at a meeting in Chicago in 1932. The group conducted a vigorous campaign for Negro repatriation to Africa and urged that Negroes support Mississippi Senator Theodore G. Bilbo's Negro

66. Chicago Commission on Race Relations, *op. cit.*, p. 62.

67. *Ibid.*, p. 480. In an interview by one of the Commission's investigators several weeks before the shooting incident, a Negro shopkeeper and sympathizer with the movement expressed the following sentiments: "I am a radical. *I despise and hate the white man.* They will always be against the Ethiopian. *I do not want to be called Negro,* colored, or 'nigger.' Either term is an insult to me or to you. Our rightful name is Ethiopian. White men stole the black man from Africa and counselled with each other as to what to do with him and what to call him, for *when the Negro learned that he was the first civilized human being on earth he would rise up and rebel against the white man.*" (Emphasis added.)

Repatriation Bill in 1939. Garvey supported the scheme in an editorial in the *Black Man,* published in London. Garvey's followers in Chicago and members of the Peace Movement launched an abortive march on Washington in support of the measure.

Members of the Peace Movement, as well as the Moors, the Iron Defense Legion (a few uniformed black fascists), and the Pacific Movement of the Eastern World are said to have been sympathetic to the Japanese during the war. In Chicago a leading member of the Peace Movement was sentenced to the federal penitentiary for advising Negroes to resist the draft and for propagating pro-Japanese sentiments.[68] The Peace Movement continues to function, although its membership is small. Its meetings are held every Sunday at 4653 South State Street in Chicago. Mrs. A. B. Baker, the current president, wrote recently:

> I feel that the greatest honor that can come to me in my life, was acceptance in a nationalist movement. It is our desire that all blood of Africa proclaim their rightful heritage. . . . We are now in a position to know the truth. . . .[69]

The Ethiopian World Federation Council, Incorporated, was formed on August 25, 1937, by Dr. Maluku E. Bayen, a nephew of Emperor Haile Selassie. Dr. Bayen was sent to the United States as a special envoy to solicit aid from people of Ethiopian descent for Ethiopia during the Italo-Ethiopian War. The Chicago branch was formed on May 27, 1938. The aims of the Federation include the promotion of "love and goodwill among Ethiopians at home and abroad, and thereby to maintain the integrity and sovereignty of Ethiopia. . . ."[70] Chapters of the Council are scattered throughout the United States, according to an officer of the local branch in Chicago. The Federation holds regular religious meetings

68. Drake and Cayton, *Black Metropolis,* p. 745. Cronon, *op. cit.,* p. 166.

69. "Baker on Africa," *New Crusader,* Chicago, February 27, 1960, p. 9.

70. Mimeographed information sheet distributed by the Council. The rest of the aims are: ". . . to disseminate the ancient Ethiopian culture among its members . . . and carve for ourselves and our posterity, a destiny comparable with our idea . . . that we may not only save ourselves from annihilation, but carve for ourselves a place in the Sun. . . . A non-Partisan, non-political-purpose is to help people of African descendant, of their history, culture and language; also help poor and unfortunate of all races and creed. . . . The Colors are *Red, Gold,* and *Green* as Ethiopia Flag. Motto: 'Ethiopia Yesterday, To-day, and Tomorrow.' "

and relies on the same biblical references to "Ethiopia" as the Abyssinians of the early twenties. It is semireligious and nationalistic.

The National Movement for the Establishment of the Forty-Ninth State was founded in Chicago during this period by Oscar C. Brown, a Negro lawyer and businessman. This movement was essentially political in ideology. Unlike Garvey, he sought political "self-determination" for Negroes by the establishment of a Negro state within the United States.[71] The movement received no support from Negroes, and unlike those linked with an idea of "self-determination" for Negroes in Africa or the religiously oriented ones, it was short-lived.

Present-day quasi-nationalistic organizations in Chicago, in addition to those previously mentioned, include the following: the Joint Council of Repatriation; World Wide Friends of Africa; American Economic League; the Garvey Club; Royal Ethiopian Jews; Washington Park Forum; and the United African Federation Council. Membership in some of these organizations is too small to justify extensive comment.

The World Wide Friends of Africa, known also as the House of Knowledge, was founded in the nineteen-thirties. Its director, F. H. Hammurabi, believes that "a race without knowledge of its history is like a tree without roots." Hammurabi sponsors a number of weekly activities to encourage Negroes "to know themselves, their nation and the world." Negroes visit the House of Knowledge on Saturdays and Sundays to seek information, read, listen to lectures, or simply to see educational films. Hammurabi is known to advise Negroes who are interested in going to Africa concerning the training they need to secure here in the United States.

The American Economic League is primarily interested in urging Negroes to invest in Africa. A representative of the League, at a meeting of the United African Federation Council in December, 1958, stressed that "the time is fast approaching when Negroes must

71. The Forty-Ninth State Movement "seeks the establishment of a new state in the Union — not an isolated, uncivilized, hostile colony around which is built a figurative Wall of China, shutting out the possibilities of travel and growth, from within and without, not a separate nation; but an interdependent Commonwealth like any other of the present forty-eight states" (*Crisis*, May, 1935, p. 137).

go back to Africa," although "there is no room in Africa for lazy American Negroes."

> We have too many organizations. I am interested in investment in Africa. I am an American. I have an interest in profits. I am of African descent. We should be represented in anything going on in Africa. Shares at ten dollars each sold to millions of American Negroes would raise substantial amount for capital investment in Africa. It's time we think about big things. Our problem is economic. Invest our money in America properly. Don't listen to the white man and what he thinks. Don't sit tight for him to help you.

The Joint Council of Repatriation is primarily interested in Negroes' return to Africa. Its members stand solidly behind a bill (similar to the Bilbo Bill) to aid persons emigrating to Liberia, which was introduced in the United States Senate in January, 1951, by the late Senator Langer. The Council, which is known to favor repatriation programs of such segregationist groups as the American Party, shares the following aims:

> To establish and finance a national home in Liberia for the American Negroes; giving them a lump endowment to each, transporting their movable assets, liquidating their resources and providing industrial, scientific, commercial and humanitarian aid to them until they have erected a substantial republic of recognition among the nations of the world. . . .[72]

On April 5, 1959, S. A. Davis, Chairman of the Advisory Board of the Joint Council of Repatriation, his wife, and seven of his aides met in Chicago with Lincoln Rockwell (white), Commander of the American Party of the World Union of Free Enterprise Socialists. According to this Nazi group's propaganda, this joint declaration was made:

> The Commander of the American Nazis and the Black Leader planned a joint demonstration by both groups at the White House to dramatize for the American people that there are already over 4,000,000 Negroes who have petitioned the government to return to Africa, but are being held here by the Jewish groups who are using the Negroes as cheap labor, and as captive voting blocs. It was felt that if the American people saw, with their own eyes, the supposedly "hate-crazed" Nazis working with dedication and mutual respect with their Negro friends to achieve a SOLUTION to their problem, rather than fighting and provoking each other, they might realize that the billion-dollar campaigns in all our Jewish

72. John Rousseau in the *Pittsburgh Courier*, June 7, 1958, p. 7

dominated mediums of public information for integration are designed only to anger and dismay both the races and to *PREVENT* a solution.

We felt that such a joint Black and White effort to achieve the decent solution of REPATRIATION, advocated by Washington, Jefferson, Madison, Monroe and Lincoln, would force our controlled press to stop driving all people, Black and White, apart by splitting into the promoted camps of Integration vs. Segregation, and demonstrate the very real possibility of a MUTUALLY satisfactory solution, — Repatriation under decent conditions.[73]

The writer interviewed three of the Negroes who were alleged to have been associated with this joint declaration. They denied some statements of the party's report:

We met at the segregated Southmoor Hotel in Chicago. Two of the Nazi leaders came from Virginia. One lives in Chicago. There were three of them and nine of us. We did not sign any joint statement. The Nazi leaders wanted us to get a large number of Negroes to march to Washington singing, praying, and carrying swastikas. The Nazi leader proposed that if they supported him to become the President of the United States, he would provide for the Negro's repatriation and the Negro problem would be solved.

He said that he loved his women. We said we also love our women. We refused to join them in a march on Washington carrying swastikas. We told him that in such a march only the Negro would get kicked and thrown in jail. We did not sign any joint statement. We reached no conclusions. Brother Davis wrote the Nazi leaders to say that we were not interested in their movement.[74]

Mr. Davis has lived in Chicago since 1905. He claims that he has been teaching nationalism for the past fifty years. He styles himself also a biblical interpreter. He may be seen at any public activity or lecture in Chicago which has some relation to Africa.

On December 1, 1958, the United African Federation Council was founded and this statement was issued:

All African groups and organizations, united together for general council, of people of African descent. To improve historical, economical, and general welfare.

73. Photographs of both parties to the alleged joint declaration were displayed in the Nazi group's propaganda material, which was published at Arlington, Virginia, undated. The March on Washington did not materialize. Activities of the American Nazi Party were covered in *The Evening Star*, Washington, D. C., April 22, 1959; *The Washington Post*, April 23, 1959; and *The News*, Washington, D. C., April 25, 1959. In June, 1960, the Mayor of New York City refused to grant a permit to Rockwell's group to hold a Fourth of July rally at Union Square. "New York Bans U.S. Nazi Rally . . ." by Philip Cook, *Chicago Sun-Times*, June 23, 1960, p. 4.

74. Interview with Brother Robert Maxi, August 15, 1959.

OBJECT: To promote love, harmony, and understanding among people of African descent at home and abroad to better their conditions educational, religious. To send technical aid and representation to Africa for economical, educational, and business purposes for all free states in the Continent of Africa.

PREAMBLE: We the people of African descent, in order to form a more perfect council for freedom and self determination, for better understanding of racial tolerance and our own heritage and freedom for all mankind, do hereby establish and ordain this constitution for the UNITED AFRICAN FEDERATION COUNCIL.

Seventeen organizations which have some interest in Africa were invited, but only six appeared at the meeting. The provisional president of the Federation, Winston G. Evans, explained that:

Many organizations arise in this Chicago among the Negroes and die out. A government never dies out and that is the kind of organization which we want. The existing organizations are numerically weak. The so-called "big shots" among the Negroes have no interest whatsoever in the masses of the Negroes. Why should they organize and demand the City Council to bring Dr. Nkrumah, or Haile Selassie, or Tubman to the South Side when they know that they can buy their way downtown? Now is our time to unite in this U.S.A. as Ghana and Guinea. The French and British empires are going down. One nation goes down and another rises up. So it is with race.

In New York City, Mr. — [a Harlem black nationalist who is connected with the African Stock Exchange Association Development Corporation] informed me that the Jews are trying their best to break up all African nationalist organizations. The Jew wants you to stay in this country so that he can continue to exploit the Negro. The Jews will raise a million dollars for the NAACP. Why not raise the same amount for resettling those Negroes who wish to return to Africa? That amount would build a sizeable town in Africa. We must look to Africa for our redemption. The Repatriation Bill is still up in Congress. The Negroes continue to feel content in spite of the conditions in America. Our only economic resource consists of the churches, funeral homes and policy. Our ministers get richer and richer. All the rich ministers of course make frequent visits to "the Holy Land" — Africa. They return learning nothing from the people out there about how to organize for freedom. . . . For all the money the Negro churches have collected there is no economic result coming from it.

African history is not taught to Negro children. We must give them this message. They are ashamed of Africa. A white kid is not. He learns the vital products of Africa and can name them. The Negro child knows only about monkeys.

His comment on Negro leadership reveals the hostility of the nationalists toward the educated Negro.

We should not wait for everyone to make up his mind. Do not expect the lawyers, doctors, and the rest of the Negro middle class here. But wait, once you have the membership, the lawyers and doctors will be here, and if you have the money, they will become members. They never start any movement themselves. They are joiners. They join the whites and the Negroes alike.

These observations represented the general feeling of members at the meeting.[75]

SUMMARY: CHARACTERISTICS OF BLACK NATIONALISM

The movements we have examined exhibit common characteristics as well as differences. Their common origins are the cultural alienation and social estrangement of the urban Negro masses from the white society, the absence of a "great Negro ethos" capable of inspiring them to work together for the ends they seek, and the confusion, apathy, frustration, and disillusionment which arise in their attempt to adjust to these conditions. Consequently, Negroes tend to perceive white society as a monolith united in opposition to their advancement and therefore as not susceptible to fundamental change through rational persuasion, let alone through coercion.[76] They become overwhelmed by a feeling of total powerlessness.

Those who do not succumb completely to this feeling of hopelessness tend to develop a distrust for existing institutions and conventional modes of action. This distrust and antagonism toward existing institutions (white or Negro) is common to the nationalist movements, reflected in their negative attitude toward political participation, conventional Negro education, the Negro church and hence Christianity, traditional modes of Negro social protest and action, Negro middle-class leadership, and the intellectuals. Some

75. Meeting of the United African Federation Council, December 1, 1958, held at the Washington Park Field House, Chicago.

76. By "coercion" physical violence is not implied but rather such activities as the "march on Washington," boycotts, and, more importantly, deliberately organized Negro vote in support of political organizations willing and able to advance their cause. The recent "sit-in" and organized voters' registration drives in the South may encourage more of such activities in the northern cities.

hostility may even be displaced from the "sacred" Christian whites to a more vulnerable minority such as the Jews. Their attitude was perhaps best summed up by S. A. Davis:

> As long as the Negro is in America there is no hope for him. The white man takes one Negro and kills the aspirations of a million others. The white man has successfully made the Negro into an individualist for himself, and denied a nation of his own to the Negro. The Negro's worst enemy is his religion. The acceptance of Christianity killed his nationalism. Christianity is his worst poisonous enemy. There are over 700 denominations among Negroes and yet the Negroes have not founded a single denomination of their own. They get together to serve white gods. The Negro will never unite until the religious struggle is won.
>
> Ask a Negro what his problem is, he says, unity. He agrees with you but that is all. His case in America is hopeless. The NAACP is the Big Niggers' organization. It was founded by whites, the bosses are whites and Jews — the biggest thief there ever was. The Big Niggers, the NAACP, don't want Langer's Bill passed. The Jews don't want it passed. The Big Niggers want to get jobs here. They are not nationalists. They have no national program. They are not interested in the plight of the masses. The Big Niggers as a class don't think. Of course they get their diplomas and stand around like any other Negro for a job from the white man. Once a Negro reaches college level he is no good for anybody. They were brought here slaves, have remained slaves, and will remain slaves.[77]

The nationalists tend to become preoccupied with the means of overcoming their sense of powerlessness, but in their preoccupation with the means, the end of building up black power appears to become less important because it seems either unattainable or utopian. Hence, they call upon superhuman or divine intervention for its realization:

> Negroes, shall we not choose between right and wrong? Shall we not pattern the lives of those men, races and nations that have prospered by justice? Surely we shall, for in so doing we will have removed ourselves from the curse of a heartless, sinful, unjust world to a new temporal sphere, where man will live in peace and die in *the consciousness of a new resurrection.*
>
> Such will be Africa's day, when a new light will encircle the earth, and black men lift their hands to their God and Princes come out of our country. For this we will not give hope, but fight and struggle on, until the *Angel of Peace and Love appears* [emphasis added].[78]

77. From an interview.
78. Garvey, *Philosophy and Opinions*, II, 14.

This phenomenon permeates the teachings of the more religiously oriented nationalist movements and, as we shall see, it is quite important in the end-doctrines of Muhammad.

The preoccupation with means and the relegation of ends to a superhuman agency is important for understanding the relationship between the exoteric and esoteric doctrines of black nationalism. It accounts in large measure for the part religion plays in black nationalism, so that even Garvey, whose nationalism was more secular than religious, could not escape it:

It is foolish for us to believe that the world can settle itself on chance. It is for man and God to settle the world. God acts indifferently and His plan and purpose is generally worked out through the agency of human action. In His directed, inspired prophecy He promised that Ethiopia's day would come, not by the world changing toward us, but by our stretching out our hands unto Him. It doesn't mean the mere physical test, but the universal and independent effort to surround ourselves with the full glory of man.[79]

RACIAL REDEMPTION

Concern with racial redemption is an important esoteric component of nationalism. The nationalists tend to perceive black redemption as a struggle between "good" and "evil" in which God is on their side. This image of the world leads to an intense feeling of persecution, since it necessarily divides the world into "friends" and "enemies":

It seems that the whole world of sentiment is against the Negro, and the difficulty of our generation is to extricate ourselves from the prejudice that hides itself beneath, as well as above, the action of an international environment.[80]

And also:

Let us pray for our enemies, whosoever they be! Let us all over the world pray daily for God's handling of our enemies! Pray hard and earnestly, at least twice a day, for God's dealing with our enemies. At twelve o'clock midday and twelve o'clock midnight let us in silent prayer for thirty seconds send up our supplications and appeal to God for the correction of those who oppose us even against His divine will that we should stretch out our hands to Him.

Surely God will answer our prayers against the wicked and unjust and

79. *Ibid.*, p. 16.
80. *Ibid.*, p. 22.

strengthen us for the great work that must be done in His name and to His glory. Remember our duty is to be firm in faith.[81]

THE QUEST FOR IDENTITY AND POWER

Theoretically, black nationalism is a special type of political behavior. The nationalists, like most people, feel a need of attachment to some power center, but this need is not satisfied in existing society. Carl T. Rowan, a Negro newspaper reporter, observes that Paul Robeson:

. . . is a black nationalist who seems to long in his heart to see the day when the power of the world's black men will overwhelm the whites whom he sees as the blind purveyors of shame and misery for 'his people.'[82]

In Mr. Robeson's own words:

I think a good deal in terms of the power of black people in the world, . . . That's why Africa means so much to me. As an American Negro, I'm proud of Africa as one of those West Coast Chinese is proud of China.

Now that doesn't mean that I'm going back to Africa, but spiritually I've been a part of Africa for a long time.

Yes, this black power moves me. Look at Jamaica. In a few years the white minority will be there on the sufferance of black men. If they're nice, decent fellows they can stay.

Yes, I look at Senator Eastland and say, 'So you think you are powerful here? If only I could get *you* across the border.'

Although I may stay here the rest of my life, spiritually I'll always be part of that world where the black man can say to these crackers, 'Get the hell out of here by morning.'

If I could get a passport, I'd just like to go to Ghana or Jamaica, just to sit there for a few days and observe this black power.[83]

The black nationalists define the power center in many ways. On the whole they tend to disassociate themselves from the power center of the ruling white society. Some think of it in religious or utopian terms, and God or Allah becomes that power center. The downtrodden feel particularly gratified by the knowledge that they enjoy a special relationship with the omnipotent or with the sacred. It is also perceived in relation to an ancient kingdom, a present African state, or a powerful black kingdom yet to come. Hence, some nationalists

81. *Ibid.*, p. 17.
82. Carl T. Rowan, "Has Paul Robeson Betrayed the Negro?" *Ebony*, October, 1957, p. 41.
83. *Ibid.*, p. 41. Quoted by Carl T. Rowan.

are particularly fond of Ethiopia, Egypt, Morocco, or the Sudan. In general, they tend to disassociate themselves from sub-Saharan Africa because it has been disparaged by the whites as uncivilized and without culture.

Related to the need for attachment to a power center is the desire for a non-white tradition and civilization. The "Ethiopians" attach themselves to the Coptic Christian tradition, the Muslims to Arabic civilization, and some to the "Moorish" or "Asiatic" peoples. The Garveyites identify themselves with "Africans at home," and essentially with their West African origins, although Garvey himself used "Ethiopian" as a symbolic term for all of black Africa. These movements seek to legitimize their attachment to these traditions by placing the black race in an exalted position in some very remote past. They entail a rejection of the "Negro heritage" in America, and of their "Negro-ness," supposedly hated by the whites. Thus the nationalists tend to view the Negro heritage in America as a period of discontinuity in the particular tradition to which they attach themselves, or as a period of God's chastisement of the black race, or simply as part of a divine plan for the redemption of the race.

The dichotomy between means and ends, the peculiar relationship between exoteric and esoteric forms of black nationalism, enables us to explain the lack of interest in political participation among the black nationalists. It restrains the nationalists' hostility toward existing institutions from finding expression in extra-constitutional means for changing or modifying the political institutions of the United States.[84] In fact, the nationalists have generally pursued a policy of self-imposed "political exile" and have not made any effort to use the vote to attain their objectives. This fact of political inaction, with the exception of a few minor incidents, is

84. Although a renunciation of politics has characterized black nationalism in the United States, the Rastafari Movement in Jamaica (West Indies) alleged to be supported by the First African Corps (a black nationalist organization in New York City) has been known to resort to semirevolutionary activities against the government of the West Indian Federation. However, the Rastafarian leaders deny both allegations. See *The New York Courier*, April 16, 1961, p. 9. As a result, the West Indian government sent a delegation to Africa to find ways of resettling these incorrigible Africans on that continent. Cf. Kingsley Martin, "The Jamaican Volcano", *The New Statesman* (London), March 17, 1961, pp. 416 and 418, also *New York Herald Tribune*, April 4, 1961, p. 15, also Janheinz Jahn, *Muntu*, translated by Marjorie Greene (London: Faber and Faber, Ltd., 1961).

particularly important for understanding the attitude toward the state of the black nationalists.

The exoteric forms of black nationalism are the "means" for coping with the material, cultural, moral and psychological problems which are purported to impede the advancement of the Negro masses. In esoteric terms, the Negro has "fallen" from the grace of God and, in the eyes of the "civilized" world, he is universally held in contempt. In other words, the nationalists take the view that the Negro is psychologically and spiritually "sick." The task of the nationalists is to "reclaim the fallen" and to bring them "a new life, pride and love of race." Consequently, they insist that the Negro can transcend his "Negro-ness," which is held in contempt by both his friends and foes, only by radically asserting his racial identity. To do this Negroes must be self-reliant and:

. . . create for ourselves a central ideal and make our lives conform to it in the singling out of a racial life that shall know no end . . . We need the creation of a common standard among ourselves that will fit us for companionship and equitable competition with others.[85]

MESSIANIC LEADERSHIP

The nationalists' emphasis on racial redemption and reclamation of the "fallen" calls for a messianic style of leadership. The leader is a national messiah. He may deliberately create this image of himself, but apparently, he believes intuitively that he is the chosen "vessel" for the redemption of his people. His followers share this image of the leader. The messianic leader legitimizes his mission — social protest and action — on the ground that he received his "commission" directly from God. His mission is further confirmed by the historical and prevailing social conditions which afflict the masses. His personal qualifications need not be consistent with conventional standards of competence and knowledge, but his ability to articulate and project the problems of the oppressed, to identify himself with them, and his sincerity and devotion to the "cause" are indispensable.

The messianic phantasy has exercised a powerful fascination on

85. Garvey, *Philosophy and Opinions*, II, 15.

the imagination of peoples in different societies and cultures.[86] It has a special appeal for the politically and socially oppressed. This phantasy has had, therefore, an appeal for some Negroes, who then tend to perceive their plight as analogous to the biblical account of the children of Israel in Egypt. Accordingly, God will deliver them in the same manner that the Jews are said to have been delivered.[87] This belief appears to soothe their temporal miseries and is made credible by the New Testament doctrine of the Second Coming of Christ with which they are familiar. Negroes have traditionally sought the "promised land" — from the slave South to the free North before the Emancipation; from Mississippi to New York, Detroit, Chicago, or San Francisco; from New York to Paris, Mexico, or Rome; from the separate Negro church to Islam, Judaism, and Voodooism.

Expectation of a messianic remedy for social ills makes the prophet-leader particularly attractive to the oppressed masses. The degree to which black nationalist leaders indulge in the theme of racial redemption and the means by which it is to be attained have given rise to two styles of leadership. The tradition represented by Noble Drew Ali appealed to the Negro's religious susceptibilities and sought to improve the status of the Negro masses through its own version of Islam. Garvey appealed to their economic plight and pointed to the political inferiority of the black race throughout the world. Garvey's declared aim was not only to improve their eco-

86. Cohn, *The Pursuit of the Millenium*. Cf. Bengt G. M. Sundkler, *Bantu Prophets in South Africa* (London: Lutterworth Press, 1948). Also Justus M. van der Kroef, "Racial Messiahs," *Race: Individual and Collective Behavior*, eds. Thompson and Hughes, pp. 357–364; Hans Kohn, "Dostoyevsky and Danilevsky: Nationalist Messianism" *Continuity and Change in Russia and Soviet Thought*, ed. Ernest J. Simmons (Cambridge, Mass.: Harvard University Press, 1955), pp. 500–549; Joseph F. Zygmunt, "Social Estrangement and Recruitment Process in a Chiliastic Movement" (Master's thesis, University of Chicago, 1953).

87. The "messiah" appeared in Negro leadership in the early nineteenth century and was a source of inspiration to Gabriel Prosser, Denmark Vessey, Nat Turner (leaders of slave revolts or plots), Sojourner Truth and Harriet Tubman (leaders in the abolition movement and the Underground Railroad), and Benjamin "Pap" Singleton (leader of Negro migration from the South to Kansas). See Bardolph's account of the lives of the first three leaders, pp. 28–34, 75. See Brown on Tubman, *op. cit.*, pp. 296–318, 537–38; cf. Sarah H. Bradford, *Harriet, The Moses of Her People* (New York: George R. Lockwood & Sons, 1897). On Sojourner Truth, see Saunders Redding, *The Lonesome Road*, ed. Lewis Gannett (New York: Doubleday and Company, Inc., 1959) pp. 65–82; Walter L. Fleming, "Pap Singleton, Moses of the Colored Exodus," *American Journal of Sociology*, XV (July, 1909), 61-82.

nomic position in the United States but also to unite them into a "vanguard for Africa's redemption." Both appealed to history in order to justify their movements, Drew Ali abstracting a history of the Negro people from the Holy Bible, and through his interpretations, bequeathing to his followers a body of racial theology which is religious and nationalistic in content. Garvey appealed essentially to social or "secular" history. The Negroes, he said, are Africans abroad, and they must seek to discover their greatness in that continent. Both believed in racial "purity" and racial separation. However, Garvey believed that racial co-operation was desirable and appealed to the "conscience" of white America in support of his program.[88] Both sought to create a "central ideal" for the race (at least for American Negroes). The nationalists differ on this point. Drew Ali had a firm faith in Islam as the central ideal. Garvey believed the focus was Africa although it seems doubtful that he actually wanted his followers to emigrate to Africa:

. . . After Marcus Garvey had returned millions to Africa spiritually, he had done his work. It was finished in the real sense. I believe if Garvey had lived, he would have studied the conditions in Africa even more than in the New World and he would have realized that the return to Africa had taken place — that the black man in the New World could make a greater contribution to Africa by remaining in America, rather than migrating.
. . . People misunderstood him. As a matter of fact, the term, back-to-Africa, was used and promoted by newspapers, Negro newspapers mostly, to ridicule Garvey. There was no back-to-Africa movement except in a spiritual sense. . . .[89]

The consequence of the disagreement among the black nationalists on what the central ideal shall be has given rise to sectarianism among them. Their past performance in this respect hardly justifies their appeal for a "United Front of Black Men."

The creation of a central ideal by these movements is further complicated by the social and cultural environment in which they function. The nationalists are confronted, as are other Negroes, with the problem of attraction to and revulsion from the existing white

88. Garvey, "An Appeal to the Soul of White America," *Philosophy and Opinions*, II, p. 5.

89. Amy Jacques-Garvey, quoted by Lerone Bennet Jr., in "The Ghost of Marcus Garvey: Interviews with the Crusader's Two Wives," *Ebony*, March 1960, p. 59.

society. This problem is highlighted by some of the behavior patterns of the nationalists. It is interesting to note that in spite of Garvey's hostility to imperialist Britain, he was attracted to the British tradition of peerages and knighthoods. Even an ardent black nationalist shared the stereotypes toward the "backward tribes" of Africa that are fostered by the whites. There are many examples of this nature in the behavior patterns of the black nationalists. Thus, the creation of a central ideal for the race is hampered by the fact that withdrawal from the object which one rejects is never complete. The sense of cultural incompleteness and the subtle attractions to the center of white power become a problem for black nationalists.[90] This may be explained as a consequence of the interaction with American society; the practical result for a viable nationalism is that the sense of cultural incompleteness and attractions to the center of white power tend to undermine and dissipate black nationalist sentiments even among the Negro masses.

In spite of the difficulties and disagreements indicated here, the black nationalist organizations we have examined are united in their rejection of the proposition that in time the Negro problem in the United States will be satisfactorily resolved. They assert that the only satisfactory and permanent solution to the problem of black-white relations is the separation of Negroes from a white majority and the establishment of a "Negro homeland" politically controlled by a black majority.

The Nation of Islam advocates this point of view and in its ideology seeks to integrate the religious and the secular traditions. Meanwhile, the Nation of Islam offers its members a sense of identity and seeks to mobilize them for spiritual, moral, social, and economic reforms within the Negro ghettos of the urban North.

90. This problem of attraction to and repulsion from the center of power and, in the case of black nationalists, to the dominant white culture, has wider implications than it appears to on the surface. In an entirely different setting we find that the idea of "African Personality" espoused by President Nkrumah of Ghana at the first Conference of Independent African States in 1958, as well as the cultural movement among Africans in French territories, suffer from this same dilemma. This contradiction has been noted with clarity by J. P. Sartre: "When the Negro declares in French that he rejects French culture, he accepts with one hand what he rejects with the other." Quoted in Thompson and Hughes, *Race. . . .*, p. 365. See also Edward Shils, Introduction, "Metropolis and Province in the Intellectual Community" (University of Chicago, Mimeographed manuscript, n.d.).

III. The Nation:

Its Rise and Growth

> I have always had a very high opinion of both the late Noble Drew Ali and Marcus Garvey and admired their courage in helping our people (the so-called Negroes) and appreciated their work. Both of these men were fine Muslims.
>
> The followers of Noble Drew Ali and Marcus Garvey should now follow me and co-operate with us in our work because we are only trying to finish up what those before us started.
>
> ELIJAH MUHAMMAD

THE NATION of Islam owes its origin to the religious tradition represented by Noble Drew Ali's Moorish-American Science Temple. However, it embodies elements of both the religious and secular traditions in its ideology and practices, since Muhammad also acknowledges Marcus Garvey as a forerunner of his movement. But he adds that both men failed to bring about the redemption of the race because they did not possess "the key" and because the "time was not ripe."[1] This chapter is an account of the rise, growth, and leadership of the Nation of Islam and of its expansion into a nationwide movement.

The rise of the Nation of Islam is inseparable from the leadership of Muhammad and the loyalty of a small group of followers who have worked patiently and persistently since about 1932. It is said that his first followers were his mother, his wife, and his six chil-

1. Interview with Muhammad. He denies emphatically that he ever belonged to the Moorish-American Science Temple or that the Nation of Islam is a splinter movement. This is in contradiction of Bontemps and Conroy's account.

dren.[2] This apparently was the nucleus about which the Detroit Temple, which is today one of the most important in the Nation, was organized. In April, 1934, he was arrested by the Detroit police for refusing to send one of his children to the public school. Prior to the arrest he had sought to set up a parochial school for the Muslims. He was charged with what *Time* described as "contributing to the delinquency of a minor."[3] *Time's* failure to explain the nature of his offence created an unfavorable impression in the mind of the public about Muhammad's character and provided a rare opportunity for a major Negro newspaper to editorialize in his defense. "*Time* magazine," said this editorial, has a "penchant for 'facts' unadorned or unexplained":

> For example, in the magazine's recent "expose" of Elijah Muhammad, two "unadorned facts" were adduced. One was that in 1934 Muhammad had been "arrested for contributing to the delinquency of a minor" and put on probation for six months. Generally, contributing to the delinquency of a minor involves some immoral or criminal act. Muhammad, as leader of a religious sect, had sought to set up parochial schools, and he and his followers refused to send their children to the public schools. That was his contribution to delinquency reported by *Time*.[4]

Later that year Muhammad moved to Chicago, where he soon organized a second Temple, called The Allah Temple of Islam. Under his leadership, the movement again came to public attention in connection with a courtroom riot on March 5, 1935, at the police headquarters building at 1121 South State Street. The riot involved "colored cultists" and police.[5] In the melee Captain Joseph Palczynski, a veteran of nearly fifty years' service in the Chicago police department, died. In addition, a bailiff was seriously wounded, two members of the cult were shot, and thirty-

2. *Elijah Muhammad* (Chicago: University of Islam, n.d.), p. 2, This brochure was issued in 1959.

3. *Time*, August 10, 1959, p. 25. In fact, Muhammad actually surrendered himself to the police after he had learned that the Michigan State Board of Education had arrested the teachers at the Muslim school and the Temple secretary. The charges against the teachers and the secretary were dropped.

4. "Time's Flippancy and Facts," Editorial, *Pittsburgh Courier*, October 24, 1959, p. 12.

5. *Chicago Daily Tribune*, March 6, 1935, pp. 1 and 10, with pictures on p. 32. The account which follows is based on this report. Its details are given because this incident has been construed by Muhammad's followers as a "miraculous" event. As such, it confirms their belief in the omnipotence of Allah.

eight others — twelve policemen, six bailiffs, and twenty cultists — were cut or bruised. Forty-three of the colored cultists "were under arrest with the possibility that some of them may be charged with the Police Captain's murder."

The incident which led to the courtroom riot had occurred about ten days earlier. A Mrs. Christopolous had sought a warrant against a Mrs. Hassan, a member of the "Moorish cult," alleging that Mrs. Hassan had broken her glasses during a quarrel. The municipal court provided for a welfare officer to hear the charges and determine whether probable ground existed for issuance of a warrant. Miss Rosemary Griffin, the welfare officer, invited the parties to her office, which was adjacent to the Women's Court. The cultists were advised by their leader that "in accordance with their vow to have unity they must go to court and stand by their 'sister' so that justice, freedom and truth would be served."[6]

On the day of the courtroom incident, the Hassans were accompanied by fifty or sixty members of the cult. Miss Griffin interviewed the Hassans and the complainant in her office and ruled that no warrant should be issued. The Hassans then returned to the courtroom: "Hassan smiled assurance to his supporters. At a signal from one of its members, the entire band rose with military precision (such military procedure is a part of their ritual) and started marching to the rear of the courtroom."

Meanwhile, another group of ten colored women were standing before Judge Edward S. Scheffler being heard in an entirely different case. The two groups — the cultists and the ten women — became intermingled. The bailiffs told the Hassan group that their proper exit was not at the rear but at the front of the courtroom, and they attempted to turn the cultists back. Several people pushed. A bailiff called for order. An excited cultist woman shouted at one of the officers: "take off your glasses, and I will whip you." In a half minute,

Coyle and Mazola (bailiff) were knocked down and kicked. Policemen standing in the courtroom rushed to their aid. The cultists seized chairs and began swinging them. Captain Palczynski, who had been sitting next to Judge Scheffler started toward the melee. Detective Harry Shelling

6. *Ibid.*, p. 10.

grabbed his arm and urged him not to get in it. Instead the Captain pushed into the crowd in an effort to restore order.

The *Tribune* reporter observed:

. . . aroused to an almost fanatical frenzy by the chain of small incidents that ordinarily would have passed unnoticed in the crowded courtroom, the cultists, their red crescent-marked fezes askew, stormed through the room with wild shouts. . . . Cries of "Freedom and Justice!" and "Onward Brother, onward!" mingled with the refrain of "Who's Afraid of the Big Bad Wolf?" sung by the women of the cult in the throes of religious fervor.

The uprising was quelled by 150 policemen and bailiffs after "a half hour of swinging clubs and pistol butts." The cultists were identified as members of the "Allah Temple of Islam":

The "Allah Temple of Islam," which propounds the theory that blacks are Moors and not Negroes, is a secret organization of national proportions, investigation disclosed. The original "prophet", one Noble Drew Ali, who began his career as a New Jersey expressman, appears to have left Chicago, which once was his headquarters. . . .

The Chicago Temple, which is said to be an offshoot of Drew's original group, holds meetings in its South State Street Headquarters on Wednesday, Friday and Sunday nights. A complete system of military procedure apparently drafted almost word for word from the Army Manual governs the conduct of the members. . . .

Most of the cultists involved in the riot were identified as clients of the Illinois Emergency Relief Commission.

A search of the forty-three cultists under arrest by the Chief of Detectives and others disclosed no weapons. No gun or knife was found on the courtroom floor. Several witnesses said they had seen bailiffs and policemen with drawn revolvers, but the investigators could not discover who had fired the shots that wounded the bailiff and the two cultists. The police captain was declared to have died as a result of a heart attack. On Thursday, March 7, 1938, forty members of the cult who participated in the riot were jailed for contempt of court.

THE NATION ON TRIAL

The Nation was put to a severe test in the early forties because of its refusal to bear arms. Members of the Nation believe that

Allah forbids them to bear arms or do violence to anyone whom He has not ordered to be killed. Thus Muhammad was arrested in Washington, D. C., in May, 1942 and charged with inciting his followers to resist the draft as well as with sedition. The charge of sedition was dropped, but he was convicted on the charge of encouraging draft-resistance and sentenced to five years in the Federal Correction Institution at Milan, Michigan. He was released in 1946.

During those years, more than one hundred of his male followers were arrested and jailed because they failed to register for the draft. One who was imprisoned recalled later that about "80 of us in Chicago were arrested in September, 1942." The government, believing that the Muslims were Japanese espionage agents, raided the Chicago Temple; according to my informant, nearly fifty FBI agents and uniformed police were involved. Although some Muslims could have avoided arrest during the raid, most were anxious to be included among the "persecuted" and submitted themselves voluntarily. The police did not "molest" the women who were present at the Temple.[7] They were each sentenced to three years' imprisonment and, upon release, placed on nine-months' probation.

In Chicago, the pre-war Temple was closed by the police who, a member of the Nation has said, "tore the place apart trying to find weapons hidden there since they believed that we were connected with the Japanese." Sister Clara Muhammad, the Messen-

7. Minister James 3X, an Assistant to Muhammad, has explained in an interview: "We were released in January, 1945 and I was arrested again in April, 1945 for failure to report for induction (the first time was for failure to register for the draft and when we went to prison they registered for us and classified us without our consent). I wrote the Draft Board a letter saying that I would not report for induction, and that is why I was arrested again. I spent another month in jail and they would not listen to my complaint. It seemed as if they were bent on railroading me back to jail again. . . . I was brought to trial after about a month, and I was sentenced to two years before I had a chance to say anything in court. After the sentence I asked the permission of the judge to say something. Then I told him that I could not be sent to prison since I still had five months of the first sentence to complete. This was my question. The judge replied that he did not know that I was still on probation. This was something that had been kept away from the judge. The judge told the prosecution attorney that he could not send me back to jail until I had completed my first term. The probation officer in charge came to verify that I was on probation. There were no arrests after that. The three years sentence was shortened by nine months on account of good behavior."

ger's wife, played a very important role during this period, acting as the contact between him and the group not only through correspondence but also through her visits to the penitentiary.

The followers of Muhammad were well behaved in prison and most of them had their sentences shortened. They generally agree that the treatment they received in prison was satisfactory.[8]

Muhammad and his followers believe that they were imprisoned because of their religious beliefs. He asserts that "the devil cooked up the charges," and that he was "tried and imprisoned for teaching my people the truth about themselves." The services of an attorney could be of no help — "because the devil wanted to shut me up any way."[9] Although Muhammad accepted legal counsel, his followers did not: "We rejected joining the war on religious grounds. We were offered legal counsel by the government and we declined the offer because we knew it would not do us any good if the government provided counsel."[10]

Muhammad's imprisonment turned out to be a blessing in disguise in helping him establish his claim to leadership. He notes with pride and without bitterness that he has paid the price for what he believes to be right for the Negro. That he has been imprisoned is an integral part of the Messenger's charisma, enabling him to liken himself to the persecuted prophets of the past. For his followers, his persecution is not only an important qualification for his leadership, but also evidence of his sincerity and the divinity of his mission.

GROWTH OF THE CHICAGO TEMPLE, 1946–1961

Prior to 1935 membership at the Chicago Temple was so small that meetings were held in homes and rented places. There was no fixed Temple. At first most meetings were held on the West Side of Chicago until, by a majority decision, the location was

8. Interview with Brother Karriem Allah. The significance of this fact is explained in chapter IV, p. 117–18.
9. Interview with Muhammad; also *Muhammad Speaks* (Chicago), December, 1961, p. 4.
10. Interview with Minister James 3X.

shifted to the South Side in 1934. For a time meetings were held at 3335 South State Street.[11] Since then the Temple has been located successively at 104 East 51st Street, 37th Street and South Wentworth, 63rd Street and Cottage Grove, and 5335 South Greenwood Avenue.

In 1946 Muhammad returned to Chicago and began to gather his followers together. An officer of the Nation describes their difficulties in securing a place of worship after the war:

> Shortly after my release [from prison] we were forced to leave the 63d and Cottage Grove Temple and we found out that it was becoming more difficult to find a place where we could hold our services. It seems as though as soon as the real estate owners found that we were Moslems they raised the rent and hence we put our money together and bought our own place and so we moved the Temple to a brother's home and held meetings there until we were able to raise enough money to purchase a Temple. We purchased a place on 824 East 43rd Street. This place was formerly a dog and cat hospital and we had quite a job rejuvenating it for Temple Services. It was quite a struggle because we had to put our pennies together to purchase the building and then have necessary conversion into a Temple. But Allah blessed us and we were able to purchase that Temple.[12]

In 1954 the present Temple on the South Side, formerly a synagogue, was purchased.[13] There are now two buildings at this site — the Temple and the University of Islam. The Temple has a seating capacity of about 500. The University of Islam contains classrooms, offices, a small library, and an auditorium. These buildings are earmarked for demolition by the Hyde Park-Kenwood Urban Renewal Program. Although the Muslims are making plans to construct a $20,000,000 Islamic Center, they see "the devil's hand" in the Southeast Chicago Commission's decision to raze their present buildings.[14] According to announced plans, the

11. Interview with Brother Karriem Allah.
12. Interview with Minister James 3X.
13. The Muslims claim they paid $93,500 for these two buildings. Some observers feel that this figure is exaggerated.
14. It has been suggested that the $20,000,000 project should not be taken seriously. It is certainly too early to judge whether the Muslims will be able to finance it. The writer believes that they may do so over a long period. The first stage of the project is estimated to cost $3,000,000. A fund-raising campaign for this has been very intense, and the Muslims have been contributing heavily toward it. The appeal for funds is not limited to the Muslims, but it is also directed to the Negro community as a whole.

projected Center will include four structures: a two-storey building which "will house the best possible teaching facilities, science
laboratories, a gymnasium for children of all ages, and a library";
another two-storey building which "will house a selected library
to guide and further the knowledge of the seers and a museum to
exhibit the art and works of Moslem scholars and an administration department"; a four-hundred-bed hospital; and a four-min-
aret mosque, "where rich and poor will stand abreast to worship
Allah — with an auditorium to seat approximately three thousand
persons."[15] Muhammad hopes that when the Center is completed,
it will stand as a "monument of black achievement."

TOWARD A NATION-WIDE MOVEMENT

By 1945 two more Temples were established, one in Milwaukee
and one in Washington, D. C. Although membership in Detroit is
said to have reached 8,000 during the depression years, the combined membership in all four Temples had declined to less than
1,000 in 1945.[16] However, the post-war period was marked by a
steady growth both in the number of organized Temples and in
membership. This growth increased in momentum after the Korean War. In 1955 fifteen Temples were scattered in various parts
of the country; by March, 1959, there were thirty in twenty-eight
cities of fifteen states and the District of Columbia; and by December, 1959, fifty Temples were reported in twenty-two states and the
District of Columbia.[17] In addition, a number of smaller missions
operate in rented quarters or private homes. This increase is phe-
nomenal compared to that of the decade immediately following the
second World War.

It is difficult to estimate the membership of each Temple or the
total membership in the movement. The Muslims have kept these
figures secret. Minister Malcolm X stated, when asked how many
members belonged to the New York Temple:

15. *The Messenger Magazine*, Vol. I (New York: Muhammad's Temple of Islam,
1959), 38–40.
16. Minister James 3X in an interview.
17. See Appendix B for a complete listing.

That is difficult to say. I would add, however, that New York has the largest active membership in the Nation; Los Angeles has the highest record attendance. I am distressed about the small membership in Chicago.[18]

It must also be remembered that every week the movement receives new converts, although, according to an official at the Chicago Temple, few remain for any length of time. The definition of a "member" is reflected in any given estimate. In general, Muslim officials make a distinction between a "registered" member and a "believer." The former is one who has fulfilled all the requirements for membership and is actively involved in the affairs of the Temple. The latter is one who has accepted Muhammad's teachings, but is in the process of fulfilling his membership requirements and may or may not participate in the affairs of the Temple. Then there are others who have heard Muhammad's teachings, sympathize with some aspects of his program and support them "morally," may contribute financially to the Nation, but have not committed themselves to the movement. Few old members drop out of the Nation. Muhammad told the writer that "a member who has been in the movement for at least seven years can be counted on to stay in."

Observers have estimated the membership at between 10,000 and 250,000. One writer has said that one Negro in every 300 is a "registered" Muslim.[19] None of them really knows. Muhammad himself has claimed a total of "half a million believers."[20] In November, 1958, a source close to Muhammad said that there were over 3,000 registered Muslims, over 15,000 believers, and nearly 50,000 sympathizers. Another informant estimated registered membership at 12,000; and in January, 1960, still another estimated it at 5,000. The lowest number offered by any officer or member was 3,000 and the highest was 12,000. We estimate, after checking and rechecking as carefully as possible, that there are at present between 5,000 and 15,000 registered followers, at least 50,000 believers, and a much larger number of sympathizers.

The Nation of Islam declined in membership from 1935 to 1940,

18. Interview with Minister Malcolm X.
19. Alex Haley, "Mr. Muhammad Speaks," *Reader's Digest*, March, 1960, p. 104.
20. *Herald-Dispatch* (Los Angeles), May 28, 1959, pp. 1, 4.

grew steadily between 1945 and the end of the Korean War, and has increased rapidly ever since. The years of crisis, 1941–46, did not bring a sharp decline in membership. The survival of the Nation in this period demonstrates Muhammad's determination and the loyalty and cohesiveness of his followers. Many business enterprises owned and successfully operated by the Nation sprang up during the post-war period. Plans for the Center on Chicago's South Side were developed by 1954.

In 1956, when the first widely publicized annual Muslim convention was held in Chicago, Muhammad came out of his isolation to appeal publicly to the Negro masses: "The Messenger has been a solitary man fighting for his ideas and principles. But he has never become discouraged or embittered. Today, he stands alone as the unacclaimed leader of the American Negro. . . ."[21]

Although the size of the Negro audience reached by Mr. Muhammad's teachings cannot be ascertained, the Muslims during the past five years have intensified their efforts to make converts. Every Muslim is a missionary in the Negro community. Muhammad and his ministers, moreover, have used public forums, the Negro press, and, infrequently, the radio. The gains in membership during recent years reflect this effort as well as an effective organization and the availability of recently trained ministers. In 1956 the *Pittsburgh Courier* took notice of the growth of the Muslim community in an article by its Chicago editor. Subsequently Muhammad began to publicize his messages through the *Courier* and, later, in other Negro newspapers. A year later he was awarded a civic plaque by the Pittsburgh Courier Publishing Company "in recognition of outstanding achievement as messenger and spiritual leader of Muhammad's Temples of Islam."[22]

Each year Muhammad makes public appearances at the various Temples. He has drawn audiences estimated to be between 5,000 and 10,000 in New York City, Washington, D. C., Detroit, Pittsburgh, Chicago, and Los Angeles. During the 1960 Muslim Annual

21. "A Thumbnail Sketch of the Messenger" in *White Christian Party Attacks the Negro Equality, Purity, Beauty and Religion* (Chicago: Muhammad's Temple No. 2, n.d) pp. 3–4.

22. For reasons explored in chapter XI, the *Pittsburgh Courier* has discontinued Muhammad's weekly messages.

Convention in Chicago, an estimated 15,000 Negroes attended the three-day activities. Of these, more than 1,100 indicated in writing their acceptance of Islam as taught by Muhammad.[23] Attending this convention were 890 followers from Temples located in the eastern United States, 471 from the Midwest, 59 from the South, and six from the West.[24]

In spite of this increase, the existence of the Nation was hardly known to the general white public until Mike Wallace brought it to public attention in a TV documentary, "The Hate That Hate Produced," in July, 1959. This presentation, together with the activities of the Muslims themselves, gave rise to articles that same year in *Time, The Reader's Digest, Cosmopolitan, U.S. News and World Report,* the *New York Times,* and other publications. Since 1959 both TV and radio commentators have taken notice of the movement, and their general reaction has been unfavorable. Many have described it as a "black supremacy movement" and as "anti-American and anti-Semitic." The Senate Internal Security Subcommittee and the House Un-American Activities Committee were said to be planning to investigate it.[25]

The reaction of Negro civic leaders to the movement has been mixed. Some have publicly denounced it. These include Roy Wilkins, Executive Secretary of the National Association for the Advancement of Colored People; Thurgood Marshall, until recently the NAACP's chief counsel; and Dr. Martin Luther King, leader of the Montgomery, Ala., bus boycott. They agree with white critics that it is a "black supremacy movement." Stating that "the NAACP opposes and regards as dangerous any group, white or black, political or religious, that preaches hatred among men," Wilkins blamed white racists and "shadow-boxing with a milk-and-water civil rights bill" in Congress for the rise of "hate white" doctrines:

23. The estimate of 15,000 was reported by the Convention spokesmen. It seems correct in the writer's judgment as well as in the judgment of many newspaper reporters who commented on it. The writer attended all activities of the 1959 and 1960 Conventions. Visitors were given forms to fill out indicating whether or not they accepted Muhammad's teachings. A count of these was reported to the writer by an officer at the Chicago Temple.

24. "Release" (Chicago: Muslim News Bureau, March 7, 1960), p. 1.

25. *Jet,* August 27, 1959, p. 6.

The so-called Moslems who preach black supremacy and hatred of all white people have gained a following only because America has been so slow in granting equal opportunities and has permitted the abuse and persecution of Negro citizens.[26]

Other Negro leaders, however, do not appear to be as disturbed by the movement as white observers and "respectable" Negroes are. It has even been suggested that leading Harlem politicians, in particular Congressman Adam Clayton Powell and Hulan Jack (until recently Manhattan Borough President), "have curried Moslem favor, even though full-fledged Moslems are enjoined not to vote."[27] In chapter XI we shall examine in detail Negro reaction to and external pressure on the movement.

The Nation of Islam is no longer a small group of "haughty, red fez-wearing and outlandish" Negroes in urban communities of the North. The writer has been impressed by the Muslims' strivings for respectability in the community and by their discipline and loyalty to Muhammad and the movement. Critics admit that they are "thus far . . . strictly law-abiding, — a fact that worries some cops more than minor outbreaks of violence."[28] The Nation of Islam appears to be firmly established and Muhammad remains its unchallenged leader.

THE MAN FROM GEORGIA

The seventh child in a family of twelve, the son of a Baptist minister, Elijah Muhammad was born on October 10, 1897, on a tenant farm in Sandersville, Georgia. For a time he lived also in Atlanta. At the age of 22 he married Clara Evans at Cordele, Georgia, on March 7, 1919. He migrated with his wife and two children to Detroit in 1923 "after undergoing severe discriminations, sufferings and handicaps in his native state for several years."[29] Little information is available about his early life but Muhammad has told the author that he worked as a field boy, a railroad laborer, and for a saw mill and a brick manufacturing concern before he came to

26. Quoted in the *Chicago Defender*, August 8, 1959, p. 1.
27. *Time*, August 10, 1959, p. 25.
28. *Ibid.*, p. 25.
29. "Elijah Muhammad," p. 2.

Detroit.[30] From 1923 to 1929 he worked in the Chevrolet factory in Detroit and he is reported to have been on relief there from 1929 to 1931. He is said to have also worked as a deliveryman for a dairy company in Chicago.[31] For a time he was a Baptist minister. Later he became an assistant minister to Prophet Fard, whom he met in Detroit. He lived in Washington, D. C. between 1935 and 1941 and was in prison from 1941 until 1946. He has lived in Chicago since his release from prison.

A man of small stature (about 5′6″), Muhammad is light in complexion and has been described as one who "might pass for an Oriental."[32] He is frail-looking, but in fairly good health. However, he was put to bed for a short period during the winter of 1959 because of high blood pressure.[33] He readily admits that he had little education. That he completed the fifth grade is authoritatively established.[34] He is a family man. His wife, Sister Clara Muhammad, born November 7, 1899, is soft-spoken and intelligent; she often comes to her husband's aid in dating events of the past thirty years. Followers admiringly call her "truly original," which means that her appearance conforms to the ideal of Muslim beauty. She has remained a housewife most of her life. They have six sons, two daughters, and twenty-seven grandchildren, all of whom are in the movement. Five of the sons are married. Four manage enterprises owned by the Chicago Temple. One son, Wallace Delaney Muhammad, is a minister in the Temple of Islam. Before assuming full-

30. From an interview. In Macon, Georgia he worked for the Southern Railroad Company and the Cherokee Brick Company where he was a tramroad foreman and builder.

31. Reported to the writer by an informant.

32. Minister Malcolm X, speaking about Muhammad during the first evening session of the 1960 Convention. kept referring to him as the "little black man." After Muhammad's arrival, one girl told the writer: "I could not believe my eyes. I was waiting to see a really black man. But who came in? A Chinese. He looks very much like an Oriental."

33. The writer visited one evening when Muhammad had been ordered to take some rest. Instead, he went out to mail a letter, then sat and spoke with his guest. He said that doctors can really do little and he had faith in Allah.

34. It has been said by one of his ministers that he went through the third grade and others have said that he went to the eighth grade. Whatever may be the truth, Muhammad is not embarrassed by it. On the contrary, the fact that he had so little education becomes an integral part of his charisma because he was not "corrupted" by conventional education. It is a source of hope and inspiration to his followers. Early handicaps become less important to them.

time ministerial duties at the Philadelphia Temple, he was an instructor in Arabic at the University of Islam. Another son, Elijah Muhammad, Jr., is the Assistant Supreme Captain at the Chicago Temple. The youngest, Akbar, is studying at the Mosque-University of Al-Azhar, Cairo, United Arab Republic. Both daughters are married. One is the Supreme Captain of the Muslim women's organization at Chicago. The other, Sister Ethel, the mother of five children, is married to the Supreme Captain of the Nation of Islam, Raymond Sharrieff.

Elijah Muhammad now lives in an elegantly furnished eighteen-room house in one of the better sections of Hyde Park in Chicago. His offices, in addition to those in the University of Islam, are in this building, on the second and third floors. These floors also have a combined total of nine bedrooms. There are additional guest rooms in the basement. One of Muhammad's sons, Herbert, lives in an adjacent building. Muhammad has five or more secretaries, and four maids to take care of the house and cook the meals. Like most of his followers, he eats only one meal a day, usually with his family and guests. His three cars — a yellow 1956 Cadillac, a blue 1959 Cadillac, and a black 1959 Lincoln Continental — are used by his secretaries and by other officers for the organization's business.[35] He says he takes no pride in such possessions:

> The reason I drive a Cadillac is obvious. Negroes place a high value on things like this. Personally, I would prefer any little old car that would take me to places. But if I did so, Negroes would begin to say "Islam made him poor." On the contrary, they can see for themselves that Islam doesn't make one poor. Look at this sister here. She came to Chicago about twelve years ago from a town seventy-two miles from Little Rock, Arkansas. She reunited

35. The Lincoln is said to have been given to Muhammad in late 1959 by the followers at the Chicago Temple in exchange for his Chrysler Imperial. The writer was informed by one of Mr. Muhammad's secretaries that for nearly a year he declined to accept a gift of a new car until the followers could raise enough money for the purchase of two city blocks of land for the proposed Islamic Center. He hastened to add that the change of cars is "desirable from the point of view of the prestige of Mr. Muhammad."

The writer was present at the first meeting which Muhammad had with his Chicago followers upon his return from a tour of the Middle East and Africa. At this meeting he told his followers that after seeing how hard the Africans were working to provide for themselves and their posterity, he felt like "throwing away every Cadillac owned by a Negro." He urged them not to give him another new car of any make.

with the Nation seven years ago. She was nothing when she came in. Now she is morally regenerated and materially well-to-do. She lives on the West Side. She owns a gas station and rents out two flats. All Praise is due to Allah for His blessings upon us the Lost-Found Nation of Islam.[36]

For many years his followers insisted that Muhammad tour the "Moslem countries" of Africa and the Middle East, but he repeatedly deferred the trip because he felt the cost was too great for his followers to bear. However, he and two of his sons, Herbert and Akbar, finally took the tour, which extended from November, 1959, until January, 1960, and was financed largely by a special contribution of $25 per member.

Muhammad's personal tastes are extremely conservative: his suits are black or striped gray and he invariably wears a bow tie. He is the only one who wears a fez. It is made of dark velvet with an embroidered crescent holding the sun, stars, and moon.[37] He speaks with a soft, but firm and persuasive voice. His manners, in his home and elsewhere, are formal, gentle, and kind. A follower who spent several days with Muhammad's family remarked:

Even his children are not common [familiar] with him. There is considerable distance between him and his children. There is nevertheless real love for them. Every one is formal in the relationship of the family. There is finesse in everything. The Messenger, the wife, children and the cook talk to one another with courtesy, finesse, and formality. Life at the Messenger's home is very cultured and gentility pervades the whole atmosphere. Sister Muhammad [the Messenger's wife] is lovable and she is a model of a Muslim woman. They have so many guests. All the secretaries eat their dinners with the family, though none of them lives there. The Messenger allows them to use one of his cars for transportation to and from their residence and for taking regular tours to the museum.[38]

Muhammad struck the writer as sincere in his concern for the Negro masses and in his view of himself as primarily a reformer. His hard-working habits are only one among many of his qualities that his followers emulate. His ministers and followers also try to imitate his speech, gestures, and walk. The Messenger's rapid walk

36. Interview with Muhammad.
37. Until 1935 Muhammad's followers wore red fezes. But this has been discontinued because the Messenger does not wish to have his followers confused with the fez-wearing Moors and other Moslem groups who "smoke, drink and misbehave."
38. From an interview with a follower.

in and out of the Temple is duplicated by officers — "he teaches us to move with the speed of light."[39] In addition to formulating the general policies of the Nation of Islam, he supervises the businesses of the Chicago Temple, answers all his correspondence personally, and writes weekly columns for Negro newspapers. His ministers are said to call him long distance every night from various cities to report on the activities of their Temples and the amount of money that has come into their treasuries for the day.

Concerning his personal character, one of his ministers has said:

. . . [He is] the most penetrating man that I know . . . the meekest man I know. He is the most courageous man I ever knew. He is most devoted and I have found in him a man whose virtues are the highest. He is the perfect example for the so-called Negro. He is fine, considerate, honest, and very understanding. Very rarely have I seen him in temper. When you fail to do your duties or fail to carry out orders as given by him, in that respect he will lash you in a very nice but stern way. He is firm and I believe that he would be just as firm with his children as with anyone else. He told me, do not fail to discipline my children, and if you do, you would spoil them. When it comes to doing wrong he would not let his children go. He has penalized his children by suspending them from the Temple.[40]

Muhammad lives a somewhat quiet life except when he makes public appearances. He speaks freely with "my dear brothers" (those whom he trusts) about his work, his mission, and the plight of American Negroes, which he considers to be the most serious problem in the world today. He feels that the moral level of the Negro masses has degenerated terribly — "you cannot find any other people in the world whose morals are so low." He discusses their economic problems as passionately as their morals and appears to be obsessed with their solution. Although he attributes much of the condition of the Negro to white oppression, he also scolds the Negro for "complacency." In his view the white man gave the Negroes a "break" when he set them free, but the Negroes are now asking to be given an "even break." Negroes must themselves labor hard to realize their full stature and identity:

Therefore, the main and basic responsibility for effecting a solution of the Black Man's problems rests upon American Negroes themselves. They

39. Interview with Minister James 3X.
40. Interview with Minister James 3X.

should supply the money and pay the price, make the sacrifice, and endure suffering to realize full manhood as Black Men.[41]

During the first few meetings with Muhammad, a visitor is likely to find him preoccupied with religious matters, but as time goes on, he speaks more and more of the problems of health, housing, family, income, and morals among Negroes. He feels that he is harassed by the Caucasian enemy — the Federal Bureau of Investigation and the Bureau of Internal Revenue — "who would get me if they knew how." "Right now," he said in an interview, "my son has a case in court and we are trying to get him out."[42] Although the impression is given that his life may be in danger, he takes walks by himself and sometimes drives alone to places of business. At public appearances, however, he is heavily guarded by a specially trained contingent of followers.[43]

Muhammad legitimizes his leadership by basing it upon the history, condition, and needs of the Negroes of the United States. He refers to himself as "one who has walked the streets with them, suffered in the hell of North America, was humiliated in the South by the devils" and who, therefore, fully understands their condition. The loyalty which they have developed for him, the bonds which bind them to him, are so strong that a few followers fear that the Muslims:

> . . . seem to worship him rather than Allah. What would happen if he dies? Even followers of Muhammad of 1300 years ago refuse to believe when they heard about his death because they had lost sight of Allah and were worshipping him instead. Our leader has taught us to worship Allah and not him.[44]

41. *White Christian Party Attacks* . . . , p. 11.
42. The case involved Minister Wallace Delaney Muhammad's alleged violation of the Selective Service requirements. See pp. 000.
42. A follower disclosed in an interview that "whenever the Messenger travels there is complete silence about his movements and what car he is in; what mode of transportation, what route he is taking, when he is leaving or arriving — there is a complete blackout of information. There is always a special bodyguard around him and special details within any one hundred yards from the Messenger. If one thought of assassinating the Messenger he would be caught dead instantaneously. There are special details at the Temple when he is speaking, at every doorway, and until he gets into his car again, when the bodyguard takes over. The detail is airtight when he is traveling. The special details place their lives at the disposal of the Messenger when he enters or leaves a place."
44. From a discussion between two officers of the Chicago Temple in the presence of the writer.

Although followers look upon him as "one among them," they show much deference toward his attributes, both personal and "divine." He has been described as the "Spiritual Leader of Moslems in the United States."[45] To followers, he is "our Beloved Leader, Divine Teacher, Last and Greatest Messenger, Holy Apostle, Reformer, foremost black nationalist, and the 'little lamb without spot or blemish.'" One minister has even referred to him as "father and mother." He is one who "has the key to the solution of the so-called Negro problem in the United States." Muslims address him on all occasions as the "Most Honorable, Mr. Elijah Muhammad, Messenger of Allah."[46] In informal face-to-face conversation they use "Dear Holy Apostle," "Yes, Holy Apostle," or "Yes, Sir."

THE PROBLEM OF SUCCESSION

Because of his overwhelming importance in the movement, the question of Muhammad's succession deserves comment.

Muhammad's followers appear to think that he is the "Last Messenger." This is official doctrine; but it does not seem to be his view. One of his brochures suggests a subtle concept of his role as "Leader and Messenger I." He himself has admitted that "if I cannot accom-

45. Abdul B. Naeem, a Moslem missionary to the United States and representative of "Jam'iat-ul-Falah" (A Pakistani organization), notes: "As we see it, Mr. Muhammad's teachings (offered through his Temples) . . . have enabled more Americans to form an acquaintance with Islam than the efforts of all other individuals seeking converts to Islam here put together.
We are aware of the fact that Mr. Elijah Muhammad as some Moslems have put it, 'operates on racial lines.' In other words he considers and speaks of Islam as a 'religion of black mankind.' However, it is not difficult for us to comprehend the wisdom of such practices on his part. . . .
Certain other friends of ours allege that Mr. Muhammad's Moslem teachings differ from those of Eastern Moslems. Mr. Muhammad readily concedes this, explaining that 'my people must be dealt with on a special basis, because their background and circumstances are different from those prevailing elsewhere in the world. You cannot use the same medicine to treat altogether different diseases." (*Moslem World and the U.S.A.*, Oct.–Nov.–Dec., 1956, pp. 8–9).
Of course, most of the older Moslem sects in the U.S. do not welcome Muhammad as a Moslem leader and some even look down upon his "so-called Moslems." This is particularly true of the "Ahmadiyyat" Moslems, and a rival sect which was formed in Chicago some years ago by a Palestinian Arab, who was formerly an employee of Mr. Muhammad at the University of Islam.
46. These terms and phrases were noted in the speeches of his ministers and followers.

plish this task, another will," but he would have "gathered the materials" for the completion of the task.[47] Besides, it appears that he is training his son, Minister Wallace Muhammad, as his successor. While still living in Chicago, Minister Wallace Muhammad said in an interview:

I am generally out of town — I am sent by the Messenger wherever there is a need. I have to be in town when the Messenger is out because the Messenger relies on me. He has confidence that I can carry out the work. The followers have come to look upon me as the second man. Besides, I had four years of the Koranic teachings. Many of the ministers are qualified but there are always people who seek information on Islam and if the Messenger is not around I am the next logical man for whom they can obtain most reliable information. People seek information continuously.

Recently it became clear that he is next in the line of succession. Several followers have told the writer that Muhammad assured them that "Allah has chosen Minister Wallace to succeed him." The Negro press has printed information to this effect which the writer believes was furnished by the Muslim News Bureau.[48]

Other ministers of Muhammad's Temples of Islam regard Minister Wallace as a possible successor. Minister Malcolm X of the New York Temple, one of the Nation's most highly regarded leaders, alluded to this in a speech at the Chicago Temple on December 12, 1958, when he introduced Minister Wallace as "the seventh son of our dear beloved Leader and Teacher who is following in the footsteps of his father."[49] In his view, it is not at all accidental that Minister Wallace should have been the seventh child of eight children.

Minister Wallace was born on October 30, 1933, in Detroit, Michigan. He received his entire elementary and high school education at the University of Islam, and spent four additional years studying Islam and Arabic in the Muslim school. An Egyptian who taught Arabic at the University of Islam rates Minister Wallace's

47. Elijah Muhammad, Speech at 1959 Annual Convention, Chicago, pp. 4–5.
48. *Herald Dispatch* (Chicago edition), December 19, 1959, p. 1: "Wallace, widely rumored to be the man who will succeed Elijah Muhammad as leader of the Muslims . . ." The *Herald Dispatch* is published in Los Angeles by one of Muhammad's followers.
49. The number seven has a mystical significance for the Muslims.

command of the language as well above the average. Before he decided for the ministry, Minister Wallace explained that he was very interested in science and electronics.

Between September, 1952, and March, 1954, Minister Wallace worked off and on for the Oxford Electric Company, Chicago, as a laborer, earning $45 a week. His employment was terminated because of irregular attendance, and his employer refused to consider re-employing him. For some time he worked also for the Temple-owned restaurant.

Minister Wallace and his family live in a four-room apartment in Philadelphia. His rent is said to be furnished by the Philadelphia Temple. He is a well-mannered young man whose devotion to his father and the Muslims is unquestioned. Both he and Minister Malcolm X represent Muhammad at public meetings. Although there is no evidence of rivalry among Muhammad's ministers now, Minister Malcolm X appears to wield a more prominent leadership role than any other minister. A split between him and Muhammad's successor could shatter the movement. If such a situation developed, particularly with Muhammad's disappearance from the scene, Minister Malcolm X could probably carry a large number of followers with him. At present, however, there appears to be no trace of any minister or member competing for power or leadership of the movement.

The followers of Muhammad are not, however, particularly concerned about leadership in the event of his death. While admitting that his death would be very tragic, those who are willing to discuss the subject are convinced that any of the ministers of the Nation would be equally capable of leading it. One optimistic member said that almost any follower, male or female, could lead them, because they have come to appreciate the importance of unity.

IV. The Way Out

> Islam dignifies the black man, and it gives him the desire to be clean, internally and externally, and to have for the first time a sense of dignity.
>
> ELIJAH MUHAMMAD

NEITHER WHITE nor Negro middle-class society offers a way out for the Negro masses. Whereas a middle-class Negro in a northern city may aspire, for instance, to move into Deerfield, Illinois, or other white middle-class communities, and may dine and wine, rubbing shoulders with the whites, in downtown hotels, the masses of Negroes must stay home in the ghettos. Consequently, the lower-class Negro who has the capacity and motivation for self-improvement must seek it within the Negro community. He cannot afford the luxury of the middle-class make-believe. He knows he is black, but he wants to be self-respecting. He may be poor, but he wants to be decent.

The need for identity and the desire for self-improvement are the two principal motives which lead individuals to join and to remain in the Nation of Islam. The Muslims are likely to claim that religion was the most important thing which led them to join the movement and religion is certainly one of the major emotional attractions of the Nation. The writer found that choices were often far more rational than would appear on the surface. He found that although there were three discernible groups of joiners, the majority were

83

alienated from themselves and estranged from their community or peer groups.

First, some joined merely because they want to lead a "better" life, subtly competing with the successful Negro middle-class, and to improve their status as individuals, as black men. The second type joined because they had "heard" something "attractive" about the movement. Their need was simple and inarticulate — they wanted to reach outside themselves for an undefined answer to their life situation. These join partly because of their dissatisfaction with the status of "blackness" in America and partly because of their disgust with the Negro middle-class social exclusiveness and leadership. The third group are those who have reacted to their own emptiness — their lack of identity — and their seemingly fixed position — and have consciously searched for a political-religious outlet. The elite core of Muhammad's followers belong to this group: their commitment to him thus has taken on a rational character, which, were it placed within a political orientation and program, would have implications for the Negro group as a whole.[1] But, as we shall see, Muhammad has no political program.

These interests and motivations are not mutually exclusive; and yet all, singly, or in various combinations, point to the view that most Muslims have joined the movement through higher levels of awareness than the members of the Pentecostal Negro religious movements. Certainly, the social consciousness of Muhammad's followers differs substantially from that of the members of the institutionalized Negro churches in America. Whatever emotional motivations underlie such choices, they are not any more excessive or detracting than may be the case in any human commitment to any movement which is viewed as being of value and consequence. The point is that the choice of the Muslim movement is not inspired by fanaticism, as most people believe. It springs from the historical and psychological roots of the Negro's situation and predicament in America.

There are, of course, various degrees of rationality in all choices. But it would be presumptuous to assume that Muhammad's fol-

1. The political significance of the movement is discussed in chapter XI.

lowers were not aware of their second-class citizenship, their double-consciousness and dual membership in American society, and their self-alienation before joining the movement.

The first part of this chapter emphasizes the needs, experiences, and motives leading up to the "crucial" moment of an individual decision to join the movement. In the second part, I shall show that in spite of the diversity of motives which lead individuals to join, they remain in the movement because the Nation offers a way out for the despised but upwardly mobile lower-class Negroes.

Sister Levinia X was attracted to the movement because it enhances one's status. She met a Muslim girl who impressed her favorably by her manner of dress and actions, which "were different from everyone else in the neighborhood." The manner of dress and, presumably, the "lady-like" behavior of the Muslim girl distinguished her markedly from Sister Levinia and from other Negro girls in the neighborhood. Sister Levinia decided to visit the Temple:

A girl in the neighborhood taught us Islam. She told us that Islam was the right religion. I believed her *because of the way she dressed, the way she acted and she was different from everyone else. Her way of life was different from what I knew.* She had told my sister that white people were the devils and that I believed because of the way the white people act and the way they treat our people. Everything that she told us was the truth just by what I know. Then she said that we are God's children people and that the Honorable Elijah Muhammad is the Messenger of Allah who would lead us back unto our own and she told us that the devil was going to be destroyed. I wanted to hear Islam and so I went to the Temple with my mother. My first impression at the Temple was that everything we had heard was true. I wanted to accept Islam that same Sunday but we came back the next Sunday and accepted Islam.

For me, acceptance of Islam was the most important thing. Joining unto your own. Most important was that Allah is God. . . Even though becoming an independent Nation is important, and we need to become an independent Nation, I think that the most important thing a people need is God more than anything else, for being here in America we have never had a God. We have thought that we had a God but we never really had one. But in the Nation of Islam we learn that Allah is our God and that we should pray to him and that he would answer our prayers.[2]

It is also clear that the Muslim girl articulated Sister Levinia's feeling of social estrangement and her antipathy toward white so-

2. Interview with Sister Levinia X (Adrine).

ciety. She had no difficulty in readily accepting everything she had heard as the "truth." She wanted "to belong" and to become one of "God's children people," where people are black and decent and where some hope of a better life is promised. She was especially encouraged by knowing that the Messenger of Allah would lead the socially estranged and despised "back to their own." She joined the Nation, like most Muslims, because she wanted to improve herself. Religion here served the purpose of offering an alternative route to social mobility:

> I learnt a new way of life: How Muslim women should act. Religion is the most important thing because it took us out of the street and help make better women of us in America. It taught us what to eat, how to act, and best places for us to go, and where we should not go, such as taverns, nightclubs, dance halls, etc. Islam helps to build a Nation. It teaches women how to raise their children, how to take care of their husbands, how to sew and cook, and several domestic things which are necessary for a family. Islam helps men a great deal because it teaches them how to treat their women. The women are taught how to dress decently.[3]

THE NEGRO WOMEN: JOURNEY FROM SHAME

One of the principal motives which lead Negro women to join the Nation is their desire to escape from their position as women in Negro subculture. The attraction of the Nation of Islam to women becomes clear if we bear in mind that both men and women in the Nation extend a great deal of deference toward each other — something they are unaccustomed to in Negro society. Womanly virtues are respected in the Nation. The Muslim male's attitude toward, and treatment of, Negro women contrasts sharply with the disrespect and indifference with which lower-class Negroes treat them. Muhammad's semireligious demand that his followers must respect the black woman has an appeal for black women seeking to escape from their lowly and humiliating position in Negro society and from the predatory sex ethos of the lower-class community. A refuge from these abuses is found in the Nation of Islam, and freedom from sex exploitation. It is a journey from shame to dignity. That

3. Interview with Sister Levinia X (Adrine).

is how Sister Elaine, and many other Muslim women see it; and that was why Sister Elaine joined the Nation.

Sister Elaine is 22 years old and was born in Chicago. Her mother was a member of the Nation from 1933 until 1949, when she dropped out. Her father also backslid in 1936. Sister Elaine was born into the Nation and remained a member until she was 13. Although she had stayed out of the Nation for about eight years, she has never belonged to a Christian church. She studied at the University of Islam, transferred later to a public school when she was in the eighth grade, and graduated in 1956. Sister Elaine recalls that she left the Nation "because I did not understand what was taught." She gave the following reasons for returning in 1957:

When I was in the dead world I went to a sanctified church once and there I found that people were just shouting and laughing. The preacher talked about what happened on the streets — prostitution — and this did not interest me.

When I went to the old world, I did not do much. I spent my time in the library, occasionally went to dance, and most often to movies. I haven't been in the movies since the last two years. I went back to the Nation one day when Brother Daniel came over to sell Ebony magazine subscription to my mother. It was then he asked me to come to the Temple if I had nothing else to do. . . . I did not keep my boy friends when I was in the old world. . . . I did not like the idea of adultery, drinking and smoking. You could not go places with boys without them asking to sleep with you. I went to few parties. The boys were possessive. I did not like that. I did not go out with boys for this reason. They wanted you to neck with them. I just didn't go for that. When they take you to a show they want you to commit adultery with them. I stopped dating and refused to go to things with them. In the Nation you are not afraid of the Brothers. They can take you to places without molesting you and *this is why I came back to the Nation.* . . . You know, like if you were out of a car after a date and the man wants to force himself on you. This is what I consider molesting. Among the dead they do not believe in treating you nicely but whenever they take you out, they want something in return. When you go out with Muslim brothers they do not make sex demands upon you. My girl friend in the dead world thinks that is nice and good.[4]

Sister X was motivated principally by the desire "to keep" her husband who had heard of Islam and apparently had decided to join the Nation without her knowledge. She was impressed by what ap-

4. Interview.

peared to be the "calm and nice" way the husband treated her after he had accepted Islam. She too visited the Temple:

I had lived in Chicago for some time and never had seen a Muslim. My husband spoke of the devil from what he had heard from his friends and told me that the white man was the devil. I hated what he said and I was enraged because my family is mixed. After my husband had heard the teachings, he became hostile to my wearing revealing pants, dancing with men, smoking and drinking.

My husband and I accepted Islam the same week . . . three days apart without one knowing that the other had accepted. It just happened that one Friday night my husband dressed up and told me that he was going to the YMCA where he participated in sports to keep himself in shape. He was an athelete. We had an argument that evening. I did not want him to go. He seemed too well dressed for sports. I wanted to go with him. He went alone. My husband came back that night quite calm and nice to me. Actually, he did not go to the Y. He went to the Temple of Islam. When he returned to the house I was very angry. But he was very kind to me. He was different. He threw out the beer and cigarettes from the house. I knew that he was changing for good. I knew that I could not keep him. I knew that I could not keep him any longer. I knew that the religion of Islam was a strong bond. The following Sunday, I came out dappy and was going out. I dressed so well so as to make my husband jealous. I went to the Nation of Islam myself. I had planned to go somewhere after the meeting. But after hearing the teaching and recalling how my husband had treated me last Friday night, I accepted Islam. Went back to the house and it was only then that we both knew the other had accepted Islam.[5]

We cannot overemphasize the prestige value to the Muslim women of the newly acquired sense of self-respect and dignity. The writer encountered a high degree of self-esteem among the Muslim girls and women and noticed some contempt on their part for the non-Muslim Negro women.

It seems clear, also, that Negro men who join and remain in the Nation are likely to be those who accept the feminine ideal and are willing and able to adjust to it. Conversely, those who do not accept this ideal are unlikely to remain in the Nation. Brother Donald X (Clark) expressed what is probably a representative attitude among the Muslim men:

The most important thing for me is my moral values, the treatment of our women. You know the way they are treated in the dead world (Negro

5. Interview.

society), and the way I used to look upon them. That is all different now because Islam gives me a sense of respect toward them. I love them more. I respect them more.[6]

The case of Brother —, who had led an unusually precocious and promiscuous sex life before joining the Nation, illustrates the adjustments which are often necessary:

Islam makes you appreciate black women. I appreciate my black women by showing them my politeness at its most highest degree [*sic*]. This applies mostly to Muslim women because a regular Negro woman would not understand such politeness. She would think that I was a queer if I tried to treat her nicely and respectfully.

During the first six months in the Nation, I felt so unclean that I would not speak to any girl in the Nation. I could not talk to the women. Now that I am clean and pure (three years after); I do not know what to do about it. You know, it is just like cleaning up a house and then the landlord looks for a tenant and cannot find one. That is the way I feel now. I would wish to get married. I met a girl in the Nation whom I like. She talks to me nicely . . . She spoke to me nicely. I would like to get married but I would need money for her maintenance.[7]

This Brother emphasized during the interview not only the problems of adjusting to the Nation's ideals about sex, but also the husbands' responsibility as the breadwinner in the family.

In another sense, which the Muslims interviewed did not verbalize, the movement has an attraction for Negro men, because their male ego has been subordinated to the female's in Negro society. Muslim women appear to accept their men as "first among equals," and in theory, at least, regard the man as the breadwinner and the head of the family. The Muslim women address the men as "sir." Wives address their husbands similarly. The reversal of customary roles between husband and wife has compensations for both parties.

The reasons for the inferior role of Negro men vis-à-vis Negro women are well known. Muhammad's emphasis on "protecting our women from enemy prowlers (white men)" has attractions for Negro men which are unrelated to the moral question. It is commonly known that Negroes were defined as biologically and socially inferior to whites during the period of slavery and that this definition has persisted in the South. The men were treated as wards by the

6. Interview.
7. Interview. Name withheld on request.

whites, but their women were thought human enough to be exploited sexually. Negro men, compelled by their subordinate social and economic status to submit to the humiliations and indignities imposed by southern white males, could not defend their women against the predation of white men:

It appears, then, not only that the Negro man is subordinated in all his relations to the whites but that his subordinate role weakens his relations with women of his own group. If he marries, his wife may at least sometimes compare him with that potential ideal, a white lover. If he seeks after the more attractive girls, or those educated or better dressed, he must compete with the white man who can offer money, prestige, and security. The hopelessness of the situation was shown in a story told by an upper-class Negro girl about a Negro boy who approaches her on behalf of her white employer. When she berated him for his action, he replied: "I'd like you myself, yes, indeed, I'd like you fo' myself, but I works for him."[8]

This white-male–black-female relationship has left deep scars in the minds of Negro men, especially in the South, where many have been lynched on the merest suspicion of sex relations with a white woman. It is no wonder that the Muslim men, mostly migrants from the South, are devoted to keeping the black woman from white men. It strengthens their ego and helps to eliminate what Negroes believe to be one source of their humiliations.

A few brief case histories illustrate the experiences, needs, and motives which in part lead individuals to join the Nation of Islam.

Brother John W. (Anthony) was born in Chicago. He is 27 years old, married, and has one child. A high school graduate, he served in the United States Army between 1952 and 1956 and was stationed in France. While there, he visited Germany, Luxemburg, and Denmark. After his discharge from the Army he took up training as a court reporter. He has four brothers and three sisters who are not members of the Nation. He was a Baptist prior to joining the Nation of Islam:

Brother Charles Betha invited me to a gathering which was held at Altgeld Gardens. If he had told me that it was going to be a religious meeting I probably would have refused the invitation. He told me that it was just a gathering.

8. Allison Davis, B. Burleigh Gardner, and R. Mary Gardner, *Deep South* (Chicago, Ill.: The University of Chicago Press, 1941), p. 38. Cf. John Dollard, *Caste and Class in a Southern Town*, Anchor ed. (Garden City, N.Y.: Doubleday and Company, 1957), especially "The Sexual Gain."

When I entered the meeting I heard Brother Minister Malcolm speaking. He was talking about the black man. He mentioned something about the Negro's language, his flag, and where we came from. These were very striking to me. I began to think about them. During his talk he kept referring to "my leader and teacher," and I wondered who this man was. I felt I would like to go to the school Malcolm went to in order to learn what he knows. . . . When Brother Charles got out of the car at the Altgeld Gardens, he told me I should not worry about anyone breaking into the car because brothers were watching it. I did not know what he was talking about, and later, when I visited the Temple I found that all the Brothers seemed to be very sincere and very friendly and warm. It seems as if they were real brothers and that they were very happy to meet me. . . .

During the meeting Minister Malcolm was speaking. He made various statements about Jesus and about there being no life after death, and this was very contrary to what I had been taught, and so at the close of the meeting I asked a question: Do you mean to tell me that there is no life after death? If you are right, what am I good for? Malcolm wrote on the black board: Life after Death. He asked, how could you have life after death? He made it so real to me and I found that it was impossible for me to have life after death. *I decided perhaps I should have life before death rather than after.*

After the meeting I told the Brothers that was the first time I was exposed to real brotherhood and I believed that it was this particular show of genuine friendship and brotherhood that made me decide to join.[9]

The interviewee did not decide to join the Nation after the first meeting, although he was "struck" favorably with Minister Malcolm's proselytizing rhetoric — his display of "knowledge" about the Negroes' language, nation, and "where we came from." He wanted to be as "well informed" as the minister who was the central figure at the meeting. However, he was undecided until he had attended the second meeting. There he was impressed by what the interviewee describes as the "genuineness of friendship and brotherhood." Thus, the need for friendship and a peer group, and the need for belonging, led him to decide to join. Second, the Muslim's emphasis on how one may attain the "good life" here and now rather than after death played a part in his decision.

Brother Thomas 5X Drake was born in Tennessee. He is 48 years old and the father of two children. His wife and daughter are Baptists; only his son is in the Nation with him. His father was a minister and farmer. Thomas came to Chicago in 1931:

9. Interview.

I was seeking a little better life and a little more freedom. I didn't think that I could put up with the restrictive conditions in the South. When I first came to Chicago I took up a job washing cars and kept that job for about six months. During that period I had more jobs than any man I ever knew. I completed the fourth grade in my education. Since then I have been educating myself — mostly in history. I would say that it is only in the Nation that I have received any real teaching from another person. Before then I always found myself better informed than most of the people in the organizations I joined. No doubt that is why I always left them.[10]

Brother Thomas is a soft-spoken, quiet man who impresses one as bent on self-improvement. He spoke coherently during the interview. His career as a black nationalist and his strivings are given in detail. It appears that he has always been a responsible individual who worked hard to improve himself and his family. He has held one job since 1947. He had neither smoking nor drinking habits. He said he was not wanting "morally or materially" when he joined the Nation. Because of his reading habits, and in spite of his limited formal education, he found himself better informed than the Negroes or other lower-class persons with whom he worked. For this reason he became disenchanted with most organizations to which he belonged before coming to the Nation.

In his search for a group which would satisfy his need for identity, he tried the Masons, the Negro church, and the labor unions, and found them all unsatisfactory. He has never belonged to the NAACP and expresses antagonism toward it. He joined the Nation because Muhammad's superior knowledge impressed him favorably and because of his strong desire to participate in organizational efforts which he believes may enhance the status of the Negro people:

I left the Baptist church [in 1948] . . . because that year was the beginning of my deep study of religion. I left the church previously, and in 1947, after becoming a member of the Masonic Order, I was told to join the church because it was necessary as an officer of the lodge to go to church for contact and good public relations. One Sunday I met a crippled man in a rolling chair sitting in front of the church and begging for money. I asked why he was not inside the church and he told me that ministers do not allow him to enter their churches. I felt that the minister should have asked him

10. Interview.

to enter the church and should ask for collections for him. I was deeply disturbed by this incident and came to the conclusion that the church was not helping my people and that ministers were interested in collecting money for themselves. I gave up all hope that the church was an instrument for helping my people. I left the church for good and began studying religion again independently. I felt my decision was right.

He participated in other nationalistic movements before he joined the Nation of Islam:

I joined the UNIA [Garvey Movement] in 1931 because I have always had a deep interest in my people. When I was a young boy back in Tennessee a fellow came to our house. He wore an impressive button and I asked him what it was about. He told me that the organization was working to return Negroes to their fatherland. I felt that if I ever came North I would join the movement. I joined the UNIA a week after my arrival in Chicago. I have always believed that a return to the fatherland is the most important thing for the Negro in America.

I lost track of the UNIA at the time they had internal difficulties which caused a split. This difficulty led to the formation of the Ethiopian Peace Movement. I joined the Peace Movement because I could not locate the UNIA, and remained in the movement from about 1949 until 1956.

I joined the Masons in 1947 and remained in it until 1957. I held the office of the "Worshipful Master" or the Presiding Officer. . . . The entire membership was Negro. Black and white of this order do not meet together. I thought that the Masons could be an instrument of nationalism if it were taught to prepare people for natural activities of life. On the contrary, its teachings are symbolic of the past. The Mason teaches what Moses did, but doesn't teach us what we should do.

I discontinued membership in the lodge when I found out that I could not live in two different worlds. The lodge leads one inevitably into western civilization and one becomes interwoven into it. One is cut off from himself and from the world of his people.

Brother Thomas joined the Nation of Islam in August, 1956, because he wanted to "unite with my own people":

I had attended meetings at the Temple before I joined. I was economically all right when I joined the Nation. Morally I was good. I had no smoking or drinking habits. Many people think that those who join the Nation are derelicts. This is not true in every instance. I found that the Muslims were tackling the same problems I was interested in. They were teaching what I was preaching. I had studied Islam before deciding to join. I joined the Nation in order to help my people.[11]

11. Interview.

ROOTLESSNESS

The vast majority of American Negroes have been victimized by the notions that their race is inferior to other races and that Africa has never contributed anything to human civilization and has never had great traditions, heroes, and men of affairs. American Negroes are ashamed of their American heritage and troubled by their African kinship. As a people they are rootless. But history does not disown them. Africa has not disowned them. American Negroes may disown their history, but they cannot deny Africa. Africa is a fact. No people can comfortably renounce their past, no matter how deprived and unhappy it may have been. The American Negro is not an exception; he may be ignorant and ashamed of his American heritage and of Africa; but he can never be indifferent to them. These are the subjective imponderables in his struggle for status and human dignity.

The need for "roots," which seriously concerns the Negro masses, especially those in the northern cities, is a problem that respectable Negro circles have shunned and long ignored. It is an unpleasant issue to raise in a "liberal" society where social facts are often glossed over by endless verbiage, and good intentions become substitutes for social policy. It is obvious that Negroes by themselves cannot resolve this problem so long as American whites control the major media of communication, all channels of information, the schools, for these institutions shape the Negro's image of himself and of his place in society. This problem was fully grasped by Walter Lippmann — his "race parallelism" notwithstanding — when he said that Americans would have to work out a civilization where "no Negro need dream of a white heaven and of bleached angels. Pride of race will come to the Negro when a dark skin is no longer associated with poverty, ignorance, misery, terror and insult. When this pride arises every white man in America will be the happier for it. He will be able then, as he is not now, to enjoy the finest quality of civilized living — the fellowship of different men."[12]

Deliberate effort among Negroes to stimulate and foster pride

12. Introduction to Carl Sandburg, *The Chicago Race Riot* (New York: Harcourt, Brace and Howe, 1919), p. iv.

in their heritage and in Africa has been minimal. Whatever information is available about their past has yet to reach the Negro
masses. The "Negro History Week" celebrated yearly is one of the
efforts aimed at giving Negroes a sense of pride in their past. But
this effort stems entirely from the Negro intelligentsia and does not
touch the Negro masses.[13] Even if such efforts were extended to the
Negro masses, it remains doubtful that much would be changed
unless they were matched with some evidence of solid Negro accom-
plishment in their present communities. There are in the northern
cities no monuments of the much-vaunted "progress" with which
the Negro masses can proudly identify themselves. It is true that
Negroes do identify themselves with the boxing and baseball
"greats" of their race. Similarly, they identify with the "greats" of
the entertaining business. However, they are also frustrated and
angered by them as well, because they feel their success has often
meant a "passport" to white society, followed by marriage to a
white person.[14] The Negro "greats" are, for the masses, brothers in
skin but not in destiny.

For many Negroes, escape from this situation of rootlessness —
the feeling of emptiness and drifting — is provided by the comfort-
ing promises of the "Holy Book." Others seek to identify themselves with a living man or with a living culture. They rediscover
themselves, their importance as human beings, and their sense of
personal dignity through these identifications.

Sister —,[15] who had studied for two years at the Chicago Teachers
College, is an employee of the Nation. She is separated from her
husband and has a fifteen-year-old son. She described herself as

13. Efforts to give the Negro a sense of a past, a myth, pride, and confidence in
the capabilities of his race have been made largely by the black nationalists, Garvey,
Muhammad, etc. The works of J. A. Rogers and Carter C. Woodson have been inspired by the same objective. Groups such as The American Society of African Culture cater to a small group of intellectuals who lack the vision or courage to relate
and interpret their findings to the Negro masses. In recent years, however, other
groups are beginning to show greater interest in disseminating information among
the masses about their heritage and African kinship. The Afro-American Heritage
Association in Chicago is one of these groups. Its effort shows some promise.

14. It should be noted that this sense of betrayal does not necessarily mean disapproval, in principle, of interracial marriages. Cf. Dan Burley, *Muhammad Speaks*
(Chicago), January, 1962, p. 4.

15. Name withheld on request.

the "breadwinner" and summed up her sense of rootlessness and striving for meaningful objects of identification:

Once your faith in mankind is shattered, you may shoot yourself. Or you must believe in something. You cannot believe in contemporary man. After years of experience of hardship it is easier to be broken in spirit. But you can't turn to whiskey, dope, Christianity, momentary drunkenness, crime, orgies for the moment. So in order to be able to cope with life of today, you must consult someone who has had great experience. You may turn to a great poet or so, but you must turn to someone who has gone through a lot of experience in life.[16]

Many turn to the Nation of Islam because they feel a need for a strong leader and an important personality with whom to identify. Such individuals derive a sense of self-importance by identifying with Muhammad, the central figure in the movement and second in importance only to Allah. The Sister we have just quoted turned to Muhammad who says, according to her, "Down with Mr. Charlie (the white man) and up with me": she gains a feeling of self-wholeness by identifying with Muhammad. Her feeling of rootlessness, estrangement, and alienation was markedly expressed when she said, "When I got there, I found myself." The need for a past which one can proudly claim and for identity are all suggested by the expressions "lost-found" and "dead" throughout this statement:

After you have gone through my experiences you cannot believe in ghost stories. That is what Christianity was to me — a phenomenon. I am a bread-winner. I have a son who is 15 years old. But I needed to believe in something. I needed some kind of God. All my life I was in darkness, I knew something was lost, I knew Solomon was black. I knew the Sphinx was in Egypt. I went to church. I got nothing out of it. I saw Ethiopia in the Bible. I looked for the American Negro in the Bible. I could not find him there. I wondered why the American Negro had no customs, no traditions, nothing. My former minister was a *strong* man. He was articulate. The man who took his place after his death was not as *strong*. He bored me. He made me tired. I wanted the customs of my people whether they are good, bad, or indifferent. I wanted something to represent what was me. If my people wore bones around their necks, I wanted to wear the same bones. I got on the blackman's trail. I followed him in the Bible. I found a friend in the Bible. He led me through the Book and out of Christianity into Islam. I now take a deep breath and relax. For me the long search is over. When I first heard the minister of Islam declare: "You are God's chosen people," it

16. Interview.

was not new to me. I can't believe anything I can't see, feel or touch. When I got here I found myself. I found my people. We may appear to be harsh, or fanatic. But we have always been told not to let Mr. Charlie know how we feel. This man (Mr. Muhammad) says to us "down with Mr. Charlie and up with me." He says, "I don't like him and I don't mind telling him I don't like him." Lots of our people don't like him but they are afraid to tell him so.[17]

A personal crisis may lead one to join the Nation. This seems especially true of young men who had previously led "fast" lives. Such people may be attracted to movements which offer an alternative to perilous living. Father Divine's Peace Movement was such a possibility. Individuals may thus join the Nation in order to withdraw from activities which seem ruinous to their lives.

Brother Leonard IX (Pound) was born in Chicago in 1939. He did not finish high school. He has been in the Nation for nearly four years and is the only member of his family in the Nation. The following is his account of a series of crises which contributed to his joining the Temple of Islam:

1956 was the turning point in my life. I lived a very fast life. Nine of my close friends died from motorcycle accidents the same year . . . I sold my motor bike which was worth $2,000.00 for $200.00 and decided to quit. I gave up race riding and everything else. But only one of these deaths struck me hardest. He was my closest friend. I could never bear to think that I shall never again have such a traveling partner. What must one do when he is unhappy? What did the dreams of accidental death mean to me? . . . I once cornered my father and put the same question to him: Why am I leading such a fast life? He could not answer because he was fearing the same thing. One of his close friends had died living fast. And here I was confronted with the same fate. . . . After raising these questions about life the next question was where to go next? What must one do? Go to Church? No. Charter a plan to heaven? No . . . People were always in a hurry. They had no time to talk to one another. This is the time I learned about the Temple of Islam.[18]

Our cases so far have been reports of the experience, needs, and motives of the rank-and-file members of the Nation. For the leaders also, religion was not the most important thing which attracted them to the Nation. Minister James 3X, Assistant to Muhammad in Chicago, was in "search" of something to which he could belong

17. Interview.
18. Interview.

and apparently found it in the Nation. The account of his conversion which follows is given in detail because it emphasizes the general problems of the Negro's identity and the restlessness to which it gives rise.

Before becoming a follower of Muhammad, Minister James belonged to the Ethiopian Peace Movement. He had heard about the Universal Negro Improvement Association as a boy in the South, and "that sort of geared" him "toward nationalism or national consciousness." He was then convinced that "Garvey's program and ideology would go a long way toward solving the black man's economic problem." In 1938 James registered and voted in an election in Chicago. That was the first and the last time that Minister James voted in any election:

I thought that I was going to be actively interested in politics and I expected that this would provide job rewards. I soon learnt of the corruption of politics and so I quitted. I realized that politics would not bring about equality and justice for my people. I wanted to see the black people receive justice and equality. I became convinced that my people could never get either of these things in this country. I wanted something more militant and someone who could speak forthrightly for black people. I wanted something which could speak forthrightly against the injustices against my people.[19]

In the nineteen-thirties Minister James could have joined the NAACP or the Communist Party but was never a member of either:

I was never a member of the NAACP. I could not accept Dr. W. E. B. Dubois' position because he seemed to oppose Marcus Garvey's program and I was on Garvey's side. I did not think that the NAACP program was militant enough because it was not dealing with the basic problems such as a high degree of economic independence. The NAACP had no program which I considered would make substantial contribution to the advancement of the black man. I still do not think much of the NAACP now, because they are trying to get for the Negroes what I am opposed to. They are trying to get integration with the white man. I am for separate but equal. I frankly do not believe that the so-called Negro can ever receive better treatment from the devil so long as they remain in the same culture. I can never forgive the devil for what he has already done to my people. I did not think that the communists were fighting for my people. I never could, you know; they did not believe in God. Before I came into Islam I did think that perhaps the communists could offer something because they advocated that all men were equal regardless of race. After studying the communist philosophy I

19. Interview.

came to the conclusion that their economic system was too harsh. I believe that the individual has right of private ownership. The idea of private property gives the individual the incentive to work hard. The communists were opposed to private ownership.

Minister James had no difficulty in accepting the teachings of Muhammad:

It did not take much convincing for me to join the Temple because it seemed Islam was what I was looking for. I joined the Nation in 1940. Before this I had done some historical research and had come to the conclusion that the white man's history of the Negro's past was not true. I never did go back to any meetings of the Ethiopian Peace Movement because Islam was just what I had been looking for.

Minister Malcolm X, who is in charge of the New York Temple, admitted frankly that he had been an atheist and against "everything." Minister Malcolm's father was a Baptist minister and a Garveyite. At the age of six, Malcolm was strongly influenced by two incidents of racial injustice which his family suffered in Lansing, Michigan:

My father was a race man, a Garveyite — a little too outspoken for Lansing, Michigan, where we moved when I was a child. I remember waking up in my room back in 1929 and seeing the house on fire. The firemen came and just sat there without making any effort to put one drop of water on the fire. The fire burned down the store that my father was building.

A typical Garveyite, he was making his first step toward economic independence by building his own store. At the time we were the only Negroes in the block. Then two years later my father was found with his head bashed and his body mangled under a streetcar.[20]

In spite of the nationalism of his father and his acquaintance with black nationalism in Harlem, he did not become a member of a nationalist organization. Instead, he was "anti-everything" and a "hustler." — As a result he went to jail twice. He admits frankly that he was a dope addict before he became a Muslim. He is not ashamed of the much-publicized fact that he was twice convicted in two different states for larceny before 1948. He discusses this past publicly, but he explains: "Yes, I am what you would call an ex-convict. I am not ashamed of this because it was all done when I was a part of the white man's Christian world. As a Moslem I would

20. *Sepia*, November, 1959, p. 21.

never have done these awful things that caused me to go to prison."[21]

This background has been frequently played up by the press. The impression given by this unfavorable publicity is that converts to the Nation come from extremely anti-social elements in Negro society. It completely misses the point that conversion has regenerated the moral character, whether or not the convert had an unsavory past. The dereliction and the extremity of Minister Malcolm's past should rather be viewed as pointing up the life-saving values which he has thoroughly incorporated into his life. Malcolm himself feels that white society would like to keep its image of the Negro "rotting in dope, drunkenness, crime and in jails" intact and uncontradicted. Such publicity, by overlooking the present moral discipline of the members and concentrating on their pasts, tends to further and promote this image.

However, it was precisely because he wanted to get out of jail and forego his previous style of life that he decided to join the Nation. Minister Malcolm told the author the following story about his conversion:

Two of my brothers (both Ministers in the Nation) were Muslims before my conversion. They had joined the Detroit Temple. One of my brothers wrote me a letter while I was in jail back in 1948 and told me that they would arrange to get me out of jail if I prayed to Allah and accepted Islam. I was a convinced atheist; I was anti-everything and my brother's promise did not impress me.

My other brother who, like myself, had the unfortunate experience of being educated on the streets visited me in the penitentiary accompanied by my sister. He told me that I would soon be released from jail if I stopped smoking and eating pork. He said that the white man was the devil. That I agreed being right there in his jail. I told my brother, however, that Jews were different and that I had known good ones who hustled with me. I knew them, men and women and liked them. My brother being a good student of human nature — something he had learnt from the streets — did not press the point. He did not try there and then to tell me that I was wrong about the Jews. He explained at another occasion that Jews were not different and that they were really using him to make money for themselves. My brother told me that God was a man, but a man who has more knowledge (360°) degrees compared with the Masons whose knowledge is 32°. I could

21. *Ibid.* Minister Malcolm said in a lecture that his critics fail to add that he is not only "an ex-convict" but also an "ex-Uncle Tom."

believe that. He then told me that a man like that met Mr. Muhammad. He explained that heaven and earth are conditions which reflect one's moral and material condition here on earth. I believed that. I wanted to know how I could get out of jail. That night and ever since, I gave up eating pork and in two months, I got rid of smoking completely. Shortly after, I was released from jail on probation and I became active in the Temple. I owe my present moral stature to Mr. Muhammad for whom I would give my life so that he may live. He has done so much for me.

Minister Malcolm is married and has a child. He lives in a spacious and modestly furnished home in Long Island, New York, and drives a "ninety-eight" model, black Oldsmobile. For all intents and purposes, his style of life is middle class, although he told the writer:[22]

I own nothing, except a record player. I have no material possessions. The house where I am living is owned by the Temple. The clothes I wear are made (sewn) by the Muslim women. When I came into the Temple, I made a vow that I was never going to own anything because frequently a very sincere leader becomes trapped by material possessions and consequently he becomes alienated from the aspirations of his followers.

Friends and critics of the Muslims are often impressed by the well-barbered, neat, and healthful appearance of the Muslim men at their meetings. The older men might be mistaken in another situation for Negro business executives, and the younger ones for "Ivy Leaguers." In spite of their long robes, the neatness and bearing of the Muslim women is equally impressive. The contrasts between them and Negro visitors at Muslim meetings are many. Few of the visitors (mainly from the lower class) are well dressed. They appear underfed, sick, shabby, and primarily *worried*. It is a pathetic-looking group compared with the "hopeful-looking" Muslims.

PATTERNS OF MUSLIM BEHAVIOR

Most lower-class Negroes have suffered and are suffering from their position in white society, but suffering in itself does not always compel individuals and groups to organize a joint program for the relief of deplorable social conditions. The oppressed must be made aware that their disabilities are remediable and common to

22. Interview. We point out these facts here because it is representative of the strides toward self-improvement which countless Muslims have made.

all, but that they can be alleviated only through purposive and communal effort. It is a well-known fact that during the present century no cause, ideology, or movement has won the active support of the Negro masses.[23]

If the fact of individual suffering is not sufficient to explain the Muslims' community, neither is the fact of Negro hostility to white society. While it is true that the majority of Negroes feel hostility to the white man, whether acknowledged or not, this resentment, like suffering, is an entirely inadequate explanation of the unity, cohesion, and perseverance of the members. The writer has found that even among the Muslims, who are perhaps more consciously aware of their hostilities than many lower-class Negroes, their hatred has been rhetorically exaggerated. Strong feelings are, of course, developed regarding present abuses and indignities, but the element of a blind, unreasoning hostility is often overdrawn:

I don't hate anyone in or outside the Nation of Islam. It is not the desire of Muslims here to hate any other nationality. Whites back up their love for Negroes with ropes and guns. They call our people "Strange Fruits." Is the murder of Emmett Till love? This may not make me hate somebody but it makes me feel strongly against the people who did it. Maybe we should not hate anybody but we should have a strong feeling for the way we have been treated. See the way they are treating our people in South Africa. How do they expect us to feel about it? We would look very stupid to sit back and say we love the way our brothers and sisters are being mistreated. I am a breadwinner and I don't want to get everything after I am dead. The Negro has to be taken out of his sleep, turned completely inside out, if he is to make progress. He is too afraid, too scared for his own good. Christianity is carrying him to death.[24]

A keen sense of injustice is conveyed by another interviewee:

We have been humble slaves for nearly four hundred years. For these years we have served them humbly. We have not harmed them. I see no reason why they should kill us and treat us the way they do. We have taken a lot of things from them for the past four hundred years which even self-respecting dogs would not have endured so meekly. In spite of this, they still hate us.[25]

The Negroes' hostility is almost inevitably ambivalent in nature, since they are compelled to admire and appreciate many features

23. The Garvey movement is generally regarded as an exception. The failure of the Communist party to attract the Negro masses is even more revealing.
24. Sister Esther X.
25. Interview with Sister Elaine X.

of white middle-class society. The sense of inferiority engendered in them, while responsible for bitterness and hostility, also causes them to reject the subculture and to strive to assimilate middle-class values. Thus, hostility is frequently found in association with emulation.

The sensitivity to the inadequacies of the immediate environment and admiration for the middle-class "style of life" is illustrated in these comments by Sister—, who had lived for a time with a white family:

We had one (white family in the South) who was a friend of the family. My father worked for him. He lent us money. In fact when I was going to college we mortgaged our house to him. I worked for one. I lived in their home. When I was living there I learned that they were not as clean as I used to think. The children were pampered. They were disobedient. One thing impressed me, however, and that is that their men respected their wives. I was very amazed that although the wife was nasty to the husband, and did not treat him as nicely as we treat the so-called Negro men, yet the husband gave his wife a great deal of respect.

Any attempt to rise above the subculture and the immediate community must exhibit some deference and conformity to the standards of the dominant culture. The following comment particularly illustrates this recognition:

I don't see how they can have anything against us. Some of them say we are lazy and dirty or filthy, and that we have low morals. Actually, many of us are guilty of these. But there are reasons for these things. I am not making excuses. Some of us are lazy and dirty; their homes and children are dirty. Of course, would you expect anything else? They have no time to take care of the home. The mothers work 12 hours cleaning the homes and children of whites. Because of the lack of recreational facilities too many children play in dirt and are dirty. The adults also have no other outlet. We have more children than they and we have more than we can take care of. These are the things they say about us.

A lot of them look at one slumming Negro and judge others accordingly. We can do the same thing to them. They have dirty and lazy ones also. Percentage-wise I do not think that the Negroes excel in these evils. Because of residential segregation the case of the Negroes becomes quite obvious. What happens is that both the clean and hardworking Negroes are forced by residential segregation to live together and therefore all of them look equally junky. Some white people who make these judgments haven't had the opportunity to know or to talk to any intelligent, educated and highly well behaved Negroes. Their only contact for the most part is with their domestic servants. They never had real experience with educated and well trained Negroes.

The business methods of the whites are recommended by Muhammad as a means of attaining economic success. In his "Economic Blueprint," he urges his followers to emulate white business operations: "Observe the operations of the White Man. He is successful. He makes no excuses for his failures. He works hard — in a collective manner. You do the same. . . ."

If fear or coercion of those in leadership, common suffering, hostility toward whites, desire for political power, or religious belief *per se* do not sufficiently explain why individuals remain in the Nation, we must ask what differentiates the Muslims significantly from the urban lower-class Negroes in general? What kind of individual remains in the Nation? What kinds of ends and incentives are offered these individuals in the Nation? What "style of life" do the Muslims appear to appreciate?

An examination of the patterns of Muslim behavior suggests rather strongly that upwardly mobile lower-class Negroes join and remain in the Nation. Most individuals perceive the ends offered by the Nation in terms of self-esteem, recognition, and status. The "style of life" that the Muslims seem to appreciate and to which they aspire is thoroughly middle class, although lacking in the advantages of education and income enjoyed generally by middle-class persons. The pervasiveness of the middle-class spirit and aspirations among the Muslims cannot escape the attention of a keen observer. This spirit differentiates them fundamentally from the vast majority of lower-class Negroes. Dollard's description of the spirit of the middle class in the southern towns he studied best sums up the writer's impression of the ethos of the Nation of Islam:

One feels their spirit to be energetic and acquisitive. In the main they intend to make their way by their exertions and personal contributions to the welfare of the community. Their personal standards of behavior, on questions of drinking, divorce, and profanity, seem to be more rigorous than those of the classes above or below them. They seem to be religious. . . .[26]

26. *Caste and Class in a Southern Town,* p. 76.

The motives which led individuals to join the Nation were largely personal, in some cases quite specific, in others general and vague, but in all cases they had to do with "improving one's self or community." This is generally true of the majority of Muhammad's followers. It is quite possible that a large number of them had not perceived or are not even aware that by pursuing the way of life advocated by Muhammad, they are in spirit, if not in fact, pursuing a middle-class style of life. We should add that although a few, prior to joining the Nation, had the capacity and motivation for upward mobility, most became imbued with this desire because of their participation in the movement. The incentives offered by the Nation also point to and illuminate the style of life which the Muslims seek as a group.

INCENTIVES

The incentives offered by the Nation to its members are largely intangible or subjective. We may dispose of the few material incentives offered by the Nation by noting that individuals who "behave" in the Nation may be assisted in time of unemployment, financial difficulties, sickness, death, or other distresses. In addition, a few who are loyal and talented may be rewarded with a "steady-paying" job in the Nation, while the ambitious may rise to a position of undreamed of prominence in their communities, as we have seen in the case of Minister Malcolm X. Individuals can improve their material position indirectly only if they closely follow Muhammad's "second commandment":[27] The pursuit of wealth is a good thing only insofar as its use is also for the common good. This can be achieved only by hard work, frugality (savings and investment), and self-discipline. The Muslims must not waste their income on alcoholic beverages, narcotics, tobacco, gambling, dancing, dating, or sports. Long vacations from jobs must not be taken, nor should money be spent unnecessarily on food or for such things as straightening and dyeing of hair and for cosmetics. Above all, they must refrain from conspicuous consumption:

27. Muhammad's commandments may be ranked as follows; (1) Thou shall pursue a moral life; (2) Thou shall pursue wealth only for the common good; (3) Thou shall act and conduct thyself as a gentleman or lady.

You must stop imitating the slavemaster. Because your slavemaster wears thirty dollar shoes or a two hundred dollar suit, you go and spend your money on these things. You have no room in which to sleep, but you go into debt for a Cadillac.[28]

GROUP MEMBERSHIP AND IDENTIFICATIONS

Although we know little about friendship patterns among lower-class Negroes, the Muslims stated frequently that "in the Negro world it was always easy to find friends for the purpose of doing wrong and very seldom for the purpose of doing right." They said that they found few "meaningful" friendships, association, or peer groups outside the Nation of Islam. They seldom found "friends who were interested in acting together for things which would benefit us," but there "was no problem in finding friends for dancing, drinking, entertainment or gambling." Those interviewed seem to value highly the friendships they have made in the Nation. It seems reasonable to infer that upwardly mobile individuals who want friendship and support from peer groups for "self-improvement" pursuits or "meaningful" identifications tend to join and remain in the Nation. Finding the Negro community at large uninspiring, they join the Nation, believing that this offers a way to pursue a "moral" and "decent" life and to improve themselves materially. In many instances they had to break away from their former friends or peer groups. In some cases they had to make difficult adjustments in their relations with former friends and relatives. Although many appear to maintain good relations with relatives and friends, a few have rejected, or have been rejected by, their former friends. The kinds of adjustments that are made and their attitudes toward their friends in the Nation may be illustrated by a few brief case histories:

Brother John W's background was discussed elsewhere. His mother lives in Chicago; his father is dead. His mother, brothers, and sisters are Baptists. John claims that he has good relationships with them. His mother has visited the Temple several times and does not condemn Muhammad's teachings, but because she is a

28. Speech, 1960 Convention.

Baptist and has been one as long as she can remember, she cannot accept Islam.

I feel at the moment that unless I am trying to introduce Islam to friends or to bring to them something nationalistically-minded, it is a waste of time to continue in their company. They like so much to talk about trivial and frivolous things and are not a help to the great work that is confronting my Leader and Teacher, the Honorable Elijah Muhammad. . . .

I have made numerous wonderful friends whom I can truly call brothers and sisters and I have lost many friends whom I thought were friends in the world of Christianity. These particular people cannot accept the way of Islam, because it takes away from them the opportunity to practice those habits which they had formed. To make the change and accept a righteous way of life would deprive them of practicing the evil habits. Consequently, they refuse to accept me and the fact that in their presence I would be an example of good would constantly prey upon their conscious mind to do good and, therefore, they are not liking it.[29]

Brother Thomas 5X (Drake) also retains his old friendships and has made many new ones in the Nation. Brother Thomas X. (Jones) is forty-eight years old and has been in the Nation since 1945. His wife and four children are also in the Nation. His eldest son is a Muslim but has been "negligent of his duties. Although he continues to visit the Temple, he is not living up to his obligations." The family relationship is good. He has made new friends and has not lost old ones:

I have made many new friends since I reunited with the Nation. In fact, my friends are increasing. I have not lost any of my old friends in my way of thinking. In fact, before uniting with the Nation I never had many friends. I used to be by myself. My friends prior to coming into Islam were not trustworthy. This is the major difference between them and my friends now. My friends in the Nation are much more trustworthy.[30]

Sister Mildred has not lost her old friends:

When I am at home they visit me, but we no longer do the kinds of things we used to do together before — night-clubbing, parties, weekend trips to have a good time, sports and games. I have made new friends in the Nation. I have not made a non-Muslim friend since I came to Chicago (August 1958).[31]

29. Interview.
30. Interview.
31. Interview.

Sister Nellie lost her friends:

I have lost friends among those who thought that we were friends when we were doing the same things together. You now find that they were not really friends. That's right! I look upon them with pity. I still have love for them. They are destroying themselves. They are trying to keep up with someone who is not like them. When you accept Islam you stop drinking, smoking and committing indecent acts that you used to do with them. They think that it is odd, and they think that you are insane. They think that you are a misfit and they don't care to be around you because you are living according to a plan, i.e., according to the righteous laws and duties of a Muslim, such as no smoking, no drinking, and no adultery.[32]

Brother Donald X, like many Muslims, finds that although his former friends do not "believe" in his way of life, they show him respect because of his "manners" toward them:

I understand my friends better now than before. The kinds of things which made me angry in the past do not any more. I show much better and fine manners toward them. Now because I have more refined manners toward my friends, naturally they treat me better and respect me more although they may not go along with everything the Messenger teaches. They respect the fact that they have seen this change in me, and really treat me nice.

One Sister joined the Nation with two other friends of her age. The others left. At the time of the interview, she was working at one of the Muslim stores; since then she has become one of Muhammad's private secretaries. She has broken away from her friends.

My friends used to come here [the store] to visit me. They are used to going to night clubs. I broke away with all of them and no longer associate with them. I rejected the nightclub. One friend continued to visit me at the store, but I decided that I could not maintain associations with kids who do not think like I do and have no love for Allah. My whole life is devoted to Islam.

This Sister, who is twenty years old, left her father and brother because her brother gambles. She now lives in a Muslim-owned apartment. "I could not live in the same place with them." Her father promised that he would join the Nation if she would return to live with them. She said, "I told him that I would not want to join on such a condition. If he doesn't really feel like joining and putting aside his way of life, there is no reason why he should join." She

32. Interview.

lives with five girls about her age and an elderly woman. Asked if the elderly woman was the matron, she said, "No. She is too old to do that. We do not need matrons. I try to live according to the laws of Islam."

We have indicated already that the Nation provides activites and opportunities for members to interact frequently and thus fosters a sense of membership, belonging, and solidarity. This is supplemented by exchange of visits between members and friends as well as through exchange of greeting cards during the Nation's festivals, especially the Saviour's Day Celebration. Two samples of greeting cards follow here:

> To the Messenger on Saviour's Day
> *As-Salaam-Alaikum:*
> You are the one
> Who met the Saviour
> And recognized Him right away
> You are the one
> Whom He has chosen
> To represent Him on this day.
> You are the one
> Who makes the effort
> To clean us up in every way
> And "You" are the one
> Who will present us
> On that Great and Dreadful Day.
>
> To My Husband on Saviour's Day
> It's truly grand
> The Saviour came
> And made Muhammad
> His special voice
> And it's really Grand
> To hold your hand and say
> You're my special choice.

Aside from the personal gratifications which members derive from the Nation, it became quite clear that the Nation provides opportunity for individuals who seek associations and identifications that inspire and legitimize their desire for social mobility. We asked several Muslims two related questions: What is your idea of a good man? What kind of person do you admire? The respondents' answers suggest that they identify largely with middle-class individuals and aspire to their standards of living and conduct. Only one Muslim said he identified with the "common" people, although it was quite clear that he identified strongly with Muhammad, whom he did not regard as a "common" man:

> I admire my own people . . . especially, the ones of the ordinary type — the common man, excepting the Messenger of Allah. I admire him. I admire people I can understand. I cannot understand the middle or upper class or educated people as I can understand the common man. I admire thoughtful, conscientious and sincere persons.[33]

Most suggested "ideal-type" individuals whom the writer believes they cannot ordinarily find in the lower-class society, white or black.

The women tended to admire the responsible and family man or woman. Sister Elaine thinks her father, a Muslim, represents her ideal of a good man. She listed some characteristics of a responsible family man which she believes her father personifies:

> My idea of a good man is one who brings his money home. A man who takes care of his family, saves his money in order to buy a home if he needs one and does not spend his money foolishly. My mother owns a home. My idea of a good man is really my father. I mean a man like my father. Father was in the Nation till about 1936. My parents are still married and father works for the U. S. Steel Co. Father is still a Muslim, though.

Apparently, many women believe that the Nation is a place to find responsible family men and also husbands for themselves.

Sister Mildred emphasized that such a man must be "a man of great moral strength." He should be "a man of decision. A man who can make his own decisions. I mean reasonable and good decisions; not a conformist." Several Sisters stressed that he must be "thoughtful, considerate, patient, honest, and loving." Several men shared the views of the women on their responsibilities in the family. Brother Vernon admires "a person who is trying to advance himself in every way that a man should advance himself." He also defined the "good" man as "a Negro who accepts Islam here in America — a man that will do things that will increase his wisdom and knowledge, a man who will take care of his family properly."

The criteria of a "good" man represent rather high ideals and

33. Interview, Thomas X (Jones).

are by no means typical of the types of persons they are likely to encounter among lower-class persons. Moreover, they may not be able to find in the Nation many individuals who incorporate the personality traits described below:

For me, a good man must be a man of deep religious faith. He must be intelligent. He must be well-balanced in the sense that he does the right thing at the right time and at the right occasion. He must be courageous when there is need for courageousness, and meek when the occasion demands. He must have the time to love (really, he must know the time to love) and when he should hate on the proper occasions. He should hate when he needs to hate, and should not hate when he should love. He should have high and noble ideas and purpose in life. He should have an insatiable thirst for knowledge, divine wisdom and understanding. He should study the attributes of God and imbue himself with those attributes.

I admire intelligent and scholarly people. I do not like a person who always cracks jokes, and wants to be humorous. I like a person with some sense of humor, but when the time comes for him to be serious, I think that he should be serious. If a person believes in a thing, let him devote his whole strength and his whole mind to it. I don't like those who straddle the fence. I like a man who has a strong character. A man who is strong. I don't like weakly people. I like people who are honest and considerate.[34]

ATTITUDES TOWARD ACCOMMODATION

Membership in the Nation assists the Negro in adjusting to the present patterns of race relations in both the North and South and in rationalizing his own subordination and humiliation. Since members come to develop more clearly defined attitudes regarding their position vis-à-vis the white man, most Muslims have expressed some admiration for the white southerner, whose beliefs are thought to be stronger, more honestly held, and more clearly defined than are the beliefs of white northerners. One Muslim expressed the idea in the following terms:

I admire the white southerner, for you know for the most part where the white southerner stands. In the north, there is confusion. I rather not go to a place that is segregated without the facts being made obvious before I go. I like people who have some kinds of values and who are convinced. . . . I do not like wishy-washy types of persons. I mean the type of person who says yes to everything. I like people who think about important things. . . .

34. Interview with Minister James 3X. There is no doubt that he identifies largely with his image of the Messenger. He is unlikely to find (at the present at least) scholarly people in the Nation of Islam.

there are so many people who spend time talking about frivolous things.
. . .

Accepting the idea of total separation of the races aids the Negro
in ridding himself of the belief that the whites are solely responsible,
and are to be continually held responsible, for the Negro's "degradation and miseries." Thus the individual who is relieved of this
feeling has less difficulty in accepting his own responsibility for
self-improvement, even within the ghetto. The following statement
is quoted at some length because of its pertinence here:

You were taught from the cradle that you were a Negro, your privileges
were few, that white was superior. When you started going to school you
knew that the whites had better schools, after a graduation from high school
you soon learnt that the colleges you could go to were limited in number.
And this is particularly so in the South. Downtown there was a white fountain, white eating places, white this and that. In downtown south you just
know it once you can make distinctions. My parents told me not to bother the
white folks and told me the don'ts when you are downtown unless you are
working for them. My father doesn't like them and would tell insurance
men or other collectors to leave his premises. If they wanted to see him they
had to come by the backdoor. I have seen him actually drive them away.
My father resents working for a white family and actually forced my mother
to leave her job with an invalid family whose husband thought it was kindness to come pick mother up in his car and brought her back. Father did not
like this idea. I was always very afraid of white people — I travelled to New
York City to visit my sister. There I saw how my sister treated them and particularly the cops when they illegally came to her residence. They would
literally be thrown out by my sister. At first I was scared and I just could
not comprehend my sister handling especially a white cop that way. From
then on I decided that when I grew up I would leave the South in order to
live in the North. Now that I know who the white people are, I would find
living in the South much easier. I accept a separation now. At first I used
to think that I must be liked by them and must be accepted by them before
I could get anywhere. Now all that is reversed.

The accommodationist attitude of the Muslims toward white hostility has been expressed in many ways. One Muslim explained that
whites despise the Negro because the "so-called Negro is trying to
walk in his image. We are trying to be their shadows. We buy black
cars, wear black suits, and imitate whites in every respect. They are
so much against us because we are trying so hard to imitate them in
everything they do." By differentiating themselves from the Negroes who are thought to ape the white man and earn his contempt,

many Muslims seek to appease the hostility — imagined or real — of the white man.

IDENTITY AND MOTIVATIONS [35]

The implication that some relationship exists between a sense of identity and the desire for self-improvement and social mobility is strongly suggested by the behavior of the Muslims. We asked several what they thought were the most important things they learned from the Messenger of Allah. Besides religion and the knowledge of Allah, several stressed "knowledge of their identity" and things which pertain to self-improvement, respect, and recognition from others. Brother Leonard IX said that because he now knows "where I originated from," he is more "concerned with self-preservation. Instead of working and throwing away my money, and leaving my body uncared for, I now take care of myself with my money and have learned how to manage my pocketbook." Another Brother said: "I am an Asiatic — a brother to all natives of Asia and that by uniting with Allah, his Messenger and my brothers in Asia, I have recognition and power."

In the past, before coming into the Nation, my life was the life of a slave because I had no training for any special position other than common labor. Since coming into the Nation opportunity for training and advancement is better. . . . Islam makes life in its totality worthwhile. . . . Now I learn to live for the Nation. I am aspiring more and more for self-independence and self-support economically. Before joining the Nation, my feeling for helping my so-called Negro brothers wasn't as strong as it is now.

Besides, it was also clear that an awareness of one's identity made members become more concerned, not only with self-improvement, but they also develop a strong sense of community responsibility. One feels that the Muslim's concern for community improvement is equally as keen as their concern for personal welfare. Brother Thomas insisted in an interview: "I would not talk about improvement in my life — materially or morally." "Many people," he said, "think that we come here because we need some improvement; this

---

35. For a discussion of identity and motivation, see Nelson N. Foote, "Identification as the Basis for a Theory of Motivation," *American Sociological Review*, XVI (February, 1951), 14–21.

is not so in every instance." He said, however, that he now has a "brighter outlook toward life" than he ever had in any other organization he had worked with; "I have a stronger will and desire to help my people; I could never have said so before joining the Nation. Islam has destroyed all doubts, or reasons I may have had for withholding my help in the cause of my people. If something can give that kind of feeling and determination for the group rather than for self alone, then I think the Messenger will succeed." The resoluteness and determination with which the Muslims try to improve themselves and thereby gain recognition from others is very evident in their outlook on life.

One Brother, comparing his ambition now with his past, said: "I had ambitions always, but it was unstable then. Since I became a Muslim, I think of it in a greater sense, and I have a chance now to be what I want to be regardless to whatever lies in front of me, whereas when I was not in the Nation, there were many loopholes." The writer asked this Brother what he meant by "loopholes?" As we have stated before, his reply suggests that by accepting the status quo of race-relations, the individual feels free to improve himself by self assertion within these limits. "When I say loopholes, I mean that I did not understand the racial balance before I came into the Nation. You know the difference between whites and colored, why they treat us the way they do, and why they do not allow us the same opportunities they allow their kids. They didn't want you to get ahead." The writer asked if he thought he could now "rise" socially in spite of the whites. "Yes, sir," he said emphatically. He added that in the past he was not very sure that an individual could advance in spite of the whites.

The sense of pride in one's past (not the Negroes' past in the United States), spurious as it may be, seems also to spur the Muslims' desire to improve themselves. Sister Nellie said she has learned in the Nation that "Africans are not savages but that the mentally dead Negroes in the United States are the real savages — they have no love for one another and they hate themselves." Comparing her life now with what it was before becoming a Muslim, she emphasized that her life is more purposeful:

My life then was from day to day existence. I had no future to look forward to. I was crazy with jealousy [referring to the competition and difficulties which Negro women have with keeping their husbands away from other women]. Then I only thought of myself. I tried to get everything that I could for myself. I trusted no one. I have trust now. I have love. I have life and I have a future. . . . My life is most eventful now. I am working with little children in the school. This means I am working with the future. I am helping to mold them and I am helping to mold that future. I have a part to play daily, honestly, and truthfully.

I used to be an entertainer. I thought at the time that the life of a singer was indeed a real life. It is a world of easy-come-easy-go . . . I was extravagant, spent money on expensive gowns, but it was a world of pressure, uncertainty, and competition. It was a false life. A competitive world. A world without security, without God. Islam is not just a thing. It is a total way of life. It is a perfect life. It is just. It is free. It is equal. You need not be a fanatic. I was always searching for something. I found it! I am a better person, a better wife.

The attitude of Muslims toward the use of their leisure time indicates that membership in the Nation enables them to devote more time to activities which are likely to benefit them. Minister James' attitude toward the use of leisure time is representative of the feeling of most Muslims:

I am too busy to have time for recreational activities. The Messenger feels that if we get too much into sports we may waste too much time and return to the old ways. There is too much work to be done. He says that we should study in order to improve ourselves and our knowledge.[36]

Sister Levinia is eighteen years old. She attends a Chicago public school and spends her leisure time doing things which she believes will improve her.

I have no occupation. I am a student. I intend to go to college. With regard to the use of my time, now instead of spending time to go to unnecessary places like movies, dances, nightclubs as most girls of my age, I get more valuable things done with my time. I spend more time at home with my mother. I spend more time studying than I would when I was not in the Nation. I do a lot of things around the house which I know would benefit me as a person — sewing, making things, cooking. I can't afford to waste my time. I want to finish high school and go to college. I want to make something out of myself that will benefit my Nation and myself. But before I became a Muslim, I didn't think very much of benefitting my Nation or going to college. Really, I never thought of going to college.[37]

36. Interview.
37. Interview.

Comparing his use of leisure time now with that of the past, Brother Vernon emphasized that he had spent much of his time at "recreation centers, taverns, night clubs, and parties." Since joining the Nation, he spends most of his time "trying to do something to help my people." Furthermore, he said, "I have no time for play. I go over to the Temple doing whatever I can to help. Some days I sell newspapers, sometimes I just work cleaning the Temple."

The writer feels (although it could not be checked) that in general the Muslims seem to take their occupations (when they are employed) more seriously than before they joined the Nation. Several expressed this attitude. Most believed that they are better accepted and respected by others and by their employers because of their membership in the Nation. They asserted that white employers treat them better than they treat other Negroes "once they know that you are a Muslim and a follower of Mr. Muhammad." Some even claimed that employment opportunities are open to them where other Negroes may not be hired. Nearly every Muslim interviewed claimed that whites do not discriminate against them in employment because of their religion. Many of these claims are sheer fantasy. One can well imagine, however, that employers may regard them highly because they take their jobs seriously, work harder, appear neater, and behave more "reliably" than some lower-class Negroes in similar situations. It is also possible that white employers may accord them some deference over other Negroes (and for that matter lower-class whites) because of their personal comportment and demeanor.

One Brother who works for the city of Chicago said that he is respected and accepted by his colleagues because he is a Muslim. The writer knows this Brother very well. He is a soft spoken, extraordinarily neat, and well-mannered person. He is pleasant to talk with and would mix with some ease with middle-class persons. It seems more likely that his personal qualities and conduct are responsible for the feeling of recognition and acceptance which he gets from his colleagues:

I have been respected and accepted by people who formerly did not respect me. I have been given attention where ordinarily I would be ignored: I have been blessed in many ways by Allah . . . When I got married I was blessed by Allah and I was able to get all the material goods which one would need when he gets married. I have been taught by the Messenger the importance of understanding the other person's point of view and therefore by having knowledge of the enemy and why he acts in certain ways, I have been able to work around him more harmoniously and without friction and misunderstanding. Once they know that you are a Muslim they immediately cease treating you as one of their tools, i.e. like a Negro.

Another Brother, who did not impress the writer as particularly intelligent, thought that whites treat him differently once they notice the emblem — a ring with the Crescent — of the Nation of Islam on him. He seems to be well-behaved and dresses neatly; but he would have grave difficulties and strains mixing in a middle-class group. His notion of acceptance and recognition by whites is, to say the least, exaggerated:

Since I began to wear my National [the ring] at my job, the white boss calls me Mr. Woods [38] instead of "boy." He opens positions for me which the other so-called Negroes can't get. At first I was mopping the floors, then I delivered telegrams [for Western Union], and then came the 'gold bricking' [explained by him as doing less work], and from there to elevator operator. Before I became the elevator operator, no other black man had been hired for that position. A black woman has since been hired.

This Brother seems to exaggerate his importance on the job when he added that the Negro girl was hired as an elevator operator "because the manager thinks that she is my wife, which she is not."

The Muslims' sense of importance and recognition is fostered especially in those situations where they are in contact with lower-class whites. It appears that in such situations white bosses confer favorable treatment (over lower-class whites) because of their personal conduct. This sense of importance is illustrated by the way Brother Karriem Allah describes his experience and that of other Muslims in a federal penitentiary during the last war:

However, I was treated differently in jail. In fact all the Muslims were treated differently from the rest of the inmates. We were the only trusted inmates in the institution. We had the privilege to go outside of the walls daily. We had no guards following us any where we went. Most of the time we were alone. There were six of us at this jail. While there, the Messenger held meetings as he did when he was outside. Our lost-found brothers who were also in jail were invited to attend our meetings. They listened to the

38. The name is fictitious, although the account is the interviewee's.

teachings of the Messenger and of Islam. Many of them attended our meetings. I do not regret having been to prison for one moment. I learnt something which I had not known before I went there: the Messenger was highly respected. He taught Islam vigorously in the prison. I admired his courage and boldness. There were many inmates that tried to match their wisdom with his but they were like a flower that had been cut down and withered by the heat of the sun. The Messenger of Allah was admired by our host — the lost-found brothers and the devils alike. The devils spoke of him as a great man, an honorable man with no likeness. I have often stood and watched officers of the prison make commendable statements about him. Often they would say, "A man like him has no right to be here." My incarceration was very easy. I liken it unto a bad dream or a hard day's work. For a time, the Messenger was put on the institutional farm. . . .

In a real sense, their feeling of recognition seems justifiable because, unlike the other prisoners, they were convicted for political offenses, not for murder, rape, robbery or other types of criminal offenses.

THE HOME

The Muslims' attitude has shifted from the maternal-centered — characteristic of the Negro subculture — to the paternal-centered family. This arrangement, although not peculiar to middle-class culture, is a significant departure from the norms of the subculture. It helps to strengthen the family, the most important unit of socialization. The father is the undisputed head of the family. Responsibility for the welfare of the family shifts significantly from the woman to the man. The writer found that, in theory at least, the Muslim men preferred that their wives should not work outside the home. Brother John W. earns a modest income and believes that so long as he remains employed, he would rather have his wife take care of the home and children. Sister Emma, his wife, was asked how she felt about her husband's attitude. She said she was quite satisfied. This arrangement was possible in a few Muslim homes. Most wives worked because of economic necessity rather than by choice. The Muslim attitude in this respect is unmistakably middle class.

The writer found that although most Muslims are in the low-income brackets, they kept their homes very clean, orderly, and modestly but pleasantly furnished. There were some homes, however, where the atmosphere was not orderly. A few of these had too many occupants or children. Muhammad discourages over-crowded homes. The writer knows at least one instance when Muhammad or the Captain of the Temple asked a Muslim family to oust their relatives. The relatives came from the South. The Muslim Brother faced suspension from the Temple if he did not oust them. He obeyed and the relatives, who were not Muslims, returned to the South. They expressed no desire to join the Nation and hence could not be assisted by the Temple.

The writer was constantly impressed by the manner in which the Muslims have assumed middle-class attitudes and symbols. Often these caused him embarrassment and inconvenience. On several occasions his Muslim friends invited him to dinner. He went without a suit to most of the dinners, except those at the Messenger's home. He noticed that the Muslim hosts, children, and guests paid special attention to formalities. The men dressed in business suits (and quite often some wore vests) for dinner. I was told that this was the practice generally, and I suppose that their behavior was not merely to impress the guest. Table manners were rather formal, and conversations were usually on "polite" subjects carried on in subdued voices. On Saturday evenings the writer visited Muslim friends for chats. Sometimes there were two or three Muslim girls and wives in the group. They took little part in the conversations. The men paid rather slight attention to them as sex objects. Often we listened to Middle-Eastern music and some jazz "classics." Although the writer was often tempted to tap his feet to the tune of jazz, the Muslims listened to it without ostensible response to the rhythm.

The formality of their manners was apparent also outside of their homes, and, as we shall see later, the students at the University of Islam are obligated to dress formally. On occasion boys who came to school without ties and jackets in the winter were sent home. A few mothers, driving station wagons typical of the middle-class suburbanites, brought their children to school every morning and returned for them in the afternoon. The younger men, especially a few who attended college or business schools, seemed to prefer the Volkswagen or other popular small cars.

On the whole, the Muslims not only verbalized their aspirations for mobility but a few were able to realize them in concrete ways. Although this could not be checked directly, it appeared to the writer that those who made fair wages tended to move away from slum neighborhoods to areas in the city which they thought to be more conducive to "bringing up" children. In a few cases, parents with sufficient income but without initiative to move from previous locations, were compelled to do so by the Captain "in the interest of the young Sisters." A few Muslims, who had managed to enter into some small businesses, very proudly informed the writer of their achievement. This was the case with one young man who worked for a white-owned dry cleaning plant. He left the job to become a salesman for an Indiana clothing manufacturer. The writer met him a few months after he had left the cleaning plant. The Muslim Brother gladly told him: "I am now on my own; this is the beginning." Similarly, Sister — who is fourteen, called the writer up to report that her mother and two other Muslim Sisters had recently bought a restaurant, and she was very happy of the fact. The writer could list a few instances when Muslims who had acquired a small business jubilantly reported the fact to him. It is also interesting to note Sister —, who proudly told the writer that she lives in a Chicago South Side neighborhood "where there are lot of teachers and middle-class people." The mobility aspirations of the Muslims are evident in their desires for their children's future. Most Muslims expressed regret that they did not "get more" education. They hoped that their children would "get all the education they need and can acquire." On the whole, the members seem to find support for their aspirations in the Nation of Islam.

It may be said that black nationalism is a tortuous route to social mobility, recognition, and status [39] or a spurious way by which the

39. This appears no less unintelligible than the resort to crime as a means of social advancement. Daniel Bell has noted: "Yet all this was acted out in a wider context. The desires satisfied in extra-legal fashion were more than a hunger for the 'forbidden fruits' of conventional morality. They also involved, in the complex and ever shifting structure of group, class, and ethnic stratification, which is the warp and woof of America's 'open' society, such 'normal' goals as independence through a

black nationalists seek to gain a sense of identity and membership in American society. It may well be, but this does not deny its immediate significance and meaning for the Muslims; nor is it so strange and unintelligible in view of the whole social history and the psychological trauma [40] which the Negro has suffered in the United States. However, the larger and more fundamental question raised by black nationalism has implications for the assimilation of the Negro in American society. Can the Negro be assimilated in view of this history as well as the psychological trauma he has suffered? Does he really want to be assimilated? This dilemma, with its practical consequences, was cogently formulated by DuBois some sixty-three years ago:

> No Negro who has given earnest thought to the situation of his people in America has failed, at some time in life to find himself at these crossroads; has failed to ask himself at the same time: What, after all, am I? Am I an American or am I a Negro? Can I be both? Or is it my duty to cease to be a Negro as soon as possible and be an American? If I strive as a Negro, am I not perpetuating the very cleft that threatens and separates black and white America? Is not my only possible practical aim the subduction of all that is Negro in me to the American? [41]

The ideology of the Nation of Islam, and of black nationalism in general, is an attempt to deal with this larger question at both the subjective and practical levels. Seen against this background, the ideology, organization, and programs of the Muslim movement will become more intelligible. The eschatology gives some "saving identity." It may not be justified, but it helps explain the Negro dilemma.

business of one's own, and such 'moral' aspirations as the desire for social advancement and social prestige . . ." (*The End of Ideology* [Glencoe, Ill.: The Free Press, 1960], p. 117).

40. For a summary of studies which bear upon this subject and a detailed bibliography of published studies, see Gergene Seward, *Psychotherapy and Culture Conflict* with Case Studies by Judd Marmor (New York: The Ronald Press Company, 1956), especially chaps. VI and VII.

41. DuBois, *The American Negro Academy, Occasional Papers*, No. 2, pp. 10–14.

V. The Eschatology

> No people strives to lose themselves among other people
> except the so-called Negroes. This they do because of their
> lack of knowledge of self . . .
> It is Allah's will and purpose that we shall know ourselves;
> therefore, He came Himself to teach us the knowledge of self.
> Who is better knowing of whom we are than God Himself?
> He has declared that we are descendants of the Asian black
> nation and of the tribe of Shabazz.
>
> ELIJAH MUHAMMAD

THEIR ESCHATOLOGY reflects the social history of the Negro in America, especially the psychological trauma and personality disturbances to which that history has given rise. On the one hand, it arises from the fact that throughout the Negro's history in America the dominant white society was successful (through the mass media and in fact) in manipulating and exploiting "blackness," with respect to the Negro in America and in Africa, as an inferior attribute, to be despised and hated.[1] For a long time, therefore, a "manipulated image" of blackness became, with varying degrees of

1. Cf. John W. Vandercook, *Tom-Tom* (New York: Harper and Brothers, 1926), pp. xiii–xiv: ". . . The fact of bondage died, but the mood lived. The four centuries during which the white race preserved its conquest of the people of Africa were ample time for the imposition of an ideal. That ideal — the gigantic, cruel absurdity that the white race is, through some weird miracle of pigmentation and force the supreme, heaven-wrought master of the world — still survives. Tragically, the Negro has accepted the truth of what was originally nothing more than an opportunist hypocrisy. . . ."

applicability to individuals as well as social classes, the "objective reality" with which the Negro identified himself. At the same time, however, the Negro was subjectively compelled to reject and to hate his "objective self" as defined by the whites. In this sense he became alienated from himself. Second, it seems obvious that the eschatology, considered against the rapid changes in the Negro status and especially the trend toward integration, reflects the tensions and anxieties resulting from the Negro's apprehension that such a trend, coupled with the possibility of assimilation and ultimately of amalgamation, promises their extinction as a people. Whether or not this apprehension has any basis in fact is beside the point. It does constitute an element of the Negroes' anxieties and, although this problem is muted by them because of racial bigotry in the United States, the writer found it widely but privately voiced. It is not the principle of integration, that is, total acceptance without discrimination, which these Negroes question, but their destiny as a people in America. Black nationalism addresses itself to both problems.

More narrowly, however, the eschatology of the Nation of Islam shows the black nationalists' desire to free themselves from the exploited image of blackness and hence from the deep feeling of self-rejection, cultural alienation, and social estrangement which pervade and corrupt the personalities of the Negro masses. It expresses the nationalist's need to attach himself in a positive way to something worthy and esteemed, some center of power, some tradition and, generally, some "central ideal" capable of endowing his life with meaning and purpose. It offers hope in a future, one in which blackness will no longer be despised. In part, this vision of the future inspires the Muslims to pursue their life activities with courage and unbending determination.

The eschatology becomes intelligible only in terms of the nationalists' insistence that knowledge of one's own identity — one's self, nation, religion, and God — is indispensable to a creative life for the individual and for the group, and is the true meaning of heaven. Not having this knowledge is hell. The instructed individual acquires a new being and outlook on life; he enjoys heaven on earth. The individual gains a new, better perspective on his past and present moral and material conditions and can initiate programs for his future and for that of his Nation. Newfound self-respect and confidence inspire him to work hard and to make sacrifices for his Nation's future. His sacrifices are justified by promises of the Nation's final, ultimate grandeur.

Consciousness of self and identity remain incomplete unless complemented by knowledge of one's "enemy." The ostensible enemy of the Nation of Islam is, of course, the Caucasian race and specifically the American white man, who is responsible for the moral and material conditions of the Negro. The enemy is not simply the white race. It is their claim to cultural, moral, and spiritual superiority, the myth of white supremacy which they have fostered so long. Their success in imposing this opportunist hypocrisy on the Negroes must be combatted. The eschatology and other esoteric doctrines of Muhammad seek, in reverse, to impose a different self-image upon the black masses that is no less spurious but is definitely functional.

It should be stressed that what follows here are strictly Muhammad's ideas concerning the eschatology of the Black Nation. These ideas are given almost verbatim from his teachings. The reader should bear in mind that the claims made in the Nation's eschatology would not meet certain tests of knowledge, logically or empirically. However, the significance of the teaching for the socially estranged lies not in its logical validity, coherence, or consistency; rather, it affords a perspective on the fundamental Negro dilemma: blackness is given a worthy status and the Negro heritage made attractive.

THE CHOSEN [2]

Although the destiny of the Black Nation and of the Caucasian race is "hidden" in the Scriptures, it has been revealed to the "Chosen" (the Nation of Islam), through God's "Messenger" (Muhammad) in the "Last Days" when the "Son of Man" would be corporeally present in the world:

2. David Riesman has noted in connection with the Jews: "Occasionally, the group's 'nerve of failure' was supported by the notion that its very powerlessness proved the Jews to be in fact the Chosen of God. . . ." *Individualism Reconsidered and other Essays* (Glencoe, Ill.: Free Press, 1954), p. 57.

We have God with us. He is not to come, but he is already here. There are many Christians, they will admit that God must be present, but there are a few people today in this fast moving world who take a moment of their time to think or even to look to see whether or not this is the day of the devil's visit, but I am here to tell you that I myself have been sent directly from the face of God. He has given to me that which is written by the prophets that will give you life, bring light to you, your understanding will return.[3]

Prophet W. D. Fard, whose activities among Detroit Negroes have already been described, is the God of the Muslims. His divinity is celebrated in Muhammad's teachings. He is known to his followers variously as "Allah (God) in the Person of Master W. F. Muhammad, to Whom all praise is due, the Great Mahdi or Messiah, as the Christians say." "He is also the Son of Man and the Saviour."[4] According to Muhammad's account, "Allah came to us from the Holy City of Mecca, Arabia, on July 4, 1930."[5]

Muhammad describes Him as one who spoke with authority and independence.[6] Prophet Fard also claimed that he came to North America by himself, that his "uncle was brought over here by the Trader three hundred and seventy-nine years ago." Continuing, he said, "My uncle cannot talk his own language. He does not know that he is my uncle."[7]

THE DIVINITY OF THE MAHDI

According to Muhammad, Prophet Fard (Master W. F. Muhammad), the Mahdi or Saviour, is the God of the Black Nation whose

3. Speech of the Most Honorable Elijah Muhammad, Sunday, March 1, 1959, at the Muslim Annual Convention, Metropolitan Community Church, Chicago, pp. 5–6, 9.

4. Information in this section was obtained partly from an interview with Elijah Muhammad at his home, partly from his teachings at the Temple, his writings in *The Supreme Wisdom* and the *Pittsburgh Courier*, and from the teachings of his ministers.

5. *The Supreme Wisdom*, II, 2: "Say: He, Allah, is One God (not three), there is no God but He and I am His Messenger and Servant."

6. "Fard" is said to mean "independent" ("Mr. Muhammad Speaks," *Pittsburgh Courier*, Part I, May 26, 1956, p. 6). July 4, the date Prophet Fard is said to have arrived in the United States, has a symbolic "political" significance for the Muslims in that it is also the date when Americans declared their independence. It signifies also the Muslims' declaration of their independence. They do not celebrate the date officially. Also Part II, June 2, 1956, p. 6.

7. Muhammad's Temple of Islam, *Lesson No. C 1* (n.d.).

birth was alluded to in the Scriptures (Revelations, 18:1 is cited in support).[8] The woman referred to in the Scriptures is said to be the Mahdi's mother. Known as "Baby Gee," she is said to have been "a Caucasian lady, a devil." Muhammad relates that "she and the Saviour's father were schoolmates" and that "she was out of Mount Teman — that strange wonder setting in Heaven (Mecca) clothed in the Sun, Moon, and Stars." The Mahdi's father, Alphonso, "was a Jet Black Man of the Tribe of Shabazz," and the "long lost uncle is none other than we, the lost-found Nation of Islam, here in the wilderness of North America." According to "prophecy," Master W. F. Muhammad, said to have been born on February 26, 1877, and to be living now in Mecca, will live for four hundred and forty-four years.

GOD IS A BLACK MAN

The conception that Allah (in the Person of Master W. F. Muhammad) is a black man is supposed to agree with "Biblical prophecy."[9] But Master Muhammad himself, the offspring of the Caucasian woman and the "jet black" man, is not a jet black man. Although his photograph is not displayed anywhere in public, a framed copy of it is enshrined at the home of Elijah Muhammad and shows a fair-skinned Arab. Muhammad explains that Allah's complexion had to be light enough to make him acceptable both to the whites, whose ways he came to study, and to the so-called Negroes:

The Saviour's mother was a caucasian raised and cleaned up so that the Son of Man would resemble the caucasians and thereby be able to have

8. *The Supreme Wisdom*, II, 12.

9. R.T.X. Ashford, "God is a Black Man," *Herald-Dispatch* (Los Angeles), May 21, 1959, pp. 1 and 5:

Compare this with the image of god of the Garveyites: "If the white man has the idea of a white God, let him worship his God as he desires. . . . We, as Negroes, have found a new ideal. Whilst our God has no color, yet it is human to see everything through one's own spectacles, and since the white people have seen their God through white spectacles, we have only now started out (late though it be) to see our God through our own spectacles. The God of Isaac and the God of Jacob let Him exist for the race that believes in the God of Isaac and the God of Jacob. We Negroes believe in the God of Ethiopia, the everlasting God — God the Father, God the Son and God the Holy Ghost, the One God of all ages. That is the God in whom we believe, but we shall worship Him through the spectacles of Ethiopia." *Stewart's Voice* (Chicago), April, 1959, p. 4.

access to the caucasian race and learn their ways. Because of this he was acceptable both to the caucasians as well as the so-called Negroes.[10]

The followers of Muhammad assign to the Mahdi (Allah) all the usual attributes of God. He is the "Creator of Heaven and Earth, Most Wise, All Knowing, Most Merciful, All Powerful, Finder and Life-Giver, Master of the Day of Judgment." They pray to Him and implore His help in everything. The death of the police captain and the wounding of the bailiff during the courtroom riot were the "vengeance of Allah" visited upon the "devil." The Muslims refer to this incident as proof of Allah's power over the universe. Some of them seem to have come to believe that under all circumstances Allah will come to their aid.

One of Muhammad's ministers gave this description of God (Allah):

I learnt that God is not a spook and that He is in every respect a real man and that He is a Superior Being in the sense that He is all wise. He is a man in the sense that He is a superman. He has unlimited knowledge and understanding. We are taught that he came from Mecca to the United States in 1930. He is the Mahdi, the only Mahdi. He is a man and yet not a man in ordinary sense. His knowledge is unlimited. He is pure, holy and undefiled.[11]

A follower who was a Roman Catholic before "reuniting" with the Nation of Islam had this to say about the Mahdi:

I could not believe what I heard. I never believed that it was possible for a man to walk with God. I had always believed in the Bible and I used to hear the preacher saying: "If you see God, you die; if you speak with God, you die!" I have gained the knowledge of myself, the knowledge of Allah and of His Messenger. When I speak of him [the Messenger of Allah], I think him the most exalted man other than Allah Himself — the Supreme Being.[12]

According to Elijah Muhammad, "white people in authority knew the Mahdi quite well," but he is said to have had difficulties with the laws of the United States and was deported in 1933. He "suffered persecution and rejection" for the redemption of the so-called Negroes whom he has chosen as his beloved children.[13]

10. "Saviour's Day" Speech by Elijah Muhammad, February 26, 1959.
11. Interview with Minister James 3X.
12. Interview with Sister Nellie LX.
13. *The Supreme Wisdom*, II, 12.

THE CALLING OF THE PROPHET

The number seven has a particular significance for the followers of Elijah Muhammad.[14] According to the "chronological history" of the world taught to members of the Nation of Islam, the white man's rule of this world and his civilization will come to an end about the year 2,000 A.D. — 6,000 years after the birth of Yakub. Yakub, who is the "patriarch" of the white race, "was born 20 miles from the Holy City of Mecca" some 2,000 years before the birth of Moses. Moses was a "prophet sent to civilize the caucasian devil." Two thousand years later, Jesus succeeded Moses. His mission was to "civilize the Jews." In this view of history, the Christian era, as well as the 6,000 years during which the white race has dominated the world, will expire in 2,000 A.D. In the seventh millenium after the birth of Yakub a new world and a righteous civilization is to be established. Muhammad's followers believe that his birth as the seventh child in a family of twelve is implied in the eschatology.

Before he became the spiritual leader of the Muslims, Muhammad was known variously as Robert Poole, Karriem, and Ghulam Bogam. According to him, "my grandfather gave me the name Elijah. My first name was Paul. Allah asked me to change to Muhammad. Allah suggested later that I take Abdul, but Abdul stands opposed to what I stand for."[15]

THE MESSENGER OF ALLAH

Muhammad claims to be the Messenger of Allah, as yet unrecognized by the Negroes and the world: "In spite of their (my people's) ignorance of Allah and myself whom He has sent — for I am not self-sent — they and the world shall soon know who it is that sent

14. *Ibid.*, I, 47: "What is the significance of this number seven? Do we not have seven inhabited planets? And a seven-thousandth year after the six thousand years of the devil's rule? Are we not reminded of this in the six work days of the week (the six thousand years of the workings of the devils) and the seventh to rest which belongs to the Lord (the original owners, the Black Man) ?"

15. Interview with Muhammad. Benyon (*op. cit.*, p. 903), has a reference to Abdul. Abdul Mohammad, one of the first officers in the Temple, seceded in revolt against Fard's position that his followers did not belong to America, owed their only allegiance to the Moslem flag, and should educate their children in the University of Islam. Abdul organized a small Moslem group of his own in which the cardinal principle was loyalty to the Constitution of the United States.

me."[16] His birth and mission are foretold in the Bible[17] and in the Holy Koran, and he is here to fulfil the promise which God (Allah) made to Abraham and his seed. It is therefore not by accident that his grandfather named him "Elijah." The Holy Koran thus attests to it: "He it is who raised among the illiterates a Messenger from among themselves, who recites to them His messages and purifies them, and teaches them the Book and the Wisdom — though they were before certainly in manifest error."[18] The people to whom Muhammad is sent are described in the Scriptures;[19] they are the so-called Negroes of the United States who were enslaved in North America in fulfillment of God's covenant with Abraham. The Jews, who claim that they are the seed of Abraham, are "pretenders." "There is no record to validate the claims that the Jews spent four hundred years in Egypt under bondage." The "fourth generation" referred to in Genesis 15:12–21 means four hundred years of Negro chattel- and "mental" slavery in the United States. The so-called Negroes were first brought to North America in 1555; thus the four hundred years predicted in the Bible have been served. The time was up in 1955.

It is time for the Negroes to be gathered unto their religion (Islam), to be reunited with their "Own Kind," and to turn their "hearts again to their Nation, their God, and their religion." It is the Messenger's duty to show them that the white race and Christianity are their enemies, and to warn that in the day of judgment, those Negroes who have not heeded his warning will perish along with the devils (the Caucasian race):

16. *The Supreme Wisdom*, II, 12.

17. Mal. 4:5–6. At Muslim meetings, as the Messenger is ushered in, the Minister declares: "Behold, I send you Elijah!"

18. Koran 62:2 quoted in *Moslem World and the U.S.A.*, August-September, 1956, p. 24.

19. Gen. 15:12–21. Minister James 3X argues: "Prophets are raised from among the people. This is true of all past prophets. It is also true of the Divine Messenger. They are raised from among the people because they know and understand the conditions of their own people. That is why an Indian, an African, or anyone else could not be the leader and divine teacher of the Negro people in America. At best they would have a partial knowledge and understanding of the Negro problem. The Honorable Elijah Muhammad was born here in the United States. He has caught hell like every other Negro in the wilderness of North America and he understands both the conditions and problems of the Negroes in America. . . . The Divine teacher must be a model and examplar for his people."

My Mission — I have been risen to raise my people here (the so-called Negroes), and to help them into the knowledge of Self, and their God Allah (who is in Person among them) and the devils (their open enemy).

My Objective — I am doing all I can to make the so-called Negroes see that the *white race* and their religion (Christianity) are *their open enemies*, and to prove to them that they will never be anything but the devil's slaves and finally *go to hell with* them for believing and following them and their kind.[20]

Muhammad claims, like the Roman Catholic Church in regard to the Pope's *ex cathedra* pronouncements, that he is "infallible."[21]

THE CONTENT OF THE ESCHATOLOGY

The eschatology of the Nation of Islam is full of Old Testament images which help to convey the sense of social estrangement of the urban lower-class Negro. According to Muhammad, all persons of African descent in North America, "the lost-found Nation of Islam in the wilderness of North America" or the so-called American Negroes, belong generically to the "Asian Black Nation" and specifically to the ancient tribe of Shabazz.[22] The origin of the Nation is traced to Abraham of the Old Testament, who is the "patriarch" of the "Black Nation" or of the "Asian Black Nation."[23] The Black Nation differs from the Nation of Islam in that it encompasses all non-Caucasian races — all the black, brown, yellow, and red peoples.[24]

20. *The Supreme Wisdom*, II, 61.

21. *Ibid.*, p. 62.

22. When the writer first met Muhammad and associated with his followers, they seemed to shun the word "African" as a term of reference either to themselves or to American Negroes. They claim that they are Asiatic black people, and that in ancient times, Africa was known as "South Asia." They consider the word "Africa" to be a European word. However, there has been a slight shift in emphasis from "Asian" to African in the last year, after both Minister Malcolm X and Mr. Muhammad made trips to Africa.

23. Members of the "Abyssinian" movement believe that their homeland is Ethiopia. Marcus Garvey appears to be the only one among the nationalist leaders who emphasized that the entire continent of Africa is the homeland of all black people. He seemed to have had a preference for "Black Africa," however.

The Moors claim that they are "Asiatics" but that they sprang from the ancient Moabites (Gen. 19:37). The Church of God (familiarly known as the Black Jews or the Black Hebrews) claims that the Negroes are the Jews to whom the Bible makes reference. They claim that the so-called Jews are pretenders. See Fauset, *op. cit.*, pp. 32–35; also, Howard M. Brotz, "Negro 'Jews' in the United States," *The Phylon*, the Atlanta University Review of Race and Culture (Fourth Quarter, 1952), 324–337.

24. Although it cannot be said that Muhammad's inclusion of all non-white races in his conception of the Black Nation is either deliberate or otherwise, the writer feels that

The world of humanity is thus divided into the Black Nation and the white race. Captain Raymond Sharrieff said at a Temple meeting:

> Black people are not a race but a nation. Only the Caucasians are a race, because the white race is racing with time and they are racing themselves just about off the planet earth.

The white race was "grafted" from the Black Nation. The Black Nation represents "righteousness," whereas the white race represents "evil." As we shall see, this conception of the world leads also to the view that the "last shall be first and the first last," or, that "Black becomes White and White, Black."

American Negroes are not only Asiatic black people; they have also been Muslims from creation. In other words, their religion from the inception of time has been Islam and their national deity, Allah. The Nation of Islam (the so-called American Negroes) has a special position in the Black Nation, for Allah has chosen the Negroes in America for the redemption of the Black Nation and as an instrument for the destruction of the present "evil" civilization. Allah has chosen them for ushering in a new world in which a righteous government under the Crescent of Islam shall prevail.

IN SEARCH OF THE BLACK MAN'S HISTORY

According to Muhammad, the black man originally inhabited the moon. People were known as "people of the moon." He claims that there are in Africa today "some tribes who still refer to themselves as people of the moon." Some several trillions of years ago, a black scientist caused a great explosion on the moon. According to Minister James 3X:

> At one time this *earth* and the *moon* were one planet, but one of our greatest scientists became dissatisfied because he could not make all the people speak the same language and so he decided to destroy all the people and caused a great explosion on the moon. The moon was blasted out, twelve thousand

this notion has served a significant function in the recruitment of followers. Marcus Garvey's emphasis on dark-skinned Negroes and his antagonism toward mulattoes was a source of weakness for his movement. This error is avoided by Mr. Muhammad's conception. Secondly, his conception undermines the minute color differentiations which are irritating factors of Negro social relations. Thirdly, it gives the Muslims a sense of belonging to a larger section of humanity, a sense that their minority position in the United States has tended to obscure.

miles from the original orbit. The earth fell thirty-six thousand miles from the original oribit. This is the earth we now live in. The part that was called the moon capsized and the life on that part was destroyed. The other part — the Earth — was able to retain its water and life. The name of the scientist who caused the explosion has never been revealed. The Messenger has taught us that at one time the whole planet was called "moon"and we were called "the people of the moon." I understand that there are some tribes in Africa who refer to themselves as people of the moon.[25]

"Original Man," the first people to inhabit the planet Earth, were black people — members of the Tribe of Shabazz. They did not originate in Africa. All that is known is that "it is our people who founded Mecca and we were first located there:"

It was the first city that our fathers founded after reimportation from the Moon. The Messenger has taught us that our people traveled fifty thousand years ago into what is now known as Africa. It was then known as South Asia. The original inhabitants were pygmies and they [the pygmies] are the descendants of the first people who went down there to Africa.[26]

SLAVERY: A DIVINE PLAN

The Negroes were enslaved in North America as part of a divine plan.

Our slavery at the hands of John Hawkins and his fellow-slavetraders and suffering here in the Western Hemisphere for four hundred years was actually all for a Divine purpose: that Almighty Allah (God) might make

25. Minister James 3X, in an interview.

26. *Ibid.* Cf. Muhammad's account in *The Supreme Wisdom*, II, 14–15. Also cf. Marcus Garvey: "I know no national boundary where the Negro is concerned. The whole world is my province until Africa is free." Quoted in Cronon, *op. cit.*, p. 3. Muhammad has gone far beyond Garvey by claiming that the whole earth belongs to Negroes by right. Garvey's claim was conditioned on Africa's freedom after which, it may be assumed, the whole world would no longer be his province.

Many Negroes, particularly some of the nationalists, do not want to be associated with black Africans. They seek to identify themselves with "Egyptians," "Ethiopians," "Moors," "Moroccans" and the "Sudanese," whom they think are not "Negroes." Among the non-nationalists one finds the same kind of "pride" expressed by those whose known ancestry includes American Indians, and even their "illegitimate" white foreparents. See Theodore P. Ford, *God Wills the Negro* (Chicago: The Geographical Institute Press, 1939), for another account of American Negro origins. Ford argues that American Negroes are descendants of the original Egyptians who were forced to seek refuge in the south by Persian, Greek, Roman and Arab invasions. They settled in the Sudan until the last decade of the 15th century (about 1492), when the Egyptian settlements "were uprooted by native African people. . . . The Egyptians were conquered by these war-like black people and sold into American slavery. From the time of their captivity, the Egyptians of the Sudan have been confused with their captors, the less

Himself known through us to our enemies, and let the world know the Truth that He alone is God.[27]

In the year 1555 when he (John Hawkins) began bringing our people away from our Native Land and away from our own people, to sell us to his white brothers in the West as merchandise for their slave markets, little did he realize at that time that bringing us here as slaves he was actually sentencing his white brothers here to their doom, for the evil that they have since done to us and are still doing cannot be forgiven.[28]

Hawkins deceived the prospective slaves into believing that they were coming to America to work and to earn more gold than in their own country. They had no idea that they were coming here to be sold into slavery or that their presence would "create a problem or problems that would take Almighty Allah (God) Himself to solve."

The Negroes in the United States are the chosen of the Black Nation (black, brown, red and yellow peoples). They are good by nature and "very religiously inclined." They are the "cream" of the earth and the most beautiful of all human creatures.

IMITATION OF LIFE

The Caucasians were not the original inhabitants of this earth, but were "grafted" from the black people. God did not create all humanity. The white race is the product of the weakness of the Black Nation. One of the geniuses of the Black Nation, Yakub, discovered that through some sort of "mutation" black people could be given brown, red, and yellow complexions. Knowing this, he made the

civilized blacks, who held the Kingdoms to the West and to the South of the Egyptian-Sudan states. To both peoples, the descendants of the Egyptians and their captors, the erroneous nickname Negro has been applied, but the American blacks were conquered and enslaved by these so-called Negro people (Bantu and West African blacks.)" They are not "historically of the same people as those Africans, to whom the modern world has in the past 400 years given the name *Negro*." In a footnote Ford, himself an American Negro, explains: "I take the so-called Negro people to be those Africans whom Leo Africanus called *cafries*, or savages, as present-day Americans would call them. It was this same *cafries* or savage Negroes who actually conquered and enslaved the dusky descendants of the Egyptians and sold them into bondage " (pp. 100–101). Ford's book is a rare treat for unsophisticated Negroes "in search of their history."

27. *The Supreme Wisdom*, II, 47. Cf. Ford, *op. cit.*, who also thinks that Negro slavery was part of "God's plan" because Negroes are "God's chill'un." Illustrative material on this element in Negro religious thinking can be found in Benjamin E. Mays, *The Negro's God as Reflected in His Literature* (Boston: Chapman and Grimes, Inc., 1938), p. 153 ff.

28. *The Supreme Wisdom*, II, 74.

first white man, a task that took him six hundred years.[29] His intention was "to make a devil," and once this intention was discovered he and his kind (numbering 59,999) were cast out of paradise (Asia) by the indignant blacks, who supposed that he was acting against the law of God. This event happened 6,000 years ago. Yakub, the black scientist, is the man the Bible refers to as Adam; he is the father of the Caucasian race. Yakub, however, was really acting according to the will of God, who wanted the "devils" to rule for 6,000 years in order to test the mettle of the Black Nation and to see whether they could rule with justice.[30] The "pale-faced, blue-eyed" people have demonstrated that they are incapable of giving justice to black people. Their alloted time is up or will be up at about the end of the sixth millenium.

Contrasted with the Original Man (the so-called Negroes), the white is inferior physically and mentally. He is also weak because he was grafted from the black. He is the real "colored" man, i.e., the deviant from the black color norm. His brain capacity is smaller than that of the black man. The original man is handsomer and his women are more beautiful. The mixing of blood must not be allowed because it will further deteriorate the beauty and strength of black people.[31]

Black people brought civilization to mankind before the Caucasian race was created. When the black man was at the height of his civilization, white people were living in the caves of Europe after they had been thrown out of Asia. At that time they were crawling on their hands and knees like the beasts of the forest and living

29. "Imitation of Life Lecture Tells Why God Created Devils" by John X, Assistant Minister of Muhammad's Eastside Temple of Islam, Los Angeles, *Herald-Dispatch*, July 9, 1959: ". . . In genetics, this is known as Mendel's Law, but Yakub used it to make Mendel's foreparents."

30. *Lost-Found Moslem Lesson No. 2*, Question No. 38, p. 10. This lesson "was given by our Prophet W. D. Fard," and it contains "40 questions answered by Elijah Muhammad, one of the lost-found in the Wilderness of North America, February 20th, 1934." Minister John X has said that: "People yearning for a change produced Yakub, who created a race of devils to rule for 6,000 years. Now, after 6,000 years, the yearning of the people has produced one wiser and more powerful than Yakub, and this one, the GREAT MAHDI, who came to us in the person of Master Fard Muhammad, is going to destroy the world *which Yakub created*" (*Herald-Dispatch*, July 9, 1959, p. 5).

31. *Ibid.*, p. 25.

on raw meat. The publisher of the Los Angeles paper, the *Herald-Dispatch*, a strong supporter of Muhammad, has written editorially:

The African people are determined to rid their land of the captors, to return to the culture and civilization which they enjoyed before the slave captors and the traders invaded their lands.

History records that the African peoples were enjoying the highest civilized society when their present-day captors were living in caves and had tails. The African people were enjoying caviar while their present tormentors were eating snails, snakes, and hogs, walking around on all fours.

The American Negro, who knows so little of himself, must learn that the history of the black man has no beginning, no ending. We must learn and understand that the days are numbered for those brutal, bestial, demoniacal beasts, who are slaughtering our people in our ancestral lands. They must know their rule is coming to an end even though they are determined to take millions of us with them. We American Negroes who have no economic security, no education, no common knowledge of ourselves, no surnames, with pure blood that has been polluted by the exploitation and sexual mixture of the slavemaster, must at this time, make a last ditch stand and demand HANDS OFF AFRICA. . . .[32]

THE POWER AND TRIUMPH OF BLACKNESS

The writer sought to determine whether or not the manipulated image of blackness had taken roots in the Muslims' image of themselves in relations to whites. Several Muslims were asked: What do you think white people have against black people? Their replies may constitute a sheer verbalization of the doctrinal views; they may, in fact, comprise the Muslims' image of themselves. Whatever the case may be, the respondents all said that whites are inferior to blacks, and that this is the principal reason for their hatred of black people. Minister James 3X stated:

First, there is fear — first and foremost there is inborn fear, and hatred for the black man. There is a feeling on the part of the white man of inferiority. He thinks within himself that the black man is the best man.

The white man is justified (in feeling that way) because he has discovered that he is weaker than the black man. His mental power is less than that of the black man — he has only six ounces of brain and the Original Man has seven-and-a-half ounces . . . The white man's physical power is one-third less than that of the black man.

32. March 5, 1959, pp. 1, 3.

Other respondents said that whites were afraid that if the blacks were given an opportunity they would surpass them (whites) within a short time. "I believe," said Sister Mildred 3X, "the whites fear that Negroes would take over the leadership if they were given a chance. . . . Whatever they have allowed us to participate in, such as sports — boxing, tennis, baseball, basketball — we have made remarkable demonstration of our potential." Sister Nellie LX said that whites know that "the black man is the best, the powerful and by nature, the righteous person. . . . They know that the black man — red, yellow, brown and the Original — outnumbers them." "The whites," said Brother Leonard IX, "are envious of the black man's hair, skin, and pretty eyes. . . . He tries to duplicate the black's skin color by getting suntan but he is very weak and weird looking." "The white man," he said, "cannot duplicate the Asiatic black man in any way." Brother Thomas Jones stressed that whites "envy the black people because we are the chosen people and the children of Allah." One Muslim, Brother Donald X, hesitated before answering the question:

Well, I don't know — I couldn't say directly why . . . I would only think the only thing they would have against our people is that they know that they [black people] are much better in many ways . . . and they know that some day they [the blacks] will be the rulers.

RESURRECTION AND THE HEREAFTER

According to the New Testament prophecy, the Resurrection is the advent of God on earth. Muhammad claims that the prophecy is now fulfilled and God is already in the world.[33] The meaning of the resurrection is that Allah (God) is the only Eternal Being, and man cannot share His immortality.[34] There is no life beyond the grave for man; he has no "soul" which will live beyond his death; there is no heaven or hell to which he could go:

Christianity speaks of Heaven which it can neither define nor prove to exist. That there is life after death is disagreeable to human nature. In man's nature, the thought of death is not cherished and even the late Pope

33. Speech of the Most Honorable Elijah Muhammad, Sunday, March 1, 1959 at the Muslim Annual Convention, Metropolitan Community Church, Chicago, pp. 5–6, 9.
34. Minister Lucius of Washington, D. C. Temple, Lecture in Chicago, October 24, 1958.

Pius XII who had everything to gain in Heaven, being the Lord's representative on earth, did all he could to stay alive. If indeed there is Heaven,
and it is said to be such a wonderful place, and there are many Cardinals
who can succeed the Pope, why then did he not willingly surrender to death
so that he might get to this divine abode? The answer is simple. Death is
disagreeable to human nature.[35]

The Resurrection does not mean, as Christians have been made
to understand, that man will arise from his grave. Instead, it means
that the time has come for the Negro to receive justice. It means that
people who have been without justice and who have lived in ignorance of themselves, their nation, history, their God, and their religion, are brought into the knowledge of these things:

You are the people that are dead in the body. You are the people that
must be resurrected in the body. It doesn't mean getting up in the graveyard among dead bodies. It means that the power and authority and wisdom
and guidance of God goes up and His knowledge, the knowledge of God,
the understanding of God rose up from a dead people — from a mentally
dead people, that's all it means. Not out of the grave. Go home and be satisfied this afternoon that you will never meet God beyond the grave. The grave
settles it all. It is justice, I say, that we want.[36]

Negroes need no longer wait for or expect God's Kingdom to
come. Heaven and hell are only two conditions of life:

Heaven is a condition. That condition the white man now has. The Bible
teaches that rich people will not go to heaven, yet the white man continues
to amass wealth, but the Negro is to be patient and wait for a reward in
heaven. If reward of hell is for the rich and heaven for the poor as the
Bible says, who is catching hell here and now. It is the Negro. If heaven and
hell are conditions, then it follows that Negroes have their hell right here
in the United States. The so-called Negroes must get out of this hell now.[37]

The Hereafter means the end of the present "spook" civilization.
It is the period after the destruction of the present world and the
authority of the "Man of Sin" to rule over it. Followers of Mr. Muhammad look forward "to seeing and living under a ruler and government of righteousness after the destruction of the unrighteous."[38]

Followers of Muhammad begin to enjoy the Resurrection and the

35. Lecture by an eighteen-year-old ministerial student at Chicago Temple.
36. Elijah Muhammad, Speech in Washington, D. C., May 31, 1959.
37. Minister Lucius, Lecture at Chicago, October 24, 1958.
38. *The Supreme Wisdom*, II, 40.

Hereafter as soon as they receive his teachings. Their lives are "transformed, morally and spiritually," and their health and material condition are improved. The Hereafter means that they will enjoy the spirit of gladness and happiness in the presence of Allah.[39]

JUDGMENT OF THE WORLD

The destruction of the present world will not mean the destruction of all mankind, but only the destruction of the devils (the Caucasians) and their religion (Christianity). It will be the judgment of Allah, which is amply revealed in the Book of Revelation as the War of Armageddon. This judgment followed from the creation of the white race six thousand years ago. The day of judgment is, however, predicated on exposing the "man of sin," on warning the so-called Negroes of the impending doom, and on gathering them together under the Crescent — the Sun, Moon, and Stars. The "man of sin" is now revealed. Muhammad has been raised to sound the warning. According to "prophecy," only 144,000 "so-called Negroes" are likely to escape the holocaust, but Muhammad and his followers are doing all they can to bring the message to as many as possible. It was not until sixty years ago that the "brothers in the East" learned of the existence of their "lost Nation in the wilderness of North America." It was then that the twelve religious leaders of the "East" met and decided that their lost-found brothers must return to their own. When these leaders met, one of them insisted that the lost-found brothers must not return until they had been reconverted into Islam and taught the knowledge of their own. Consequently, the judgment of the Caucasian world, which was to take place in 1914, was postponed to allow time for the so-called Negroes to hear the message.[40] That year marked the expiration of the period

39. *Ibid.*, p. 40: "Everyone of us — the so-called Negroes — who accepts the religion of Islam and follows what Allah has revealed to me will begin enjoying the above (Hereafter) life here, now! . . . Joy and happiness is yours for the asking, my people . . . You will be clothed in silk, interwoven with gold, and eat the best food that you desire . . . The present Brotherhood of Islam is typical of the life in the Hereafter. The only difference is that the Brotherhood in the Herafter will enjoy the spirit of gladness and happiness forever in the Presence of Allah. . . .

40. *The Supreme Wisdom*, II, 76–77. It is interesting to note the similarity between Muhammad's biblical interpretations and those of the Watchtower Bible Society (Je-

which was given the whites to rule the world and dominate the darker peoples. The destruction of the world will definitely occur some time before the year 2,000 A.D. and the year 1970 has been suggested by the Messenger, although the "exact day is known only to Allah."

The judgment of the world will come in two stages. According to an account by Minister James 3X, the first stage is the "spiritual sounding of the trumpet," and the Messenger is doing that now. The second is the Day of the Apocalypse. This will not come suddenly. For it to do so would be unjust. Allah has promised that eight to ten days' advance notice will be given to enable all the righteous to escape destruction:

> People will be given a chance to decide. The first chance is the spiritual sounding of the trumpet which is the work the Messenger is doing. We are living in the Day of Judgment according to the Book. The last trumpet will be a siren coming from a plane in the sky. It will be heard everywhere and it will be so loud that it will shake the earth. The plane will drop pamphlets written in Arabic and English and everyone will have between eight to ten days during which they may decide to get out of this hell. There will be people posted at strategic points to tell us where to go. These people will ask everyone which side they are on. The Book says that we should not worry about carrying our property and belongings with us. We are going to leave everything behind. The Messenger is sounding the warning now.[41]

Evidence of all this is found in the Scriptures, in history, and in contemporary events. The decline of European imperial power in Asia and Africa and the struggles of the liberated people for independence from further white domination are examples of the great changes at work. The Bandung Conference, the Accra Conference of Independent African States, the All-African Peoples Conference and similar Asian-African or Afro-Asian conferences are indicative of the unity of black mankind. The rapid growth of Islam in Black Africa in the last fifty years and the decline there of Christianity points to the coming of the end of the era.

hovah's Witnesses) as far as the stories of creation and the judgment of the world are concerned. Of course, the Jehovah's Witnesses' doctrine does not make God and the Devil human beings, nor is the judgment confined to a particular race. *New Heavens and A New Earth* (Brooklyn, N. Y.: Watchtower Bible and Tract Society, Inc., 1953). The Mormons make similar claims.

41. Interview.

Widespread corruption is evidence of the decline of the Caucasian civilization. Muhammad says that the life of the present white civilization is one of "sport and play." What is good is not wanted by it. The world of the "devils is against the Truth."[42]

America is particularly vulnerable to the destruction because it is here that Allah wishes to make Himself known and felt.[43] Allah has found His people (the so-called Negroes) and He is angry with the slave-masters of America for the evils they have done to them.[44] America has tampered with the "Sacred Vessels" (the so-called Negroes) that "she took from their Native Land and people and filled with wine and whiskey."[45]

America, that is, the white people of America, is going to the limit in doing evil, and "as God has dealt with ancient people, so will He deal with modern Babylon (America)." Evidence of America's fall is already manifest in retributive acts of God.

Minister James 3X has said that "judgment will not come to all of the wicked at once," and that the "Caucasians in Europe will last longer than those in America."[46]

Muhammad claims that Allah has warned that He will destroy the world with bombs, poison gas, and fire which will consume and destroy everything of this present world so that none of white civilization will be left. A dreadful plane "made like a wheel" was pointed out to him in the sky by Allah. Its dimensions were half a mile by half a mile. It was a "human-built planet":

. . . (I won't go into all of the details here, but it is up there and can be seen twice a week; it is no secret.) Ezekiel saw it a long time ago. It was built for the purpose of destroying the present world. Allah has also hinted at plaguing the present world with rain, snow, hail and earthquakes.[47]

42. *The Supreme Wisdom*, II, 29–30.
43. *Ibid.*, p. 10.
44. *Ibid.*, p. 12.
45. *Ibid.*, p. 16. It is interesting to note that some Negroes who are not followers of Mr. Muhammad also tend to interpret certain kinds of disasters as retributive acts. The writer encountered this particularly among some members of the Masons (and similar fraternal societies) with whom he had contact. These persons interpreted the recent fire at a Roman Catholic school in Chicago which took nearly one hundred lives and the explosion of a gasoline truck in the South which killed a number of persons as divine retribution against white civilization.
46. Interview. Of course it is in America that Negroes have had direct experience with the oppression of the "wicked" ones.
47. *The Supreme Wisdom*, II, 30.

BLACK REDEMPTION

Redemption of the Black Nation will come after the final judgment. The "New World" will come into being here on earth. The chosen, namely, the righteous blacks who hitherto have been oppressed by the Caucasian race, will inherit power over the whole earth. This will be the culmination of history, and the Black Nation will surpass in glory all previous regimes. It will have no successors and black men will rule forever under the benign guidance of Allah. In this "New World" there will be eternal peace and happiness.

"Some Muslims," said Sister—, "are unhappy because the final judgment or the Last Day hasn't arrived soon enough." Others are not, however, intensely preoccupied with expectation of the "Last Day." Some do not expect it to happen in their life times. Sister—, a native of Mississippi who has lived in Chicago for over twenty years, is an example. She became a "registered" Muslim about a year ago. For herself,

The day itself seldom comes into my mind. It is not that it is not important. We have a work to do. We do not know when it will come, maybe today or a long time from now. In any case, we can't put all hope on one day.[48]

That the day is coming all Muslims believe. Adult Muslims spoke about it in 1959 and some actually looked for signs in the skies on fine summer evenings. Two Muslim Sisters reported that another Muslim had told them of seeing a "huge machine" in the skies on a Tuesday evening during the summer of 1959. When such things happen, Muslims alert their neighbors and friends either by word of mouth or by telephone. Stories about "flying saucers" are taken seriously. Recently a Sister, hearing on the radio that scientists at an astronomical observatory had seen an "unidentifiable object," interpreted it as a sign of the impending destruction of the world.

Twenty high school and thirty-five seventh and eighth grades students at the University of Islam were asked whether they would want to see the final judgment in the immediate future. Not one of them was ready for it. The most frequently given reason for wanting a delay was that they have not attained the degree of "righteous-

48. Interviewee requested that her name be withheld.

ness" which would qualify them. Some felt that they had not lived long enough to enjoy the "things of this world." Probably the adults would respond in very much the same way. Sister Mildred said:

I have mixed feelings about it. I guess I would be glad provided I was living a completely righteous life. But then it would be a dreadful day. I would be sad to leave my parents and close relatives behind to be destroyed. It would be a dreadful day for me and I would say, give them one more chance. I would search myself to see if I am ready. Maybe I would need another day, a week or a month.[49]

Brother — said: "It's (judgment day) coming. We are not ready. Our people are not ready. Yes, Sir, we are not ready. I get scared the way this white man is skidding so fast."[50]

Sister — said: "I would be ready anytime. I have been here too long in the United States."[51]

49. Interview.
50. Interview.
51. Interview.

VI. Organization

> Up, you mighty race. You can accomplish what you will!
> Build your future on these foundations: Freedom, Justice and
> Equality.*
>
> ELIJAH MUHAMMAD

AUTHORITY IN the Nation of Islam on all matters of ideology, theology, and policy resides solely in the Messenger of Allah.[1] He is the only leader of the Nation. Ministers and other officers perform some leadership functions, although they deny that they are leaders. Their authority comes from Muhammad, hence they must be respected and obeyed by the followers.

While members claim that there is no hierarchy in the Nation aside from the "special" role of the Messenger, because "all Moslems are brothers and sisters and they are all equal," others hold conflicting opinions on this question.[2]

* This is one of the permanent mottoes written in bold letters on a large bulletin board at the auditorium of the University of Islam.

1. There is scope for both members and officers to make decisions on details, provided they are not in conflict with general policies and rules. Ministers at temples outside of Chicago assume such responsibilities. In Chicago the Messenger is likely to be consulted on many more matters of detail by the minister and officers than would be the case with a minister in New York or California.

2. There is no question but that there is a hierarchy of relationships among the officers of the Nation. The equalitarian claim is far more "spiritual" than real. The difference in the conception of hierarchy in the Nation was voiced by two officers. In an interview one minister stated unqualifiedly and emphatically: The Messenger is the supreme leader of the Nation of Islam. The ministers in charge of the Temples are next to him. Next is the Captain of the Temple. The Captain who is at the Temple where the Messenger resides is the Supreme Captain.

THE NATION

The Nation of Islam is comprised of Muhammad's followers, the majority of whom are organized into nearly fifty Temples in various parts of the United States. Thus the basic organizational unit of the Nation is the Temple. Each Temple is autonomous, although consultation with the Messenger is highly recommended in matters of general policy. Temples are theoretically equal, and each has direct access to the Messenger. Some Temples may appear to be more important than others because of their numerical strength and ability to contribute financially toward the general welfare of the Nation. Chicago, the headquarters and the Messenger's permanent residence, is increasingly assuming the character of a Mecca for Muhammad's followers. There individuals as well as ministers and officers come to meet "The Man."[3] However, the ministers and a few other officers are in closer contact with the Messenger than the rest of the followers.

Muhammad appoints all his ministers and those officers who have national responsibilities. The most important officers of a Temple are the captains, secretary, treasurers, and the investigator. Their appointments must be confirmed by the Messenger. In Chicago, however, the Messenger makes the appointment or may authorize some other official such as the captain to make an appointment subject to his approval. In effect, all appointments to the key offices of the Temple are ultimately subject to the approval of the Messenger.[4]

According to an official, "no one but the Messenger can dictate to a minister." Although his jurisdiction is confined to his Temple, a minister's load of work is in general heavy and exacting, since he is in charge of its operations and management. He presides and teaches at religious meetings which are held three times a week, on Wednesday and Friday nights and on Sunday afternoons. He attends all Temple activities during the week and may be delegated to represent the Messenger at other Temples and at public functions. He

3. Ordinarily, when Negroes speak of "going to meet the Man," they mean a white man or a white boss.

4. In an interview, a minister who has been at one Temple for nearly twenty years and is close to the Messenger claimed that there have been no instances to his knowledge when the Messenger failed to confirm an appointment made by one of his ministers.

counsels the followers. Where there is a school, he may be on its staff. In Chicago, the minister in charge of the Temple is relieved of some of the managerial responsibilities because of the presence of the Messenger and a comparatively larger secretarial staff. In spite of this, his load of work is heavy.[5]

The next ranking officers are designated Supreme Captains. There are two, one male and one female, for the Nation as a whole. They occupy command positions. Both take orders from the Messenger and are responsible to him. At the head of the men's organization within each Temple, which is known as the Fruits of Islam (F.O.I.), is a captain. The Supreme Captain oversees all the captains. The captains are responsible to the Messenger through the Supreme Captain. The women's organization, which is known as the Moslem Girls' Training and General Civilization Class (M.G.T.–G.C.C.), is headed in each Temple by a female captain. M.G.T.–G.C.C. captains receive instructions from the female Supreme Captain and are responsible to the Messenger through her. Captains at Temples outside of Chicago receive instructions also from the local minister. Temple captains are assisted by officers ranked as first, second, and third lieutenants. The lieutenants must recognize the captains as their superiors.

The Supreme Captains reside in Chicago. Besides them, there are captains for the Chicago Temple. Supreme Captain Raymond Sharrieff was born in Atlanta, Georgia, is in his late thirties or early forties, and is the father of five children. He is the Messenger's aide-de-camp and the chief liaison officer between the Messenger, the ministers, and the followers. He is, aside from the Messenger, the only officer who has full knowledge of the day-to-day activities of the Nation. As the "eyes and ears" of the Messenger and the friend of the followers, his authority, more than that of the Messenger, is most felt by both officers and the rank and file who are more directly in contact with him. Captain Sharrieff is also the Messenger's son-in-law. He earns his living as a full-time "servant" of the Nation. He is one of the Trustees of the Nation. Ten years ago, according to

5. In addition to Muhammad's personal secretaries, there are two secretaries whose duties include keeping records and public relations for the Chicago Temple.

one of his children, the Sharrieffs lived in an apartment hardly large enough for the family. Now they live in a well-furnished apartment, in a building owned by Muhammad, in one of the better sections of Chicago's South Side. He owns a black 1954 Cadillac.

Sister Lottie, a short, alert woman, unassuming in manner and mother of five children, is the Supreme Captain of the Moslem Girls' Training and General Civilization Class. Her husband, Brother Ali Muhammad (not a relation), works as a sign painter. She is the Messenger's second daughter.

The male captain at the Chicago Temple, also assistant to Supreme Captain Raymond Sharrieff, is Brother Elijah Muhammad, Jr. He is married but has no children. He is the Messenger's fourth son. He works for the bakery shop owned by Chicago Temple and also as the night watchman for the Temple and the University of Islam.

Although formerly only the Messenger and the two Supreme Captains had national responsibilities, an office of National Secretary has recently been created. Brother John 11X (Simmons), secretary of the New York Temple, was appointed to this office. However, his duties have not been clearly defined. At present he is generally responsible for "establishing new Temples, coordinating statements issued to the press by the Temples, giving news stories to the press and accompanying the Messenger at press conferences." His office is in New York.

TEMPLE INCEPTION

Before a Temple is organized, an informal group which has heard the teachings of the Messenger invites him or one of his ministers to deliver lectures on Islam and the Messenger's teachings to them. After hearing the lectures, the group may decide to accept Islam and the teachings of Muhammad. It may then apply to the Messenger to establish a Temple of Islam. Until a few years ago, a minimum of fifty persons was required for the establishment of a Temple. Now only twenty-five are necessary. At the end of two years the Temple is assigned a number by the Messenger and a minister is appointed. After a period of organizational work and teaching, the minister may appoint temporary officers of the Temple from among the "registered" members.

OFFICERS AND THEIR DUTIES

Only members of the Fruits of Islam and the Moslem Girls' Training and General Civilization Class are eligible to become officers of a Temple. Members of these two organizations are the most trusted among the followers of Muhammad and form the elite core of the Nation's leadership within a Temple. They are members who have "completely" submitted themselves to the will of Allah and of His Divine Messenger and are willing to devote their entire lives to the service of the Nation.

Ministers and captains are the principal officers of a Temple. They are assisted by Temple secretaries who are recorders, and work closely with them. Secretaries may be female or male. Each Temple also has two treasurers, one being in charge of the general income and ordinary expenditures of the Temple. The other is entitled the Poor Treasurer. His duties include the management of funds for assistance to the sick and needy and for funerals. In Chicago the Messenger is also the general business manager and treasurer. For the moment there is no business manager who coordinates all the business enterprises of the Chicago Temple. Each business has its own manager who is directly responsible to Muhammad or to someone designated by him. A few of these business enterprises are managed by the Messenger's sons. Brother Herbert, father of six children, is manager of the bakery; Brother Emmanuel, father of four children, manages the dry-cleaning plant and is assisted by Brother Nathaniel, who also has eight children. Brother Akbar until recently was one of the two bookkeepers at the Temple.

The next important officer in a Temple is the investigator. There are two investigators, one man and one woman; they are responsible to the captains for the general welfare and for the conduct of the Muslims. They determine the material needs of members and make recommendations for whatever assistance is necessary. They investigate family disharmonies, or disharmony among members, settle disputes, or refer them to the appropriate officers. In addition, the Messenger gives assistance to Negroes in prison — incidental items such as soap.

There are, in addition, junior captains who have no national responsibilities but who supervise the youth organizations for boys and girls in the Temples. These organizations are modelled upon the adult organizations.

The Supreme Captain of the F.O.I. and the male captain of the Chicago Temple are full-time employees and receive salaries, but the amount of their salaries is unknown. There is no evidence that the women captains are paid employees. The Temple secretaries, however, are full-time employees.

THE UNIVERSITY OF ISLAM

All officers of the University of Islam are appointed by the Messenger. He is also responsible for the appointment of the teaching staff, either personally or on the recommendation of the principal. Although most of the teachers are Muslims, in the past he has appointed Negroes who were not followers to the staff. The governing body of the University of Islam consists of a Board of Trustees including Muhammad, Raymond Sharrieff, the Supreme Captain, and Brother John Hassan, who has been in the movement since the founding of the Chicago Temple.

Many other offices are held by members in the Temple. These are not full-time positions. Members are recruited for such jobs as Temple guards during meetings and as chairmen of various business committees. Guards are responsible for searching persons before they enter the Temple for worship or the F.O.I. or M.G.T.–G.C.C. meetings. Other followers volunteer their services for various tasks of the Nation. A multiplicity of activities makes it possible for a great many members to be intensely and continuously involved in the activities of the Nation of Islam. The ability of the Nation to find some job for everyone who is able and willing is an effective therapy during the process of initiation and withdrawal from their previous activities. Young people feel that they are genuinely wanted. Temple activities become a substitute for the dissipation of the Negro lower-class life, its sports, tavern life, and gambling. Many find the camaraderie among the Muslims far more attractive than the more impersonal relations of their previous environment. The channels for recruitment of officers and initiation of members belong to the Fruits of Islam and the Moslem Girls' Training and General Civilization Class.

THE FRUITS OF ISLAM

As a general rule, each Temple has set up for the men an organization called the Fruits of Islam. However, a newly established Temple may not be permitted to organize one until two years have passed. The F.O.I. has described itself as a "military" organization within a Temple, but it is a military organization which bears no arms and seems to have no military objectives, since, according to official doctrine, "Allah in His own good time takes the devil off our planet." One of the teachings of Muhammad is that his followers must never carry any kind of weapon. The extent to which he emphasizes non-violence will become clear later.

The Fruits of Islam does have some features of military training in its organization, discipline, and ranking of officers. When the writer asked a Muslim whether there was a "military organization" at the Chicago Temple, he replied:

You know about the Fruits of Islam. Its functions are primarily to protect and defend the Nation and its nationals. To protect the Nation we are under. . . . We receive military training. We get education also in the F.O.I. By protecting the Nation we mean one hundred per cent protection of everything in the Nation from the pin to the Temple and all the nationals, and even the doorknobs on the doors of the Temple. Anyone that violates this or does some injury to the Nation would be severely dealt with, and if need be, physical violence would be used in defense of the "national interest" of the Nation of Islam.

We have no firearms. Our training is without firearms. We are trained in self-defense. What an F.O.I. would do or can do without firearms, a cook can do with potatoes. We are the Fruits of Islam and we need no firearms. It is a Brother's duty to defend the life of a Muslim Sister with his own life, and he must defend the life of a Brother with his own life.

Many Muslims do not consider the F.O.I. a military organization in the sense that this term is commonly understood. This description is inadequate for understanding the ideological as well as the practical functions of the organization. One explanation is that:

Fear of trouble with the unbelievers, especially with the police, led to the founding of the Fruit of Islam — a military organization for the men who were drilled by captains and taught tactics. . . . [6]

Ideologically, the organization fits into the general belief of the Muslims that the Nation of Islam is a nation within a nation, and as such must have its own government. This belief is given some semblance of reality in the organization and functions of the Fruits of Islam. The organization makes its members feel the "importance" and "serious mission" of the Nation. It inspires both respect and fear for those in authority within the Nation. As the organ of indoctrinating and disciplining initiates and maintaining their enthusiasm and morale, it is a unique instrument of the Muslim community. Above all, the Muslims feel secure that the Nation has an organization to enforce discipline within the ranks and, particularly, to protect them against assaults or external threats of violence. Members of the F.O.I. enjoy a certain amount of prestige within the Nation and regard themselves as protectors of the interest of the Nation and especially of the dignity of black womanhood.

The organization and practices of the Fruits of Islam also reflect the fear that disorderly conduct is likely to offend the civil authority. The Muslim community as a whole may be provoked by outsiders. They want to prevent this. They know that disorderly conduct can arise from a number of sources. The first source, a minister told the writer, stems from their unorthodox views about Christ, Christianity, and white society. He argued that there are Negroes who would be provoked into violence upon first hearing the teachings of Muhammad — "fanatic" Christians who would protect with their own lives the "sanctity of Christianity and the dignity of the white race." The second and the most important source of conflict may be the presence of an *agent provocateur* deliberately planted in a meeting to foment an incident and provide an excuse for government to "crack down" on the movement. The Muslims continuously worry about this prospect. Their desire for acceptance and respectability

6. Benyon, *op. cit.,* p. 902.

in the community enforces the demand that Muslims must never be the aggressors and must never provoke violence.

The fear that violence may be provoked among the Muslims from external sources was discussed at length at a strategy meeting between Muhammad and one of his ministers on August 15, 1959, at which the writer was present. The meeting was held at Muhammad's home; the atmosphere was somewhat tense, and although Mr. Muhammad remained calm and drank coffee along with the rest, he was evidently worried. This meeting was called because of a letter sent to the New York Police Commissioner by the "Imperial Wizard of the Christian Knights of the Ku Klux Klan," J. B. Stoner. The letter, dated August 6, 1959, read in part:

> National Headquarters
> P.O. Box 48
> Atlanta, Georgia

> Honorable Stephen P. Kennedy
> Police Commissioner of New York City
> New York, N.Y.

> *CONFIDENTIAL AND TOP SECRET*

> Dear Fellow Whiteman:

> Re: the black Muslims

> The Christian Knights of the Ku Klux Klan is composed of all loyal White people, both Catholics and Protestants, native born and foreign born, young and old. We are working to unite all of the forces of White Christendom in the struggle to Preserve the Great White Race. The future of civilization depends upon the survival of the beautiful intelligent White Race — the bearer of Christian truth.

> I have received a report from one of our Klansmen on the New York police force informing me that the nigger Muslims are in rebellion against White law and order. He reports that these blacks have no respect for your honest White Christian policemen. Therefore, in the interests of law and justice, I am offering you the support of the CHRISTIAN KNIGHTS OF THE KU KLUX KLAN.

> * * * * * * *

> Police Commissioner Kennedy, my dear friend, I now offer you the service of the Christian Knights of the Ku Klux Klan for the purpose of maintaining White Supremacy in New York City and for keeping New York niggers in their place. I think 5,000 Klansmen could clean up Harlem for you if you would give them police badges and N.Y. police uniforms to wear instead of their Klan uniforms. They will leave their Klan robes at home so the New York niggers won't know that your police reinforcements are White Christian Klansmen. You can use our Christian Knights as guards

to protect every White business in Harlem and also in other New York areas where nigger customers are giving trouble to white business men. After all, how do the black jig-a-boos expect to live without White business to sell them what they need. You can also use our Klansmen to escort White salesmen into Harlem and other parts of New York City that are suffering from the black plague. . . .[7]

Neither Muhammad nor anyone else at this meeting knew how a letter purportedly sent to the Police Commissioner and marked as "confidential" got out of the Commissioner's office a week after it had been sent. However, Muhammad's copy was mailed to him from New York by an "unknown" person. He was led to take the allegations in the letter quite seriously. On the basis of this letter, Minister Malcolm X had charged:

We suspect that the Ku Klux Klan is active in New York City, specifically on the police force. Because of the Miles Davis incident and the incident where a Negro was murdered in the 79th police (district) ; the Massey case, which involved police brutality; a near riot, which occurred at the 28 precinct, in which Ray Robinson had to come to the rescue, and other near riots caused by the police . . . we feel that there is physical evidence to indicate the KKK is very active on the New York police force, as this suggests.[8]

Emphasizing the "peacefulness" of the Muslims, Malcolm also said:

The Moslem record in Harlem has been one of courtesy, and law abiding. We have never given a hint or sign of any kind of violence; yet, for the past few weeks, we have been the target of some of the most vicious anti-Moslem propaganda, which leads us to believe that we are being penalized for being law-abiding citizens.[9]

When the *Amsterdam News* asked the Police Commissioner's office to comment on the letter, the Deputy Commissioner, Walter Arm, said:

We would not dignify a letter of this sort with an answer. We would not allow the stationery of the Police Department to fall in the hands of those people whom we do not need for advice in telling us how to police the City

7. Letter published in *Amsterdam News* (New York), September 12, 1959, pp. 1, 2.
8. *Ibid.*, p. 9.
9. *Ibid.* The propaganda value of this sort of incident is immense in lending internal cohesion. They have not failed to exploit such incidents to their own advantage.

of New York. We get a lot of crank letters and a letter of that sort, if we received one, would be returned to the proper authorities.[10]

In spite of the Deputy Commissioner's calm appraisal of the importance of such a letter, Muhammad took it seriously and did not dismiss the possibility that "someone could be planted at one of our meetings by an hostile group to start a fight." Commenting on the attitude of the police authorities toward his followers, he said:

It is strange that the government, the police departments and the F.B.I. actually want to see the Muslims become aggressive. They do not want to see decent and peaceful Negroes. The government doesn't like the Negroes to be peaceful. They are more disturbed that my followers are peaceful than if they were not. They dislike the idea that my followers are not derelicts. . . .[11]

The writer then asked: "What would happen if a Negro were to hit one of your followers at a meeting?" He replied confidently that the idea of any of his followers hitting back was "unthinkable because all of them are taught to refrain from doing any kind of violence, including hitting a brother or a wife." "To do so," he said, "would be a violation of the law of Islam, which is punishable." However, he was issuing a firm directive to his ministers "to drum it into their ears that they must never be aggressive nor resort to violence except in defense of their own lives when such is clearly in danger." On this, as on other occasions, Muhammad drove the writer home in his recently acquired Lincoln; and in the course of the ride, the writer expressed some doubts about Muhammad's optimism on the faithfulness of his followers. He was still confident that "a brother would not attack another brother. Planting of pimps at our meeting would not help provoke trouble. This tactic of our enemies is bound to fail. Both the beliefs of Islam, the laws, and the punishment which would be imposed on a follower are enough to check outbreaks of violence. Islam is peace, and it teaches against violence."

Although F.O.I. is enjoined from carrying weapons of any sort, in the required exercises which are part of "good health" activities, its members are regularly engaged in drills. These exercises are

10. *Ibid.*, pp. 1, 9.
11. Meeting with Muhammad.

held once every week. The meetings at which they drill are not open to the public. However, the F.O.I. occasionally exhibits its skills for the Muslim audience. Such exhibitions impress both Muslims and visitors. The general procedures of these exercises embody some form of "police" behavior, such as the ranking of officers as captains and lieutenants, and displays of the art of self-defense, such as boxing and judo. Members of the F.O.I. may be called upon by the Messenger or the Captain for any Temple duties for which they are qualified. They are expected to follow all "Islamic Laws" more strictly than other followers. The members of the F.O.I. are assigned numbers; for example, "Special F.O.I. 105." This "conspiratorial" make believe in assigning numbers to members is one of the ideological disguises which give the Muslims a feeling of the importance of their mission. The letters "F.O.I." are even sewn on their clothes. In 1958 there were approximately one hundred F.O.I. members at the Chicago Temple and within its organization, numerous units charged with different duties. The most important unit is the "Special Honor Guard" headed by a lieutenant who is also its secretary. This unit, which is made up of young men (most are under thirty), provides the special bodyguard which is thrown around Muhammad at public meetings.

FUNCTIONS OF THE F.O.I.

Meetings are held regularly on Monday evenings. Members are divided into groups for purposes of instruction, physical exercises, Temple jobs, such as cleaning and painting, and F.O.I. business meetings. It is during these meetings that the investigator makes inquiries about the welfare of the Brothers. Brothers found to be in financial difficulty are generally assisted. The unemployed are given assistance if jobs cannot be found. The technique employed is for those who are employed to "keep their ears open" for job opportunities at their places of employment. Such opportunities are reported promptly to the Fruit of Islam Captain, who in turn alerts unemployed members about the vacancy and urges them to apply for the position(s). In many instances, an unemployed follower may be given assistance indirectly by being employed at one of the

Temple's businesses, even though there may be no need for additional workers. In this way, they are not given the impression that they are receiving "hand-outs" — a practice which is not encouraged.[12] Minister Wallace observed that "a Brother will not receive the necessary assistance if he is found to be untruthful, unfaithful, or unreliable":

All of the Muslim Brothers are good men. Not to be good would be unusual. We do not expect perfection but you can tell if a Brother is seriously trying to be good or not.[13]

The officers of the F.O.I. include the Captain, and First, Second, and Third Lieutenants. Respect for officers is part of the general orders and procedures of the F.O.I. The proper salute must be shown to superior officers. The following are some of the general orders for the F.O.I. members:

1. To take charge of any post given.
2. To be a soldier, keep on the alert, and be quick in actions.
3. To report all misunderstanding under any circumstances.
4. To stand my post correctly — a member on post may not shake hands and he must stand at attention.
5. To leave my post when and not before properly relieved.
6. To receive and Obey Orders from the commissioned and noncommissioned officers and guards.
7. To be careful of what I say and do in the line of duty.
8. To salute all officers and private "soldiers" when a meeting is in process.[14]

The "Prospectus"[15] for the training of the Junior F.O.I. members includes the following:

1. Cleanliness: Physically, mentally, and property of the Temple — school, Temple and outside property.
2. Love and Unity:
   a. Love of our Leader and Teacher, the Honorable Elijah Muhammad.
   b. Love of each other.

12. Interview with Minister Wallace Muhammad.
13. *Ibid.*
14. "General Orders" (typed, n. d.).
15. "Prospectus, Jr. F.O.I." (typed, n.d.)

    c. Knowledge of unity.

    d. Purpose of uniting with one another.

3. Religious view:

    a. Brotherhood of Islam read at every meeting (from the Book *Al-Islam*).

    b. A portion of Muhammad s Life as told by Maulana Muhammad Ali.

    c. *The Supreme Wisdom* (Solution to the So-Called Negroes Problem by Elijah Muhammad, Published by the University of Islam).

4. Physical Training: Hikes, healthy games, exercises and drilling.

5. Military Courtesy:

    a. Giving proper respect.

    b. Saluting an officer by his rank.

    c. Addressing an officer by his rank.

    d. Obeying all orders given by an officer.

6. Educational Trips:

    a. Museums.

    b. Zoo.

    c. Planetarium.

    d. Aquarium.

7. Drawing Class — If interested:

    a. Drawing of own creations.

8. Woodcraft Class — after accumulating some money:

    a. Ideas from the class to be shaped out of wood.

9. Self-defense

    a. Art of boxing.

    b. Judo.

    c. Wrestling forms.

Other duties of the F.O.I. include the following:

> "Oh you F.O.I.
>
> Keep —   1) The Messenger Happy
> 2) The Dead Before Him
> 3) Up the Spirit of February 26
> 4) The Prayer Formula of W. D. Muhammad
> 5) The House Fire Burning"[16]

A nineteen-year-old member of the F.O.I. gave the following account of some of their responsibilities:

On Friday night I was on 63rd Street on Fishing Detail.[17] I went back to the Temple on time for the eight o'clock meeting. We were there not only selling the *Pittsburgh Courier* but we particularly draw the buyer's attention to the Messenger's Message. It is rather strange if I say that most of our people don't buy that paper. . . . I am responsible for thirty-five copies a week and I sell about a half of that number and lose on the remainder. Each Fruit member is responsible to sell at least thirty-five copies of the paper weekly. Some Brothers sell more copies than that.

F.O.I. members also organize the entertainment for Temple functions. At a PTA turkey fund-raising dinner held in the University of Islam auditorium, a quartet consisting of a saxophonist, a "tom-tom" drummer, a cornetist, and a guitarist played soft, popular music. "Tea for Two" was one selection. All four musicians were introduced as people who had been professional entertainers before joining the Nation. The Junior Fruits of Islam, boys between thirteen and eighteen years of age, performed what was described as a military drill. The performance was precise and disciplined. The writer was very much impressed with the performance, which included "original salute" as well as "special salutes"; the original salute was the traditional salute but facing the East; the special salute was an improvisation.

MOSLEM GIRLS' TRAINING AND GENERAL CIVILIZATION CLASS

The Moslem Girls' Training and General Civilization Class is "[t]he name given to the training of women and girls in North America how to keep house, how to rear their children, how to take care of their husband, sew, cook, and in general, how to act at home and abroad."[18] Only women who feel that they can participate in all the activities of the Temple are members of the M.G.T.–G.C.C. They may be called upon to perform any duties within their competence in the Temple. They are officers of the Temple and servants of

16. From a permanent poster displayed at the University of Islam auditorium.

17. Interesting Negroes on the streets to attend Temple meetings. This street is notorious for the large number of lower-class Negroes who hang around there.

18. Answer to Question 14 in Lost-Found Moslem Lesson, No. 1, "First Term Examination Assignment of Mr. Elijah Mohammad" (Mimeographed, n.d.).

the Nation. Most of them hold jobs outside of the Temple. There are at present about seventy-five M.G.T. women at the Chicago Temple. The M.G.T. is organized along the same lines as the F.O.I., although they do not perform all the duties required of the latter. Among the women, hygiene and personal cleanliness are emphasized. They are taught reading and writing (especially those who were not privileged to receive formal education), history, and domestic science — sewing, cooking, housekeeping, etc. They are concerned with the training of good Muslim women and watch over the conduct and behavior of the female followers.

The M.G.T.-G.C.C. meets regularly on Thursday nights. Below is a typical schedule of its activities:

M.G.T. and G.C.C. Schedule [19]

Section 1	Section 4
7:00–7:03: Prayer	8:00–8:20: English
7:03–8:00: Actual Facts	8:20–8:35: Spelling
Section 2	8:35–8:55: Penmanship
7:03–8:00: Sewing	8:55–9:10: Refinement
Section 3	9:10–9:25: Beauty
7:03–7:30: Art	9:25–9:35: Hygiene
	9:35– : Cooking

The M.G.T.-G.C.C. requires that all women from about the age of thirteen report for a weight check twice a month. According to an interviewee, every woman and girl in this age group must keep a certain weight level. A fine of one cent is imposed for every additional pound beyond the required weight for all women. Records are carefully kept by Sister Rosie Lee 2X, the secretary. According to this informant, the women do not object to the fine because they believe "nothing is for the worse but all for good." In other words, whatever Muhammad commands is in their own interest.

The M.G.T.-G.C.C. welfare program consists of inquiring into the welfare of Muslim Sisters at meetings and trying to satisfy their wants. Both the F.O.I. and the M.G.T.-G.C.C. are subdivided into the Sick Committee and the Poor Committee. The Sick Committee looks after those who may be sick and visits them. The Poor Com-

19. Copied from a blackboard at the University of Islam the morning after an M.G.T.-G.C.C. meeting.

mittee investigates the conditions of the poor or unemployed members and makes recommendations for their assistance.

In general, the F.O.I. and the M.G.T.–G.C.C. serve the adult education and initiation policies of the Nation. Members of these organizations are considered servants of the Nation. Study of the
Koran and *The Supreme Wisdom* is a special requirement for the
F.O.I. and M.G.T.–G.C.C. members.

SOLIDARITY ACTIVITIES

Aside from the formal relationships and organizations described
above, building the Nation requires the continuous participation of
the membership. Co-ordinating the activities of the Nation at other
levels is also necessary both for the smooth operation of the Nation
and for the mutual solidarity of the members. The Messenger cannot maintain a direct personal contact with all his followers, except
through correspondence, for various reasons. However, his presence
is felt by his followers through his "Messages" to the Temple and
appearances by his ministers or by a member of his family, most
often Minister Wallace. The New York Minister, Malcolm X, represents him frequently. The Messenger's visits to Temples outside of
Chicago are rather infrequent. In fact, he has visited only one Temple in the South — that in Atlanta, Georgia — and only recently.
Muhammad's followers often travel great distances to hear his
teachings at other Temples or to see him in person. In 1959 it was
reported that over 3,500 Muslims traveled to Washington, D.C.
from various parts of the country to hear his teachings and to honor
him. This figure may be somewhat exaggerated. The most important
occasions for co-ordination and for involving members in national
activities are the Saviour's Day Celebration and the Annual Convention.

SAVIOUR'S DAY

Followers of Elijah Muhammad look forward to a spiritual re-
union with their leader and one another each year on February 26,
which is the occasion of the birth of the Great Mahdi (Allah) in the

Person of Master Wallace Fard Muhammad. Most Muslims worship on that occasion at their Temples, but many travel to Chicago to worship and to attend the Muslim Annual Convention, which begins on February 27.

February 26 is a day of worship, contemplation, and rejoicing. On Saviour's Day and at the Convention acquaintances are renewed, new acquaintances made, and gifts are exchanged. In 1960, greeting cards were exchanged among the Muslims and sent to their friends. About 20,000 cards were printed and sold at $1.50 per box of eleven cards.

Saviour's Day is to the Muslims what Christmas is to the Christians. The Muslim Sisters dress in immaculate white gowns and the men appear in suits with special handmade ties specified by the Supreme Captain for the occasion. During the 1960 Convention as well as during the previous ones, male members were required to wear the following:

1. First Day: Blue suit with white (knitted) tie
2. Second Day: Brown suit with brown (knitted) tie
3. Third Day (final session): Grey suit with black (knitted) tie.

However, a member or visitor without these colors or suits is welcomed, "if you are black."

The speaker's platform at the Temple of Islam in Chicago, which is usually undraped, is decorated with flowers and draped with white linen on this occasion. The chair which the Messenger occupies is green.[20] He is flanked by the Supreme Captain, two or more of his sons, and by a few ministers. Ministers from many Temples speak in praise of the Messenger's work among his people. Muhammad expounds the divinity of "Elijah's God" whom the followers and visitors have heard so much about. He recounts the Saviour's birth, his life and activities in the United States, and his promise to the so-called Negroes in North America.

20. Muhammad's appearance at the Temple on Saviour's Day in 1956 was described on the printed program as: "3 P.M. . . . Royal entrance of the Messenger, Honorable Elijah Muhammad — A New Leader for a New Day." At the final session of the 1960 Convention, Minister Malcolm X asked the audience to remain seated while the Messenger was leaving the hall and pleaded: "Please pay the same respect to this black man you know loves you, that you would pay to the President of the United States, who you think loves you."

MUSLIM ANNUAL CONVENTION

Although the 1960 Convention was described as the "Thirtieth Session," there is no evidence that these conventions have been held continuously since the founding of the Nation. If they were, the early meetings were small and did not attract public notice. The first widely publicized one was held in a Chicago Protestant church in 1956. The convention draws a large number of Muslims from various sections of the United States where Temples are to be found. A large number of them come from the East and the Midwest. Few come from the West or the South. However, the convention also draws a large number of Negroes who are not Muslims. The 1959 Convention was attended by about 2,000 persons.

In 1960, the Muslims used every possible means of publicity, posters, stickers on cars, press releases, handbills, newspaper ads, radio and television spot announcements, in the hope of drawing a larger audience. The convention was widely publicized in the local press, radio, and television. Reports in some of the local white press before and during the meeting were hostile, and according to the Muslims, their objective was to discourage Negroes from attending. Nonetheless, local radio and television announcements and commentaries assisted by giving publicity to the convention. The Muslims were generally pleased with the average attendance during the three-day activities, but they were somewhat disappointed by the "apathy" of Chicago Negroes. According to Muhammad, if Chicago Negroes were not afraid of their white masters, more than 50,000 would have been present on the opening day of the convention:

> If you are afraid to listen to me, then you should suffer the consequences! I am the Messenger of Allah, and I don't have the time to beg disbelievers to believe.[21]

Considering the amount of money and effort which the Muslims spent on publicity, the attendance was disappointingly low. However, for Chicago, the attendance was high when compared to previous records.[22] The writer attended Muslim conventions in 1959

21. Speech of Muhammad, from writer's notes.
22. Attendance at the 1956, 1957, 1958, and 1959 conventions did not exceed 2,000 for any of those years.

and 1960. The procedure and activities of the two conventions varied. The former lasted three days and was held in a Negro church. The latter was held on "neutral" ground in the Chicago Coliseum. In 1959 Saviour's Day was celebrated at the Temple, but in 1960 it was a public affair held at the Coliseum. At the previous convention, ministers reported on the activities of their respective Temples and at the latter, a "consolidated" report was given by the National Secretary.

The ministers' reports at the 1959 Convention were mainly testimonials, presented few facts, and were heavily weighted in favor of "bearing witness" to the work of the Honorable Elijah Muhammad. For three days, followers and visitors listened to reports from the Temples. The Messenger appeared briefly during the first day's session but did not make a speech. At the last session he delivered a major address which lasted nearly four hours and consisted of general ideological teachings and specific plans for subsequent years. The conventions have emphasized different themes each year. In 1956 the theme was "Unity or Death — Our Wants, Our Needs, Our Hopes, Our Fears, Our Opportunities — A Way Out." In 1957 the "Protection of Black Women" from the "beasts" and "non-enemy" prowlers was emphasized.[23] In 1959 the Messenger emphasized his long-term plans for Chicago, and expressed the hope that these will become the general community plans among his followers in other cities. The keynote address in 1960 was "The Birth of Jesus": the point was made that "Jesus died for what he believed to be the truth" and not for any other reason. However, the theme of the 1960 Convention was "What I have Seen and What I have Heard During My World Tour: What the so-called American Negro Can and Must Now Do For Himself — Our Unity Will Make Us Self-Dependent."

Few non-Muslims speak at these conventions. In 1956, however, F. H. Hammurabi, Director of the House of Knowledge, Chicago, showed films on Africa and other parts of the world. In 1959, James R. Lawson of the United African Nationalists Movement, New York,

23. "Beasts" refer to whites and "non-enemy" prowlers refers to Negroes and other persons of color who seek to have illicit sexual relations with black women.

delivered messages from President Nasser of Egypt and President Tubman of Liberia to the Convention. Other activities included exhibits, bazaars, and performances by students of the University of Islam.

There are no debates on the reports given at conventions, nor are decisions made by the delegates. The business of the Nation is conducted behind the scenes during the convention. Ministers and other Temple leaders meet in conferences with the Messenger and with the Supreme Captains. Groups of followers are also invited to the Messenger's home. In this way the Messenger is able to meet and talk with his followers.

ECONOMIC NATIONALISM
AND ORGANIZATION

Few Negro leaders have stressed the importance of economic self-sufficiency as an instrument of racial advancement.[24] For the Garvey movement, however, economic self-determination was fundamental to the realization of the political objectives of black nationalism. A contemporary Garveyite writes:

> . . . Respectable incomes would mean elimination of a great portion of the social and political adversities existing in our communities. . . . *So long as you sojourn in America* [emphasis added], support the resident or racial merchant . . . until such time you realize exactly what BLACK NATIONALISTS have preached over the years, that the future of the blackman is within and lashed to that of AFRICA. the land from whence we all came. . . .[25]

24. Frederick Douglass, *Life and Times of Frederick Douglass Written by Himself* (Hartford, Conn.: Park Publishing Company, 1882), p. 501: "A race which cannot save its earnings, which spends all it makes and goes in debt when it is sick, can never rise in the scale of civilization, no matter under what laws it may chance to be. Put us in Kansas or in Africa, and until we learn to save more than we spend, we are sure to sink and perish. It is not in the nature of things that we should be equally rich in this world's goods. Some will be more successful than others, and poverty, in many cases, is the result of misfortune rather than of crime; but no race can afford to have all its members the victims of this misfortune, without being considered a worthless race." Cf. Booker T. Washington, *Up from Slavery*, pp. 223–224: "The wisest among my race understand that the agitation of questions of social equality is the extremest of folly, and that progress in the enjoyment of all the privileges that will come to us must be the result of severe and constant struggle rather than of artificial forcing. No race that has anything to contribute to the markets of the world is long in any degree ostracized. It is important and right that all privileges of the law be ours, but it is vastly more important that we be prepared for the exercises of these privileges. . . ."

The Nation of Islam affirms this with greater emphasis. In fact, among the Muslims, hard work, thrift, and accumulation of wealth have a semireligious sanction.

Mr. Muhammad's economic teachings and organization are inextricably tied up with his religious and nationalistic advocations for the "solution of the so-called Negro problem in the United States":

The Black Man in America faces a serious economic problem today and the White Race's Christianity cannot solve it. You, the so-called American Negro, with the help of Allah (God) can solve your own problems.

The truth must be recognized by the Black Man. He himself has assisted greatly in creating this serious problem of unemployment, insecurity, and *lack*. Before the Black Man can begin to gain economic security, he must be awakened (from the dead), gain knowledge, understanding and wisdom which will enable him to follow my teachings. Islam and only Islam will point the way out of the entanglement of *"want in the midst of plenty"* for the followers of Islam, the true religion of the Black Nation.

The Black Man in America is a Lazarus, begging for crumbs from the rich man's (white man) table. To solve his problems, I repeat, Lazarus must be called out of his grave. . . .

The believers in truth, Islam, must stop looking up to the White Race for Justice (Jobs). . . . [26]

The following is Muhammad's "Economic Blue Print for the Black Man":

1. Recognize the necessity for unity and group operation (activities).
2. Pool your resources; physically as well as financially.
3. Stop wanton criticisms of everything that is black-owned and black operated.
4. Keep in mind — *Jealousy Destroys From Within*.
5. Observe the operations of the White Man. He is successful. He makes no excuses for his failure. He works hard — in a collective manner. You do the same. . . .

The White Man spends his money with his *own kind*, which is natural. You, too, must do this. Help to make jobs for your own kind. Take a lesson from the Chinese and Japanese, the Puerto Rican and the Cubans, and go all out and support your own kind. Through such support of their own kind, the Chinese and Japanese are able to give employment and assistance to their own kind when they are in need. This is the first law of Nature. Defend and support your own kind. True Muslims do this.

25. A. N. Nwokeoji, *Go East Young Man* (New York: African Nationalist Pioneer Movement, 1957) pp. 48–49. The author of this pamphlet is known also as Charles Peaker.

26. Elijah Muhammad, *Herald-Dispatch* (Los Angeles), November 21, 1959, p. 8.

Because the so-called American Negro has been deceived and misled, he has become a victim of deception and is too deaf, dumb, and blind (dead) to support his own kind. He is today in the worst economic condition of any human being in the wilderness of North America. Unemployment is mounting and he feels it worst. He assisted in reducing himself to his present insecure economic condition. You, the Black Man, are the only member of the human race that deliberately walks past the place of business of one of your own kind — a black man, and spend your dollars with your natural enemy. The so-called American Negro has never in the history of America been known to boycott or criticize the White Man as he does his own kind. He thus shows love for his enemy and hatred for his own kind.

A true Muslim would never boycott the place of business of his fellow Muslim or black brother. A true Muslim is proud of the success of his black sisters and brothers. He recognizes that their success is his success. He recognizes the law of Islam. If one brother has a bowl of soup, you have half of that soup.[27]

COMMUNALISM

The organization of the economic activities of a Temple is described by Muhammad as "communalism." It is a system in which his followers voluntarily and regularly give part of their income toward the establishment of businesses. These contributions are given as "alms" (for the "cause of Islam") by members and are not considered to be individual shares in the business enterprises. Members are required to contribute one tenth of their weekly or yearly earnings toward the support of the Nation. This contribution is known as "Duty." During Sunday meetings there is usually a queue of followers making payments to the Temple secretaries. Although most followers appear to contribute regularly, they are under no obligation to do so when they cannot afford it. One follower stated that he made a regular contribution of not less than ten dollars every week until he began to support his unemployed father. Another claimed that she "has never failed to give her share" and contributes an additional dollar every Sunday for current expenditures. The writer found that members took their financial contribution to the Nation seriously. Several followers were asked: "Is there some respect in which you feel you are lacking? Do you think that you are living up to your obligations in the Nation?" The respondents said, among other things, that they were not satisfied with their

27. Elijah Muhammad, *Herald-Dispatch*, February 19, 1959, pp. 3, 10.

financial contributions to the Nation and wished they could contribute more "to this great cause." The writer asked twenty-five
high school students to draw a circular graph showing how a Muslim family would spend a theoretical yearly income of $4,500. The
idea was to discover whether or not the students had also been imbued with the idea of the "Duty" to the Nation. The entire group
responded. A study of their graphs revealed that everyone allocated
ten per cent of income for contributions to the Nation. Their response also indicated a general tendency to allocate a sizeable
amount of income for savings.

Our evidence is by no means conclusive, but it appears that Muhammad's communalism is aimed at fostering three related sets of
values among Negroes, especially among his followers. First, he
seeks to inculcate, through encouraging habits of saving, a sense of
responsibility for economic self-improvement. Second, a channel
for investments is created through the collective business enterprises
owned by the Temple. Third, he demands a sense of responsibility
for the welfare of the community — the Muslim community. These
values, which are said to be lacking among American Negroes, are
the goals of communalism. The "Duty" (tithe), with its semireligious sanction, is the mechanism for inducing the habits of savings.
Part of the Duty is invested in collective business enterprises. These
enterprises serve as models for members. The followers also expect
to profit from their contributions to the Nation in time of sickness,
unemployment, or old age. In Chicago the decision to invest in a
business is the Messenger's responsibility. The profits realized from
the businesses are turned over to the Temple and, according to one
of the officers, "the high officers of the Temple decide what they
wish to do with it." These officers consist of the Supreme Captain,
the Treasurer, Brother John Hassan, one of the trustees of the Temple, and the manager of the particular business. In all cases, their
decision is made in consultation with the Messenger or "someone
close to him."

Most of the Chicago Temple's businesses were established in the
last ten years. Before 1957 profits were invested in new businesses.
Since 1958 net profits have been used to support members who are

too old to work. About seventy-five per cent of the profits is used for the aged, operations of the Temple, and the assistance of smaller Temples. The remainder, twenty-five per cent, is reserved for the support of the University of Islam.[28]

The Chicago Temple now owns and operates nearly fifteen businesses. In 1947 the Temple purchased a 140-acre farm in White Cloud, Michigan, because the Messenger believes that "the Nation should be able to feed its own members." The farm is operated by two Muslim families who are assisted during weekends by volunteers from Chicago. Wheat, beans, other vegetables, and chickens are raised. In addition, the farm is said to produce enough milk and butter to meet the demands of the Chicago followers, though this is difficult to believe. These products are sold through the Temple's grocery store, which also handles products from its bakery. The farm is said to be one of the more profitable businesses. Among other important businesses are a dry-cleaning plant with its own deliverymen, a restaurant which serves "American and Arabian-styled foods," a dressmaking shop, two fair-sized clothing stores — one for men's wear and the other for women's goods —, a barber shop, a gas station, and a number of apartment buildings.

These businesses are small enterprises. The Muslims claim that they are continuously expanding and that the Messenger contemplates eventually moving into industrial production, but the Muslims obviously do not have the capital for a large-scale industrial venture. Even if sufficient capital were available, they are limited by the lack of skilled and experienced personnel. They cannot hope to compete successfully without these prerequisites. The Garvey movement floundered in part because of its premature expansion into ambitious enterprises. It had no skilled and experienced business managers who were also devotees of the movement. Such was also the fate of Noble Drew Ali's enterprises. Both Garvey and Ali paid a high price when they sought to employ people outside the movement with some skills but who were "more cunning than scrupulous." Such lofty aims as moving from small business enterprises to industrial production serve to inspire enthusiasm and morale

28. Interview with Minister Wallace Muhammad.

among the followers, but they have often led to sporadic, unplanned, and unprofitable ventures, such as their publishing enterprises. The Muslims have attempted during 1959–1961 to publish five newspapers and magazines — *The Islamic News, The Messenger Magazine, Mr. Muhammad Speaks to the Black Man, Salaam,* and *Mr. Muhammad Speaks.* The first four have been discontinued and only one, *Mr. Muhammad Speaks,* which is published in New York, pays for itself. Minister Malcolm X expressed the need for consolidation of these papers. This would enable the Muslims to use their limited skills and resources more effectively.

The enterprises owned by the Muslims are those traditionally operated by Negroes — barber shops, small restaurants, etc., which can be managed by comparatively untrained personnel. The writer visited these enterprises and interviewed their managers and employees. A brief account of a few will indicate their scope.

There were 32 full-time employees at seven business establishments at the time of our visit, in November, 1958. In addition, 12 persons were reported employed on part-time bases. The full-time employees were distributed as follows: the dry cleaning plant, 5; the grocery store, 4; the dressmaking shop, 3; the clothing stores, 6; barber shop, 8; bakery, 2; and restaurant, 4.

The dry cleaning plant, located at 608 East 63rd Street in Chicago, is fitted with cleaning machines. One of Muhammad's sons is the manager. The Temple owns two pick-up and delivery trucks. In addition, two Muslim Brothers, Thomas 5X and Cheatem LX, operate their own trucks for pick-ups and deliveries. Each is paid a 35 per cent commission on what he collects from his customers. The business is patronized by both followers and non-Muslims. The manager told the writer that he does not contract business from other dry cleaners. He reported that he was operating at a profit.

The dressmaking shop is managed by Sister Ethel Sharrieff, the Messenger's daughter, and employs three full-time Muslim Sisters. When there is a "boom," reported one of the employees, additional persons are hired. Although Muslim Sisters who can sew are preferred for employment, non-Muslims have been employed occasionally. The plant is small and equipped with modern sewing machines; the Muslims hope to expand it into a garment industry. Dresses are made mainly for Muslim women and children, and occasionally hand-made ties and suits for men. The shop is patronized also by non-Muslim women. Its goods are merchandised through the Temple's clothing stores.

The Chicago Temple owns two clothing stores, one for men and one for women. These stores serve partly as outlets for the small quantity of goods made in the dressmaking shop; but most of the goods in these stores are bought from the open market. They consist mainly of current American fashions for men, women, and children. The store also handles jewelry and other accessories for men and women. Prices of these items appeared to be a little higher than the prices in Chicago's larger department stores. Two Muslim Sisters, June X, a public high school graduate, and Lorraine X (she did not complete high school) were in charge of the store. Asked whether they thought the store was operating at a profit, Sister June said: "It could be better. It is all right." The writer asked why she thought "it could be better." She replied: "Oh, maybe we haven't now in stock what the people want. We are operating at a profit, however."

The Temple's grocery store and the restaurant are adjacent. Brother Milton (not a relation of the Messenger) is the manager of the grocery store. There are three employees at the grocery store. One is an electrician who serves both the grocery store and the restaurant. The grocery store maintains a large supply of foods and kosher meats, and sells neither pork nor cigarettes. The manager told the writer that it was a "very successful business." Prices of meat were comparatively higher than elsewhere in the neighborhood.

Employees who were interviewed in these stores felt generally that they were better paid than Negroes working for comparable businesses. They expressed frequently that they were working in "our own businesses." They are not members of any union and have no desire to be organized. The writer is inclined to believe that their wages were perhaps lower than they might have received in similar employments in the area. Wage differentials are compensated for, however, by their sense of involvement in "ownership," pride in their collective effort, enthusiasm in the movement, and the general feeling of camaraderie among the employees.

The Nation's biggest plan is the proposed Muhammad's Islamic Center. Two city blocks have been purchased for its site.[29] It was expected that construction would commence in the summer of 1960.

Although members are encouraged to establish businesses through co-operative effort, a vast majority of the Muslims have to earn their living from other sources of employment. Not more than fifty are currently employed by the Chicago Temple. This figure includes employees at the University of Islam and the Messenger's personal secretaries. Similarly, members are urged to support Muslim and Negro-owned businesses; but they are forced to depend largely on white-owned stores and services because of the limited scope of Negro enterprises.

The Muslims claim that these businesses are profitably operated. There is, of course, an increasing need for executive talent as the businesses expand and become more complicated. Their places of business are noted for cleanliness in comparison with the majority of similar business places in the Chicago Negro community.

Members of the Nation appear to be economically more secure than many Negroes from similar low-income backgrounds. Elimination of expenditures on such "non-essential" items as tobacco, liquor, games of chance, and popular entertainments has enabled them to utilize their income more effectively. The dietary rule that they must eat only one meal a day is another source of savings. Although we could not test the impression that some Muslims have moved to better-situated apartments in the city and others have attempted to buy their own homes, this seems to be the case.[30]

29. This area is bounded by East 85th and 86th Streets and by South Park and South Prairie Avenues. The Chatham-Avalon Park Community Council opposes the Muslims' plans for the site. See the Chicago *Southeast Economist*, March 27, 1960, p. 1. In August, 1960, the Chicago Park Commission, which had sold the land to the Temple, expropriated it for a park. The Muslims won a $165,000 court settlement, an amount larger than the Park District Commission was willing to pay before the court's decision. See *Mr. Muhammad Speaks, Special Edition*, I, No. 6 p. 19.

30. An improved economic status tends to moderate the militancy of the members. In fact, this interest in the acquisition of wealth appears to be one of the important internal constraints on the possibility of the movement becoming politically significant or revolutionary.

Politically and socially, followers of Muhammad tend to isolate themselves from the Chicago Negro community and also from the larger American community. However, they participate in the normal economic activities of the community as employees, producers, consumers, and as members of trade unions. Consequently, their social isolation is more apparent than real. The economic organization of the Nation of Islam is the most effective point of contact and interaction between Muslims and other Negroes. It seems likely that they are gaining status in the Negro community in proportion to their improved economic position.

FINANCING THE NATION

The income of the Nation of Islam is a well-kept secret. It is impossible for an outsider to determine the Nation's annual income or expenditures because almost all business transactions are made in cash or by cashier's check. An insurance company reports that the Muslims bring at a time as much as $1,500 of premium payments in cash.[31] No bank account kept by the Nation (if any is kept) would reflect the total income. We can only describe the sources of their income.

The movement is supported primarily by its members and secondarily by Negroes who are interested in its programs or make contributions at meetings. Each Temple raises its own funds and determines how they are to be spent. Most of its funds come through voluntary contributions of members. Occasionally levies are imposed, such as the twenty-five dollars which each follower contributed toward Muhammad's tour of Africa and the Middle East. The principal sources of income are the "Duty" and profits from the business enterprises. All contributions are designated as "charity" on receipts issued to subscribers and the purpose is indicated: Duty, C.P. (Charity for the Poor), Land Drive, Muhammad's Center Fund, Traveling, and Saviour's Day. Saviour's Day subscription is a pledge made by members for special projects such as the proposed Muhammad's Center. Additional funds are derived from

31. Reported to the writer by Robert C. Nelson, a Chicago correspondent for *The Christian Science Monitor.*

such public functions as bazaars, dinners, and collections at public meetings.

Annual income from all sources has been estimated at $300,000 to $500,000.[32] For the years 1958 to 1959 each Muslim pledged a minimum of $105 toward Muhammad's proposed Center. We do not know how many fulfilled the pledge. In 1959–1960 the minimum pledge was $125 per person. Each donor's name was listed on a large bulletin board at the auditorium of the University of Islam after he had completed his pledge. An asterisk was placed beside the name of anyone who had completed his payment. Those who made more than one full payment received two or more asterisks. The data which follow are taken from that list:

Location of Temple	Number of Persons Reported To Have Completed Payment Before February 26, 1960	Total Number of Stars	Totals of Each Temple
Chicago	96	115	$14,375
Hartford, Conn.	30	30	3,750
Miami, Florida	10	10	1,250
Washington, D.C.	14	15	1,875
Cleveland, Ohio	15	15	1,875
New York City	172	186	23,250
Buffalo, N.Y.	5	5	625
Roxbury, Mass.	29	29	3,625
Philadelphia, Pa.	26	26	3,250
Springfield, Mass.	12	12	1,500
Newark, N.J.	17	19	2,375
Newark, N.J.	undetermined	5	725
			$58,375

We should bear in mind that only eleven out of fifty Temples reported prior to February 22, 1960, and that many made their reports during the convention. There is competition among the Temples as well as among individuals in making these payments. This list does not show members who contributed but were unable to complete the pledge before that date. This figure, though incomplete, is indicative of the determination of the Muslims. It is even more impressive when we consider that this represents only one of their sources of income.

32. *U. S. News and World Report,* November 9, 1959, p. 112.

We have already noted other sources of income, such as the sale of copies of the *Pittsburgh Courier* until the summer of 1959. Since then the Muslims have been selling the Los Angeles *Herald-Dispatch*; in March, 1960, *The New Crusader*, a Chicago paper, was added. These papers carry "Mr. Muhammad's Messages."

Since Muhammad believes that Negroes have too long been given to the idea that "someone else must bear their burden for them," he insists that the Nation must be self-supporting. As a "nation of people" they must tax themselves for their own purposes. He adds that over the years they have been taxed by the United States government "without any substantial good" accruing to them. They are under a severe strain in trying to stretch their meager income to cover the expenses of the Nation. In Chicago the maintenance of the University of Islam is an additional burden. The cost of running the school is well over $40,000 a year. Until January, 1959, no fees were charged; since then a small fee has been added.

The apparent financial success of the Nation is due to the voluntary basis of its officialdom and service personnel. Employees of the Nation are paid minimal wages which are described as "charity." Each employee is given a sealed envelope marked "charity." Employees are not supposed to discuss their wages with others. In all instances an employee negotiates his wage with the Supreme Captain and only infrequently with the Messenger.

The writer could not determine the amount of charity which employees received. However, Minister James 3X said that he was "satisfied" with what he gets: "it takes care of my family." A full-time employee, eighteen years of age, who works at one of the businesses establishments, gets $35 a week. Another, who uses his own truck for collecting and delivering laundry, is paid a commission of about 35 per cent of whatever he collects from his customers.

Employees are given no opportunity to bargain collectively. In 1959 teachers at the school tried to bargain collectively for increments in their charities. Until September, 1959, the school operated four hours a day of a four-day week. When in September it became necessary to operate on two shifts, the same teachers had to teach on both shifts. The Muslim employees did not press for an increment, although they would have welcomed it; but the non-Muslim teachers felt strongly that they should receive increments because of the additional work which they were asked to do. A meeting was held with the Messenger and the Supreme Captain. The principal presented the case for the teachers. Muhammad's attitude toward their demand was a firm and unequivocal rejection. He told them that he was prepared to accept "resignations here and now." This threat was followed by a dissertation on the needs of the Temple, what he is trying to do for "our people in the mud," and the sacrifices which his followers are making. He dilated on the task of "resurrecting the dead" as the moral duty of every enlightened Negro. He was aware that they could receive better wages in the public schools, but added, "Charlie can afford it because he has the resources," meaning that since white people control the economy and the government, they can afford to pay public-school teachers better salaries. In the end all the teachers capitulated to his moving plea. Not one demurred after the speech. However, after the Messenger had left, the Supreme Captain admonished the teachers to be patient, for better days were coming. It seems likely that he negotiated with some of the teachers individually. Two months later, all but one teacher received increments ranging from $5 to $15 per person. The teacher excepted from this general increment had been paid a higher salary than most, and although she was unhappy, she did not resign. At this meeting, the writer learned that employee "charities" — teachers, secretaries, bus drivers, janitors and others connected with the school and the Temple proper — totaled about $500 per week. These expenses are met from weekly collections at Temple meetings.

Muhammad receives gifts from time to time from his followers or from the Temples. Minister Wallace once said, "you would be surprised how handsomely they can give." He added, however, "the Messenger of Allah usually gives more in return to the donors."

At the present Muhammad is making a public appeal to Negroes for support of the proposed Muhammad's Center. Aside from this, he refrained from seeking support of nonfollowers. Until the 1960 Convention collections were not taken at public meetings, although exception was made in the case of the Center Fund. He has firmly rejected suggestions from some of his followers that he should seek the financial support of white people, especially of segregationists. Those who have made this suggestion believe that many white people would contribute financially to his program of racial separation.

It has been suggested that Muhammad is receiving aid from foreign sources, but the charge appears to be without foundation. He has received some free literature from other Islamic groups — most religious groups distribute such materials. Muhammad has denied all such allegations:

> I have been charged, because of the continued progress that I am making toward enlightening my people, I am now being charged indirectly of receiving outside aid which is absolutely false. There is not one dime that has come to us from any source other than our own selves. I have been charged with communists. I have been charged with trying to get aid from the United Arab Republic. I am not after aid from anyone but the God that has sent me. I don't particularly need any from any other source. Allah is sufficient. Allah has offered to you and me if we will submit to Him, the entire universe. I will not walk around Capitol Hill or go to the White House begging the President and the Congress for anything of America. I have no need to do so. What right do I have if I preach to you the doom of America and preach to you that God is present with me; what right have I to go begging any other person. I have met with God as Moses met with Jehovah, so I have met with Allah and He has revealed to me what He has revealed.[33]

PROBLEMS OF ADMINISTRATION

The administrative structure of the Nation has not kept pace with its recent growth and expansion. The most important problem to overcome is the inability of the Nation to attract persons with trained skills and special competence. This handicap is partly the result of limited financial resources and the high premium placed on loyalty. Muhammad explained these difficulties as follows:

> Some of our problems include the fact that out of every nine converts only one may be intelligent and competent to be usefully occupied for rendering services of educating other members. The Negro middle class or the so-called educated ones are not at all inspired with a feeling of wanting to render service to their own people and to make the kind of sacrifice necessary for assuming this responsibility.

33. Speech, Washington, D. C., May 31, 1959, p. 7.

The only people who come into Islam with the exception of a few are the poor and ignorant and it is a very tedious task trying to uplift these people.[34]

The lack of qualified personnel in the Nation is particularly acute not only in the administration but also in the teaching staff of the Muslim school. The Nation is consequently limited by the capacity of the Messenger's chief subordinates, most of whom did not complete their high school educations and some of whom, like Minister Karriem of Baltimore Temple (Maryland), were "completely illiterate" prior to joining the Nation. A few, like Minister James 3X of the Chicago Temple, completed high school. Minister Malcolm X of New York completed the eighth grade. The careers of both these ministers, both unusually able and talented, in the Nation illuminates the capacities and limitations of Muhammad's chief lieutenants.

Minister James 3X was born in Camden, Arkansas. Before becoming a follower, he was known as James Anderson. His father was a Baptist minister for over fifty years. In 1934 James left Arkansas for Chicago at the age of eighteen after completing high school. Since then he has not traveled "behind the Cotton Curtain." When he first came to Chicago, he "sought employment for about a year." In 1935 he was employed at $13.00 per week at a laundry plant. He kept such jobs until 1939 when he heard about the Temple of Islam through an ex-member employed on the same job.

He joined the Nation of Islam in 1940, and was among those imprisoned during the second World War. Before and after the War he helped as an instructor at the University of Islam during the day and worked in a factory at night. In 1954 he began training for the ministry and about 1956 became an assistant minister. In the last five years he has also acted as an assistant to the principal at the University of Islam, and for brief periods he has acted as the principal. He is now a full minister.

Minister James' duties include teaching Islam at the University of Islam. He is the first to arrive at school early in the morning and the last to depart. His day is fully occupied with both ministerial duties and administrative responsibilities. He lectures two nights a

34. Interview with Muhammad.

The Messenger of Allah, Elijah Muhammad,
spiritual leader of the
Nation of Islam.

Scene at the Chicago Temple on Saviour's Day, 1959. Elijah Muhammad, his wife (seated immediately on his left), his daughters and several ministers are listening to eulogies of his work.

A view of the 1959 Muslim Annual Convention, showing the separation of
the sexes and the theme of economic self-sufficiency.

Scene at the 1960 Muslim Annual Convention in Chicago. Minister James
3X, Muhammad's assistant in Chicago, is at the rostrum.

Akbar Muhammad, the youngest son of Elijah Muhammad, teaching Arabic to a group of Muslims.

Four young California ministers of the Nation of Islam.

Muslims and visitors waiting in line to be searched before entering the Temple, a customary procedure at all Muslim Temples. The one shown here is Muhammad's Temple of Islam No. 27, Los Angeles, California.

Muslims in New York congratulate one another upon winning $75,000 in damages in a celebrated police brutality case.

A large crowd standing in the rain in Harlem to listen to Minister Malcolm X, one of the most forceful and articulate of Muhammad's spokesmen. Malcolm insists that integrationists could not gather such a large audience even on a sunny afternoon.

Minister Malcolm X presenting Muhammad's call for separation of the races to a Harlem crowd of over six thousand persons who stood in the rain to hear him.

Minister Malcolm X (*center*) and Walter C. Carrington (*right*) in a debate on Negro problems at the Harvard University Law School Forum. Mr. Carrington is at present the United States Peace Corps Commissioner in Sierra Leone, West Africa.

The restaurant attached to New York Temple No. 7.

In this scene from the Muslim play, "Orgena: A Negro Spelt Backwards," the actors on the left are wearing the costume which the Muslims believe to have been their authentic dress before they were robbed of their culture, traditions, and religion in America.

week at the Temple as well as on Sundays and attends all Temple activities during the week. His ambition is to continue to "improve" himself as much as possible so that he may become "a greater helper in this cause."

Malcolm X Shabazz, known formerly as Malcolm Little, tall, slender, light-skinned, and an eloquent speaker, has risen from an extremely depressed lower-class environment to a position of prominence among the Muslims. His full "Muslim" name is Malik El-Shabazz. He is — in his own right — one of the better-known black nationalist leaders in Harlem. Now 36, he was born on May 19, 1925, in Omaha, Nebraska. Malcolm's parents moved to Lansing, Michigan, when he was six years old. He received his formal education in Michigan, but left his family for Boston, where he lived from 1941 until 1942, finally moving to New York City in 1943. Minister Malcolm told the writer that he spent most of his time in jail during the nineteen-forties and was converted to Islam in 1947. Asked if he was ever employed for any length of time, he said:

At 15, I was my own boss — the go-easy-way. I was a hustler. The only job I ever had was waiting tables. I had no education. I went to school down there [pointing to the streets in Harlem]. I mean, on the streets. Everything I have learned has been since I became a follower of Mr. Muhammad. I was never interested in education. At 19 I was in prison.

Minister Malcolm represents Muhammad at many public meetings in the United States. Early in July, 1959, he was sent on a tour of Africa and the Middle East as the Messenger's personal envoy, visiting the United Arab Republic, Saudi Arabia, the Sudan, and Nigeria. Other Muslims regard him very highly and look forward to his addresses. He was the editor of the now defunct *Messenger Magazine*. Muhammad regards him as a "great minister."

Last summer, July the 5th and 6th visiting Number 7 Temple, New York, with my beloved Minister Malcolm who just sat down — you will find him everywhere you find me. Only at the table I ask him to excuse himself there because he is so much taller, he will eat up my meal. But anywhere you will find me you will find him. . . . He is one of the most faithful ministers that I have. He will go everywhere — North, South, East or West, to China if I say go to China, he will go there. So I thank Allah for my Brother Minister Malcolm.[35]

35. Speech in Milwaukee, Wisconsin (typed), pp. 3–4.

Very few followers appear to be sensitive to the organizational problems of the Nation. Those who are aware of these problems are not likely to discuss them with an outsider. The officers are well aware of the needs of the Nation, particularly the need for a competent staff, but because of the premium placed on loyalty and deference to the Messenger, they cannot often find desirable personnel. A few of the more educated followers were critical of the Supreme Captain. They complained he had too much power and that half of the time the Messenger did not know what was going on. The few who felt this way believed that "if you want to get anything done, you must go directly to the Messenger." There is much truth in this criticism but it is also a displacement of criticism of the Messenger upon a more vulnerable officer.

One of the most important problems facing the Nation is the failure of the Messenger to delegate enough power to those below him, with the possible exception of the Supreme Captain. When such powers are delegated, they go to unqualified but loyal individuals. This is one of the difficulties of the school and a great handicap in its administration. During the course of this study only one follower criticized the Messenger and the organization of the Temple in Chicago. He emphasized that he supports the Messenger's program wholeheartedly, but expressed deep concern over certain aspects of the organization:

I am concerned over the policies and attitudes of the Messenger and of those immediately surrounding him. I worry about the secrecy in this place. The whole place is surrounded with secrecy. Frankly I do not know what I am supposed to do around here. It is a family oligarchy. ———— seems to be the nearest man to the Messenger. The Messenger seems to trust him. I guess it is because both of them went to jail together. Maybe this is a basis for trust. The Messenger just doesn't seem to trust me. He makes all the decisions. My decisions concerning administrative matters never seem to be carried out. The Messenger says that he wants suggestions. He appreciates it when suggestions are made. That is as far as it goes. He seems to distrust those below him except for a few. I really like what the Messenger is doing. I believe in everything that he is aspiring for our people. But I just do not seem to understand what he wants me to do. The Messenger's secretary has little education. The organization is really poor. They haven't begun planning for the Annual Conference yet. The planning is done within the same month.[36]

This follower deplored the concentration of all policy-decisions in one office. He proposed that the Nation, like any other government, should have a cabinet to advise the Messenger.

SUMMARY: THE NATURE AND CHARACTER OF THE MUSLIM COMMUNITY

Organized life and activities of the Muslims described in this and subsequent chapters constitute what we have described as nationalistic exotericism. However, the interplay of esoteric beliefs, previously described and organized activities is what gives the movement an active and cohesive existence. This we shall call the "Muslim community." It is not a physical community; it is a community of believers, essentially a pariah group within the Negro ghetto, a self-conscious community whose members strive by hard work, self-discipline, and sacrifice to live in accordance with a "central ideal" — Islam — as they understand it. It is also a community in which the anxieties and frustrations of its members are accommodated.

The Muslims claim that they find "peace of mind and happiness" in this community, that in it they enjoy "freedom, fraternity, justice, and equality." To them the real meaning of freedom, justice, and equality is to be sought in one's own community and among one's "own kind," not with "strangers," and not in integration, as many Negroes believe.

However, the discovery of one's identity and community is not enough. This knowledge must be translated into a deliberate course of action intended to promote one's "self-interest" and that of the community as a whole. Although the "interest" of the community is to a very large extent defined by the leader, members may modify its details. Organization is needed for the purpose of translating the community's interest into action. But this requires a certain type of organization; it is oligarchic, militant, and highly disciplined. Its

36. The interviewee asked that his name be withheld. He has since left the movement.

oligarchic characteristic is inherent in the ideology of the Nation, but it is also a function of the leader's beliefs about the capability and responsibleness of the followers. It is also worthy of note that the oligarchical structure of power and differentiations between the leadership and the rank and file do not bother the Muslims because of the overwhelming importance which the followers attach to their "common purpose." This phenomenon was noticed by Joseph F. Zygmunt in connection with the structure of power in the organization of the Watchtower Society (Jehovah's Witnesses). His description is applicable to the Nation of Islam:

> With all of this structuration [sic] and apparent differentiation, it is noteworthy that the movement is imbued with a commonness of purpose that exercises a profoundly 'equalizing' and equilibrating influence. This equalitarianism of purpose tends to soften the hierarchical distribution of authority. All are 'brothers.' . . . If some have more authority than others, they are still 'servants.' Truth has made them free though their lives are highly regulated.[37]

It is militant in the sense that the defined interests of the Nation are vigorously asserted and aggressively pursued. It is disciplined partly because this is thought to be "what the Negro masses need," and partly because attainment of the ends of the Nation depends on the ability of its members to forego many things which are said to impede the advancement of the Negro masses. Maintenance of discipline is important for internal cohesion and loyalty to the movement.

Within the limits of this community, every one is "important," the loyal and talented are rewarded, and the ambitious may rise to a position of prominence. Hard work, self-sacrifice, discipline, and loyalty are required. There is no room for laziness.

> If a man is lazy let him go to the Christian church. But if you are ambitious and hardworking, come to the Temple of Islam. We are not interested in what you wear. Come out and follow the Honorable Elijah Muhammad. We want you to wear Islam in your heart and to help expand our stores. Let's expand our store into a garment industry. If the white man can do it with your labor, why can't we use our labor to build our own garment industry? We must have something of our own — jobs for every black man and woman. . . . We've got to get out and work. We must have our women at home for creative arts. We must remove our women from the white man's

37. Zygmunt, "Social Estrangement and Recruitment Process in a Chiliastic Movement" (Master's Thesis, University of Chicago, 1953), p. 97.

kitchen. No one's mind should be in the sky. In Islam every one works. All of the Messenger's children work. Heaven demands hard work. There is no room for laziness and no room for ignorance in the Nation of Islam. . . .[38]

Division and subdivision of labor enable many members to participate continuously in the activities of the Nation. Numerous offices and titles, most of them honorary and prestigious, are created and conferred on many a lower-class Negro who never before anticipated he would "count" anywhere. Members are inspired by both the remoteness of the esoteric ends and the definitiveness of the exoteric goals — e.g., moral and economic self-improvement. The interplay of the esoteric and exoteric ends enables the Muslims to act together for the "common good." It gives individuals a sense of direction:

Let us here in Chicago unite, and begin setting up a standard that will serve as a guide for the 20,000,000 Negroes, throughout the black man's world in this U.S.A. This would make the God of heaven and earth proud of you and me. The plan has already been drawn, it is an Educational Center to teach our people the knowledge of self — Libraries, Recreational Center, Medical Center, and a beautiful Mosque of Islam, to teach the religion of our God and our Fathers, which will cost a very very small sum of $20 million compared to its value. To you and I this $20,000,000 can be raised right here on the Southside. You have it, for such a worthy cause, to which your children, and their children's children, can one day point with pride to this monument of their salvation.[39]

38. Minister Malcolm X, commenting on movies he made when he visited Africa and the Middle East.

39. Elijah Muhammad, "Think For Self," *The New Crusader*, March 26, 1960, p. 5.

VII. Recruitment and Initiation

THE OFFICIAL policy of the Nation of Islam, Muhammad told the writer, is to recruit the "Negro in the mud" into the movement and to "alienate him from giving support to middle-class Negro leadership" or to "such leaders as Father Divine, Prophet Jones, etc." He has concentrated effort on lower-class Negroes in the urban North. Recently he began to organize in the South and sent a minister to Atlanta, Georgia, where a Temple was established about 1956. He has small "missions," under the supervision of the minister at Atlanta, in a few towns of the Deep South. Many Negroes visit the Temple of Islam because they were invited by a Muslim friend or "missionary" in the Negro community; some visit because they learned about the Muslims from the press, radio or television, but few join the Nation and remain in it. An officer in Chicago stated that although about ten per cent of visitors at meetings express the desire to join, only two per cent fulfil the requirements for membership. Another officer estimated that an average of fifty voice the desire to join at the three meetings held weekly. Of this number, he said, not more than five become registered members. For reasons

stated previously, we have no supporting data. We suppose, however, that the turnover rate of new members is very high.

Most Chicago Muslims were born in the South. The majority
of the migrants probably did not complete elementary school, and
very few completed high school. Some were illiterate, and most had
no skills for industrial occupations in the Northern cities. Many
came North seeking "a way out" of their miseries in the South.
Subsequent experience taught most that the Northern city was far
from being the "promised land": because they lacked education
and skills, their employment and cultural opportunities were limited. They found that discrimination in jobs and housing in the
North, just as in the South, is sanctioned by custom. These migrants
were strangers not only to the white society but also to the urbanized
Negro community. The established Negro residents resent them because of fear that the "ignorant" migrants would inundate their
neighborhoods. They fear that the newcomers' rustic ways would
impede the "advancement of the race," check the "gains" which
they have already made in race relations, and impair their acceptance by whites. They are ashamed of the newcomers — aptly described by a Negro reporter as the "unwanted from Dixie."

Muslims born in the North are a little better educated than those
born in the South. Many attended high school but few completed.
Few attended college for more than a semester or more. College
graduates number less than ten in the Nation as a whole, although
the Muslims claim that there are five physicians in the movement.
There are two college graduates among Chicago's registered Muslims; both are graduates of southern Negro liberal arts colleges.
There are a few who completed one or two years of college or are
currently enrolled in colleges.

The vast majority of those who visit the Temple of Islam are the
"unwanted from Dixie"* who, because of their social background
and racial origin, are in the Negro ghettos of the northern cities. In
these ghettos, the community's "mood" is uninspiring; enduring
friendships are rare; opportunities for moral deterioration and
self-debasement are abundant, and only the upwardly mobile, en-

---

* Johnnie A. Moore, *Chicago Defender*, January 23, 1960, pp. 1, 2.

dowed with character, determination, and capacity for self-improvement, seek to escape from the general indifference of the Negro community or from the "facts of being black" in a hostile white environment. Unemployment, broken homes, and sickness are their common experience. Bitterness, frustration, and disillusionment are the constant ingredients of their daily lives. Most are compelled by their feeling of social estrangement and cultural alienation to seek escapist remedies for their problems, to gambling, alcoholism, dope, and crime. Some end up in jail. Others turn to fortune-tellers, to "spiritual" remedies; not a few join a nationalist organization and some join the Nation of Islam. All engage in a continuous search for some way out of their present miseries.[1] They take different routes, most of which, however, lead to further misery, frustrations, and moral degeneration. Few lead to self-enhancement and to moral regeneration. The Nation of Islam is one of these routes for lower-class Negroes who seek to enhance themselves. The Nation points a way out for those who have the capacity and motivation for developing character through self-discipline, hard-work, and individual sense of responsibility.

ELIGIBILITY

Theoretically, black people — and all red, yellow, or brown peoples — are eligible for membership in the Nation of Islam. In practice, however, only American Negroes are members. Students from the Middle East have sought to attend Temple meetings but were excluded. Mr. Jalil Jawad, a student from Iraq, relates that three years ago he and Hussair Ali Al-Salih (both Moslems) went to the Chicago Temple and were denied admission in spite of the fact that they showed their identification cards as proof that they were from Moslem countries. They were told by the guards that the Temple was being cleaned that night. The visitors wondered "if the guards thought that we were drunkards." The guards "almost physically prevented us from entering the Temple." They left. Three months later, according to this informant, Dr. Jawad Maurib

1. These impressions on the background of the Muslims in Chicago were formed as a result of the writer's extensive association and conversations with members.

and his American white wife visited the Temple and were also refused admission. They were told that if they should leave their
addresses, they would receive communication from the minister.
No communication was received. This informant was rather
shocked that "a brother Moslem would be discriminated against
because of his race" and stated that "even the Caliph is an equal
to any Moslem at the Mosque." Moreover, "the Mosque is open
twenty-four hours a day and nobody going to worship would ever
be accosted by anyone."

An officer of the Temple explains that their exclusion has nothing
to do with race but that it is done because "they are already familiar with Islam" and followers of Muhammad are at this time "mere
babies in Islam." The Messenger recognizes his Brother Moslems
from the East and many have dined with him at his home. However,
he feels that some of the Eastern Moslems residing in this country
have forsaken the teachings of Islam:

> Here we might add that Mr. Muhammad doesn't think too much of some
> of the Eastern Moslems anyway, particularly those residing in this country
> where, he claims, "their contact with a strange civilization has turned them
> into hypocrites of the worst type." The fact that Moslem grocers in Iowa,
> Ohio, California and Michigan handle liquors and pork products and nearly
> all Moslem diplomats at the United Nations and in Washington, D.C., New
> York and San Francisco freely indulge in drinking greatly disturbs him.
> The "behaviour" of many Moslem students in America doesn't impress him
> either.[2]

As a result of this misunderstanding, Mr. Naeem notes:

> A few of the Moslem groups in the United States have alleged, in letters
> to a prominent Moslem leader abroad, that Mr. Elijah Muhammad's follow-
> ers "aren't taught to perform their daily prayers." Mr. Muhammad em-
> phatically denies this, saying that "the day is nearing when you will see
> them climbing to the top of minarets, proclaiming the Glory of Allah, and
> flocking to the mosques as good Moslems do in Saudi Arabia, Iraq, Morocco
> and Pakistan. . . ."[3]

American Negroes who indicate their desire to "reunite" with
their "own kind" and are prepared to "submit totally to the will
of Allah" and to Muhammad are readily accepted. The theory of

2. Naeem, *Moslem World*, Oct., Nov., Dec., 1956, p. 9.
3. *Ibid.*, p. 9.

"reuniting" is that Negroes have always been Muslims, although because of the many years of slavery in the United States they have lost this knowledge. For them, therefore, the act of becoming a Muslim is not an act of conversion but a "reconversion" to the religion of their forefathers and a return to their Nation.

TECHNIQUES OF RECRUITMENT

An officer told the writer that there was a time when Muhammad promised to give a dollar to each Negro who would come to hear him. It is not unusual that unemployed persons are enticed to attend a meeting by promises of a job or assistance of some sort. Some may even be treated to a free meal at the Temple's restaurant. However, Muhammad discourages direct enticements of this sort although he "is always ready to assist the needy." Prospective members may even be invited to dinner at the Messenger's home, an honor which overwhelms the unsophisticated.

It is the duty of each Muslim to invite the "so-called Negroes" to Temple meetings. An organized effort is made to "keep the dead before the Messenger," that is, to confront non-Muslims (Negroes) continuously with the teachings of Muhammad. One such effort to bring Negroes to meetings is known as "Group Fishing." Generally, it involves teams of followers going to lower-class neighborhoods in the cities to interest Negroes in attending meetings "rather than spending time in the tavern." A nineteen-year-old follower described how he came to know about Islam through a Brother and how he went "fishing":

I first heard the teachings from Brother — who was working with me at the same job. He told me about what the Messenger was doing for the so-called Negroes. I heard the teachings. I could not ignore it and I had to become part of it. The Brother who told me is a patient man and strong believer in the Messenger. I would say the Brother literally picked on me. I went to the Temple of Islam and accepted Islam the first five minutes I was there and in two weeks I was accepted by the Nation. My first impression at the Temple was to go out and get every Negro man, woman and child and to put them right in the Temple of Islam as quickly as possible. I feel the same way now whenever I go out fishing on 47th and 63rd Streets. We see a man. He is drunk. We tell him to come to the Temple. He tells us what he wants is a bottle. He tells us he has no time, and I say to myself, for all I know, he has too much time. I feel like taking the dead on my shoulders. But I can't force him. He should be at the Temple of Islam.[4]

A department of public relations was added recently to the organization of the Chicago Temple. It is headed by Brother Charles X Betha. For purposes of establishing wide contact in the Negro communities, neither the Chicago department nor the recently created National Secretary's office has developed an extensive program. However, both seek to establish contact with Negroes. In Chicago, in groups of two or three, the Muslims attend public events and rallies involving Negroes.[5] There they sell Negro newspapers which carry Muhammad's writings and speak to the buyers about Islam, and especially about Muhammad's economic programs. In addition, small groups visit Negro churches on Sundays. After the service they mingle freely with the members and suggest to them that they attend Temple meetings later that afternoon.[6] This approach seems to be effective. In this way groups of churchgoers, especially those from "storefront" churches, and sometimes their ministers have been persuaded to visit the Temple of Islam and hear the teaching.

Although the Muslims do not sing or use any kind of music at

4. Interview.

5. The writer met the Muslims at a number of public events in Chicago — "African Freedom Day" sponsored by the Afro-American Heritage Association, and at a rally resulting from the lynching of Mack Parker, sponsored by the Negro Voters' League (both events held at the Packing House Union Building).

6. The writer also met Muslims at Quinn Chapel, an all-Negro church, on Sunday, June 21, 1959, when Congressman Adam Clayton Powell was the principal speaker. The following incident was related to the writer by Miss Lillian Jenkins, then a graduate student at the University of Chicago: Miss Jenkins had attended an interracial church in Chicago. While the congregation is now predominantly Negro, white attendance is good. A group of Muslims came before the service and asked the minister in charge, who is white, to allow them to make an announcement after service. The minister agreed and did not bother to ask what the subject of the announcement was. At the proper time, one of the Muslims went over to the speaker's stand and told the congregation of Mr. Muhammad's plans for the Negroes and invited them to come to the afternoon meeting at the Temple. Miss Jenkins reported that after the minister had heard the announcement, he was "embarrassed, dumbfounded" and the "interracial congregation showed great displeasure toward him." The minister tendered an apology, explained that he had not known what would be announced, and commented that he did not think members of his congregation should attend the meeting because "that man is down there teaching race hatred." In Boston a Negro lady reported a similar incident in her church and stated that "the Muslims were very very rude to the minister when they were ordered not to distribute their literature in the church and to leave."

religious meetings, Minister Louis X of Boston Temple, a former popular entertainer, recently made a record entitled "A Moslem Sings: A White Man's Heaven Is A Black Man's Hell." The lyric is a synopsis of Muhammad's teachings. Minister Louis X is accompanied by piano, guitar, and bass. The rhythm is similar to a subdued West Indian calypso. This record is played in a juke box at the New York Temple's restaurant in Harlem. The Chicago Temple has not adopted this practice although it seems likely that this may become a generally accepted recruiting technique. Minister Louis is young, light-complexioned, handsome, and his delightful voice has a special appeal for young women. It is no wonder that he has made several appearances at Muslim rallies in New York and at Temples in the New England states.

Motion pictures portraying business and educational activities of the Muslims and the Messenger's visit to Africa and the Middle East are used for attracting new members. The writer has watched two such films, one on Muslim activities and the other on Minister Malcolm's visit to Africa and the Middle East. Nearly 500 persons, Muslims and non-Muslims, were present. Muhammad watched the films as Malcolm X narrated the highlight of his tour. The technique of his appeal emphasized business activities and the Negroes' connection with Africa:

> We said, we would take you to Africa, but before that we must show you the Africans who have been right here in America for the last 400 years. Let me add, this (pointing to Mr. Muhammad) is the man who made us African-minded. The man who taught us that we have a home, if we can't get one here, where we can return.[7]

While commenting on the film showing Muslims at work in their various business establishments, Minister Malcolm introduced a shoe-shiner whom he described as "an expert leatherologist" and emphasized that he is employed at the barber shop, even though he is not a Muslim. The motion picture on this trip deserves some comment because it reveals the kinds of appeal they make in their recruitment efforts.

First, Minister Malcolm concentrated on two Egyptian cities —

7. From the writer's notes.

Alexandria and Cairo — and then, with a group of Muslims in Khartoum in the Sudan, visited a Muslim girls' school there. In both Egyptian cities and in the Sudan, the best in housing, office buildings, etc. was portrayed. Homes and office buildings in Alexandria along the Mediterranean shores were the central attractions. Malcolm was careful, however, to refer to Alexandria or Cairo not as Egyptian cities, but as African cities — "Alexandria-Africa or Cairo-Africa." "Most homes in these cities," he told his audience, "could be yours if only you are a follower of Mr. Muhammad." These pictures of Egypt, the Sudan, or "Moslems" in general, were perhaps salutary in counteracting the deplorable extremes of Hollywood's image of Africa!

PUBLIC MEDIA

For many years Muhammad reached the public exclusively through pamphlets, which he distributed mainly at meetings. In 1956 he began to seek followers through the Negro press. Several Negro newspapers have published or continue to publish his articles — The *Pittsburgh Courier*, Los Angeles *Herald-Dispatch*, *Amsterdam News*, *Milwaukee Defender*, Chicago *New Crusader*, etc. He or his ministers have occasional access to a few small local radio stations.

He has also ventured to publish his own newspaper and magazine. The *Messenger Magazine* and the *Islamic News* are examples. Only one issue was published and both have been discontinued. The *Magazine* was launched in April, 1959. It was to be a quarterly publication. The only issue of the *Islamic News* was published on July 6, 1959. *Mr. Muhammad Speaks: A Militant Monthly Dedicated to Justice For the Black Man* was started in May, 1960, and several issues have since been published. In addition, two pocket-sized magazines were published. One, *Mr. Muhammad Speaks To The Black Man*, "the only publication that says things others dare not mention," edited by Dan Burley, was published in June, 1960. Only one issue has been produced so far. The writer was told that nearly 50,000 copies of the first issue were printed. It sold for

15 cents a copy. Sales were high, but it is doubtful that more than 30,000 copies were sold. *Salaam*, a monthly magazine "with a slick format like Coronet and Pageant," edited by Masco Young, a nationally known Negro newspaper writer, is the latest of Muhammad's publishing ventures. This publication is financed by the Pittsburgh and Philadelphia Temples. The first issue, published in July, 1960, dealt exclusively with Muslim activities. It sells for 20 cents a copy.

The content of his appeal through these media is substantially religious. This was especially true of all his writings in the *Pittsburgh Courier*, in which only occasionally and almost in passing he took notice of social and economic problems. He deals with social and economic problems in the *Herald-Dispatch*, a Los Angeles paper. His critique of Negro social life is ably represented by one of his followers, Randolph Sidle, whose column, "Our Way of Life," appears regularly in the *Herald-Dispatch*. However, there has been a marked shift in Mr. Muhammad's public appeal since March, 1960. His articles in the *New Crusader* reflect this change of approach. There is some religion, but it is considerably "toned down." Little or no reference is made to white people as "devils." His effort since the last annual convention reflects his sensitivity to accusations that he "teaches hate." The "hate-white" image of the movement has been a powerful handicap in his effort to recruit Negroes. He is trying to change this and other "unattractive" images of the movement. Masco Young, editor of *Salaam*, wrote recently:

Question: Does Mr. Muhammad teach "white hate" and "black supremacy?" Answer: Mr. Muhammad teaches that all black men should be proud of their African heritage — not ashamed to be black. Other racial and religious groups, such as the Jews, Italians, Irish and Catholics, are strongly proud of their cultural heritage and are constantly doing things to perpetuate it. So why is it wrong for the black people to be proud of theirs?

* * *

Question: Does Mr. Muhammad absolutely refuse to grant an interview or an audience with a white person — say, for example, a newspaperman? Answer: This is not true. Mr. Muhammad has said very very sincerely that he will willingly grant an interview to any white man who is willing to tell or write the truth about him or his Nation of Islam.[8]

8. *New Crusader*, July 2, 1960, pp. 1–2.

Personal contact still appears to be the most effective way by which Muslims gain converts. Muslims concentrate their efforts first on their relatives. This was illustrated by the response to our question: How did you first come to know of Islam? Thirty Muslims responded. Twenty-nine said that they heard about Islam through relatives. Only one, a former prostitute, said that a Muslim Brother "saw me walking the street, explained Islam to me, and invited me to attend a meeting that night."[9] The extent to which Muslims are able to influence other Negroes depends on their conduct and behavior, and on an appearance of well-being. However, the Muslims have not always been very effective in either presenting themselves or the teachings of Muhammad to a prospective convert. Because of their lack of education and finesse, they fare rather badly with educated Negroes.

The collective effort of the F.O.I. members ("Group Fishing") brings large numbers of working-class Negroes to hear the teaching of Mr. Muhammad. During the May visit to Washington, D.C., an observer reported that Muhammad's followers were so effective in handing out leaflets about the meeting that nearly four thousand people (non-Muslims) attended. This observer added that the Negro press in the area did not consider the visit "newsworthy and were caught unprepared by an influx of people who came to hear him."[10]

Only a few members are recruited through personal correspondence with the Messenger. These live in areas where their number does not justify the organization of a Temple. Muhammad teaches them by correspondence. In addition, a few members are converted while in prison. The Messenger maintains contact with Negro prisoners who have heard his teachings and have expressed a desire to join the Nation. He sends (as previously indicated) money and lessons to them and advises them. Below is a form letter which the prisoners receive after they have made their intention known to the Messenger:

"As-Salaam-Alaikum:

In the Name of Allah, the Beneficent, the Merciful; Master of the Day of Judgment.

9. Interview. The figure includes persons who answered only some of our questions.
10. Evelyn O. Chisely, in a communication with the writer.

Dear Brother:

Your letter of   has been received and I was very happy to hear from you. I am happy to know that you desire to join onto your own Holy Nation of Islam.

We have recorded your name in the "Book of Life," as a Believer. The following are the five fundamental Principles of Islam:

(1) A belief in the One God Whose proper Name is Allah.

(2) Believe in His Prophets.

(3) Believe in His Scriptures.

(4) Believe in the Resurrection.

(5) Believe in the Judgment Day.

Enclosed is one of our small Muslim Daily Prayer Books. Learn the prayers by heart and pray five times daily facing the East. When you are free, you will be able to attend the Temple of Islam and be qualified as a Believer.

May the peace and blessings of Allah be upon you.

> As-Salaam-Alaikum: (peace be unto you)
> Your brother
>
> Elijah Muhammad
> Messenger of Allah

More than four hundred prisoners were "converted" to Islam in 1958.[11]

PROSELYTIZING RHETORIC

The proselytizing rhetoric of the Nation of Islam deserves some observation, first because it serves as a means of attracting Negroes to the movement, and second because it conceals the real significance of the movement for both its leaders and followers. Third, although the rhetoric serves as a means of recruitment, it is also one of its major limitations.

The rhetoric presents the Nation simultaneously as "religion" and as "nationalism." Both have an appeal for lower-class Negroes in search of identity and status in the existing society. Muhammad understands the religious susceptibilities and the superstitious mentality of lower-class Negroes. He understands also the latent black chauvinism born of the degradation of the Negro masses. Their religious susceptibilities, superstitious mentality, frustrations, hopes, and aspirations are all exploited in the proselytizing rhetoric. Con-

11. Report by Minister James 3X at the 1959 Annual Convention. This represents the total for the Nation as a whole. See "Muslim Negroes Suing the State" by Lawrence O'Kane, *New York Times*, March 19, 1961, pp. 1, 46.

cealed in this rhetoric, however, is the appeal of the movement for upwardly mobile lower-class Negroes who have the capacity for self-improvement, materially and morally. This, as we have seen already, is the major attraction and constitutes the importance of the movement to most of his followers.

There are two levels of appeal in the rhetoric; internal and external. Internal appeal, discussed later, is directed primarily toward the Muslims. The primary object is to assist them in their effort to improve themselves; to help in building the movement by maintaining solidarity and loyalty to it and also to reinforce beliefs, morale, and enthusiasm among the members. External appeal is aimed first at persuading non-Muslims that the solution to their problems lies in Islam; second, that they should unite with Muhammad for the nationalistic goals which he has proclaimed; third, that they should take cues from what he and his followers are doing, even if they do not accept his leadership.

There appears to be neither consistency nor restraint in this rhetoric. Whatever appeals to Negroes is exploited so long as it helps to attract them. In fact, this is illustrated by Minister Wallace's instructions to other ministers asking them "not to play up religion" to their audiences. He actually asked them to tell their audiences that "religion is not important" and that they should stress in their lectures the concrete activities of the Messenger.[12] The same deemphasis on religion in favor of appealing to Negroes on the basis of "bread and butter" was revealed in an interview with a prominent Muslim minister:

There is something which just doesn't reach the Negro community. You know, our people have had enough spiritualism from Christianity. Our emphasis has been religion, and this wouldn't appeal to them partly because they are ignorant, and partly because of the discipline in Islam — the worldly things they have to forego, smoking, drinking, loose habits, etc. I believe therefore, that the concrete work of the Messenger should be portrayed. The people are concerned with material things. You can see it in New York. All the nationalists — Lawson of the United African Nationalists Movement, Carlos Cooks of the African Nationalist Pioneer Movement — in Harlem preach materialism. Our people want to improve their shelter, food and

12. "Condensed Outline" (typed), undated. Under ". . . Welcome Address" Minister Wallace's instruction reads "State Religion not important; but we are all same color."

clothing and we should gear our propaganda to that. Carlos and Lawson
and other nationalists get over the teaching to the masses but they lack organization.[13]

Negro visitors to Temple meetings are treated to a long session
during which the minister outlines the doctrines of Muhammad,
the injustices which black men suffer in America, the failure of
Christianity in remedying their ills, and the wickedness of the white
rulers. Above all, they are assured that Muhammad is a "fearless"
and "courageous" black man, "who exemplifies the longings and
aspirations of every intelligent Black Man and Woman in America":

. . . If Allah bless us with his presence this afternoon you will see a man
who exemplifies the longings and aspirations of every intelligent Black Man
and Woman in America. You will see a real, capable Leader who understands the needs of the so-called Negroes and how to achieve them. You
won't see anything freakish about this man and his program for his people.
The so-called Negroes will never be anything if they continue to place their
hopes in the likes of freaks with a lot of mumbo jumbo. Our problems here
in America are real and we must be realistic in going about to solve them.
We must wake up and see that such leaders as Father Divine, Daddy Grace
(deceased), Prophet Jones and the likes are a big joke and cannot get the
so-called Negro anything but the ridiculous before the eyes of the civilized
world.[14]

Visitors listen to "success" stories of "Brother or Sister X or Y
who has opened a restaurant, a barber shop or a small business enterprise." The entrepreneurial initiative of such persons is said to
be the result of the teachings of Muhammad. Stories such as the
following are likely to impress some visitors:

Many of our people (who are) without goals or achievements, on hearing
the Message of Messenger Muhammad attain great heights such as Bro.
Curtis X of New York who before hearing Messenger Muhammad was employed as a mechanic on the streets but who now has his own five-story
garage storing over 120 cars, with 5 service and towing trucks, employing
people, exclusive AAA Service in upper Manhattan, secured his own de-
tached home, became a two-car family, and father of four girls and a boy.[15]

Others who seek good health or relief from worries are told:

13. Interview.
14. Lecture by a Minister (typed), p. 1.
15. "Condensed Outline," p. 3. Compare the impression of a New York school
teacher, non-Muslim, who visited the New York Temple: "What impressed me is that
they do seem to be financially successful and success is always impressive. . . ." Miss
Ruby Maloney, in a communication with the writer.

And many people suffering from continuing headaches, allergies, over-weight, under nourishment, ulcers, fevers, constipation, food poisoning, acid-ash, indigestion and other illness have been greatly relieved or cured by practicing healthful life giving diet prescribed by Messenger Muhammad. Many of the food habits taught by Messenger Muhammad are now being put into practice by the Medical doctors of today such as weight control, values of food and their effect. The list of those who have benefitted from His Healthful eating habits is numerous for it includes each one of us.

Mr. Muhammad has saved many of our people from being victims of Spiritual advisors who offer non-helpful advice for pay, home cure doctors, luck sellers, charm sellers, dream interpreters, symbols readers, number givers, number writers, love solvers, success finders, one world friend finders, Pennsylvania Dutch Hex signs seller, Horoscope readers, prayer candle sellers and readers . . . spiritual blessing sellers, just arrived from Mars sellers, Special blessing sellers, Extra special blessing sellers, twig branch, stump and root sellers, clay from the Delta swamp curers, water from Alaska cure all, and the dirt from my back yard will get you money sellers. All these $2.98 specialists, Muhammad exposed as being blood suckers on our poor people.[16]

Conversions of "prominent" persons to Islam assures visitors and members of the worthiness of the Muslims' cause:

Many musicians and fighters have come into the Temples. Fighters such as Henry "Toothpick" Brown, Paul 4X who was known as "Mike Jacobs." Musicians such as James Moody, Sonny Stitt, trumpeter Adam D. Rice, The Calypso Kid, Louis Walcott, Raymond Orr.

Similarly, the conversion of two Negro physicians into the movement was widely publicized:

Typical of the Negro professionals who are turning to the teachings of The Honorable Elijah Muhammad are Doctors Leo X McCollum of Newark, New Jersey and Boyce E. Jenkins of St. Louis, Mo. . . .

Asked why he turned to Islam, Dr. Jenkins (formerly president of the Greenville, Mississippi branch of the NAACP) said, "I saw the light and in Mr. Muhammad I found a man who was doing something for his people."[17]

The conversion of a few preachers who were not particularly "prominent" is often used as a means of attracting those who may have reservations about the Muslim religion:

16. *Ibid.*, pp. 4–5.

17. *Mr. Muhammad Speaks*, New York, July 1960, I, 2, p. 6. Detailed accounts of both physicians and a photograph of one were printed. Dr. McCollum is reported as the captain of the Fruits of Islam at Temple No. 25, Newark, New Jersey. His wife, Sister Edwina, described as a former secretary at the Treasury Department's Internal Revenue Service, is the Temple's Secretary.

Many preachers have come to Messenger Muhammad with their problems which he solved for them. We have many preachers among us who have come into Islam, Min. Lucius X of Temple No. 4, Washington, D. C. was formerly a Seventh Day Adventist Minister and Presiding Elder of the Church, Rev. L. Davis, in Los Angeles who turned his entire church over to the teaching of Islam this year. The Minister in San Francisco . . . is a former Bible Scholar. The Baptist Minister in Richmond, Virginia turned over his church this summer and it is now Temple No. 24. And recently in nearby Trenton, Rev. R. Hall of Holy Cross Church invited a speaker in from the Temple of Islam and on hearing Islam closed their Church and advised their members to attend the Temple of Islam. R. Hall began attending the Temple in N. Y. C(ity). Preachers and Bible scholars come every day and write that they now have a better understanding of the Bible since Messenger Muhammad started revealing the true interpretation than ever during the many years in the Ministry.[18]

Although the Muslims insist that "Garvey was one of the greatest Black Men ever to come to America," they do not want the followers to become sentimental about him. For example, they claim that Garvey's inspiration for coming to America "to tackle the world's greatest burden of awakening and uniting the so-called Negroes" came from an African Moslem:

What made Marcus Garvey so different? What changed his mind? What opened his eyes and freed his thinking power? When Mr. Garvey went to England, it was an African Moslem there who exposed him to the natural religion of the Black Man. . . the militant religion of ISLAM. This awakened him, freed him from the religious chains of the white man's christianity, and started him thinking once again like a Black Man, for the COLLECTIVE benefit of all Black Mankind.[19]

Followers are told they must not worship the dead or romanticize the accomplishments of departed leaders:

Will we never learn from the foolish mistakes of others? . . . In modern times Marcus Garvey came to America . . . to instill a Black-Nationalistic spirit into us, but most of us were too busy paying tribute to the "dead leaders" of the past, and some of us were even IGNORANTLY waiting for those "dead leaders" to return from the grave . . . and many are following a dead Garvey. . . . Mr. Garvey himself taught that a "greater than he" was coming. . . . Why must we always worship dead men? . . . all who

18. "Condensed Outline," p. 4.
19. *Mr. Muhammad Speaks*, July, 1960, pp. 3, 13.

really loved Mr. Garvey could not help but recognize, accept and follow MESSENGER ELIJAH MUHAMMAD today.[20]

The proselytizing rhetoric places the Muslims as the forerunners of the Negro's growing interest in Africa; but their interest is not an unrestrained enthusiasm. Muhammad does not want his followers to be sentimental about Africa and thus forget their problems in America. Their interest, while it is genuine, serves nevertheless as a means of attracting new members. The July issue of *Mr. Muhammad Speaks* printed six pages of news, articles, profiles, and pictures of African leaders. Minister Malcolm X was photographed talking with Mr. Kaunda, leader of the Northern Rhodesia African Nationalist movement. Like the African leaders, Muhammad was pictured as "seeking Black Nationhood." The writer's observation (confirmed by one minister) is that the Muslim leaders do not feel that they would attract many members by overemphasizing Africa because many Negroes still think of Africa as a "vast jungle." The expression, "Asiatic blacks," the writer was told, is more "neutral" and does not evoke the feeling of shame which the word "Africa" does among Negroes.

DILEMMAS OF THE RHETORIC

Apart from the general lack of motivation among the Negro masses in "getting ahead" by their own effort and the formidable rigors of self-discipline and sacrifice which Muhammad demands from his followers, the proselytizing rhetoric is a powerful limitation on the Nation's ability to attract a mass following. We shall mention only a few of these limitations. The rhetoric creates a public image of the Nation which is at variance with the concrete, visible, and perfectly sensible activities of the Muslims. This incongruity produces intellectual dilemmas for potential followers. Thus, only Negroes who can disentangle in some measure the concrete activities of the Nation from the rhetoric are likely to join and remain in the movement. For instance, Negroes who seek the "old-time religion" cannot find a satisfactory substitute in the Nation. Those who

20. *Ibid.*, p. 5.

seek "genuine" Islam, i.e., religion divorced from nationalism, will not find a clear-cut distinction in the Nation. Others who seek assurances of their racial identity (unbelievable as this may sound) will not find it in the rhetoric of the Nation of Islam. Such persons are baffled and confounded by Muhammad's insistence that they are "Asiatics" or "Muslims." Many who had once thought or were taught that their ancestors were brought from Africa to America are thoroughly confused. Several Negroes who had heard the teachings of Muhammad asked the writer quite sincerely: "Are we really Asiatics? Are we Muslims? Or did our forebears come from Africa?" A Negro girl, about 21 years old, told the writer that after she had heard Muhammad's teaching she was no longer able to say what "race" she belonged to! She said that she had been used "to thinking that I am a Negro; now I am confused. I don't know what I am." Some of Muhammad's followers raised the same questions but were usually constrained in trying to find an answer.

Muhammad's emphasis on the prehistoric Black Nation or the transcendentally placed Kingdom of Paradise seems utterly ridiculous to most Negroes. They ask: "Where is it located? Is it in Africa, the Middle East or in Asia?" In any case, most Negroes disapprove using the word "black" or "dark brown" to describe themselves. In fact, they take pride in distinguishing themselves as "brown, light brown, low yellow, medium yellow, yellow, high yellow," *ad infinitum*. They hate and despise their black-ness. A great many still do not wish to be associated with Africa. They consider it "degrading." Muhammad tries to circumvent the Negroes' aversion to Africa by asserting that they are Asiatics, of whom Africans form only a part.

Negroes who have always had some attachment for Africa or are now "reclaiming" their African ancestry are openly anti-Muhammad. A Negro visitor at one of Muhammad's meetings noted some of these conflicting images of the Nation:

In addition to what information I have, these people regard Mr. Muhammad as a prophet. However, it would seem that they look to him as a nationalist leader rather than one who has contributed a new religious insight. They do manifest brotherliness and warmth. There appear to be marked differences between them and traditional Moslems. It appears to me that in embracing Islam they are attempting through religion to give the black man a sense of a past as well as a destiny that would transcend temporal economic and historical developments. In this way, their organization has gone beyond Garveyism, which was strictly a rational economic and nationalist program. Bearing in mind that I do not have sufficient knowledge of their teachings, it would seem to me to be somewhat of a noble lie. It seems like a far-fetched way to give the American black people a sense of identity. Historically, what do we have to do with Islam? . . . When they discuss economic and social matters, I am very much in sympathy with what they say. . . . [21]

However, the Muslims seem to believe that their recruitment effort is impeded by "Uncle-Tom leaders, Negro preachers, fear of the slavemaster, ignorance of the black man's heritage, love of the frivolous, fear of losing jobs, and the love of Jesus." As Brother Herbert Hazziezz said, "Negroes are not ready to pursue a decent and moral life. They are not ready for civilized life. They don't feel responsible and they enjoy their irresponsibility. They think white. They desire to be white; made to hate black. Islam teaches us to be ourselves; to love ourselves, our brothers and sisters; to act for ourselves; stop being liars, being afraid; stop being the laughing stock of the world; to become men among men, women among women; stop being boys and girls all our lives."[22]

One Muslim explained that Negroes think that followers of Muhammad are not educated. She spoke of her sister who is a high school graduate but who would have nothing to do with the "uneducated" Muslims:

My sister doesn't like uneducated people. She is ashamed of the Muslims because she thinks that we are not educated. She thinks that only ignorant people come to the Temple, and especially, migrants from the South. . . She tells me she finds socializing with uneducated people difficult but she cannot find educated ones to socialize with. Her life is sort of sad. She can't be with the educated and can't socialize with the uneducated![23]

Thus the rhetoric powerfully limits the ability of the Nation to enlarge its membership. Negroes are conformists, not to any comprehensive social or political values, but to the material necessities of survival even if this means further degradation and debasement. The rhetoric is entirely too threatening to many.

21. Ruby E. Maloney, In a communication with the writer.
22. Interview.
23. Interview. Name withheld.

INITIATION INTO THE NATION

The first step in becoming a member is attending a meeting at a Temple of Islam. After the teaching, the presiding minister says: "How many believe what they have heard to be true? Hold up your hands." After that they are asked to "come forward" if they believe what they have heard and wish to reunite with their "own kind," in this "great cause." Those who indicate acceptance go forward to shake the hand of the Minister or the Messenger, who says to each: "You are not a Negro from this day on. You are now a Muslim, a member of the Black Nation with Brothers (Sisters) throughout the world. You are now free."

They are directed to register with one of the secretaries. The men go to the F.O.I. secretary and the women to the M.G.T.–G.C.C. secretary. After attending at least two or three meetings, the prospective member receives the following letter:

THE SUPREME WISDOM
By Allah to we the

Lost-Found Nation of Islam	ISLAM-JUSTICE,	The Problem:
in the Wilderness of	FREEDOM	Allah has declared
North America	EQUALITY	that we must return
Can you qualify?		To our Native Land
You Can		and People or be
Get on to your Own Kind		destroyed
	As-Salaam-Alaikum	

In the Name of Almighty Allah, the Beneficent, the Most Merciful, Sole Master of the Day of Judgment; and in the Name of His Divine Messenger, The Most Honorable Elijah Muhammad

Dear _____

The Nation of Islam is very happy over your return to your Own Holy Nation. We desire to inform you that you are no longer a slave, but Free, Independent, Asiatic Muslim with Allah, and a billion of brothers and sisters on your side as friends.

Please report to the office of the Temple, Sunday for instructions and lessons.

May Allah bless you.

As-Salaam-Alaikum
(signed by the secretary)

The prospective member, upon reporting at a Temple, is given a letter of application to copy exactly in long hand and return to the Temple. The letter follows:

> (Applicant's) Address
> City and State
> Date

Mr. W. F. Muhammad
4847 S. Woodlawn Ave.
Chicago 15, Illinois

Dear Saviour Allah, Our Deliverer:

I have attended the Teachings of Islam, two or three times, as taught by one of your ministers, I believe in it. I bear witness that there is no God but Thee. And, that Muhammad is Thy Servant and Apostle. I desire to reclaim my Own. Please give me my Original name. My slave name is as follows:

Those applicants who are able to copy this letter accurately then proceed to receive lessons and instructions for membership. However, some members have difficulty doing so themselves and must, if they wish to become members, learn how to write. If those who can write make mistakes, the letter is corrected in red pencil and returned to them. Some applicants are able to complete this step within a short time and are then admitted to the instructions.

A few applicants are known to have waited for more than two years before they were able to produce their letters without mistakes. One applicant's letter was returned because he spelled the word Saviour according to the American spelling, Savior, and for lower-casing the O in Own. However, his letter was accepted the following week, after he had submitted an accurate copy.

Initiation of new members is aimed at facilitating their withdrawal from society, re-orienting their values, and maintaining discipline, cohesion, loyalty, and enthusiasm in the movement. The first step at withdrawal and emotional detachment from the "normal" society and the individual's beliefs about his past is the neophyte's negation of his "Negro-ness," i.e., all the stereotypes associated with Negroes. He is taught to believe that his nationality is "Muslim" or "Asiatic." He is made to change his name — a process of disassociating himself from the manipulated image of the Negro. He is taught to submit himself totally to the will of Allah and Muhammad. Withdrawal is facilitated by lessons which are intended to give him new perspectives and values. This continues long after the individual has become a registered Muslim.

Once the initial letter has been accepted, the believer begins to attend open meetings and receives lessons which he studies and on which he is examined. These lessons are committed to memory. We may note that memorization is part of the process of un-doing the "tricknowledgy" which they had learned in the Caucasian world. Lessons based on "Actual Facts," the Koran, *The Supreme Wisdom* (Muhammad's doctrines), and practices of Islam are offered. A record of the progress of each member is kept and students are rated in such things as cleanliness, conduct, co-operation, effort, and reliability. Lessons are offered to others in penmanship, reading and spelling, languages and general civilization, astronomy, chronological history from 13,000 B.C., solar system, spook being displayed for 6,000 years, chronology, ending of the spook civilization. More ambitious members may take courses in Arabic, arithmetic and the metric system, algebra, general geometry, and trigonometry. A candidate who fails in any subject may present himself as many times as he desires for re-examination. However, no candidate may proceed to any subsequent lessons until he has passed examinations based on the "Actual Facts."

Advanced students — those who have completed all the required lessons — turn to problem-solving. Members spend considerable numbers of hours among friends tackling these problems. The close relationship between the problems and the teachings is clear in the following examples, which were selected from thirty-four such problems:

13. After learning Mathematics, which is Islam, and Islam is Mathematics, it stands true, you can always prove it at no limit of time. Then you must learn to use it and secure some benefit while you are living, that is luxury, money, good income, friendship, in all walks of life. Sit yourself in Heaven at once! That is the greatest desire of your Brother and Teachers. Now you must speak the Language, so you can use your mathematical Theology in the proper terms, other-

wise you will not be successful, unless you do speak well, for she knows all about you.

The Secretary of Islam offers a reward to the best and neatest worker of this problem.

There are twenty-six letters in the Language and if a Student learns one letter per day, then how long will it take him to learn the twenty-six letters?

There are ten numbers in the Mathematic Language, then how long will it take a Student to learn the whole ten numbers (At the above rate)? The average man speaks four hundred words, considered well.

14. The University of Al-Azhar, in Cairo, has a Student population of thirty-six hundred, all but one-tenth taking other than his own Language, three-tenths taking Construction Engineering, two-tenths taking Civil Engineering, three-tenths taking Mechanical Engineering, and the rest taking Teachership.

One, one hundred and eighty-fifth of one had more than eight absent charges to their credit, so at the end of their Courses, they do not receive Diplomas.

How many were there in number that did not take other than his own Language? How many were Construction Engineers? How many were Civil Engineers? How many were Mechanical Engineers? How many were Teachers? How many were in number that did not receive Diplomas?

Upon completion of a required number of lessons, a believer who is found to meet an additional test of reliability is accepted as a registered Muslim and is given a name. The member drops his last name and any middle initials. In place of these, the Messenger of Allah assigns to him a certain number of X or some other symbol. For example, Charlie Cotton may become Charlie X, Brown Roundtree may become Brown 5X and so forth. Others may still be known as James W. The names which individuals bore before becoming registered Muslims are said to be "slave names," which were given by the Caucasian devils or by the slavemasters. It is important for a member to change his name as a step toward the declaration of his full independence. Commenting on the change of names, Minister James observed at a Temple lecture:

Many Negroes protest against the teachings of Mr. Muhammad. They claim that they have had other teachings from among their own people. They ask, "What about old Reverend Roundtree?" Well, Rev. Roundtree doesn't even know who he is, because he's learned all he knows from the white man. He even bears the name of some white man who owned his grandfather. This is the trouble with the Negroes — they don't know who they are and since they only learn from their own enemies, they can only teach what the enemy has taught them. We still have names like Anderson, Robinson, Culpepper, and these are white man's names. Negroes who go to college just get taught what the white man wants them to know. They go into college named Culpepper and they come out still named Culpepper. They don't even know who they are.[24]

Many Muslim parents continue to give their children the "slave-master's names" as their first names; others assign to them "Muslim" names which may be Arabic or, exceptionally, non-Arabic African names.[25] Early in the movement initiates were required to pay ten dollars before they were given their "Original" names but this practice appears to have been discontinued.[26] Few Muslims have been able to obtain their "real" names in place of "devil's" first names. In fact, very high-ranking officers of the Temple in Chicago who have been in the Nation for more than twenty years have not as yet obtained their "real" names. Minister James 3X has been in the Nation since 1940 and until now has not received his Muslim surname. His Muslim last name is "Shabbazz." The surname is supposed to have been given by Allah Himself. Many followers are proud that they have at least dropped part of the slavemaster's names and hope that some day Allah will bestow upon them their real names. Brother Karriem Allah, whose names are all "Muslim," told the writer, "receiving my Holy names was the second most important thing that ever happened in my life.[27] In any case, the Mus-

24. It is interesting to note a similar situation among African nationalists. Most of them were brought up as Christians and at baptism were invariably given what the missionaries considered "Christian" names as part of initiation into Christianity. Many of these people have dropped the European or biblical names completely. Examples include such persons as the President of Ghana, Dr. Kwame Nkrumah, and Dr. Nnamdi Azikiwe, Governor-General of the Federation of Nigeria. Minister Malcolm X once asked a white university professor of sociology: Have you ever known a white man answering to the name Kasavubu? The professor told the writer that this had never occurred to him.

25. It is quite possible that members would be as happy to give non-Arabic African names to their children but most of them have never had any contacts with Africans. In the course of the study one member named his newly-born son "Essien," which is a West African name.

26. Benyon, op. cit., p. 901. Members deny that fees are charged for this.

27. "I wouldn't give up my righteous name. That name is my life." Ibid., p. 902. They are ashamed of their old names and consider it an insult to be addressed by the slave names. During interviews with members they frequently asked, "Do you want to know my slave name?"

lims are happy that their names have been recorded in the "Book of Life," which is kept by the Messenger.

Occasionally, teachers at the University of Islam have had difficulties in identifying students because of a slight mistake in recording the number of "X's" in the record of a student who bears the same first name as other students. The majority of the Muslims use their old "devil's" names in their business relations. Many use X as the middle initial. Those who have received full "Muslim" names drop their previous names completely. The writer knows of only one instance in which a Muslim tried to change his name legally.[28]

An African who sought membership in the Nation was informed that it was not necessary for him to receive a new name because he had no "slave" name. He was not required to pay any admission fee. Although he could attend Temple meetings, he was not required to undergo the training which is offered to all initiates. He was recognized as a "Brother Muslim" or "believer," as contrasted with a registered Muslim.[29]

The instructions given to Muslims include hints about things which are supposed to be good for their health and welfare. For instance, every Muslim is given an eighteen-page mimeographed diet which he is supposed to follow. The following is a list of foods which Muslims may or not eat:

Some of the Foods We Eat and Do Not Eat [30]

Some We do Eat	Foods We Do Not Eat
Small navy beans	Lima beans
Small pink beans	Butter beans
String beans	Black eyed peas
June beans	Green cabbage
White cabbage (not Green)	Collard greens
Cauliflower	Pinto beans

28. Ira Sidney Pulliam, Jr. and his wife, Callie, of Los Angeles, petitioned the Superior Court to change their names because of their "decision to join the Moslem religious faith." Ira wanted his name changed to Abdul Hamid Akoni and Callie asked that her legal name become Callie Cobb Akoni. The *Pittsburgh Courier*, September 26, 1959, p. 6.

29. This was not really being accepted into membership as defined by the Muslims. He was not expected to participate in activities other than meetings when he cared. He had no obligations to them and none was asked of him.

Egg plant
Okra
Carrots
Mustard greens
Turnips (white)
Spinach
Tomatoes
Celery
Lettuce
Green and hot peppers
White potatoes (be careful they
  are easy to put on weight)
Fresh corn (milk corn)
Radish
Asparagus
Whole wheat bread

Meats we do Eat

Of course no meat is good for us;
  but if we are going to eat meat
  the best is:
Lamb
Beef
Squabs (young pigeons, we eat
  chickens but they are not good
  for us).

Fish we do Eat

White fish
Trout
Bass
Salmon
Pike

Kidney beans
Brown field peas
Corn bread

Meats we do not eat

Pig (Hog – Swine) The *Hog Meat*
  is *divinely Forbidden* by
  Almighty God
Rabbit
Possum
Squirrel
Coon and any other animal of the
  family
No wild games (sic), that which
  walks, crawls, runs or flies

Fish we do Not Eat

Carp
Cat Fish
Buffalo
Eat no fish without scales weighing
  over 50 lbs.
Eat no fish that sucks its food
  (Sucker fish)
No sea food such as Lobster, Crabs,
  Oysters, Shrimp, Frogs, Clams,
  etc.

This is what the Muslims mean when they say Islam teaches them not only what to eat but also when to eat. As we have noted previously, they are supposed to eat one meal a day, the dinner meal, with the entire family present.

The duties of members may be divided into two categories, moral and material. First and foremost among moral duties is to love one another, to live in complete unity, and to share all the burdens of

30. Exact copy. The daily dietary prescription is omitted.

the Nation of Islam. The spirit of unity is demonstrated when a member comes to trial before a court. In such instances, followers of Muhammad have been known to travel to the city where the case is being tried in order "to stand by their Brothers and Sisters so that justice may be done."

Other duties are aimed at control of the conduct of members. The following "laws" were given to members in May, 1959, by the Supreme Captain, Raymond Sharrieff:

"In the name of Allah, the Beneficent, the Merciful:" Violations of these laws are subjected to 30 days to indefinite suspension from the Temple:
1. Sleeping in the Temple
2. Keeping late hours
3. Using narcotics (dope, heroin, marijuana)
4. Married and taking up time with other sisters
5. Abusing your wife
6. Socializing with Christians
7. Drinking alcoholic juices
8. Unclean homes
9. Personal hygiene
10. Watching the movements of the sisters
11. Lying and stealing from one another
12. Gambling (shooting pool, dice, cards, etc.)
13. Eating pork
14. Gossiping on one another
15. Fornication
16. Adultery
17. Disobeying your officers
18. Disrespecting Ministers and the Supreme Captain
19. Talking about your Leader and Teacher
20. Misrepresenting the teachings of Islam
21. Disrespecting the Messenger of Allah

The rules which govern the conduct of Muslim Sisters are similar. In addition, Sisters are required to wear clothes which do not expose their legs or arms. They do not wear lipstick or conspicuous cosmetics. The headtie is required for all Sisters. Dresses and colors are prescribed for boys and girls at the University of Islam. Detailed requirements of conduct are numerous.

The only sanctions available for enforcement of these rules are the sense of moral guilt, fear of incurring Allah's displeasure, the opinion of members, denial of assistance in time of need and, lastly, suspension from the Temple or expulsion from the Nation of Islam for persistent violations. Muhammad claims that the maximum period for suspension or expulsion for serious violations is seven years: "Allah told me to make this the maximum punishment for the most serious violations." Illicit sex relations are among the violations punishable by expulsion. During the period of this study a few persons were suspended for short periods of time. The stiffest penalty administered was five years. This involved persons who had pre-marital intercourse with other Muslim members. The writer interviewed a few of those who had been suspended from the Temple and found that all anxiously wished to return to the Nation. The case of Brother — is described to show how the sanctions are enforced and how individuals may react to their loss of membership.

Brother — had been in the movement for three years before he got involved sexually with a non-Muslim girl. He related his case as follows:

I have been out of the Temple for two years. I got involved sexually with a non-Muslim girl and left the Temple voluntarily. I was a good Muslim for three years before this happened. I abstained from sexual relations during that period. There was a girl in the Temple I wanted to marry but we just couldn't get married fast enough for me; so I took up with this other girl. After being out for two years drinking, smoking, and whoring I decided there was nothing in this dead world and wanted to get back into the Temple. I went and told the Captain that I wanted to rejoin the Nation. Tuesday is the interrogation day and for four successive weeks I was interrogated by the Captain and others — both formally and informally. You know, they keep at you for a long time to see if you are telling the truth. You know, if you lie you cannot remember the same lie next week and you don't always know when you are being interrogated. You may just think that you are having a conversation with a Brother, but he is taking careful note of everything you say. After these four weeks of questioning I was brought before the entire Muslim congregation at a Wednesday night meeting, and court-martialed. The Captain acted as judge and jury. I was denounced in vigorous terms for adultery, fornication, gambling, drinking, smoking, and for breaking nearly all the laws of Islam. I was asked if I had had sex with any of the Muslim Sisters and when I truthfully denied this, the Captain said: "It's a good thing you didn't." After this period of humiliation I was asked how I pleaded to the charges. Guilty was my only plea. The Captain found me guilty and suspended me from the Temple for another year. I was placed also in "Isolation." This means that no Muslim can speak to me and I cannot attend any meeting, public or private, of the Temple. There are a few Brothers who say hello to me now, but most will turn their backs if I meet them on the street. I want more than anything to get back into the Temple. My time will be up next year and I'll go right back for life. You know I had worked my way up to being a member of Mr. Muhammad's bodyguard and felt that I was on my way to the ministership. I moved from the fifth car to Mr. Muhammad's car. I have to start it all over again. I know that once I serve my term I will be welcomed back into the Nation. I'll be eligible for consideration and I have to prove myself all over again. The Captain said to me: "Do you think that the Honorable Elijah Muhammad is joking? Do you think that he is playing games? What right have you to go risk disgracing his efforts?"

It is interesting to note that although this Brother had been suspended from the Temple, he told the writer that he has continued to send $20 every week to the Nation. Only one officer is known to have violated the sex regulation and was promptly stripped of his office and suspended from the movement.[31]

The personal comportment and politeness of the followers of Muhammad is widely appreciated in the Negro community. Even those Negroes who do not approve of other aspects of the Nation of Islam have "great respect" for the conduct and discipline of the followers in their private lives and relations with other Negroes. Many believe that Muhammad's success is to be explained by his ability to discipline his followers. The need for respectability explains, in part, the severity of punishment for infractions of rules of behavior.

There are obvious disadvantages arising from the austerity of the working class Muslims. In general, Negroes who may share Mr. Muhammad's views on the race question find it difficult to give up their "carefree" life for the promises of Islam. Consequently, while rigid discipline is an asset to the moral and social life of the members and for the solidarity of the movement, it is also a check on its expansion. There is no evidence that discipline and control are likely to be relaxed in order to increase membership.

This dilemma manifests itself, as we have seen, in the nature of the appeal Muhammad makes to potential members who agree in

31. Because such matters are guarded secrets of the movement, observers have been baffled in explaining the expulsion of an officer in recent years.

principle with some of his teachings but feel that this doctrine is "openly anti-white."

Withdrawal and alienation of Negroes from the society is achieved partly through the process of initiation and partly through constant repetition and dramatization of Muhammad's doctrines at Temple meetings. This is why attendance at meetings at least once a week is required of all members.

A new convert to the Nation is subjected to a program of memorization which prepares him for further lessons and keeps him constantly busy during the early period of conversion. In this way, he is given new and exciting directions about the world around him. He sees himself, his people, his society and the world in a new light and he is encouraged to assimilate "new" values for self-improvement. He acquires a new sense of personal worth and responsibility.[32]

32. Chapter IV describes the extent to which the Muslims have assimilated these values and how they have become the operative elements which fashion the ethos of the Muslim community.

VIII. Religious Ritual and Ceremonial Life

A BILLBOARD in front of the Chicago Temple extends a standing invitation to meetings:

> Hear The Honorable Elijah Muhammad,
> Messenger of Allah, Speak On Freedom,
> Justice and Equality for the Blackman in Islam.
> Every Sunday at 2 p.m., Wednesday and Friday, at 8 p.m.

All "so-called Negroes" are welcome, provided that they are not drunk.

There is virtually no religious ceremony or ritual at Temple meetings except the prayers said at the opening and closing of meetings and perhaps a verse or two read by the minister from the Koran or from the Bible during the course of his lecture.

The followers of Muhammad do not worship in accordance with the prescribed traditions of Eastern Moslems. Their meetings are devoted to lecturing. But it seems evident that the present form of worship has grown out of the particular conditions under which the movement started. For instance, the present Temple seating arrangement makes it possible to worship and to hear lectures at the same time without physical discomfort, whereas a true mosque has no

211

seats. Muhammad requires his followers to study the Moslem procedures for prayer and to practice them, and to say the daily prayers, five or seven as the case may be.[1]

Muslims are instructed to prepare themselves for prayer:

Washing the hands to the wrist;
Rinsing the mouth three times;
Cleansing the inside of the nose with water three times;
Washing the face three times;
Washing the arms to the elbows three times (the right arm should be washed first);
Wiping over the head with wet hands;
Wiping the ears with wet fingers;
Wiping around the neck with wet hands; and
Washing the feet (the right one first) to the ankles.[2]

The order of worship is simple, but it has not been written up and no calendar of events is distributed at regular meetings. Ministers are instructed, however, on how to make appeals to the audience, especially at the meetings attended by the Messenger. This is embodied in a seven-page document prepared by Minister Wallace Muhammad. It reads in part:

Acquaint the people with the Messenger's Program (Not Teach)
A. Extent of Message
B. How Messenger Got into the *Courier*
C. Muhammad as a Benefactor
D. Relations with outside Groups
Make Welcome Address (State religion not important; but we are all the same color)
. . . Someone acts excited (State that they are getting envelopes in the back. Encourage them on putting money in the envelopes)
Mention what the Messenger has done.
Introduction of Speaker to introduce the Messenger (Build them up)
Speaker introduces the Messenger

1. Eastern Moslem daily prayers are five in number:
   1. The Dawn or Early Morning prayer (*Fajr*), before sunrise.
   2. The Early Afternoon prayer (*Zuhr*), after the noon hour.
   3. The Late Afternoon prayer *(Asr)*, about four o'clock in the afternoon, or close to two hours before sunset.
   4. The Sunset or Evening prayer (*Maghrib*), just after sunset.
   5. The Late Evening prayer (*Isha*), nearly two hours after sunset or before retiring to bed.
A Muslim is required to pray five times a day and twice at night if he awakens from sleep. *Muslim Daily Prayers*, pp. 8–9.
2. *Ibid.*, pp. 9–11.

The Messenger

(Note: When the Messenger is shaking hands, the M.C. should say: We do not want to do anything to disrespect this Great Man . . . So let us not leave until he leaves.

A few sisters should speak out spontaneously when the women stand up to accept (the teaching) — such phrases as "walk on up there sister."

A brother should say, "We'll die for you sisters; nobody will mess with these sisters.") [3]

Meetings begin promptly. Members must be punctual, and unless they have good excuses for being late, they may be suspended from the Temple for repeated offenses. This is an effort to "correct" the tardiness which is considered by Muhammad to be one of the habits "formed by the so-called Negroes in the old world [i.e., before coming into Islam] and this was disadvantageous to them in the eyes of others." The Messenger wants to rid them of this stigma as well as others. All registered members are required to attend at least one religious meeting a week or one of the F.O.I. or M.G.T.-G.C.C. meetings. The religious meetings are generally well attended by both members and visitors. An average of about four hundred persons attended Sunday meetings during the winter months of 1958–59. About fifty of these were visitors. Wednesday and Friday meetings are smaller because few visitors attend and because Sisters without escorts may not attend. Sunday meetings normally last for about three and a half hours for visitors and four and a half for registered members, who remain for a business session after worship. Wednesday and Friday meetings last two hours as a rule, but sometimes extend an additional half hour. Children attend a separate meeting on Sunday morning.

PRELIMINARIES

The visitor to Muhammad's Temple of Islam cannot fail to be impressed by a number of unusual procedures. One visitor has described what happened when he first went to the Temple:

I went straight to the Temple where I was redirected to the adjacent building. Here smartly dressed young men examined my credentials — and

3. Wallace Muhammad, "Condensed Outline." This document is actually an outline of propaganda techniques aimed at non-Muslim visitors.

asked the following questions: Is this your first time here? Name? Address? City or town of birth? Length of time of residence in Chicago? The answers were carefully recorded and I was given a slip, which was my permit to enter the Temple. These officers explained that it is their custom to gather information for the purpose of their mailing list. I was advised to bring friends to the next meeting.

After registering the visitor is directed to the Temple. All entrances are guarded. Only one entrance to the Temple is open; it leads to a waiting room for visitors.

THE SEARCH

All persons entering the Temple for worship, for F.O.I. or M.G.T.-G.C.C. meetings, or for other public meetings must be searched. "Undesirable" property is "seized" and returned after the meeting. Apparently only the Messenger and the Supreme Captain are not searched. Everyone else — men, women, children, followers, and visitors — is subjected to a rigorous search from head to toe. Billfolds, cigarette packages, fountain pens, pencils, etc., are examined. A visitor wearing overshoes must remove them in order that his feet may be searched. The visitor quoted above relates:

A ball-point pen which I had was carefully examined: the cap removed and inspected. All other things I had except the billfold and pen were taken away from me and were returned in a paper bag after the meeting.

Men are searched by F.O.I. members, women by M.G.T. members. A woman visitor reports:

. . . I went to the women's check room. A brother stationed outside the door asked if I had registered and when I said I had, he knocked at the door. A sister came out and asked if this was my first visit. She thought she had recognized me when I told her I had been there once before. She and the other sisters wore floor-length white rayon satin robes and headdresses, white low or medium heeled pumps, pearl earrings. Face powder was the only makeup used and most of the sisters wore no powder. The women's checking area was crowded with sisters and visitors, but service was swift and the atmosphere a friendly one. A different sister was summoned to search me and when she found I had been there before she commented that I understood they would inspect my purse for cosmetics, cigarettes, matches and nail files. She went through the purse thoroughly and, without indicating any disapproval, extracted the items which were not permitted in the Temple's auditorium, placed them in a paper bag, and gave me a ticket. I was asked to leave my overshoes in the check room and was given a ticket for them. My coat pockets and person were not searched as they had been on my first visit. All the sisters smiled and spoke and the three who remembered my previous visit gave especially friendly greetings, saying they were glad to see I had returned. A sister opened the door leading to the auditorium, and a sister stationed outside asked if I had been there before, led me to a seat about halfway down the aisle.

The search is undeniably an unpleasant and embarrassing experience for a visitor at the Temple of Islam. Some feel that it is humiliating. For one persistent visitor, it never ceased to be offensive:

At first I felt that the search was ridiculous. But when I discovered that it was taken so seriously and done so thoroughly, I was frightened. For the first hour at the Temple, I was exceedingly uneasy and afraid. The members looked at the visitors with curiosity, if not with utter suspicion. There was much handclapping and it appeared that someone was constantly watching to see whether the visitor approved of, or enjoyed the quips about, Negroes, and particularly those about whites. After some time, I just felt that I should clap my hands and laugh whenever these things were said. From then on I felt less uneasiness. After the meeting I felt a great warmth and friendliness among the members and I decided to continue my visits. However, after nine months of regular attendance, I have not discovered any relaxation in the manner I am searched. I have not adjusted to the search. It is the most annoying experience I have ever encountered.

In an interview, Minister James admitted that in spite of the unpleasantness of the search, it was necessary because there are many "erratic so-called Negroes" who may come there to cause trouble should they find the teaching too "challenging against their beloved Jesus." Another explanation of the search was offered by Minister Lucius in a Temple lecture:

The Temple of Islam is the Holiest place in the United States. The visitors are coming from the Old World to the New World. In the Old World, the so-called Negroes had been used to carrying knives, guns, cigarettes, liquor, etc., with them. In coming to the New World they must leave these things behind. They have no need for knives and guns. In the New World all blacks are brothers and they live as such. The occasion for using these things does not exist in the New World. Besides, Allah's protection is sufficiently adequate.

It may be added that the guards who conduct the search also come close to the visitor to smell his breath. If the odor of liquor is detected, he is not admitted.

The fear of a disturbance arising from a public meeting is an important reason for the search. It is also thought to be necessary because of threats on the life of Muhammad.[4] Such threats, real or fancied, serve to reinforce the Messenger's sense of persecution. His followers, identifying their fears and anxieties with his, share this sense of persecution. These rumors not only focus the attention of his followers on him and help draw them closer to him; they also facilitate withdrawal from the "enemy" who poses a continuous "threat" to the welfare of the Nation of Islam. However, the search also creates an atmosphere of awe and inspires fear and anxiety among visitors. An important aspect of the initiation process, this invasion of the privacy of the individual person humiliates him and makes the visitor feel guilty about his previous way of life. In some measure, it prepares him for what he imagines to be a better way of life. Initiates are thereby readied for submission and obedience to the will of Allah and Muhammad, and to the many exacting demands of personal discipline and loyalty. Last, and perhaps not as important, the search helps initiates during the early period of transition from the "Old World" to discontinue carrying such items as blades, knives, or cigarettes, even if they use these items surreptitiously. Initiates are assisted to forego "undesirable" habits gradually because it can be quite embarrassing when infractions are discovered.

After these preliminaries, the visitor is escorted into the Temple. The officer marches briskly down the aisle, comes to a stop, salutes the other guards, and shows the visitor to a seat. Male visitors normally sit on the front rows in the aisle to the right of the speakers' platform, separated from the followers and believers. Female visitors sit immediately behind the male visitors, separated from them by a few rows of empty seats unless there are too many visitors to maintain this separation of the sexes. The registered Muslim women

4. *Islamic News*, p. 1; see also Eddie Hawkins, *New Crusader*, March 12, 1960, p. 14.

sit in the center aisle behind the Temple officers, who occupy the front row of this aisle. All male registered Muslims and believers sit in the left aisle. Other men may also sit in the balcony on a crowded day. Women are separated from the men partly because this is the tradition of Islam and partly because undivided attention is required. The Temple is not a place for socializing; mixing the women and men together might cause distractions. Sister Nellie LX told the writer that she resented separation from her husband when she first visited the Temple:

> I thought they had a whole lot of nerve to search my pocketbook. . . . I really felt they had nerve. I resented being led by one of them to a seat as if I couldn't find a seat for myself. Worse still, I was separated from my husband who sat on the men's side. I felt that another woman may talk to him or may look out for him. After the meeting, my husband told me that the procedure would in the long run make me a better woman and a better wife.[5]

The Temple, a former synagogue, seats five hundred persons and is well maintained. The floor is carpeted with a reddish rug. The speakers' stand is a simple structure which seats four persons. At its center there is a microphone. Temple lectures can be heard through a loudspeaker system in the adjacent school building. A blackboard stands on an easel at the left of the speaker. An American flag appears in the upper left corner of the blackboard and directly below it, painted against a white background, a tree with a black man hanging from a branch. This symbolizes justice under the United States government. Opposite the tree is the cross, another symbol of oppression, shame, suffering, and death. Below the cross appears the word "Christianity." In the upper right corner the flag of the Nation of Islam is painted — the moon and stars in white against a red background which represents the sun. The letters, I., F., J., and E. are inscribed on the flag, one on each corner. These stand for Islam (Peace), Freedom, Justice, and Equality. Below the flag and directly opposite the word "Christianity," is inscribed "Islam." Between the two flags and the names of the two religions is a large question mark with the question: Which One Will Survive The War of Armageddon?

5. Interview.

Two guards are posted on each side of the speakers' stand. They face the audience and are relieved every thirty minutes. A guard relieving another marches forward, stands at attention, and exchanges a salute. They lean toward each other and whisper some words. The guard to be relieved then marches swiftly up the aisle and the other does a smart about-face and takes his place. This goes on throughout the meeting.

Guards are posted at the front entrances, both inside and outside the Temple. They make sure that no one sleeps in the meetings, and anyone who dozes is promptly awakened and politely warned. Sometimes the offending person is asked to go to the washroom and bathe his face with cold water. The guards also see that members and visitors do not chat. Anyone who is caught turning his eyes toward the women may be reprimanded, and "neck-twisting" may be punished by suspension from the Temple for at least thirty days.[6]

The meeting begins as soon as the presiding minister rises and greets the audience, saying "As-Salaam-Alaikum," to which the congregation, standing, responds, "Wa-el-Alaikum-Salaam." The minister then instructs the visitors on the procedure for prayer. The prayer is short. With the congregation standing, the minister announces that they are facing the East.[7] They are asked to raise their hands with palms up, eyes closed, and heads bowed for prayer. The minister turns so that he too faces East. The prayer is usually said in English, but occasionally in Arabic. The congregation repeats it silently after the minister:

"In the Name of Allah, the Beneficent, the Merciful. All Praise is due to Allah, the Lord of the Worlds; Master of the Day of Judgment. I bear witness that there is none to be worshipped, but Allah, and that Muhammad is His Servant and Last Messenger. O! Allah, Bless Muhammad here in the Wilderness of North America, and bless the followers of Muhammad too, as Thou didst bless Abraham, and the followers of Abraham. O! Allah, make Muhammad successful, and the followers of Muhammad successful, here in

6. The rules of decorum are so strict that one visitor was even asked to button the coat of his Ivy League suit before he entered the Temple.

7. The Universal Negro Improvement Association and the Ethiopian World Federation Council also face the East when they pray. This appears to be true of other black nationalist groups. The African Nationalists Pioneer Movement in New York, which is extremely secular, is an exception. Members merely stand and repeat: "One Aim! One Goal! One Destiny!" at the opening of a meeting.

the Wilderness of North America, as Thou didst make Abraham successful, and the followers of Abraham. For surely Thou art Praised and Magnified in our midst. Amen."[8]

Seriousness of purpose and sincerity in prayer are emphasized.

There is no singing. "Shouting and wailing" is considered characteristic of Negro Christian preachers who want to arouse the emotions of their congregations in order to get money "which is tied up in churches and Cadillacs." In general all such emotionalism is discouraged:

> I am here not to preach a great sermon for you to make you shout too much because it's a little too cold; you will get a little warm and may catch cold when you go outside. So I am not a man to preach to you to make you shout a lot. I am a man that preaches to you so that you will listen a lot. We want you to listen. If you listen well, then that is the thing. You can shout when you get home.[9]

After the prayer, the minister salutes the congregation again, saying, "As-Salaam-Alaikum," to which the followers respond, "Wa-el-Alaikum-Salaam." Frequently the minister asks the congregation, "How do you feel, my dear brothers and sisters?" and makes impromptu remarks to establish rapport. His duty is to bear witness to the teachings of Muhammad and to affirm that "Allah is our God and the Most Honorable Elijah Muhammad is His Last and Divine Messenger."

Owing to the presence of visitors, the minister, or the Messenger when he is presiding, begins the lecture by explaining a few things, such as the reason for the use of Arabic in greetings:

> You have perhaps been hearing people say "Al-Salaam-Alaikum" and the people referring to the God Allah. Let me acquaint you with just what you have been listening to. "As-Salaam-Alaikum" means peace to you brothers and sisters in the Arabic language. Now you say, well, I could just say Peace. No, in the Islamic World each Muslim must greet the Muslim in his own language and that is why we use "As-Salaam-Alaikum." That is the Arabic tongue, the Mother Language of all. Arab or Arabic as it is called is the mother of all the languages. All of the other languages came after that and the fact about it is that it is the first — it is the last. It is the purest language and the most beautiful language and has the most beautiful char-

8. Cf. *The Supreme Wisdom*, II, 64 for a shorter version. The "Amen" is pronounced "Ameen." After the Amen the members pass their palms over their faces.

9. Elijah Muhammad, Speech, Milwaukee, Wisconsin, January 18, 1959, p. 1.

acters that you ever studied in your life—it is just the best. I don't say that because I am a Muslim but it is just the best.[10]

Muhammad's introduction explains little about Arabic, which he neither speaks nor writes. It is significant, however, as a means of mitigating the tensions arising from the humiliating experience of the search and the apparent strangeness of the Muslims. It is also a way of explaining to the visitors why the Muslims may appear in some ways to be alien. Humorously, but obviously with serious intent, he strikes at what he considers the root of the Negro problem, his identity—by emphasizing the uniqueness of the "Islamic World," of Allah, "our God," and of Arabic, the "language of our Nation." All of these serve to focus attention on the "attractions" of Islam and his movement by stressing the "national" language (Arabic) as the "most beautiful, mother of all languages, the language of peace" and Islam, the religion of brotherliness, of love and unity. Both Arabic and Islam are presented as unifying and dignifying symbols for a people divided and despised. On the other hand, English and its forms of greeting are discredited for the purpose of alienating his listeners emotionally from any lofty sentiments or notions they may have for this "difficult, young and scrapped-up" language they have spoken all their lives.

The Messenger or minister explains next why Muslims refer to themselves as "Brothers and Sisters," in the "Brotherhood" of Islam. The symbols on the blackboard, as well as the flag of the Nation of Islam, are explained. The flag is said to be a "sign of life" for the so-called Negroes, for, according to the teaching of the Messenger, it came into existence several trillion years ago. The symbol of the star was "put on our flag seventy-two trillion years ago" and the "moon was put on six trillion years ago." It is not known when the sun "was put on our national flag."[11]

Minister James explains that the symbols of the flag of the Nation of Islam have a great deal of meaning for the "so-called Negroes" who need a "good sign for life." The sun, the five-pointed star, and the moon represent natural and universal elements indispensable

10. *Ibid.*, pp. 3–4.
11. Minister James in an interview.

to life: The sun stands for freedom; the moon, for equality (the force of the moon exerts an equilibrium in the physical world by maintaining the levels of water of the earth); the star, for justice. The five points correspond to the five senses of man, which justify his freedom and equality. Compared with the flag of Christian government, this is a symbol of life.

That flag and the cross have been symbols of misfortune and slavery for black people. The sign of the cross represents murder and wickedness since its inception, Christ the Prophet was lynched on that cross and ever since the so-called Negroes started bearing it they have been catching hell on it. Does it require any argument to show why the so-called Negroes should rally under the flag of the Nation of Islam?[12]

The teaching on Sunday is usually long, the minister or the Messenger trying to cover every aspect of the doctrine. Much time is often devoted to the discussion of Negro problems, both contemporary and "historical." Most of the ministers address their listeners in a calm manner.

Minister Malcolm X appears to be able to hold an audience interminably. Unlike the other ministers, he is used to "street speaking," a familiar sight in Harlem during the summer months. Like most of Harlem's "street speakers," Minister Malcolm inveighs against traditional Negro leaders who have betrayed the true aspirations of the Negro masses and lists the ills of the Negro community, such as drunkeness, juvenile delinquency, drug addiction, prostitution, skin and hair bleaching, lack of desire for self-improvement among the Negro masses, and the evil deeds of the white man. Frequently, he seeks the audience's response by leaning close to the microphone at the end of a sentence and asking, "right or wrong?!" The audience echoes, "right!" and applauds. His English is good, his presentation forceful.

If the American Negro, who has been lynched, seen his women raped, worked as a chattel slave, fought in wars for a democracy which he himself cannot enjoy, disenfranchised, segregated against, denied his rights as a first class citizen, finds it necessary during this twentieth century to have the army protect his children in order for them to attend schools which he pays taxes to maintain, does not hate those who inflict these ills on him

12. From a Temple lecture.

can the Honorable Elijah Muhammad teach him hate? I ask you this, audience.[13]

Speaking before a huge African Freedom Day Rally in Harlem, he proposed an immediate "Bandung Conference" of Harlem leaders:

. . . If the people in Africa are getting their freedom, then 20 million blacks here in America, instead of shouting hallelujah over what is happening 9,000 miles from America, should study the methods used by our darker brothers in Africa and Asia to get their freedom.

It has been since the Bandung Conference that all dark people of earth have been striding toward freedom . . . but there are 20 million blacks here in America yet suffering the worst form of enslavement . . . mental bondage, mentally blinded by the white man, unable now to see that America is the citadel of white colonialism, the bulwark of white imperialism. . . the slavemaster of slavemasters.

. . . The first step at Bandung was to agree that all dark people were suffering a common misery at the hands of a common enemy. Call him Belgian, call him Frenchman, call him Englishman, colonialist, imperialist, or European . . . but they have one thing in common: ALL ARE WHITE MEN! [14]

Occasionally there is handclapping and ovation as a minister or the Messenger speaks. These interruptions are usually brief, although at times the applause is prolonged when the Messenger speaks. Minister Malcolm at times evokes a response not unlike that received by revivalists, particularly from the older men and women who enjoin, "Yes! Yes! Give it straight! All Praise is due to Allah!" "Spell it out! That's right! Make it plain for the people!"

Women do not normally speak at the Temple, but occasionally they are invited to make an announcement or a report. Then they speak from the rostrum. Distinguished guests are also occasionally invited to the rostrum. At the end of the lecture, the minister asks the audience to raise questions but warns that if he cannot answer all of the questions he will refer those too difficult to his beloved teacher and leader. Few questions are asked. The minister may then declare: "Negroes must get out of this hell now." Next he may ask: "If there are any among the visitors wishing to get out of this hell here and now, they should rise up and go to the secretaries to register." The standard procedure for those who indicate their accept-

13. Quoted in the *Herald-Dispatch*, December 5, 1957, p. 1.
14. Quoted in the *Herald-Dispatch*, April 23, 1959, pp. 1, 5.

ance of Islam is to march forward to the base of the platform where they shake hands with the minister or with the Messenger if he is there.

Finally, announcements are made, and visitors' attention is called to the Muslim business establishments, which they are asked to patronize.

CLOSING OF THE MEETING

At the Chicago Temple many visitors are able to hear the Messenger of Allah. When he is not out of town, there is always an expectation that he will come to the Temple. The presiding minister prepares the audience for his visit. But when the Messenger does not come, the minister advises the visitors to return since the Messenger will be there on one of the days. To the followers, the minister says that their Teacher and Leader is busy and that "he works very hard every hour for the seventeen million dead so-called Negroes." Undoubtedly, a sense of frustration is created in the visitors who had come to hear him speak. For the followers, this sense of frustration, if it exists at all, is compensated for by the presence of the Supreme Captain, Minister Wallace, or another member of his family, who delivers "the greetings of our beloved Leader and Teacher, As-Salaam-Alaikum." The members respond, "Wa-El-Alaikum-Salaam, and return our greetings of peace to the Messenger from the F.O.I. (women, M.G.T.)." The greetings and the response are repeated three times, the closing prayer is said, and the minister offers the following advice to the followers and visitors:

My dear beloved brothers and sisters, I warn you as you now leave this Temple, in everything you do, you shall not do unto others what you would not wish them to do unto you. Never be the aggressor. But if the wolf should bite you on the jaw, do not turn the other jaw. Show the wolf that you also have teeth and that you can bite.

The registered Muslims remain at the Temple for a while to consider the business of the Nation. Non-registered members (believers) are not admitted to the business meetings.

Wednesday and Friday night meetings follow the same general order, although issues of the day or topical discussions of various aspects of Islam are featured.[15] Student ministers are invited to speak for about ten to fifteen minutes on Wednesday nights.

RECREATIONAL ACTIVITIES

Tuesday evenings are set aside for a social get-together known as the Unity Party. Muslims and non-Muslims meet in a relatively informal atmosphere. The men come dressed in suits, and most of the women in their Muslim dress. The Muslim girls are less "traditional" than the older women, and they frequently come in blouses and skirts, but with a headtie. The party is held in the auditorium of the University of Islam, where food and soft drinks are served.

There is usually no program and no speech making. Men and women sit together at long tables and chat. Occasionally three or more people stand together and talk. On the whole the atmosphere appears rather subdued. Conversation is carried on in low voices. The party is orderly, and Muslims are particularly cordial to the visitors. A visitor is impressed by their friendliness and decorum.

Organized entertainment is provided on feast days. Feasts may be given by the Messenger, the Temple, or one of the organizations within the Temple — P.T.A., F.O.I., M.G.T.–G.C.C. Recitation of poems, music by a band consisting of followers who were professional entertainers before joining the Temple, and "fire-eating" demonstrations are featured.

Sometimes the members present a concert or play. The most popular play is "Orgena," subtitled "A Negro Spelt Backwards." It is a portrayal of a stereotyped American Negro. The "Trial" is another play usually combined with "Orgena" into one play. It is a harsh indictment and trial of the white man for all his "crimes" against the so-called Negroes (The Nation of Islam). The trial takes place before an all-black jury which finds the white man guilty of the charges. The play was written in 1956 and directed by Brother Louis X and Lonnie X of the Boston Temple. Minister Louis X plays the leading role in it. A brochure distributed to the audience states: "Orgena was not written out of malice toward any racial

15. A typical discussion at meetings is reproduced from the writer's notes as Appendix C.

group, but . . . to show the so-called Negro that he is someone with a great culture, history, and heritage. . . ."

Other organized activities include the showing of documentary films on such topics as education in Muslim countries, sanitation, and some scientific themes. Teams of Muslims visit the museums regularly. "Places of Educational Interest" recommended to Muslim visitors during the 1960 Annual Convention included the following: "Adler Planetarium, Natural History Museum, Museum of Science and Industry, Art Institute of Chicago, Lincoln Park Zoo, Cortez W. Peters Business College, Stock Yards, Merchandise Mart, Supreme Liberty Life Insurance Company."[16] Private swimming parties are arranged for the F.O.I. and the M.G.T. members. Followers are not participants in popular spectator sports.

Saturday is about the only day for which there is no scheduled activity. Many members, especially unmarried male adults and new converts, spend considerable leisure time in activities of the Nation, which help them to withdraw from participation in activities of the "normal" society to which they were accustomed and facilitate their adjustment to the "new" way of life. Several members were asked what changes took place in their use of leisure time since joining the Nation. Many members felt that they were too busy for recreation.

Before I joined the Nation I went out Friday nights and all weekend night-clubbing and drinking. This started when I was twelve-and-a-half years old . . . running around with girls and getting into trouble because of speeding. I began having sex life at eleven and my first girl friend was about fifteen. I was never introduced to dope habits. I had two friends who were real dope fiends. . . . Now, instead of chasing women and nursing liquor bottles, I spend my spare time at the Temple of Islam. Mondays: 7 to 11 p.m. studying Arabic, English, writing, social science, arithmetic, and *The Supreme Wisdom* at the F.O.I. meetings. After that I go home to bed. On Tuesday nights, I am at the Unity Party. Wednesdays, I attend the regular Temple meeting. Thursdays, I am on M.G.T.'s Guard Duty. This means that I along with other members of the F.O.I. to guard the doorways to the Temple and to the University of Islam in order to protect the Sisters, the divine and righteous Muslim women. Friday nights are regular meeting nights. I work eight hours a day. On Saturdays, I work at my laboratory — a mechanical shop. Sunday afternoon is regular meeting. There is no time

16. "Places of Educational Interest" (Mimeographed).

for visiting friends except on Saturdays and Sundays. I usually spend my free time experimenting on all sorts of things in the laboratory.[17]

NOTES ON SECRECY

Early in the development of the Nation of Islam, the "secrecy" which surrounded its activities and paucity of knowledge about its aims and objectives led to speculation that members practiced some unusual "primitive" rituals, and the speculation continues.[18] Two reasons seem to account for it. First, this speculation has been fostered by lack of understanding of some of the teachings of Muhammad by both his initiates and outsiders. Secondly, not many scholars have studied the Nation closely. The whites are excluded, and most Negro scholars appear to be uninterested.

THE "SECRET" RITUAL

Rumors of human sacrifice arose after an incident in Detroit in 1932. Benyon says that Prophet Fard's "position on this question was never made clear." He then continues:

He taught explicitly that it was the duty of every Moslem to offer as sacrifice four Caucasian devils in order that he might return to his home in Mecca. The prophet also taught that Allah demands obedience unto death from his followers. No Moslem dare refuse the sacrifice of himself or of his loved ones if Allah requires it.[19]

As a result of this teaching, according to Benyon:

On November 21, 1932, the people of Detroit became conscious of the presence of the cult through its first widely publicized human sacrifice. A prominent member, Robert Harris, renamed Robert Karriem, erected an altar in his home at 1249 DuBois Street and invited his roomer, John J. Smith, to present himself as a human sacrifice, so that he might become, as Harris said, "the Saviour of the world." Smith agreed, and at the hour appointed for the sacrifice — 9:00 A. M. — Harris plunged a knife into Smith's heart. After constant recurrences of rumors of human sacrifice or attempted sacrifice, on January 20, 1937, Verlene McQueen, renamed Verlene Ali, brother of one of the assistant ministers, was arrested as he prepared for

17. Interview.
18. This assumption seems to underlie Benyon's description of the Nation of Islam as a "voodoo cult."
19. Benyon, *op. cit.*, p. 903.

the ceremonial slaying and cooking of his wife and daughter. This sacrifice was, as he said, to have "cleansed him from all sin."[20]

Although some followers of Muhammad admit this incident took place, they deny that human sacrifice is the teaching of the Nation. They deny that the followers who performed the sacrifice understood the "science" of the teaching. They claim that the teaching is symbolic, representing the "Four Beasts" in the Book of Revelation which are said to stand in the way between the destruction of the present world and the emergence of the New World. In an interview, the Messenger, Minister James, and some followers all denied that this teaching meant that each follower must kill four Caucasians before he can return to Mecca.

Although the controversial passage on what appears to be "human sacrifice" is contained in the "secret rituals," there is no reason to doubt the interpretation which the followers and officers offer. In fact, if the earlier interpretation were correct, Muhammad, it would appear, has since modified its implications. Secondly, it would appear from the teachings of Muhammad that the "destruction of the four beasts" is predicated entirely on an act of God (Allah) in the same way that the destruction of the present world is "left to the Will of Allah."

In spite of this explanation, neophytes seeking membership in the Nation continue to give erroneous interpretations of this passage. An applicant who was recently released from jail, on reporting to his parole officer, let it be known that he was a Muslim and that he was required to bring in the heads of four white people. The white parole officer was disturbed, and reported what he had heard to a Negro work trainee.[21] The trainee wanted to learn the truth and approached an officer of the Temple. He was told that the parolee had not been around long enough to understand the teaching.

These rumors, like the search, are not significant in themselves. The incidents have become myths which serve as a means of inspiring fear among initiates. Such fears make the initiates feel helpless, emphasizing the demand for personal sacrifices which they may be

20. *Ibid.*, pp. 903–4.
21. A student at the University of Chicago School of Social Service Administration. Information obtained in an interview with the trainee.

required to make in the interest of the Nation. They inspire loyalty in the movement and dramatize the extremes to which individuals may resort in demonstration of loyalty.

Exclusion of whites from membership in the movement (and from attendance at Muslim meetings) is another subject of speculation, and some whites seem to think that the Muslims are engaged in "conspiratorial" activities. For the first time, however, the white press was invited to send reporters to the 1960 Muslim Annual Convention. No white reporters attended. In his speech Muhammad angrily said: "When they were not invited, they complained. This time I invited them and they didn't show up." Some white papers were represented by their Negro reporters — the *Chicago American* by Messrs. Wesley South and Les Brownlee, and the *Chicago Sun-Times* by Mr. Fletcher Martin. The *Reader's Digest* was represented by Mr. Alex Haley and his research assistant. Government agencies (such as the Chicago Commission on Human Relations) sent their Negro representatives. White F.B.I. agents sat in parked cars outside the main entrance of the Coliseum.

This secrecy of the Muslim movement is more apparent than real. However, the Muslims' exclusiveness serves different functions for Mr. Muhammad's followers and for outsiders. First, secrecy, like rumor and myth,[22] seems to compensate members for the lack of genuine religious rituals and ceremonial rites. This point is illustrated not only by the lack of such rituals or ceremonies in worship but also by the Muslim's attitude toward death, a subject of deep concern in most religions.

Death is de-emphasized in the movement as it is in Father Divine's movement and perhaps in the Negro subculture generally. Lack of concern for the dead has a semireligious sanction in the teachings of Muhammad. Islam, as taught by him, rejects the view that there is life beyond the grave. Minister Lucius once observed that "Allah has no use for dead people." As a consequence, burial rites are not part of the religious life of the Muslims. The followers live, work, and pray with reference to their conditions here and

22. Also the claim (reported earlier) that Allah was responsible for the death of the police captain in the courtroom riot.

now — their Nation, the lot of the black folks in general, and with the hope of living to see the Hereafter, or at least to "live and die as good Muslims."

During the period of this study three deaths occurred at the Chicago Temple. The announcement of one death was made by Muhammad himself at a Sunday meeting. He spoke movingly of the loss to the Nation of the deceased whom he described as "a faithful Brother who had served his Nation and people loyally." He expressed deep regret that, because of his own ill health, he was unable to visit the Brother at the hospital when he was ill. He eulogized him at length. He thanked Allah that the "Brother lived and died a true Muslim." He would demonstrate his love for the deceased, he said, through ample support of the bereaved family. Followers were urged to attend the burial.

Funeral services are not held at the Temple. The remains of the dead are taken directly from the funeral home to the cemetery. The minister attends the burial along with other followers, but no prayers are said for the dead. Deprived of religious rituals and ceremonial rites, the Muslims derive some gratification from the rumors and apparent secrecy, and from the hidden powers of Allah; these are the sources of awe and dignity for the movement.

Secrecy is also a factor in the attraction of new members. The tradition of secret-fraternal societies among Negroes has been discussed. Many Negroes are traditionally attracted to such societies, partly as a route to social status and partly because they offer pomp and pageantry.[23] Many a lower-class Negro, however, is excluded from either fraternities or sororities of the Greek-letter class or the fraternal orders of the lodge-type. Their admission to the Nation of Islam, which shares some of the characteristics of these fraternal societies, is looked upon by many as a privilege — an alternative route to social mobility — because they are denied admission into fraternal orders and sororities due to lack of education, wealth or social standing.

Negroes traditionally have used the forum provided by the sep-

23. Cf. Edward Nelson Palmer, "Negro Secret Societies," *Social Forces*, XXIII, No. 2 (October, 1944), pp. 207–15.

arate Negro church and the secret-fraternal societies for releasing their pent-up feelings of frustration and bitterness against the injustices of the white society and for the uninhibited castigation of what they consider to be the internal weaknesses of their community. They are spared the embarrassment of critically discussing their own weaknesses in the presence of whites. The exclusion of whites saves both races from direct confrontation and reduces the occasion for violent conflict.

IX. Education of Muslims

> The education and training of our children must not be limited to the "Three Rs (reading, 'riting and 'rithmetic)" only. It should instead include the history of the black nation, the knowledge of civilizations of man and the Universe, and all sciences. It is necessary that the young people of our Nation learn all they can. Learning is a great virtue and I would like to see all the children of my followers become the possessors of it. It will make us an even greater people tomorrow.
>
> ELIJAH MUHAMMAD

PAROCHIAL EDUCATION among the Muslims is almost as old as the Nation of Islam. The first Muslim school, styled the University of Islam, was established in Detroit in 1932, and the second in Chicago in 1934. Both schools have been in continuous operation ever since. The distrust of conventional educational institutions by black nationalists was noted previously. No other nationalist group has attempted to establish a parochial school.

Elijah Muhammad believes that the education of Negroes has been a failure because it was "designed by the slavemasters or their sons, to keep the Negro in his place." Consequently, the educated Negro is not a whit better off than before he went to school: "He goes to school bearing the name the slavemaster gave him and comes out bearing the same mark of oppression." Negro education has not enabled him to think for himself, to inquire into his past, to be proud of his heritage prior to slavery, and to have a desire to become independent economically or otherwise. Above all, the educated Ne-

231

gro elite is irresponsible; their education has not made them feel responsible for the community or for the people. Comparing the education of Negroes with that of many foreign students from Africa, Muhammad has said:

We should acquire an education . . . that will make our people put to better use the knowledge they acquire . . . an education that will make our people willing and able to go and do for self.

Is this not the aim and goal of the many foreign students who are studying in this country? Don't these students return to their own nations and give their people the benefit of their learning? Did not Nkrumah return to Ghana to lead his people to independence with the benefit of learning he acquired in America and elsewhere? Did not Dr. Hastings Banda return to give the benefit of his education to his people who are striving toward independence in Nyasaland? Did not Dr. Azikiwe of Nigeria give the benefit of his education to the upliftment and independence of his people?

Does not America offer exchange scholarships to smaller, weaker, and dependent governments so their students will acquire knowledge to aid the people of those countries? Then why shouldn't the goal of education be the same for you and me?

Why is scorn and abuse directed toward my followers and me when we say our people should get an education which will aid, benefit and uplift our people? . . .[1]

The education of the "black pharisees"[2] has not brought them justice; nevertheless, Negroes are proud that they have made advances in education:

One hundred years up from slavery. You still today feel that you have been schooled. You have a few diplomas and degrees. You can do little things educationally, but that does not yet even get you justice in America. You still suffer injustice with an armful of diplomas and degrees from colleges and universities. . . .

How pathetic a sight many of us make as we boast of our meagre education and the attainment of a degree of economic growth. All these things are an illusion. When rightly viewed, your education has been designed by your oppressors with the specific intent of keeping you in servitude. . . . Our oppressors own and control everything we have. What, then, is the basis of our vaunted and foolish pride? Something must be wrong upstairs.[3]

1. *Mr. Muhammad Speaks* (New York), March–April, 1961, p. 8.
2. The "black pharisees," Dan Burley reports, is the term used by Muslims to describe middle-class and educated Negroes "satisfied with things as they are so long as they are permitted to be comfortable and to live out their lives as 'carbon copies' of the white man who maintains his own social and economic spheres as solidly lilywhite." *Ibid.*, p. 8.
3. Speech, Washington, D. C.; also *The Islamic News*, Vol. I, No. I, p. 7.

The objective of "Muslim" education is, presumably, to stem the tide which has produced the black pharisees:

To re-educate the so-called Negro, who has been the victim of centuries of mis-education. . . . to attain his rightful place in the sun as a Black Man . . . A cardinal fact of its teachings, is to give the students a feeling of dignity and appreciation of their own kind.

It also places especial emphasis upon the daily Moslem duties, the teaching of Arabic, the observance of the dietary laws, and the development of a child's character.[4]

Education of boys and girls is equally important. The Muslim girls must, in addition, be schooled in their special duties and responsibilities as future wives and mothers:

The Muslim girls of our Nation should spare no effort to learn their special duties and responsibilities as future wives and mothers. The University of Islam in Chicago and the one in Detroit are both equipped to give them the finest training in their special fields. Those who are unable to attend one of these schools should take advantage of the instruction available in the Temple of Islam M.G.T. (Muslim Girls' Training) classes.[5]

Mr. Muhammad believes that "integration" of Negro and white children in schools is undesirable:

You must teach and train your boys and girls in your *own* schools and colleges. And keep your little children, especially your little girls, from mixing with white children. When you do this, then your own people who are the Original People of the Human Family will respect you as a Nation.[6]

THE UNIVERSITY OF ISLAM

The University of Islam is only a University in name. However, under this name, both the Chicago and Detroit Temples have operated elementary and high schools since the early nineteen-thirties. At that time, the University of Islam in Detroit was in trouble with the Board of Education, which wanted to close it.[7] Again it was under fire in 1959 because of inadequate physical facilities.[8]

4. *White Christian Party Attacks.* . . . , pp. 7–8.
5. *The Supreme Wisdom*, II, 58.
6. *Ibid.* In a speech at the 1960 Convention, he said that integration at college level is not as bad as integration prior to the age of sixteen.
7. Bontemps and Conroy, *They Seek a City*, p. 182. The resistance from the followers of Fard was "so great that the court in order to avoid a race riot suspended the sentence of almost all the rioters."
8. *Detroit Free Press*, August 14, 1959, pp. 1–2.

Until 1953 the University of Islam in Chicago provided only elementary school curriculum, but a high school was added in 1954. The University is a two-story building without a basement. The first floor is divided into five classrooms, the principal's office, a little storage room, and rest rooms for boys and for girls. In addition, the students have a large closet where they leave their coats and other belongings. The second floor contains an auditorium which is used for both classes and other activities of the Temple at night. There is also a small library for the use of students and faculty members. In winter the library may be used as a classroom if an additional room in the Temple used for classes becomes too cold. Displayed in the library is the Civic Plaque awarded to the Messenger by the Pittsburgh Courier Publishing Company.

The auditorium, like other parts of the building, is well maintained. The picture of the Messenger of Allah and the flag of the Nation of Islam are the principal decorations of the auditorium, aside from a mural of the Taj Mahal.[9] When Mr. Naeem visited the school in 1956 he reported that the assembly hall was "decorated with large flags of Turkey, Arabia, Pakistan, Morocco, Egypt and other Moslem countries of Asia and Africa."[10] Until December, 1958, printed replicas of flags of all predominantly Moslem countries were displayed along the walls of the auditorium. Beneath each flag was a brief history and factual account of the country. Since then, these have been removed. Missing in this display is the United States flag. There was no flag of Liberia, Ethiopia, or Ghana, which are not considered "Moslem" countries. A flag of the Algerian government-in-exile was on display.

ENROLLMENT

The present enrollment is about three hundred and fifty. There has been a marked increase in the last fifteen years: the total enrollment for 1945 was fifty students. In 1954, when the present building was purchased, the total enrollment was estimated at one hundred and twenty-five. Although a few non-Muslim children are

9. F.O.I. members entering the auditorium must salute the flag of their nation.
10. *Moslem World and the U.S.A.*, June–July, 1956, p. 25.

enrolled, the school primarily serves Muslim children. A few non-Muslims have sought admission for their children, but the present facilities do not permit expansion. The writer knows a few teenage girls enrolled at the University of Islam whose parents are not Muslims.

"SEPARATE BUT EQUAL"

Boys and girls receive instruction in the same building but in separate classrooms. Segregated instruction has been part of the tradition of the school since its founding. However, in the kindergarten and the first grade, the sexes are integrated "because they are innocent" at that age. Even in these integrated classes, the little girls are seated behind the boys. Until February, 1959, the "separate but equal" rule was rigidly enforced. A new principal was hired about that time. He was concerned with economy and maximum utilization of the existing staff and physical facilities, and decided to integrate the classrooms. The decision was put into effect without consultation with Muhammad. However, the change was brought to his attention after it had been put into operation. He vetoed the principal's decision promptly. A faculty meeting at which Muhammad was present was called. The principal's main argument at this meeting was based on "economy and student achievement." He stressed that there were only six classrooms for elementary grades two through eight and four high school grades. In practical terms, students in two or more grades had to be instructed in one room if separation of the sexes was to be maintained. The second and third grades were in one room; grades four, five, six, seven, and eight met in the same room, and all grades of the high school were in one room. In grades two and three, the teacher instructed each class for twenty minutes in a forty-minute class period. In grades four through eight, each grade generally received ten minutes of instruction, and a similar plan was followed for the four high school grades. However, each teacher used the forty-minute period in the manner he or she thought to be most effective. The principal's integration plan made different classrooms available for the second, third, and fourth grades, which are the larger classes. Five and six, seven and eight, nine and ten, and eleven and twelve would have remained combined, each pair in a separate classroom. To some extent, this would have been more practical an arrangement than the former grouping. The Messenger was sympathetic toward the principal's plan but said, "I am first and foremost, a reformer," and "until the new Islamic Center is built we must endure the present difficulties."

This incident reveals both the aims of education and the work of Muhammad among the most economically underprivileged class of Negroes. In the exchange which followed between him and the principal, he demonstrated that in spite of his long public speeches he is a man of few words, firm and determined. He knows exactly what he wants and also his limitations. Although he needs the advice of trained people for the administration of the school, he is the one to give general directions.

The principal is an Egyptian who has lived in the United States for nearly ten years. In the conversation between him and Minister James which followed after Muhammad had left, the principal appeared to be wholly ignorant of the background of the students and their parents. Minister James explained to him that most of them came from homes whose parents "are the poorest in this society — homes in which more than two or three families are crowded together in the same apartment, and where the youngsters had been exposed to all kinds of adult activity." These overcrowded conditions, James said, "contribute to juvenile delinquencies, immorality, and early pregnancy at ages as low as twelve in the Negro community." He explained that the task of the Messenger is "to rehabilitate not only the morals of adults but also of the children." "The Messenger at the moment is confronted with the choice of either giving them what is considered the best education which they probably could receive in the public schools or training them to be morally fit citizens. The choice of a reformer is clear; in fact, the Messenger has little choice." "These children," said Minister James, "are underprivileged from birth. . . . There is no reason to believe that a majority of them would benefit from attending public schools, and there is no assurance that they would acquire the rudiments of civilized and moral life." The end of education in the Nation is character building. Muhammad believes that if basic "moral" virtues are inculcated in the individual, his happiness and the welfare of society would be enhanced.

The problem of classroom space was partially tackled in November, 1959, when a two-shift system was introduced. Under this arrangement, pupils from the sixth grade through high school attend classes from 8:00 A.M. to 12:00 noon. The kindergarten through fifth grade pupils attend classes from 12:30 until 4:30 P.M. The same teachers teach both shifts.

The two-shift system was inspired partly by difficulties which the school in Detroit was having with the state and local Departments of Public Instruction during the summer of 1959. The Detroit school had an enrollment of one hundred and two students and was housed in a "crumbling" former theater building at 5403 John C. Lodge. There were five instructors at the school, three male and two female. The three male instructors were said "to be qualified in accordance with the laws of Michigan."[11] The two female teachers were not. However, the school was closed because it was considered "educationally and physically inadequate." It has never been approved by the Department of Public Instruction. The Muslims secured a new building shortly thereafter and classes resumed.

Prior to the introduction of the two-shift system, the school week at Chicago consisted of four days (four hours per day) of instruction, from 10:00 A.M. to 2:00 P.M. Under the new arrangement, just as in the previous one, there is no interval for recreation or for lunch. Although the period of instruction is short for each grade in a classroom, the students attend school throughout the year except for a two-week vacation in August. Two additional weeks of vacation may be added for the annual convention, public holidays, and forced closing because of weather. To some extent the long school year compensates for loss of time due to the present staff shortage and multiple-grade rooms.

No classes are held on Tuesdays. This day is given over to varied activities, such as a party, or a trip to a museum or zoo. Different activities are arranged for the various age levels, designed to meet

11. *Detroit Free Press*, August 14, 1959, p. 2.

their special needs and abilities. For example, teenage girls may receive additional training in home economics on Tuesday, while the younger children are taken to the Museum of Science and Industry.

THE FACULTY

The faculty of the University of Islam has never exceeded ten members. The principalship changes hands rather frequently. Since 1953, there have been five principals including the present one. All of the principals in recent years have been believers in Islam. Of the four past principals, three were male and one was female. A former principal and the present one are Arabs.[12] The first Arab principal, also an instructor in Arabic, Shaikh Jamil Shakir Diab, is now a rival Moslem leader on Chicago's South Side. Arab students in the area describe him as an *Imam* (priest).

The job of the principal consists generally of supervising the teachers and the curriculum. He may teach one or two courses in addition. The principal's powers are very limited. Two of the principals worked only part-time. The principal's relationship with the Messenger is actually advisory. Insofar as it is known, only one non-Moslem has been appointed principal although there are non-Moslem Negro teachers on the staff.[13] There are two non-Moslems at present: both were formerly public school teachers. Moslems are preferred and it is important that they be married. Some exceptions are made for followers of Muhammad. Of the present staff, the principal, who is a part-time employee, studied at the University of Michigan, one teacher has a Master's degree, and three have Bachelor's degrees. Four have completed at least two years of college work, and are now studying for their degrees or hope to do so in the future.

12. The writer was told that the former principal had never attended a single Temple meeting. Some Muslims complained also about the present principal's lack of interest in "religion." He has never attended any religious meeting. The Muslims feel that the Arabs are not interested in identifying with them. Both Arabs are immigrants. [Since this study was completed, the Egyptian-born principal has been replaced by Sister Christine C. Johnson, a Chicago public school teacher of many years experience.]

13. It is exceedingly difficult for the school to keep the non-Muslim teachers for any length of time. Only few have served in the school for more than a year.

CURRICULUM

The curriculum is patterned, with some modifications, after that of the public schools in Illinois. A report card listing the program of study of 1959–60 reads as follows:

Reading and Spelling
Penmanship
Languages and General Civilization
Arithmetic and Simple Metric System
Advanced Arithmetic
Algebra
Advanced Algebra
General Geometry and Trigonometry
Astronomy
Chronological History From 13,000 B.C.
Solar System
Spook being displayed for 6,000 Years
Chronology
English
Reading
Writing
Composition
Literature
Science
General Science
Biology
Chemistry
Hygiene
Languages
Arabic
Social Studies
History: American History
World History
Geography
Sociology
Civics
Art
Typing
Shorthand
Home Economics
Religion
Islam

The writer spent much of his time at the University of Islam and closely followed the courses offered during the period of this study.

At no time was a separate course offered in the following subjects, although they are listed: astronomy, chronological history from 13,000 B.C., spook Being displayed for 6,000 Years, ending of the spook civilization, and chronology. These subjects properly belong to "religion" and are taught by the minister in the class on Islam.

Arabic is taught from the fourth grade through high school. The Muslims consider Arabic their "national" language. The writer noticed that religion was entirely divorced from the academic subjects and could be obtained only in the class on Islam. The history of the world's civilizations was emphasized. Although the history of the Black Nation is supposed to receive greater emphasis, there was no special course devoted to it. Instead, beginners in the high school studied American history for one year and world history as they advanced. The textbook used for world history is *The Past That Lives Today*, by Carl Becker, Sidney Painter, and Yu-Shan Han. The writer accompanied Minister James when he went to the Follett Book Company to buy textbooks. The salesman there said that "Brother James has been our customer for the past ten years." Minister James and the history instructor solicited the salesman's suggestions for the "most widely and currently used" American history text. They selected one from the list recommended by the salesman.

Until early in 1959 no tuition was charged at the University of Islam. Since then parents have been charged the following fees: fifty cents per week for the first child and twenty-five cents each for the second, third, and fourth child. No fee is charged for the fifth or additional children of the same family. The Messenger was first opposed to the requirement of fees but was later persuaded to concede it on an experimental basis.

The estimated annual cost of operating the school is about $40,-000. Although the school has no fixed budget, current expenses are met partly through weekly contributions from members. The Messenger told the writer that he was planning to reserve funds on a long-term basis for the school. At the present students pay $6.00

annually for textbooks. Free bus transportation to and from the school is provided for all students.

Within the limitations shown above, the performance of the school appears to be reasonable. However, Mr. Naeem appears to have been very much impressed when he wrote in 1956:

> During my visit to the School, I had the great pleasure of seeing young adults (boys and girls) recite passages from the Koran from memory and perform the prayer ritual in a perfect manner. They were also able to carry on conversation in Arabic, using authentic Arab accent. (Needless to say, I was greatly impressed to see such a progress made by converts to Islam. In fact, when a group of eight or nine girls sang for me a popular hymn in Arabic I was moved to tears. Such was the beautiful and unforgettable sight that my eyes saw there!) [14]

Although no student was encountered who could speak Arabic, all of the high school students seem to know their prayers in Arabic. A few can read and write simple sentences in Arabic. Two or three high school graduates of the school have gained entrance to colleges and universities on the basis of their performance on admission tests. Some enter trade or business schools. Others do not go beyond high school.

EXAMINATIONS

In addition to grades for regular subjects, the teacher is required to assign grades to students with regard to the following:

> Attendance
> Conduct
> Cooperation
> Effort
> Reliability

Although students had been graduated prior to 1959, there had never been a formal graduation ceremony. On June 23, 1959, a combined elementary and high school graduation exercise was held for students from Chicago and Detroit Schools. Twelve students from Chicago and six from Detroit received their elementary school diplomas. Four students, two from each city, were graduated from high school. Diplomas were also awarded to the twelve stu-

14. *Moslem World and the U.S.A.*, April–May, 1956, p. 23.

dents who finished high school in previous years. The students wore academic caps and gowns and marched to the tune of "Pomp and Circumstance." The commencement address was delivered by Minister Wilfred of the Detroit Temple, and the Messenger, as President and Founder of the school, made brief remarks before awarding the diplomas. Humorously, he said that he also "needed a diploma!" The staff and members of the Parent-Teacher Association awarded him a silver loving cup inscribed, "Mr. Elijah Muhammad, Messenger of Allah, Founder and President of the University of Islam . . ." And Muhammad was especially happy on this occasion; for him this had been "a long awaited dream" and the fruit of more than twenty-six years of labor and hardship. Never before had Mr. Muhammad been seen to be so joyous—he came forward and bowed several times in acknowledgment of the long applause.

DISCIPLINE AND CONTROL

Students and teachers are required to come to school in prescribed uniforms.

By Order of the Messenger of Allah
The Most Honorable Elijah Muhammad

October 19, 1957

— Girls —

Approved: — Jumper Dresses for the girls, and Head Pieces to match the color of their dresses. The colors are: Brown
Beige, and
Blue

I Length of Dresses:
    1. For Teenagers — 8 inches from floor — age 13 to 17 years.
    2. Girls: Kindergarten to 12 years.
II Length of dress skirts: Well below the calf of the legs.
III All blouses are to have ¾ length sleeves, and high neck bands.
IV Sox — knee length to match dresses.
 V Shoes — Black slippers — for all.

— Boys —

I Boys Suits. The colors are: Blue,
Brown, and
Grey.
II Caps to match the color of their suits.
III Shoes: — Black or brown.

NOTE: All students to be outfitted at once — or within the time required to fill orders, at the M.G.T. Dress Shop or (Dress Salon). Make a $5.00 deposit at the Shop at once.

Teachers are to be outfitted in colors approved for students. Outfits to be made alike.

Per: /s/ *Sis. Lena (Durroh)*
Muhammad's University of Islam
No. 2 Director

The majority of the students dressed neatly. Invariably, the boys wore a suit and tie. The prescribed uniform was not widely used although the school authorities tried to enforce it. The Muslim teachers did not adhere to the colors although they all wore long robes. The non-Muslim teachers used jumpers while they were on the premises.

The majority of the students come from working-class families, which accounts for the minor problems of discipline which one encounters in the school. Every student is searched each morning before he or she enters the classroom. All undesirable articles found on them are confiscated. These include such items as razors, pocket knives, chewing gum, and "indecent" literature. A school day begins with a prayer. But before prayer is said, a guard from the Junior Fruits of Islam shouts, "Attention!", and on the pronouncement by the minister, "Original Salute!", they salute the flag of the Nation. Prayer follows immediately. The minister takes about five minutes every morning to remind the students of the virtues and aspirations of the Black Nation and of their role in its advancement. His emphasis is on good morals and manners.

The responsibility for maintaining discipline is shared by the teachers and officers of the Temple. The Supreme Captains and the Captains visit classes regularly, and students dread being taken before any of them. Often students who misbehaved were sent home and they were not to return unless accompanied by their parents. The "bad" ones were expelled. Usually the parents were reprimanded for the misbehavior of their children. They might even be suspended from the Temple for "failure to look after the morals" of their children. An interesting case involved a father of a fourteen-year old girl. He works for a steel mill, owns a 1958 car, and lives in a blighted neighborhood. He was called in by Temple officers and was ordered by them to move to a better neighborhood "for the sake of your children." He was instructed to find a "place away from the slums" or else face a ninety-day suspension from the Temple. Temple officers and the PTA try to make the parents assume major responsibility for the conduct of their children in and outside of school.

Students in the high school worked relatively hard on their lessons, were obedient to those in authority, but quietly (and sometimes openly) resented restrictions imposed on them. Both the boys and the girls appeared to be more friendly with the non-Muslim instructors, whom they believed to be less austere. Also they showed signs of resentment toward the prohibition of dating. The sex taboo tended to drive the girls together and to seek much stronger ties of friendship with the same sex. It would not be surprising if this taboo was one of the main reasons why six girls transferred at the end of the 1959 school year to the public schools. The major reason given by the girls was that some desired subjects were not being offered at the University of Islam. They emphasized the absence of a course in typing. A similar exodus on the part of the high school boys began, but the Messenger moved in time to check it. For the girls, typing was introduced immediately and an instructor hired for that purpose. The Supreme Captain's boy transferred to Hyde Park High School. In his case the Messenger's permission was obtained by the father. The reason for his transfer appeared to be that he was not studying hard enough inasmuch as he believed his father had some influence. It was felt that a transfer would place him on a competitive basis with other students in the public school.

There were twenty-five students in the high school, twenty girls and five boys. They were asked to answer in writing a few factual questions and to state their ambitions. Most of the students did not co-operate. The responses received follow:

Bobbie Jean X, sixteen years old, was born in Marshall County, Mississippi, and has been in Chicago since February 23, 1958. Her father is a worker. Neither of her parents is in the Nation. She has been a registered Muslim for about a year. Her ambition is "to be a nice Muslim, and a better helper to the Messenger, Most Honorable Elijah Muhammad."

Phenoy Karriem, sixteen years old, was born in Chicago. Her grandparents have been members of the Nation for the last twenty-five years. Her grandfather works at a supermarket. Phenoy, who is a rather bright student in the eleventh grade, wants to become a stenographer.

Louise Armstrong is fifteen years old and was born in Chicago. She transferred to the University from the public school system. Her father works in a steel mill. Neither parent is in the Nation. Louise had been in the Nation for about a month at the time of this report. "My ambitions are to finish high school, take a year or two of college, then take two years of nursing. After I have taken up nursing for two years, I plan to work in our own Muslim hospital that we are planning to build."

Ruth Helen X, born in Chicago, is fourteen years old. Her family has been in the Nation for ten years. Her ambition is to be a seamstress.

June Eveline X was born in Hamilton, Mississippi, and she is fourteen years old. She and her parents have been in the Nation for four years. She would like to become a secretary or nurse upon completion of her education.

Carol June X is thirteen years old. She was born in Fort Worth, Texas, and has been in Chicago since 1954. Her father is self-employed. She and her parents have been members of the Nation for seven years. She wants to "help the Messenger of Allah in any way I can."

Mary X is fourteen years old and was born in Memphis, Tennessee. Her parents came to Chicago in 1946. Both parents were unemployed at the time of this study. Her parents have been in the Nation for nearly sixteen years and she has been a Muslim since she was born. Her ambition is to be a teacher "exactly like Brother James," or a nurse.

Clara Marie Sharrieff, twelve years old, was born in Chicago. Her father is Raymond Sharrieff, the Supreme Captain. Her mother operates a business. Her mother has been in the Temple for twenty-eight years and her father for twenty-six years. Clara's ambition is to be a medical doctor.

Alice X is fourteen years old. Born in Greenwood, Mississippi, she came with her parents to Chicago about 1952. Her father is a machine operator. They have been in the Nation for three years. Her ambition is to finish college and "become a teacher like Sister Ray or maybe a high class nurse or secretary . . ."

Christine 2X is almost thirteen years old and was born in Mississippi. Her family came to Chicago about 1950 and have been in the Nation for seven years. Christine would like to become a nurse or doctor. She and Clara are very close friends.

Twenty-five boys in the seventh and eighth grades were asked the same question. All of them expressed a desire to go to college upon completion of high school. A few of their responses follow.

Glen 3X is twelve years old and in the eighth grade:

I have given some thought to it. I want to study law. My uncle is a lawyer. My father and mother are in the Nation. My aunt has government bonds up to $3,000.00 and insurance policy for my education.

Wallace Muhammad is the Messenger's grandson. He wants to become a physician, and as far as he knows, no one in his family has ever been a doctor.

My mother is trying to save money so that I can go to college and then to a medical school. I have two jobs myself. I earn $28.00 per week on both jobs. Out of this sum, I save $15.00 a week and mother adds $10.00 to this. We save weekly $25.00 with a bank for my education.

Wallace's cousin Elijah hopes to be an industrial engineer because "I understand that they make lots of money." He said that both his father and mother are working and saving money toward his college education.

Timothy Earl Garrett is fourteen and both parents are in the Nation. He hopes to become a chemist. His father is an interior decorator and his mother works for Spiegel Company. Timothy told the writer that his father and mother have already saved up enough money for his education.

Although this survey is limited, a marked difference was shown between the aspirations of the boys and the girls. The majority of the boys hoped to go to college, whereas only a few girls were interested in a college career. However, what impressed the writer was the relationship between their career plans and the opportunities which they perceived to be available or likely to be available in the Nation. Medicine seemed attractive because one of the Nation's projects is the building of a hospital. Also evident was an interest in industrial training and, for the girls, in secretarial work. The Messenger's secretaries hold attractive prestigious positions in the Nation. Although the exclusive life of the Muslims tends to narrow their perception of opportunities which may be open to Negroes, most Muslim parents expressed the desire that their children receive college education.

A few adults were asked what they would like their sons or daughters to become. Their responses follow.

Sister Mildred:

Let me speak about my son. I want him to be a good Muslim. I want him to become a doctor, but he must be a good Muslim first.

Brother Thomas Jones:

I would like my children to become teachers at the University of Islam. To have them qualified so that they can better render service to the Nation in any capacity which pleases Allah and His Messenger, I certainly hope that they would go to college and I shall put every effort toward it.

Brother Karriem Allah:

I would want Osman to become a teacher of Islam [minister]. I desire that my other children become believers in Allah and Islam. I hope to send Osman to college and also to the University of Al-Azhar in Egypt.

Brother Donald X:

I would like them to become anything they wanted to, as long as they do it the right way — a doctor, lawyer, etc. By right way, I mean, I would not want them to get a good education and use it to aid the Caucasian people and not their people.

Sister Elaine X:

I want them to be good Muslim children. I want them to respect adults. I shall let them decide what they want to do professionally. I don't think that I want anyone to decide what I should be and I do not want to decide for my children.

Brother John W:

Basically, I would want him to be a good Muslim and would like for opportunities to be so that he could choose a field whereby he could make a very great contribution to the advancement and uplifting of Islam.

Among the adults the range of choice was wider, although emphasis was on the children being first and foremost "good" Muslims and also on using their education to advance the Nation of Islam.

ADULT EDUCATION

Facilities at the University of Islam serve also for the education of adults. Information on the progress of adult education at the Chicago Temple was limited because these classes constitute part of the F.O.I. and M.G.T.–G.C.C. activities which are open only to registered Muslims. However, Arabic classes held at 4:00 and 6:00 P.M. were attended also by non-members. The other courses are offered at night, and they are said to be tailored to suit the interests of small groups. Perhaps the courses which more members take advantage of than any others are those in writing, reading, and arithmetic. There appear to be among the migrants from the South a few whose ability to read and write is markedly limited and the night school offers an opportunity for them to study.

Interest in learning is particularly keen among the men under thirty. Among this group, many take advantage of evening schools in the city where training is offered in technical skills or business. During the period of this study, five young men and two women who had quit after a year or two of college were back in school to complete their work. Many attribute their renewed interest in education to the teachings of Muhammad. They claim that their ambitions have been "heightened" by these teachings. Minister Karriem in an interview said that he was the "fruit" of the work of Mr. Muhammad among the so-called Negroes. Minister Karriem is now in charge of Temple No. 6, Baltimore, Maryland, which he claims has four thousand members. He joined the Nation of Islam in 1943. He claimed that, prior to joining the Nation, he was "completely illiterate" and that the Messenger taught him "how to read and write." He proudly noted that not only can he now read and write, but he also types and lectures to many Negro colleges and organizations. A few examples of the changed outlook of followers in terms of their ambitions now as compared with the past illustrate this point.

Sister Elaine X:

Three years ago I didn't have any ambition — I mean, I didn't quite know what I wanted to be. Now I know what I want to be. I want to be a comptometer operator. That's all. Some day, I would like to be a house-wife and get two children. I want a boy and a girl. I want to have a home of my own. I want to save a little money before I get married and I want to be married to a Muslim.

Elaine is currently taking courses in a business school, training for her chosen career.

Brother John W:

My ambition at present is to qualify myself in some way whereby I can be of some help in the Nation of Islam. I have tried to be more studious in various fields. I feel I am now best qualified with the stenographic ma-chine. If this doesn't work, I would like to be a minister. I would like to have my mind definitely made up and I want to be as successful when and if I become a minister. In the past, my ambition was very low. All I imagined myself doing was to get married, get a job, and raise a family. I still did not want to work as hard for my living as my father did.

Brother John W recently completed a three-year course in court-stenographic reporting.

Brother Kwrmenr X (Crowley) is currently studying Arabic and Russian and also studying for a college degree. These and other adults showed keen interest in education both in the liberal arts and, particularly, in the sciences. However, the majority of this group were interested in the trades.

Ministers of the Temples of Islam are drawn from the members of the F.O.I. They receive a major portion of their training tutori-ally from the Messenger, but also from the University of Islam's adult education program. During the course of training, a prospec-tive minister is regularly tested for his comprehension of the teach-ings and his effectiveness in public speaking. Student ministers, as has been indicated, speak for brief periods at the Wednesday night meetings.

X. Black Zionism

> It is entirely natural for man to want to be equal of man. It is natural, again, for man to love the Brotherhood of Man (except the man devil).
>
> Further, it is natural for man to love FREEDOM for himself, for Freedom is essential for life, and to love JUSTICE for himself, for without Justice there is no joy in freedom and equality.
>
> THE SUPREME WISDOM

IN ITS ideology the Nation of Islam is political: its objective is expressed both in terms of a Negro homeland and in the wishful image of the post-apocalypse Black Nation. The former, improbable as its realization may be, lies within the realm of human experience and is therefore theoretically possible. The latter is a paradise located outside of society in some sphere transcending historical experience. In practice, however, the Nation of Islam is apolitical. If it has political aims of a practical kind, they are not clear. At present, at least, it is a nation within a nation — a vanguard of Negro exodus and nationhood. Its Zion is not clearly defined.

The political doctrines of the Nation seem inconsequential except insofar as Muhammad attempts to define the sources of political life and authority, stipulate the conditions under which individuals (especially American Negroes) may enjoy such rights as freedom, justice and equality, and asserts his attitude toward democratic claims of the United States. Important for us, however, is the relationship of the movement to other political or leadership groups in the United States and possibly with foreign groups or governments, as well as the function which his proposed political solution contributes to the movement.

Political life and authority emanate from Allah:

In the Name of Allah, the Beneficient, the Merciful. Let us give Praise to Allah, our God, for His Love, Mercy and Blessings upon us in this wilderness for giving us a Flag that represents the Universe, Sun, Moon and Star. It also means that we are FREE, JUSTIFIED, and made EQUAL of all mankind.[1]

The same person is both the religious and political leader of the Nation. This conception is theocratic. Allah brings about the New World in its completeness, and He will be the Ruler of that world. The religion of the New World will be the New Islam. For the moment, Muhammad, as Messenger of Allah, holds both political and religious leadership.

Political authority is based on the distinction between "right" and "wrong" and, more specifically, on the notion of justice. Justice is inherent in the nature of God. Hence, political authority is predicated on this essential nature of God:

Justice is a very common thing. Justice is right, justice is righteousness. Justice is opposed to wrong. Justice is the nature of God. It is the law that distinguishes right from wrong. Justice is the weapon that God Himself will use to bring judgment and justice to the world on the day of Judgment. Justice is the purpose of the coming of God to judge. To give justice to those that are the deprived of justice of all the people of earth. The so-called American Negroes are more deprived of equal justice than any people on the planet. Justice is one of the most greatest principles of righteousness, fair dealing with one another. If justice were to prevail throughout the world there never would come a day of Judgment. The unjust judges of the world are not concerned with justice for the black man of America. I am here pleading for your justice, not pleading to unjust judges to give you justice. I am pleading to a just judge to give you justice. That just judge is Almighty God Allah. We have arrived at the end of the time of these unjust judges. Therefore you must know the truth of all.[2]

Knowledge of Allah and His true religion and, especially, knowledge of justice, righteousness, and righteous government is indis-

1. This is the inscription on the flag of the Nation of Islam. "Islam," "Freedom," "Justice," and "Equality" are also inscribed, one word on each corner of the flag.
2. Speech at Washington, D. C., May 31, 1959, p. 2.

pensable to the ruler. This knowledge has been revealed to the Nation of Islam through the Honorable Elijah Muhammad, Messenger of Allah. It comes from Allah Himself, who is All-Knowing, All-Wise, Creator and Ruler of the Universe. Only one who has knowledge about these things can rule with justice. The ruler must love justice. In addition, he must possess the qualities of kindness, mercy, and love.

Citizens of the Nation must have knowledge of these truths. They must love justice not only for themselves but also for others (excepting the man devil). The rights of individuals, such as freedom and equality, can be enjoyed only if the citizens have knowledge of these things. They must seek freedom and equality for themselves and for others, for these are natural and essential to man. Without a passion for justice "there is no joy in freedom and equality."

In addition, the individual must have knowledge of himself, his language, his religion, his God, and his Nation. He must live a righteous life — the life of a Muslim. The knowledge and love of "One's Own," knowledge of the "enemy," and of what is right and just constitute the life of a Muslim. In practice, this means living in accordance with the laws of Islam as taught by Muhammad.

We have noted that nationalism facilitates the Muslims' withdrawal from the white society and from the Negro subculture. Muhammad's views toward established political authority in the United States serve the same function. He attacks principally the Negroes' sentimentalism toward the claim of the United States to be democratic. He says that the Negroes have been distracted from ever-present injustices by their unrealistic attachment to the "promise and heritage of basic American documents." This attachment exists because of their lack of knowledge about their past. It is the cause of the Negroes' mental slavery, a slavery which is as bad, if not worse, as physical slavery. Negroes regard Lincoln as their emancipator, a notion which Muhammad believes misguided:

The truth will make you free. . . . You say, "We are already free. Abraham Lincoln freed us." That is not the kind of freedom I speak of. Abraham Lincoln was not your friend. Abraham Lincoln was not instrumental in trying to free you. Remember that. Abraham Lincoln wanted a United

States of America. . . . They didn't want two Presidents. They didn't want
two governments ruling America. They wanted only one government, one
president for them all. Not that they were so full of love for the so-called
Negroes, that he wanted them free from the hands of his brother. But this was
a good weapon to bring his brother into submission to his idea of a United
States and one President of that United States. So, therefore, you were just
lucky that you got freed from servitude and slavery at that time. Otherwise
you would probably still have been in servitude and slavery today. You say
you love Lincoln. You love him because he freed us. He is your emancipator.
I say to you, my beloved brothers and sisters, Lincoln was not your brother.
He was not your friend anymore than George Washington.[3]

Social conditions in the United States have never permitted Negroes to enjoy the freedom they are said to have gained. Their treatment by whites shows that they are not yet free:

We as a people numbering between seventeen and twenty million people
in America have worked and slaved for America for four hundred years,
only now to be denied justice even by the Federal Government. We have
fought in every war that the country was involved in. The so-called Negro's
blood has been shed on his own soil and foreign soil, only today to be denied justice in the government that he has fought and bled and died for.
The government allows lynchers to lynch you and me at will and he even
goes so far as to hide the identity of the lynchers. Turn the lyncher over
to the brother who is in sympathy with him. Our daughters and wives are
beaten and raped before our eyes by the white men and boys of America,
and the government will not put a stop to it; but will allow lynchers to
lynch you and me if we are charged with an attempt to rape one of them.
All of this you suffer. The lynchers live right next door but are not brought
to justice. All of this grief, you and I are burdened with. . . . We killed
the white man in Germany; we killed other white men's brothers for him;
we killed our own brothers for him. Yet we still are without any justice, we
still are without anything. Our sons and daughters are lynched, kicked,
beaten, hung up in the sun. Drowned in the river, in ponds and lakes, their
bodies are found in the street, on the highway, in the bushes — killed by the
very people for whom they have slaved away their lives for four hundred
years. Our women are attacked, insulted, disgraced, right in our homes, in
our eyes, in the street, in the white men's cars, in his house, in his businesses.
They are disgraced in his factory, everywhere our women are trampled under

3. *Islamic News* (Chicago), July 6, 1959, p. 7. This attitude is widely shared
by black nationalists who recall "how Negroes went about the streets of Harlem mourn-
ing the death of President F. D. Roosevelt," whom they consider one of their great
benefactors. In their 4th of July speeches New York black nationalists denounced
Negroes for wasting their hard-earned income on fire-crackers and celebrating an
occasion when their forefathers were still in chains.

foot by the white man. When we go to them for justice, they laugh at us and say, "that's good for you, nigger."[4]

The federal government has not protected Negroes against violations of rights guaranteed them by the Thirteenth and Fourteenth Amendments to the Constitution:

If you consult your history, you will find that you and I have been in this part of the world for some four hundred years. We have served out of that four hundred years a little better than three hundred years in servitude slavery. And about ninety-four we have been so-called free. And we have been called citizens for about that time, is that right? But why are we seeking civil rights if we are citizens of America? We don't have the need of going to the government begging the government to grant us civil rights. We don't need to beg the government to give us those glorious benefits that are laid down in the Constitution, but you and I are still begging for justice, is that right? Well, to whom were these particular Amendments applying to? We know today that we are having trouble trying to sit in classrooms with white people, is that right? If they hate us and despise us so much that they don't want their children educated in the same classroom with you and I, then what should we do? Should we continue to beg for freedom, justice and equality from people who don't want to even sit beside you in an educational institution or ride with you on the same vehicle? Should we continue to beg for freedom, justice and equality from a people that have all of these written in their Constitution and then fail to give it to us? And yet we bleed and die for that same Constitution.[5]

All of these things are happening under a government that is reputedly the most powerful in the world:

It is beyond comprehension that the American government, — mistress of the Seas, Lord of the air, conqueror of outer space, squire of the land and prowler of the deep bottoms of the oceans — is unable to defend us from assault, rape and murder on the streets of these concrete jungles. What sane man can deny that it is now time that you and I take counsel among ourselves to the end of finding justice for ourselves.[6]

We have observed that Muhammad and all black nationalists consider the dependence of Negroes on the initiative of whites for their advancement and for community improvements as one of

4. Speech, Washington, D. C., May 31, 1959, pp. 3–4. References are made to the recent lynching in Mississippi of Mack C. Parker, who was awaiting trial for the alleged rape of a white woman, and to the Florida rape of a Negro college coed by four white men.

5. Speech, 1959 Convention, pp. 3–4. During the 1960 Convention Muhammad stressed the prolonged filibuster by southern Senators over the civil rights bill.

6. *Islamic News* (Chicago), July 6, 1959, p. 2.

their real enemies. For reasons stated previously, Negroes seem to perceive their problems as well as their communities *solely* as the creation of the white society, and hence, they exert their efforts almost exclusively in the direction of making the white society recognize and assume *full* responsibility for the solution of these problems. This attitude, laying blame solely on the whites, tends to obscure serious weaknesses within the Negro community: the lack of cohesion, of a sense of mutual concern; their amoral attitudes toward one another and their lack of "will" to join together for the very demands which they make on the white society. Although the whites are largely responsible for the conditions which have produced these attitudes, American Negroes must now share the responsibility for them.

Muhammad as well as other nationalists insist that Negroes have been free for several decades, but have not yet created conditions necessary for their freedom: Negroes have now reached maturity and should assume a major responsibility for the solution of their own problems. They must stop "begging for freedom, justice, and equality" from others so long as they have not learned to practise these "virtues" among themselves:

Then what shall we do, if we are not going to beg them for freedom, justice and equality? Who are we to turn to? We must remember that if we are to enjoy such rights, we first must create such in ourselves. We have not been able to unite and respect each member of our nation as a brother. We have not been able to respect any of our Kind from abroad as a brother. What is wrong with us? If we want freedom, justice and equality, shouldn't we practice it among ourselves. . . . We have not been able to do anything worthwhile since we left the cotton fields of the South under the lash of the southern white slavemaster. What do I mean, worthwhile? That worthwhile I refer to is toward self-independence. We have been a lot of great things.
. . .
It is only fear that keeps you and I from becoming a great nation, just fear. It is not the white man so much as the fear that is in you about the white man. You are today indeed free, but you don't exercise the right of a free people. But yet you are free. The government of America will agree with me that you are free to go for yourself. The government of America will agree with me that you are free to believe in any God that you choose and any religion that you choose. . . . *Your leaders are preaching the wrong thing. They are not preaching the Gospel of self-independence, as you now have grown to that particular age that you need self-independence. Not serv-*

*ants, not workers for another one. You need now to turn and go and work
for yourself.*

I don't know why the leaders are not preaching to you self-independence.
All of your black kind all over the earth today are rousing them to self-
independence — in the spirit of independence for self. Here you are numbering a nation — here you are around begging the white people. They
claim that they have freed you. You are still begging them to allow you
equal chance on his job that he has made for himself and kind. And then
you are foolish enough — think over that — to think they are doing an injustice to you for not hiring you. It is not injustice for a white man to tell
you and I tomorrow morning, he doesn't have a job for us and that he will
go and hire all of his kind. He could easily say to you and I that we have
had near a hundred years to make jobs for ourselves. Go make one for
yourself. Why do you now continue to hang around the factory gates of the
white man of American begging for a job when we have qualified scholars
and scientists among ourselves that are helping that white man to carry on
his work, to build his factories, keep his people employed. Why don't you
and I get hold of his hand, that man of ours, and pull him out of the factory?
You are not preaching the gospel of self-independence. You are begging
for jobs. It was for that purpose that they brought our forefathers here —
to give them a job to labor for them and not to want self-independence.
Don't fight and quarrel among yourselves. Stop quarreling and fighting
among yourselves. Don't make the whole world look down on you as a
crazy people. Go on, love one another. Do good to each other. . . . [7] (Emphasis added.)

What Muhammad seems to be saying is that there exists in fact
inequality of "conditions" between whites and blacks in the United
States which transcend inequality of "procedure," such as voting
rights (in the South), access to jobs created by whites and other
facilities owned and operated by them. Inequality in procedure, he
believes, is the main concern of such organizations as the National
Association For the Advancement of Colored People and the Urban
League.[8] Black nationalists are in general antagonistic to these or-

7. Speech, 1959 Convention, pp. 3, 15.
8. The nationalists' disdainful attitude toward the NAACP's approach to the Negro
problem rests partly on their belief that the inner weaknesses would not be resolved
by "integration." They seem to ignore the important relationship between procedural
rights and substantive rights. The complaint frequently voiced by them against the
Urban League is that it wants to "fill opportunities created by whites, whereas it should
be teaching them to create or help create opportunities for themselves." Minister Malcolm X has told the writer that many Negro leaders tend to confuse "integration" as a
"means" with the "end," namely, the "overall quality of Negro life or human dignity."
Because of this confusion of means and ends, Malcolm insists that these leaders have
absolutely refused to re-examine the means in relation to the end. He wondered why

ganizations and to the traditional Negro leader because they believe
that these leadership groups have obscured the "real" issues. Inequality of conditions, the nationalists say, result largely from the
Negroes' cultural backwardness, moral dispositions, and the collective image of their place in American society and in the world.
These have prevented the Negro masses from moving. For Muhammad a *total* re-orientation of the social and moral values of the
Negro masses is a prerequisite to the enjoyment of real political
rights. This leads him to ask, "What is to be done?" if the inequality
of conditions between whites and blacks is to be ameliorated, if not
eliminated. Politics, he says, will not help:

> You plead to politics. I want to say to you this afternoon politics will
> not answer your prayers that you are praying. Politics will not solve the
> problem of the Negroes any more than it did for the Hebrews of Israel in
> Egypt.[9]

The Negro is now at the crossroads. He must not be deceived by
the effort toward integration:

> We must not be deceived by the rush toward integration that has become
> the theme of the past few years. Just as the Romans were to beware of the
> Greeks bearing gifts, so must we beware of slavemasters bearing integra-
> tion. Why, I ask you, after four hundred years of murder, rape and slavery-
> dom, do our oppressors now come waving the olive branch of integration?
> Is it that they really love us; is it that they are sincerely sorry for their
> sins and seek restitution? If they love us then why was there no evidence of
> this love in the hearts of their forefathers when they sold our forefathers
> like cattle on the auction block? If they are really seeking to atone then why
> do they not offer us some measure of restitution — an area of this country
> we can call our own — to the sons and daughters of the embattled?
>
> They are not come to this hour because they love us nor is integration a
> sign that they are sorry for their sins. The blunt fact is, our oppressors see
> fire coming. They see the handwriting on the wall and know what it means.
> They would have you believe that the days ahead hold glory for the Chris-
> tian world.
>
> My beloved, I, Elijah Muhammad, who must speak if it kills me and who
> will die rather than lie, tell you this: I know tomorrow, I know the end of it
> all. Tomorrow is not heaven for the Christian world; tomorrow is hell for
> the Christian world. . . .[10]

Negro leaders have failed to communicate with the masses while they have perfected
their communication with whites!

9. Speech, Washington, D. C., p. 2.
10. *Islamic News* (Chicago), July 6, 1959, p. 7.

Negroes must find justice or commit suicide.

What is your life and my life if it has no protection? This thing has come to the point of explosion. I am your brother. Your hurt is my hurt. How many years have you been frightened? "Keep your mouth shut. Don't say that. It is not time." When is it going to get time for you to speak up for yourselves? You can't blame the government for not giving you anything. The only thing that you are pleading for is a job. Is it not true that John Hawkins, the slavetrader of our people, brought you and me here for just the purpose of working for the white man? He didn't bring you here to make you the white man's equal. He didn't bring you here to make you a citizen of America. He didn't bring you here to make you an owner or President of America. He didn't bring you here to make you feel that you are equal with the white people, or that you should demand from the white men equal justice in their court, because in the first place he brought you here to be a slave.

Are you satisfied to be a servant in America for white people forever? To suffer injustice at the hands of the white murderers or satisfied to see your women free to be taken from your side and used by them at their will. Are you satisfied? Where is your intelligence? You have none. You care less. Why? Because you are blind, deaf, and dumb.[11]

THE POLITICAL OBJECTIVES OF
BLACK NATIONALISM

Black nationalism assumes that the distribution of political power between whites and blacks in the United States will not allow of a solution of the Negro problem. Therefore, they have not sought to change either the prevailing American ideology or institutions. Some nationalists have disassociated themselves from politics. Others have sought to use the legislative process.[12] These efforts have been abortive.

The significance of the Nation's political aims is dubious. In the short run, its separatist ideology assists the Muslims to withdraw from political involvement and participation and to devote their attention to the narrow problem of economic self-improvement and the larger problem of moral reform among the lower-class Negroes.

11. Speech, Washington, D. C., p. 6.
12. Efforts of the Peace Movement of Ethiopia and the U.N.I.A. in the thirties and forties to get congressional support for the so-called "Repatriation Bill" are examples. In matters ideological, they have staunchly resisted communist infiltration of their movements, and in the thirties, the Nation of Islam successfully rejected efforts of Japanese and other subversive groups to exploit the movement.

The broadest political objective of the Nation of Islam is expressed in its doctrine of the hereafter, which has already been discussed. It will be recalled that members of the Nation look forward to living under a government of righteousness after the destruction of the present world of unrighteousness. This is the New World of Islam, in which eternal peace and the harmony of black mankind will be realized. Its realization depends upon divine intervention.[13]

Meanwhile Muhammad advocates:

1: Separation from the white people.
2: A home — some good earth where you and I can call our own home.
3: Support for you and me on this earth until we are able to go for ourselves.
4: Complete unity between you and me from this day on and forever.[14]

TERRITORIAL SEPARATION

The Nation of Islam advocates, in addition to the black Utopia, some sort of territorial separation of Negroes and whites. It maintains that separation offers the only solution to the race problem in America:

Separation of the so-called Negroes from their slavemasters' children is a MUST. It is the only SOLUTION to our problem. It was the only solution, according to the Bible, for Israel and the Egyptians, and it will prove to be the only solution for America and her slaves, whom she mockingly calls her citizens, without granting her citizenship. We must keep this in our minds at all times that we are actually being mocked.[15]

13. Non-Muslim black nationalists often ridicule this aspect of Mr. Muhammad's teachings. A member of the Ethiopian World Federation, commenting on Muhammad's "New World" at a meeting of the United African Federation Council previously reported, said: "We did not invite him to this meeting because his movement is a religious cult. They want to stay here until this man (the white man) falls in a millennium. We are not waiting for any miracles. In any case, when this man has fallen, I wonder what will be left for Mr. Muhammad to fall on. His group is doing all right otherwise."

14. Speech, Washington, D. C., p. 16.

15. *The Supreme Wisdom*, II, 39. Cf. Speech, Washington, D. C., p. 13: "Why should not you and I unite too, to our own God and people? Why shouldn't we wake up and unite and demand some earth for our own selves, as other nations are doing? There are small nations only three or four million, that are demanding homes for their people. Here you are numbering six times their number and you are not asking for any earth whatsoever. All we are asking for is: Treat us like you treat yourself and give us a place at your table and in your home and allow us to marry your daughter as you marry mine. What do you look like, asking the white people to swallow you up?"

SYMBOLIC RETURN

The concept of "return to our own kind" is frequently employed by Muhammad. This means the spiritual identification of the members of the Nation with the "Islamic" world and with other non-Caucasian peoples. In a sense, therefore, acceptance of Islam as a religion of black people is a symbolic "return to our own kind."

I have brotherhood, friendship with all the world of Islam, regardless to where they may be. I have friendship and their brotherhood. You need friendship, you need sincere friendship, you have to get it from people like yourself.

Don't look for strange people, members of another race that are not members of your own nation for friendship. They are not your friends, you will be greatly disappointed.

I say, my friends, let's unite with all of the dark people of the earth, but first with ourselves, then with all of our kind; for friendship, brotherly love and protection. Be like white people; they are in unity with all their kind. Be in unity with all our kind. Then you will be like civilized people. Don't let the white people classify you as an enemy of our own people to their own like. They like you to be divided and as long as they have you and me divided, they know that they can rule. A united people is hard to rule.[16]

Muhammad demands a portion of the United States for the settlement of Negroes and the eventual establishment of a Black Republic. The Nation of Islam, it appears, is to be the vanguard of the Black Republic. It will request the United States not only to give land but also to provide material assistance for a time. This, Muhammad says, is not too much to ask in return for the four hundred years of exploitation of the Negroes:

If they don't want us to mix with them in their equality, give us a place in America. Set it aside. . . . Give us three, four or more states. We have well earned whatever they give us; if they give us twenty-five states, we have well earned them. Give us a territory. Give us the same instrument that they had to start a civilization in that terriory. Take care of us. Give us what we ask them for, for the next twenty or twenty-five years until we are able to go for ourselves. Demand something. Don't demand a job. Demand some earth. We have come to the point we must have a home on this earth that we can call our own. You pray for help to be sent to Africa, money to help them be free from England and America. It is like a blind man praying for eyes for the other blind man that can't see and yet doesn't realize that he doesn't have any eyes. It is a shame. . . .[17]

16. Speech, Washington, D. C., p. 14.
17. Speech, Washington, D. C., p. 10. Cf. The United African Nationalist Move-

Elsewhere in this speech Muhammad notes:

They will never give us three or four states. That I probably know, but that doesn't hinder you and me from asking for it.[18]

Does Muhammad really expect the United States to offer Negroes land here in the Western Hemisphere? The writer's impression is that he would make such a request only if he had an impressive number of followers to justify it. On the other hand, his real intention may be no more than to get Negroes to pool their resources for the purchase of property both in the cities and in the rural areas. He is impressed with the great wealth of the United States and "sees no reason why Negroes have to go elsewhere to look for anything more." When a Negro reporter from *Jet* magazine who came to him with what Muhammad thought were "loaded" questions, asked, "Where do you want to establish the Negro state?" he replied, "some portion of this good earth — factories, farms, homes, jobs, etc." Muhammad is very anxious to have Negroes own property and business enterprises, and preparation for this is one of the most important aspects of his teachings. He is a propertied man himself and rents a few apartment buildings to his followers. He points to the businesses owned and operated by the Chicago Temple as examples of what Negroes could do "if only they had enough sense." Those who seem to grasp the significance of this aspect of his teachings point out that he cannot really intend his followers to emigrate because "he is tying up the Nation's money in property." These people say that if he really had emigration in mind he would not be planning to spend so much money for an Islamic Center.

Although Muhammad has made it clear on several occasions that he wants "*some* portion of this earth" for the Negroes, his ambiguity allows his followers to read many meanings into his teachings. As Brother Leonard IX recently explained:

The President of the United States, Mr. Eisenhower, should take all of his white people, willingly or unwillingly, and should give to Mr. Elijah

ment and the African Nationalist Pioneer Movement, both in New York, are now advocating that the United States should pay back to Africa approximately $500 billion as compensation for unpaid African labor which helped develop this country during the entire period of chattel slavery. This is not to be confused with existing foreign aid programs of the United States government.

18. *Ibid.*, p. 11.

Muhammad all of the black people, willingly or unwillingly. This would cut away the confusion of discrimination. One would have no other responsibility as a living human being but to his own. Ike would then put his people on so much land there and give Mr. Muhammad so much land for his people. There would be a buffer zone of one hundred miles separating the two nations right here in America until Allah comes to destroy the devil. . . . We should keep on building the little nation that we now have throughout the [then] forty-eight states until we get enough of our people together so that the Messenger will not have to beg for any agreements but the devil will be glad to make an agreement of that type for he has no other way out.[19]

RETURN TO OUR NATIVE LAND

Although the alternative to a black republic in the Western Hemisphere is return to "our native land," what constitutes "our native land" has never been made clear. Apparently Muhammad means any country outside of the Western Hemisphere, but preferably the Arab regions of the East. Since he claims that the so-called Negroes had their first home in Arabia and that they founded the city of Mecca, it would appear that Saudi Arabia is a logical homeland! The last known settlement before "the so-called Negroes" were brought to the Western world was the Nile Valley. They may, therefore, claim that region of Africa as their homeland. The preference for the Arabic-speaking countries in Africa and in the Middle East is made very clear in Muhammad's teachings. These emphasize the history and cultures of the Arabic people. Ghana, Liberia, Ethiopia, and the other non-Moslem countries of Africa have not received the same emphasis, although in the last year or so Muhammad has become increasingly aware of political developments in tropical Africa.[20]

Followers of Muhammad romanticize all Arab countries, but they have a special affinity for *Afrique Noir* and particularly for the areas of Africa in which Islam is the dominant religion. On many occasions Muhammad has given his followers the impression

19. Interview.

20. This awareness seems to have been sharpened by his recent visit to Africa. The tour, which lasted fifty days, took him to Istanbul, Damascus, Beirut, Jerusalem, Cairo, Khartoum, Addis Ababa Asmara, Medina, Jidda, Mecca, Dharan, Karachi, and Lahore.

that these predominantly Moslem countries are ready and willing to help them to leave the United States if they are persecuted. These countries, he says, would give them refuge as "brothers in Islam." Some followers believe that only those American Negroes will be welcomed in Asia or Africa who are followers of Muhammad. But Muhammad, obviously, does not want to lose his followers and thus he discourages individuals who are eager and perhaps able to emigrate from doing so. A follower in Los Angeles is reported to have emigrated to the Sudan, and Chicago Muslims believed that the Sudanese government would not admit him because he had not received Muhammad's "blessing." A Chicago follower, known to the writer, was discouraged from going to Egypt even though he said he was going there to study. The order that he should not go came after he had begun making inquiries with shipping lines about the cost of transportation. Muhammad is said to have explained that his trip would not be wise because of the international situation (it was June, 1960 — the time of the collapse of the Summit conference). These claims seem to have no other significance than as myths for the consumption of followers — myths intended to facilitate the psychological withdrawal of the followers from society and to enhance the solidarity of the movement. There is, however, an element of "sincere self-deception" in Muhammad's doctrine of separation. This is to say that he believes sincerely and profoundly that each of his proposals for a negro state is desirable and feasible. He seems to think that the real problem lies in uniting Negroes before proposing the ultimate course of action — land in the United States or exodus. He firmly believes that separation would enable "American Negroes to discover themselves, elevate their distinguished men and women to exalted positions, give outlets to their talented youth and assume the contours of a nation, once given opportunities for self-expression beyond the white world."[21]

Other black nationalists, especially the Garveyites, insist, with some justification, that Muhammad indulges not only in self-deception but also in purposeful deception which assists him to "put his message across." They are quick to point out that Muhammad's

21. *White Christian Party Attacks* . . . , p. 11.

promise of exodus to his followers is spurious and that he has no intention whatsoever of encouraging Negroes to emigrate. Generally, those Negroes who might readily leave the United States for settlement in some part of Africa, if they had the means, are probably not attracted by Muhammad's promises and claims.

POLITICAL PARTICIPATION

Neither Muhammad nor his followers participate in local or national politics. The reason they give is religious. The government is unjust and corrupt in the eyes of Allah. It would therefore be sinful for righteous Muslims to participate in its affairs. Furthermore, the government has been condemned to destruction by Allah, and it would be contrary to His will for the Muslims to help in postponing the day of judgment. This is consistent with Muhammad's teaching that "to integrate with evil is to be destroyed with evil. If we know a man is doomed, we should try to get as far away from him as possible." Followers of Muhammad have been enjoined by Allah not to vote. They hold that their nationality is not "American." They are "Muslims" or "Asiatics." They seem to equate "Muslim" with nationality: a young follower who was seeking admission to the Chicago Technical College, 2000 South Michigan Boulevard, asked the writer to be one of his references. On his application form he gave his "race" and "nationality" as "Asiatic" and "Muslim."

Some members indicate, however, that political participation would be unwise at this time. A few of these believe that Negro unity (under Muhammad's leadership) is essential to effective political participation. A minister speaking of one of the northern urban centers said that "the whites are leaving to the suburbs" and "with the unity of black to black" the latter could control the city. Many Muslims are aware of political currents in the United States, particularly as these affect Negroes.

There is no reason to believe that followers of Muhammad vote surreptitiously. The writer inquired of two precinct captains on this point. One said, "they simply do not vote." The other said that he had once managed to get "one of the weaker sex" to vote. "She had some difficulties," he said. "She needed my help and I guess that's why she voted."

There is speculation, however, that the Muslims may, as they feel more secure, take an active interest in local politics in the major northern cities. This speculation arises in part from a statement made by Minister Malcolm X. At an outdoor Freedom Rally in May, 1960, sponsored by the New York Temple and reportedly attended by 10,000 Harlemites, he told the gathering:

> The Honorable Elijah Muhammad and his thousands of followers will place their weight behind "any fearless black leaders who will stand up and help the so-called American Negro get complete and immediate freedom."[22]

It is said that the statement came just after Minister Malcolm had reminded the "enthusiastic crowd that a big election is coming up this year and then asked what kind of leaders the masses will support." They will not support leaders "who are hand-picked for us":

> If these leaders are afraid to be identified with us then they can no longer expect the support of the masses. . . . They charge us with being extremists but if it was not *for* the extremists the white man *would* ignore the moderates.[23]

The nature of support the Muslims would give Negro political leaders is not clear, since they do not vote. Of course, they may contribute financially to an "approved" Negro candidate seeking an elective office either through existing political parties or independently of them. They could do so without necessarily voting. We believe, however, that in cities like New York their support of Negro candidates would be important, not from the standpoint of their voting strength or of their financial contributions, but as voluntary workers for the candidates. Because the Muslims are highly organized, disciplined, and enthusiastic, they would certainly be an asset to a candidate who had their support. On the other hand, they may also be a liability for a candidate openly supported by a group considered by many as advocating black supremacy. In Chicago

22. Quoted in the *New Crusader*, June 4, 1960, p. 3. Cf. *Mr. Muhammad Speaks* "The Voice of Harlem," New York, May, 1960, p. 5.
23. *The New Crusader*, June 4, 1960, p. 3.

their influence may not be significant, partly because of an effectively organized Negro political machine, but particularly because of the profound insensitivity and apathy of Chicago Negroes to "racial" leaders or issues.[24]

The Muslims are not likely to participate in politics in the foreseeable future. First, this would require a significant change in their beliefs and ideological orientations. The writer interviewed Minister Malcolm X a few weeks after he had made the statements quoted previously to ascertain the Muslims' political plans, if any. He told the writer that the Muslims were not planning on voting and do not expect to participate in the politics of the United States:

> That we are not going to the polls does not mean that we are not voting. We abstain from voting and abstention is a kind of voting. We do not believe in voting Negroes to go to Washington and serve the white people. We want our own nation and if Negroes are good enough to serve in Washington, they should be good enough to serve in their own nation. Lots of newspaper people have asked me the same question you are asking since I made that statement. The Honorable Elijah Muhammad will support those Negroes who demand an independent Negro state. Let me add: we should not foreclose what we may do in the future.

The writer is inclined to believe that Malcolm's statement was for the purpose of "testing" public reaction, especially the reaction of Negro politicians. However, on July 31, 1960, Muhammad told nearly 10,000 Negroes in Harlem to "go to the voting polls with their eyes and ears open."[25]

ATTITUDE TOWARD CIVIL AUTHORITY

Muhammad teaches all his followers that they must submit to the just acts of those in authority in public or private life, provided these do not conflict with their religious beliefs. In a speech in

24. It has been suggested that the existence of an efficient Negro political machine capable of providing reward through patronage and other services accounts for the Negro's lack of enthusiasm for "race" leaders or issues. In New York Negro response to "race" leaders seems to be more evident.

25. Quoted in Los Angeles *Herald-Dispatch*, August 11, 1960, p. 1. The editor, in the same issue, urged Muhammad to organize Negroes to vote in the coming presidential election: "We trust Mr. Muhammad recognizes the necessity for an all out drive, led by his followers, to get the Negro, all over America, to register and vote in November. . . ." The editor implied that seeking a separate state in the United States was a vain hope.

Detroit in 1959 he advised his followers to "obey those in authority" and admonished them: "Be yourself — yourself is a righteous Muslim. Follow the Golden Rule. . . . Be polite, courteous and respectful so that you may inspire respect from the police officers. . . . If you are attacked when peaceful, God comes to our rescue. If you are aggressive, you must fight your own battle without Allah's help. If attacked, the Holy Koran says to fight back."

Questioned about his attitude toward civil authority, Minister James 3X responded:

I have all the respect for civil authority. I learnt earlier in life that there can be no peace or stability in society without the highest respect of the citizens for the constituted authority. I would respect the laws of any land provided they do not conflict with the laws of the Holy Koran.[26]

Except with regard to military service, Muhammad's followers are law-abiding citizens. They stubbornly resist induction into the United States military forces. During the second World War most of the eligible ones preferred the penitentiary. Their attitude has not changed. They refuse military service on the ground that Allah enjoins them to abhor war and not to contribute in any way to preparations for it. Some have claimed the status of conscientious objectors, and in at least two known instances — those of Wallace Muhammad and his brother, Akbar — these were granted.

Minister Wallace was eligible for the draft in 1953. On January 20, he was classified 1-A. He appealed that decision, claiming the status of a conscientious objector. This was granted by his local board. In 1957 it was explained to him that as a conscientious objector he would have to serve two years' civilian duty, and he was assigned to the State Hospital at Elgin. He failed to report to the hospital and was therefore indicted, tried, and was found guilty by the U.S. District Court in 1958. However, during the trial his attorney argued that he had not been duly ordered to report to the hospital because the order bore the signature of a clerk, not that of a draft board member. On this ground the judge ordered a new trial and Minister Wallace was found not guilty because the order for him to report was invalid. Meanwhile he was properly

26. Interview.

ordered by the draft board to report to the hospital. When Minister Wallace failed again to report, he was indicted a second time, in January, 1959. At this trial, the defense attorney argued that as a regular minister, Wallace was exempt and that the proceeding was a denial of his client's constitutional rights. Minister Wallace was found guilty of failing to report for civilian duty at the hospital.[27] The judge said that there was no "factual basis" to Wallace's claim of being a minister in the Muslim faith. He ordered a pre-sentence investigation and on April 21, 1960, Wallace was sentenced to three years' imprisonment. The defendant's appeal was denied by federal judge Edwyn Robson in late October, 1961.

The followers regarded the verdict as another evidence of religious persecution but were not outraged. The Muslims feel that their status as a religious body was the unstated premise upon which the case was decided. They insist that Brother Wallace is a minister and that "the facts are there."

Minister Wallace was calm throughout the period of the trial and often drove his own car to the court. He anticipated being found guilty but expressed the hope that the "sentence would be light." As a logical successor to the Messenger, some sentence would be to his advantage and enhance his charisma. It would assure the followers of his mettle as well as of his right to step into his father's shoes. He wanted to "get the sentence over with because it had dragged on for seven or eight years." He yielded, however, to his attorney's advice that "important" constitutional issues were at stake.

A case involving an assistant minister at the Philadelphia Temple seems to have taken a different course. Brother James 6X, the assistant minister, is twenty-two years old and a high school graduate. He became a follower of Muhammad about three years ago. The following is his account:

While I was in high school and before I reunited with the Nation of Islam I registered with Local Board 137 in Philadelphia and I was placed un-

27. U.S. v. Wallace Delaney Muhammad, "Memorandum On The Defendant's Motion For Judgment Of Acquittal" (Typed) and "Defendant's Memorandum In Support Of His Judgment Of Acquittal" (Typed), William R. Ming, Jr. & Co., Attorneys for Defendant. Both documents were made available to the writer by Mr. W. R. Ming, Jr. The writer is grateful to Mr. Ming who placed at his disposal files connected with this case.

der I-SH classification. Upon my graduation my classification was changed to I-A and because I got into some trouble I was later classified 4-F. In late 1959, the draft board sent me a letter wanting to know whether there was a change in my status. I wrote to say that there was no change and that I am an assistant minister of Islam. I asked that I be given the status of a conscientious objector, but the clerk replied that I should appear for physical examination. I was examined and I passed.[28]

Brother James' 4-F classification had hitherto made him ineligible. After he passed the physical examination, the clerk asked him about his beliefs. He replied that he was a Muslim and that he "would not serve anyone but Allah":

I said to him, how could I preach peace with a gun in my hand? The clerk asked me what I would do if I saw a black man and a white man in a pit. "Would you save them?" he asked. I said I would save the black man. "Then what?" said the clerk. I told him Allah is the best knower. He said, "Do you wish to say that Allah would intervene then?" I said yes, because he is everywhere as far as I am concerned. He gave me the thoughts I am now speaking. The clerk said, "I am trying to talk to you as an individual," and I said, well, when you talk to one Muslim, you are talking to all Muslims. There is no such thing as an individual Muslim. We are all one.[29]

According to him, the draft board wrote later to say that "I was unacceptable even though I had passed the physical examination."

Apparently, not all Muslims seek the status of conscientious objector. A former follower, Milburn J. Davis, is now serving in the Air Force and still thinks that he is a conscientious objector and "if it's Allah's will, I'll stay one."[30]

FREEDOM, JUSTICE, AND EQUALITY IN ISLAM

The national principle is the ideological basis upon which the Nation of Islam is organized. The organization of the Nation and the symbols of authority suggest to the members a form of "private"

28. Interview.
29. Interview.
30. In a letter to the editor of *Sepia* (January, 1960, p. 5), Mr. Davis wrote: "I am the only Muslim in the United States military services. At the time I enlisted I had been active in Muhammad's Temple of Islam. . . . Why did I come into the Air Force? I was a fool, that's why. . . . I signed up professing to be a conscientious objector. . . . How do I like the military? I don't. Because I sought adventure, I turned my restlessness to the Air Force. But since I have been part of it, I haven't known a day of rest or serenity. . . . I wish I were free from this service life so I could partake in Islam. . . . I am a conscientious objector and if it's Allah's will, I'll stay one."

government where they seek freedom, justice and equality, among themselves rather than in the larger American community. Consequently, members feel that they belong both to a nation and a government of their own. It will be recalled that the Nation of Islam has its own head of government, the Messenger of Allah, who combines both spiritual and secular authority in his office. In addition, the Nation has its own flag and its own corps of private police who maintain discipline within the Nation. It is within this framework that the members speak of equality in the brotherhood of Islam. They regard themselves as "brothers and sisters" and as equals within the Nation. In a very real sense, they enjoy fraternity, equality, and fair play in the Nation. Their freedom is limited by both voluntary self-restraint and by the demands of the New Islam and the leader. The following discussion of one of the organizations within the Chicago Temple is illustrative of the degree of membership participation in the business of the Temple.

THE PARENT-TEACHER ASSOCIATION

Within certain limits the Parent-Teacher Association of the University of Islam is an example of democratic participation. Parents and teachers who comprise the organization meet regularly, and decisions concerning the welfare of the students and the progress of the school are made by this body. The PTA elects officers, and its meetings are conducted according to simplified parliamentary rules. Members discuss freely and vote on matters concerning the school. The Messenger is not a member, as he has no school-age children. The PTA may make recommendations to the Messenger on any subject.

During the period of this study, the PTA held several functions in order to raise money to reimburse the Messenger for purchase of textbooks issued to students of the University without charge, and was able to raise most of the amount. The PTA also took the initiative in planning for a biennial health examination of the students at the University of Islam. A committee was appointed to investigate what services would be available and at what cost. The committee's investigation proved that it would be financially feasible.

The decision was forwarded to the Messenger, who promptly cooperated with the PTA. The students of the University of Islam have since received free physical, dental, and eye examinations. Children found to have sight defects were provided with glasses if their parents could not afford them. In some cases the cost of glasses was to be repaid on an installment basis by the parents. In such matters the followers have much discretion. The Messenger has a veto power, but he is likely to use it rarely for fear of losing the good will of his followers.

THE NATION AND THE NEGROES IN THE UNITED STATES

Muhammad declares:

One of the chief purposes of Islam in America is to bring about unity of our people. . . . When this is achieved, we would have a greater weapon in our hands and possession than all the atomic bombs the West can manufacture.[31]

Accordingly he calls for a "United Front of Black Men of America":

Unite, my people, and regardless of your faiths and beliefs, form yourselves into one Nation of Brotherhood (the love and help of each other). You will see that unity will solve the greater part of your problems before you know it.[32]

To what extent does the Nation seek in practice the unity and brotherhood of Negroes regardless of their "faiths and beliefs?" On the whole Muhammad and his followers have been careful not to antagonize other Negro leaders and organizations. He is disgusted with the "so-called" leaders and, particularly, the middle class and the Negro intellectuals, and he paraphrases approvingly Frazier's remarks in *Black Bourgeoisie:* "The Negro elite in the United States subsists on the crumbs of white philanthropy, the salary of public servants, and what can be squeezed from the meager earnings of the Negro workers (*sic*)".[33]

31. *The Supreme Wisdom*, II, 83–84.
32. *Ibid.*, p. 84.
33. Quoted inaccurately in *White Christian Party Attacks* . . . , p. 10.

Although Muhammad's appeal is directed mainly to the "Negro in the mud," he has recently begun to seek support from the Negro middle class. This change was evident at the 1960 Convention. Negro professional and other middle-class persons who attended the final session were seated in a reserved section near the rostrum. Muhammad appealed to them to unite with him:

> Let's unite into a great nation. Get behind me you professional people. Back me up. . . . Why do you tremble when I ask you to join me? Join up with me and you won't have to open your mouth. I'll do all the talking and take all the chances. Just don't throw stones at me. If I had one million Negroes behind me today the other nineteen million in the United States would be free tomorrow. . . . With all your diplomas you are ready to rob your own people just like the white man.[34]

A Negro newspaper reporter correctly observed that in his appeal Muhammad "begged, cajoled, threatened and ridiculed American Negroes, especially the well-educated ones and leaders."[35]

Another indication of Muhammad's changed attitude toward the middle class was the Unity Bazaar at which Negro businessmen were given an opportunity to display their products. More than one hundred Negro businesses and organizations were represented at the bazaar. These were mostly small businesses, although two savings and loan associations were represented. There is some evidence of more co-operation between Muhammad and Negro businessmen in the future.

A sustained business relationship existed between the Nation of Islam and the Pittsburgh Courier Publishing Company from 1956 until the summer of 1959. Owing to adverse publicity given the movement, the *Courier* was allegedly pressured into terminating the relationship. A local NAACP secretary reports pressure exerted on his group:

> In the time since the Muslim group has been brought to the nation's attention, the local NAACP office has been advised by several sincere individuals that we must denounce the Muslims in no uncertain terms . . . They advised full-page ads in local newspapers, and some even offered money to help underwrite the project. They further urged that The Pittsburgh Cour-

34. Speech, from the writer's notes taken at the Convention.
35. Wesley South, in the *Chicago American*, "Prophet Tosses Dud Bombshell," February 29, 1960, p. 3.

ier, which each week publishes a column by the Muslim leader, Muhammad, be condemned for this action, and that we use our influence to get the column removed.[36]

The relationship was beneficial to both parties, for in 1958 followers of Muhammad sold 1,164,110 copies of the *Courier* and realized a total of $23,282.20 in commissions at two cents per copy.

Here is a fact. From little acorns big trees grow. Let's take the principles of this statement, convert and use them to help our Nation's progress. Our pennies can be the acorns and our goal like unto a tree.

Thanks to Allah we sold 1,164,110 *Pittsburgh Couriers* during the year of 1958. Multiply this figure by two cents and you get $23,282.20. . . .

Brothers, let's give those two pennies more of our *Courier* sales money to our future and make this tree grow tall and strong.[37]

In addition to the financial return to the Nation, Muhammad had the advantage of being able to publish his weekly Message in the *Courier* for nearly four years.

A similar relationship now exists between the Messenger and the *Herald-Dispatch,* a Los Angeles weekly. The paper has become a mouthpiece for Muhammad; its editorials are mainly restatements of his arguments. The Muslims sell the newspaper in various parts of the country. A number of other Negro newspapers give regular columns to Muhammad's writings. Although for some time in 1959 the *New Crusader* (a Chicago Negro weekly which calls itself the "Militant Voice of the Negro People") carried anti-Muhammad articles inspired by a rival Negro Moslem sect, it has since ceased doing so, and Muhammad has begun to write weekly articles for it instead.[38]

36. Derrick Bell, Executive Secretary, Pittsburgh Branch, NAACP, writing in the *Pittsburgh Courier,* September 5, 1959, p. 3 (Magazine section). Although he disagrees with the Muslim doctrines he felt that it would be unwise for the *Courier* to discontinue Muhammad's column. It has been alleged also that white advertising agencies threatened to withdraw their support if Muhammad's columns were not discontinued.

37. Circular letter to Muslims from Captain Raymond Sharrieff, undated. Until the severance of relationship between the *Pittsburgh Courier* publishers and Muhammad, the paper sold for fifteen cents. The company received thirteen cents per copy. On this basis, it grossed $151,334.30 in 1958 from sales which were made by the Muslims.

38. Muhammad's followers are currently selling the *New Crusader* in Chicago and arrangements are being made between the publisher and Muhammad for nationwide sales through various Temples.

The Nation avoids connections with Negro organizations and leadership groups in Chicago or elsewhere. When some Negroes who opposed the Hyde Park-Kenwood Urban Renewal Project approached the Muslims for support, the Temple leadership took no interest and declined to co-operate. Muhammad has emphasized that he is "not organizing his followers to be turned over to any group to exploit." Most of his followers do not belong to any other organizations. Many have an aversion to labor unions. If they belong, their participation is limited to payment of dues. Brother Thomas 5X (Drake), a member of the AFL-CIO Meat Packers Union, resigned his position as a shop steward when he became a follower:

> I joined the Union about nine years ago and was quite active in it. I think that the principles of trade unionism are good, but it would stand for a lot of improvements. The union runs into the same control one finds in politics. Therefore, this stopped me — any time anything is controlled by whites. The good one sees in the union is that they take advantage of the worker. The Negro needs the union for some kind of unity to stay away from the wrath of the boss. I was a steward in my local. As an officer of the union, we run into difficulties. The low culture and lack of understanding among the Negroes in general makes the leader feel very disappointed. He fights alone and he has only the contract to fight with against the management. The rank and file do not give him the support which is necessary. I did not feel that I should continue to fight for a man who was content lying low down. . . . The orientations of the union are essentially different from the struggle of the Negro. At one time I was hopeful that workers' solidarity through trade unionism would go a long way toward solving the Negro problem. I no longer believe that this is possible.[39]

The attitude of Muslims toward labor unions is evidence of their distrust of white institutions and leadership. Significantly, by withdrawing from active participation in the unions, they disassociate themselves also from the widespread allegations of corruptions in these unions. Thus, they place themselves in a position of moral "superiority" over whites who lead the unions. Similarly, they disassociate themselves from "contamination" by Negroes who, because of their ignorance, have been corrupted by white leadership. Withdrawal from active participation in this and in other organizations (black or white) helps to inspire undivided loyalty in the movement.

39. Interview.

BLACK HEGEMONY AND MOSLEM BROTHERHOOD

Muhammad wants not only to unite Negroes of the United States under the Crescent of Islam but also to "reconnect" them to their "own kind" by establishing bonds of friendship with other Islamic believers and with all darker peoples of the world. In his effort to give his followers a sense of identity with a civilization, tradition, culture, and a center of power which they have been denied in the United States, he tends to romanticize the Middle-Eastern and Arabic-speaking African countries, as seen in his report on his African-Asian tour:

On November 21, 1959, I left New York with my two sons for a tour of Asia and Africa where Islam is the dominant religion of the black man today. We landed in Turkey on November 22 to be greeted in an atmosphere entirely different from what we knew in America. It was like being in a different world.

There was friendship and brotherly love in Turkey when it was learned we were Muslims. If you are drunk of the white man's Christianity, don't go over there. They don't like Christians.

We could live anywhere over there without thinking someone was going to throw a stone because we were in the wrong place. We could go about without feeling someone was going to say "hey nigger . . . where the hell are you going." I felt for the first time like I was getting into a land of freedom. . . .

It was a paradise to be among them. I had to leave Egypt to keep from staying. I was offered a beautiful home in Cairo while there for thirteen days. Egypt is a Muslim nation with a Muslim ruler.

But you can't go into the nation of Islam with the white man's name. You must change the name and take on a name of your own nation.[40]

Apparently some Moslem groups in Africa and Asia have heard of the Islamic movement among Negroes in the United States and are interested in knowing about it. We do not know how well Muhammad's movement is known among Moslems abroad. Individuals write, however, to obtain information about either the movement or the University of Islam. A Moslem African from Sierra Leone, West Africa, sought admission to the University of Islam. The principal explained that the school does not offer college courses. The applicant had already completed high school in Sierra Leone. Sim-

40. Speech at the 1960 Convention. From the writer's notes.

ilarly, a few foreign visitors in the United States who have heard or read about Muhammad's movement have paid visits to him. Such guests include students from Africa and the Middle East. Mr. Muhammad in his speeches has given the impression that he has friends among officials of Afro-Asian countries.

The Moslem World and the U.S.A., a magazine published in New York, was the main organ which attempted to introduce Muhammad's movement to the "Moslem" world. The first issue was published in January, 1955, and five additional issues were published between then and the end of the first half of 1957. The editor-publisher, Abdul Basit Naeem, has been mentioned as a representative in the United States of the Jam'iat-ul-Falah, which is described as: ". . . a Moslem religious organization of Pakistan, the sole aim of which is to work for the exposition, propagation and implementation, in all its fullness, of the scheme of life promulgated by Islam and, thereby, to promote the all-round well-being of humanity."[41] About the same period, Naeem was also the editor-publisher of the *African-Asian World,* a magazine published in New York and devoted to the discussion of African-Asian affairs. American Muslims (including the Nation of Islam) were not discussed in the latter magazine.

The Moslem World and the U.S.A. addressed itself generally to Moslems in the United States and also to black nationalists. It contained news about Moslems abroad and about politics in the Middle East. During the Suez crisis it sought to mobilize opinion through its editorials in support of President Nasser's nationalization policy:

President Gamal Abdel Nasser has done it again! This time it's the nationalization of the Suez Canal Company. . . .

Whatever measures the West wishes to take to seek a reversal of President Nasser's historic decision, we believe the "seizure" of Suez by its rightful owners is good news from Egypt and an action worthy of sincerest commendation and whole-hearted support by all Moslems.[42]

Naeem sought also to influence opinion in the United States in support of the Algerian independence movement.

41. *Moslem World and the U.S.A.*, October, November, December, 1956, p. 3.
42. *Moslem World and the U.S.A.*, August–September, 1956, p. 4.

. . . Brave sons of Algerian mothers continue to lay down their lives for the precious Cause of their homeland's freedom from colonial rule. The enemy remains as merciless as ever. . . .

Believing that ALL COLONIALISM AND IMPERIALISM MUST GO, and that the people of Algeria have just as much right to freedom and sovereignty as do the French or other nations of the world, we cannot help praying that Paris would come to its senses, soon, and recognize the independence of Algeria as she has of two former colonies — Tunisia and Morocco. Meanwhile, we feel compelled to say also: "Keep it up, Algeria!"[43]

Aside from Muhammad's teachings, and news about his followers, which comprised about one-third of the magazine, Naeem was largely responsible for interpreting the Nation of Islam. He became Muhammad's propagandist for Moslems in Africa and Asia.[44] In an editorial entitled "Mr. Elijah Muhammad and MOSLEM WORLD & THE U.S.A.," Mr. Naeem said, however:

The publication of our articles on the Moslem movement of Mr. Elijah Muhammad in the last three issues of the MOSLEM WORLD & THE U.S.A. has created considerable interest in the world of Islam and among Moslems in the U.S.A. . . . Many of the readers have requested "more information" and "the truth" about Mr. Muhammad and his teachings; a few have expressed their desire to know of the "true relationship" between Mr. Muhammad and this journal.

On these pages we shall attempt to explain our "relationship" with the Moslem leader. . . .

MOSLEM WORLD & THE U.S.A. is an independent publication. It is not the property of Mr. Elijah Muhammad or, for that matter, of anyone else other than its publisher. However, realizing . . . that both Mr. Muhammad and his Moslem movement have become an inseparable part of the over-all picture of Islamic affairs in America, we consider it our duty to print periodical, detailed reports on their progress.[45]

The nature of the relationship between Muhammad and the *Moslem World and the U.S.A.* cannot be determined. Naeem's explanation does not appear to be entirely complete. There is no reason to think that both parties did not profit from the relationship. Since

43. *Ibid.*, pp. 4–5.
44. See his "The Black Man And Islam," *ibid.*, pp. 11–13: and "Is Islam a So-Called 'Negro' Religion?": "As for Islam being *your* religion, dear friends, of course it *is*! It is *your* religion because it is professed by your own kith and kin in Africa. Islam has been described as a "Faith best suited to the needs of Africans;" so it *must* best suit *your* needs too! . . ." October–November–December, 1956, pp. 15–17 and 50.
45. *Ibid.*, p. 8.

Muhammad had a supporter in a Moslem leader who tried to interpret his work to other Moslem groups in and outside of the United States,[46] legitimacy was given in some measure to the claim that his followers are "true" Islamic believers. Naeem found support among Muhammad's followers, whose $4.50 per annum subscriptions to the magazine may have constituted one of the major sources of its income. More importantly, perhaps, Naeem used the magazine effectively to spread news and opinions about the Middle East and particularly about President Nasser's policies. Although the *Moslem World and the U.S.A.* contained short news items about Moslem countries and Islam, the teachings of Muhammad, and the progress of Muhammad's followers, Egyptian and Arab affairs were in fact the dominant features of the magazine. In 1956–57 the Anglo-French-Israeli attack on Egypt became the dominant news.

Publication of the journal was discontinued in 1957. In the January–February issue of that year the editor announced that "articles of Mr. Muhammad are no longer printed in *Moslem World and the U.S.A.* because these are now being made available to his followers (and others interested in his Message) in the form of a Special Book to be released in February, 1957."[47]

Mr. Naeem became the General Secretary of a new group known as the American Islamic Education Society with headquarters in Brooklyn, New York.[48]

It is interesting to note that publication of the *Moslem World and the U.S.A.* was terminated shortly after Muhammad had discontinued writing for it. This coincidence raises some questions. Was the magazine subsidized by Muhammad? Was the main source of support the annual subscriptions of Muhammad's followers? There is some reason to believe that the magazine was largely supported by Muhammad and his followers and that it was discontinued because this support was withdrawn.[49] We believe that Muhammad withdrew his support because he did not wish to be too closely asso-

46. Letters to the Editor suggest that the magazine had readers in countries as far apart as Pakistan and the Union of South Africa.

47. *Moslem World and the U.S.A.*, January–February, 1957, p. 18.

48. *Ibid.*, pp. 4–5.

49. The writer was assured by two officers in the Nation of Islam that the magazine was discontinued because the "Messenger withdrew his support."

ciated with an instrument which tended to emphasize the interests of foreign governments. The relationship between his movement and Naeem's pro-Arab propaganda may be one reason for speculations about Nasser's "relationship" to the black Muslims in the United States.

Muhammad does enjoy some recognition from a few prominent persons in foreign lands. During the 1959 Annual Muslim Convention James R. Lawson, President of the United African Nationalist Movement, delivered messages alleged to have been sent by President William V. S. Tubman of Liberia and President Gamal Abdel Nasser of Egypt.[50] President Tubman's message read in part:

> We look upon you people of African descent living in the United States as our kith and kin, as well as twenty million prospective Liberian citizens.
> . . .

President Nasser's message read:

> I would like you to convey my words to our brother peoples; namely, that unity and solidarity are the two indispensable factors for realizing our liberty. This lesson must be seriously taken to heart and maintained against the imperialist forces seeking to undermine our integrity and convert us into disintegrated groups which can easily be victimized and made to serve their selfish interests. Our unity's capable of bringing the external world to recognize our liberty and independence provided for by the right of man.
> . . . [O]ur great religion and traditions and ways of living will serve as the cornerstone in building the new society based on right, justice and equality.[51]

Muhammad himself takes the initiative in seeking a "hearing" and recognition from Afro-Asian leaders and groups. He does this primarily by sending congratulatory messages to them. In 1957 he sent the following message to the Afro-Asian Solidarity Conference meeting in Cairo:[52]

50. Mr. Lawson, an American Negro, attended the All-African Peoples Conference in Accra, December 5–13, 1958. It is alleged that his tour of Africa was partly financed by Muhammad. Lawson has since disassociated himself publicly from Muhammad.

51. Cf. *Herald-Dispatch* (Los Angeles), March 12, 1959, pp. 1, 5.

52 The Afro-Asian Solidarity Conference is a non-governmental organization comprised of representatives from African and Asian countries. The first Conference held in Cairo was financed largely by President Nasser. The Conference met last in Guinea, West Africa, in the spring of 1960.

Lt. President G. A. Nasser

In the Name of Allah, the Beneficent, the Merciful. Beloved Brothers of Africa and Asia:

As-Salaam-Alaikum. Your long lost Muslim Brothers here in America pray that Allah's divine presence will be felt at this historic African-Asian Conference, and give unity to our efforts for peace and brotherhood.

Freedom, Justice and Equality for all Africans and Asians is of far reaching importance, not only to you of the East, but also to over seventeen million of your long lost brothers of African and Asian descent here in the West. May Allah open and guide the hearts and minds of our people who are acting as our rulers and our leaders and especially those who are participating in this great Conference.

May our sincere desire for universal peace which is being manifested at this great conference by all Africans and Asians, bring about the unity and brotherhood among all our people which we all so eagerly desire.

> All success is from Allah
> As-Salaam-Alaikum
> Your long lost brothers of the West
> /signed/ Elijah Muhammad . . .

Muhammad sent the following message to Ghana when it became independent in March, 1957:

The Muslims of America Salute Ghana

The Muslims of America join me in saluting Mr. Nkrumah, the Prime Minister, and the citizens of Ghana in your newly won status as a free nation. We are familiar with the bitter taste of servitude, thus our aching hearts burst with pride and joy to see our once-enslaved Brothers and Sisters of Ghana getting their priceless independence. May they forever treasure it! And may they never again allow the BLACK GOLD to be hauled away from their shores to enrich and strengthen other nations . . . but may this priceless LIVING GOLD be forever used in the future, not only to strengthen the nation of Ghana, but also to help secure the same priceless freedom for all of our downtrodden Brothers and Sisters.

May the One God, Allah, be thy God. May thy Freedom be as the Sun, and thy Justice be as the Stars, and thy Equality be as the Moon.

New York Muslims seize every opportunity to make their feelings known to some African and Asian leaders visiting the United States. They do so at receptions for the visitors, sometimes initiated by the Muslims, but frequently held in conjunction with other groups.[53]

53. James R. Lawson and Hajji Talib A. Dawud, Negro leader of a rival Moslem sect (the Moslem Brotherhood U. S. A.), are said to have been responsible for blocking Muhammad's followers from participating at a Harlem luncheon and reception for President Sekou Toure of the Republic of Guinea during his state visit in the United States. See the *Pittsburgh Courier* (Chicago edition), November 21, 1959, p. 11.

When Dr. Sartono, leader of the Indonesian National Party and chairman of the Indonesian Parliament, and Mr. Sunito, the secretary of the Parliament, visited the United States in 1957, Minister Malcolm X and Congressman Adam Clayton Powell were among those who welcomed them to Harlem. Minister Malcolm, in welcoming the guests, said:

The 80 million Moslems in Indonesia are only a small part of the 600 million more in other parts of the dark world, Asia and Africa.

We here in America were of the Moslem world before being brought into slavery, and today with the entire dark world awakening, our Moslem brothers in the East have a great interest in our welfare.

In the future, the growth of Islam in America, and especially here in Harlem where there is a larger concentration of our people than anywhere else in the world, is a factor that must be taken into consideration in all future deliberations.[54]

There is widespread suspicion that Muhammad's movement is actually being used by some foreign government, especially by the United Arab Republic. We shall examine this and other fears expressed by critics of the movement before offering our evaluation of the political significance — domestic and international — of the movement.

CIVIC SAFETY AND NATIONAL SECURITY

Muhammad's teachings are of concern to political and civic leaders and to observers of the movement. First, there is concern that his teachings may precipitate violence, especially in the big city slums.[55] Second, there is concern that Muhammad advocates the use of violence for the attainment of his objectives. These allegations have never been substantiated. His critics are satisfied merely to point to dramatic statements he has made, for example:

Why do you tremble when I ask you to join me? Join up with me and you won't have to open your mouth. I'll do all the talking and take all the chances. Just don't throw stones at me. If I had one million Negroes behind me today the other 19 million in the United States would be free men tomorrow.[56]

54. *Ibid.*, July 10, 1957, sec. 2, p. 1.
55. *Time*, August 10, 1959, p. 25. Also *U.S. News & World Report*, November 9, 1959.
56. Speech, 1960 Convention. From writer's notes.

Muhammad's statement referring to the "Mosaic Law" is often described as proof that he is seeking to use violence for the solution of the Negro problem: "We must take things in our own hands. We must return to the Mosaic law of an eye for an eye, and a tooth for a tooth. What does it matter if 10 million of us die? There will be 7 million of us left, and they will enjoy justice and freedom."[57] A Negro leader reacting to this statement is reported to have said: "There is something ominous about all this — like seeing a class B scare movie all over again. We seem to be standing idly by watching history repeat itself. I guess it was too much to hope that we had learned our lesson from Hitler."[58]

A third issue of public concern is related to the question of national security:

It is for these two reasons — civic safety and national security — that both federal and local authorities are keeping close tabs on the strength and influence of this "black supremacy" movement.[59]

The movement has been described as a "strange politico-religious sect" which has "proved attractive to bitterly frustrated men and women and to extremists who identify themselves with Black Africa and take pride in the emergence of the new nations of that continent."[60] Another says: "the quality of the Moslems' discipline seems a portent of trouble to come."[61]

United States Senator Kenneth B. Keating, addressing the National Bar Association (Negro), said that the Muslim movement requires the attention of Congress:

A very disturbing development has been the emergence of a new hate group in the United States, which calls itself Moslem and whose leader preaches a cult of racism for Negroes and extreme anti-Semitism.

It obviously serves Communist interests to promote dissension among

57. Speech, Washington, D. C. May 31, 1959.
58. Lestre Brownlee, "Elijah's Theme — Hate Whites," *Chicago-American*, February 23, 1960, p. 12.
59. *U.S. News & World Report*, November 9, 1959, p. 114. See Robert Colby Nelson, " 'Nation of Islam' Stirs Up Debate," *Christian Science Monitor*, April 11, 1960, p. 11.
60. Raymond Moley, "Black Supremacy Cult Teaches Race Hate," *Chicago Daily News*, February 8, 1960, p. 18.
61. Thomas B. Morgan, "The Lure of Secret Societies," *Cosmopolitan*, January, 1960, p. 53. See also "Hate Groups Sow the Wind," by Mrs. Eleanor Roosevelt, the *Chicago Sun-Times*, April 5, 1960, p. 26.

the Negroes in this country and to incite hatred against Americans of Jewish faith.

The name adopted by this fanatical organization is an insult to the members of the Moslem religious faith, which has absolutely no relationship to this group.

These developments require the attention of Congress. We must always be on the alert to efforts by subversives in our midst masking under one false front or another to strike at the core of our democratic principles and freedoms.[62]

Mr. Thurgood Marshall, then NAACP chief counsel, speaking at Princeton University on October 21, 1959, is reported to have said that the movement is "run by a bunch of thugs organized from prisons and jails and financed by Nasser or some Arab group."[63] At its fifty-first annual convention the NAACP tabled a draft resolution directed against "black nationalism" or "black chauvinism" as represented by the "Black Muslim" movement. Opposition to the resolution is reported to have been against the language rather than its substance. Delegates from the floor complained that objections to the allegedly clandestine "Black Muslims" were not sufficiently spelled out.[64]

Muhammad and his followers deny that their objective is to achieve freedom, justice, and equality for American Negroes by means of violence. In reply to these allegations, Minister Wallace Muhammad accused *Time* magazine, which spearheaded, among newspapers and magazines, the "expose" of the Muslims, of "purposely twisting my father's words to make him sound as if he is plotting for the Muslims to overthrow the government." He denied emphatically that "Muslims preach, think or act violence. The magazine attempted to make it clear that my father planned on committing treason. Actually he meant that the white man will probably destroy himself by that time (1970)." Minister Malcolm in New York termed the charges against Muhammad "inaccurate, half-truths and misleading information." He said that "no white man in America who knows his own history should ever charge anyone

62. Quoted in the *Pittsburgh Courier*, August 29, 1959, p. 6. See *U.S. News & World Report*, November 9, 1959, p. 114.

63. Quoted in *Jet*, November 5, 1959, p. 6.

64. *New York Times*, June 26, 1960, p. 50. However, a resolution condemning the movement was passed during the NAACP's Annual Conference of 1961.

with teaching race hate or racial supremacy." The "Negro news-papers," he said, "have never written anything about Mr. Muham-mad's good works, but as soon as *Time* magazine attacked him many of these same papers, instead of checking with the Muslims to see if the charges were true or not, were satisfied to reprint and parrot the exact false charges of the white man."[65]

Muhammad has denied on several occasions that his movement receives support from any group whatsoever, although his critics continue to charge him with receiving support from communists and especially from the United Arab Republic.

Few Negroes consider the Nation of Islam a political movement.[66] The Senate Internal Security Subcommittee and the House Un-American Activities Committee, as noted already, reportedly plan an investigation of the leaders of the movement, including Muham-mad. The *Herald-Dispatch,* in an editorial, asked rhetorically, "Who is Un-American?":

> The HERALD-DISPATCH deems it worthy of note that these two Commit-tees, so zealously concerned about the tenets held by American citizens and the reputation of the United States, make no apparent effort to bring before their councils the white citizens groups and other white supremist organ-izations; the leaders of the various states including senators and congress-men who boldly yelp against civil rights. The HERALD-DISPATCH sees in this daring move against the Moslems a strong hint of fear for their fast-slipping domination over the black race and a fatalistic grasp of the world-wide knowledge that the white race is a gradually dying race, that the white man's brutal rule is a thing of the past.
>
> Islam, definitely not a cult as derogatorily termed by the . . . Negro publication, is a peace-loving, progressively minded religious organization of black men and women who believe in absolutism of the black people. In order to attain their leader's ordained status, however, they are not wan-tonly destroying what is not theirs or those who own it, as has consistently been universally done by the white race, but are building up what they possess, resorting to resistance only for self-protection against their cring-ing persecutors. . . .
>
> We . . . deplore the exaggerated efforts of the Un-American Activities and Security Committees to explore the privacy of the Moslems while hypo-critically turning their attention away from the devil-inspired white suprem-

65. *Pittsburgh Courier,* August 29, 1959, p. 6.

66. P. L. Prattis, *Pittsburgh Courier,* September 5, 1959, p. 12. Also Dan Burley, "Muhammad Has 'em Worried," *The New Crusader,* May 28, 1960, p. 2. Neither writer considers the movement political.

ist groups and national political leaders who defy the precepts of the United States. . . .[67]

IDEOLOGY AND CIVILITY

Much of the alarm and concern expressed by critics about the dangers of Muhammad's movement, or of black nationalism in general, to the civic safety and national security of the United States, is largely the result of fears and prejudices furnished by the American environment and of public ignorance about the style of Muhammad's leadership and the ideology of the Nation of Islam. Such fears about the political significance, domestic and international, of the movement are grossly exaggerated. Most of these critics, being far more concerned with vilification of the movement than with understanding it, obscure the issues to which the movement addresses itself and thus have left the behavior of the Muslims unexplained.

Whites in the major urban cities fear generally that the Negro's frustrations in the overcrowded ghettos may find expression in acts of violence against them — not simply individual acts of violence but an organized assault. This fear is compounded by guilt about the continued subordination of Negroes to them — the denial of their rights and opportunities either by law or by custom. The fear of black revenge intensifies the white suspicion of Negro movements which do not openly support the existing etiquette of race relations or of white paternalism, which the black nationalists reject. Respectable Negro leaders, for reasons which range from concern with personal security to dedication to integration, are similarly alarmed about the black nationalists' agitation against paternalism. Thus, both whites and these Negro leaders help perpetuate paternalism, considered by nationalists as the Negro's worst enemy.

The possibility of spontaneous eruptions of violence between whites and blacks in the major urban cities need not be denied. It exists in spite of Muhammad's movement. The movement, however, tends to stop the believer's aggression from finding expression in acts of violence against both whites and Negroes.

Evaluation of the political significance of the Nation of Islam

67. August 27, 1959, pp. 1–3.

must be based on an examination of the logic of its ideology, the style of its leadership, the aspirations and fears of its members and the actual behavior of the Muslims.[68] A distinction must be made between ideology and civility. By civility is meant here all methods of social and political protest and all activities intended to bring about change which do not infringe the rights of other citizens or do violence to the established political procedures or institutions of the state. It excludes, therefore, all extra-constitutional methods for modifying or changing either the procedures or the institutions of the state. The evaluation which follows, tentative as it must be, should be understood in terms of the relative importance attached to the ideology and to the actual performance of the Muslims.

(1) The Nation of Islam is not a political movement. Although black nationalism is ideally a separatist type of political ideology, the Nation of Islam is in fact apolitical. It is also nonrevolutionary. The teachings of Muhammad reveal his utter distrust of political action, other than in a Negro-controlled state, as an effective means for the Negro's attainment of status, apart from civil rights, in American society. The political alternatives he propounds appear just as impracticable as the prophetic expectation of the Kingdom of Righteousness. In spite of the formidable obstacles against the realization of a Negro state and the utopian character of the Kingdom of Righteousness, these expectations lend a certain coherence to Muhammad's ideas and, in a significant way, they inspire the concrete activities of the Muslims. This relationship between ideology and the actual forms of social life within an existing order of things has been correctly noted by Karl Mannheim:

> One can orient himself to objects that are alien to reality and which transcend actual existence — and nevertheless still be effective in the realization

68. Karl Mannheim's caution in studying chiliastic "mentality" seems appropriate here: "If we are to come closer to an understanding of the true substance of Chiliasm and if we are to make it accessible to scientific comprehension, it is first of all necessary to distinguish from Chiliasm itself the images, symbols, and forms in which the Chiliastic mind thought. . . . The essential feature of Chiliasm is its tendency always to disassociate itself from its own image and symbols. . . . Likewise, the investigation of the careers of Chiliastic revolutionaries is apt to be misleading, since it is of the nature of Chiliastic experience to ebb in the course of time and to undergo an unremitting transformation in the course of the persons' experience." *Ideology and Utopia*, trans. Louis Wirth and Edward Shils (New York: Harcourt, Brace and Company, 1936), p. 215.

and the maintenance of the existing order of things. In the course of history, man has occupied himself more frequently with objects transcending his scope of existence than with those immanent in his existence and, despite this, actual and concrete forms of social life have been built upon the basis of such "ideological" states of mind which were incongruent with reality.[69]

The political ideology of the Nation of Islam is no more than a rationalization of the existing distribution of political power between blacks and whites in the United States. It offers them a final hope, a way out of their political impotence in the existing society. The eschatology which predicts the judgment of the world gratifies the oppressed, who believe that in an unspecified future (or, as Muhammad says, in 1970) the oppressor will be destroyed by Allah or that whites by their own follies will destroy themselves. In this way, the politically powerless will become powerful. The final hope is timeless. It is placed both in the present and in the future. For the present, the Muslims become preoccupied with the techniques of attaining the good life in the here and now. This is their "proper" concern. The attainment of black power over the whole world is relegated to the intervention of "Almighty Allah" sometime in the future. Theoretically, the Muslims are absolved, as it were, from political schemes or programs intended either for changing the present regime or modifying its institutions. Hence their withdrawal from emotional involvement and participation in the political life of the United States. Thus, a peculiar pacifism characterizes the teachings of Muhammad: Allah's protection and power will render all secular power superfluous during the final struggle. The revolutionary possibilities of the movement are thus mitigated by the ideology of the Nation and by the Muslims' need for achievement and status. The most the Muslims may hope for is work, watchfulness, and prayer. Not unlike other religionists, the Muslims too may wait for all eternity for the coming of the Messiah, the predicted apocalypse in 1970 notwithstanding.

(2) The Muslims will not deliberately resort to the use of violence or themselves create a situation which is likely to impair the civic peace of the community. They may, however, defend themselves against unprovoked assaults. The possibility of their engaging in

69. Mannheim, *op. cit.*, p. 192.

violence even in self-defense is also a speculative question. Twice in recent years, the Muslims have been assaulted physically by the police; in each instance they sought redress in court. In New York City two policemen assaulted Muslim families in their homes. The Muslims sued and collected $75,000 damages. Presently, they have a suit for damages pending against the police of Monroe, Louisiana, for "unlawful entry and denial of their constitutional rights." The police are said to have forced their way into a Temple meeting during worship and to have assaulted the minister and several followers. The writer can well imagine the Muslims resorting to litigation rather than violence. In fact, civil suits for damages appear as a deliberate strategy they may employ with not inconsiderable financial return.[70]

Some of Muhammad's critics argue that although the movement may be nonrevolutionary in its aims, Muhammad's incendiary speeches pose grave problems for the civic safety of the community; but it is possible to place Muhammad's utterances within another perspective. We should not disassociate his speeches from his style of leadership, or from his psychic disposition, or from the effect which he intends to produce. Muhammad is a "man of God" and he is "inspired by Him." For this reason a show of courage and sometimes of defiance is an integral part of his personality. He, like most Negro preachers, is an independent leader whose support comes almost exclusively from his followers. His independence of white support gives him a certain amount of freedom which most Negro leaders do not enjoy. His utterances are for the consumption of the Negro audiences. They are aimed at "shocking" them from their slumber, and the specific function of this "shock treatment" is to alienate them from dependence on white initiative or on the promises of American democracy for the solution of their problems. Obsessed with putting across this message, he tends to be bombastic and histrionic in his statements in the hope that he can arouse the Negro masses into awareness of their own responsibility for their present misery. In any case, a careful examination of his speeches does reveal not only the conscious dramatization of his

70. These and other instances are discussed in Chapter XI.

doctrines but also the interrogative and tentative character of his "incendiary" statements.[71]

From the point of view of practical considerations, we should bear in mind that Muhammad makes his speeches to closed and highly controlled audiences.[72] It has been pointed out that unless he were psychotic (which the writer does not believe), no revolutionary would make his intent so obvious to a powerful opponent such as the United States government or the overwhelming majority of the white population. It has also been said that he is another Hitler in religious disguise. This analogy ignores several important considerations: Where is his army? Where are his arms? Where is the personnel fomenting political intrigues? Why do the Muslims abhor bearing arms of any sort? Why do they surrender this opportunity for training in the use of arms or even for infiltrating the military installations?

The Muslims abhor violence as a matter of religious belief, although they believe in self-defense. One of the injunctions of the movement is: "Never be the aggressor under any circumstances." There are good reasons why the Muslims abhor violence. First, Muhammad is deeply concerned about "fighting, cutting, shooting and killing" in the Negro ghettos:

. . . It struck me recently, that among whites, Negroes seem on their best behavior.

THEY SEEM TO GO out of their way generally to be inoffensive, courteous, in most instances, and on their best behavior in order to convey to the boss whites that they represent the "best" Negroes and are not at all like

71. The writer believes that this verbal "aggression" is intended largely for the consumption of Negroes. Mr. Muhammad seems to be conscious of this fact; the writer has heard him repeat frequently that he wants "to save the Negroes alive rather than dead." This warning helps allay the fears of those in his audiences who may believe that he might lead them into conflict which could result in their death.

72. The extent to which Mr. Muhammad discourages violence-oriented behavior among his followers, the methods he employs for controlling aggressive tendencies of his audiences, the function of "secrecy" to the movement which causes his critics to view the Muslims as a conspiratorial group were discussed in great detail previously. It is important to note that as a result of a few incidents which arose from street-corner speaking four years ago, Mr. Muhammad has stopped his followers from engaging in such public forums. It seems to us preposterous that a large section of white and Negro opinion is so gullible as to believe that a few thousand Negroes led by Muhammad is going to overthrow the government! By their exaggeration, they have actually given the movement a greater sense of importance than it deserves.

those who raise hell and have no respect for racial opinions of the whites who have on occasion encountered them under adverse circumstances.

But among their own, or once they "get back home," that's when the butting and cutting, shooting and booting takes place. For they seem to lose all sense of values as they wreak their pentup original dislike of whites on those of their own blood, color and bone.[73]

Muhammad believes that the way of life offered by Islam would alleviate this problem. Thus his own kind of "non-violence positive action" is aimed at restraining the internal problem of self-destructive violence within the Negro community, especially in the major urban centers. The movement helps to channel the latent hostility of some of its members into activities aimed at self-improvement and the improvement of the Muslim group. Muhammad and his subordinates are in their own self-interest sensitive to possible repercussions from law enforcement agencies and they, more than their critics, are painfully aware that acts of violence traceable to them may doom any usefulness Islam may have in Negro life or the very survival of the movement. They do not want intervention from the political or civic authority, and if they can avoid it, they will not give cause for intervention. Last, but very important, is their desire to gain acceptance and respect within and outside the Negro community. Tendencies toward violence among the Muslims decrease in proportion to their increased sense of security in the community. Thus, as they continue to invest their resources in profitable economic enterprises and as they become individually and collectively more secure, they become more conservative in their social attitudes.

(3) The Muslims are, to some extent, alienated from the white-power complex, which they regard as the instrument of Negro oppression. They identify themselves emotionally with Moslems in Africa and Asia as co-religionists and with black Africans in general. They are not likely to align themselves with the governments of those states against the political or military interests of the United States, as many of Muhammad's critics believe.

The Muslims are gratified, in large measure vicariously, by the apparent influence exerted on world affairs by the Afro-Asian states, especially at the United Nations. They feel some pride, like many

73. Burley, *The New Crusader* (Chicago), June 18, 1960, p. 2.

Negroes in the United States, as more African states come into existence and as white rule over their black brothers is mitigated or reversed. The Muslims' identification with Moslems in North Africa
and the Middle East satisfies the Negro's need for attachment to
some tradition in the Middle East, the home of Islam, which has
a past they esteem more highly than sub-Saharan Africa where
most of the black slaves in the New World actually came from.
The convert to Islam is no longer a member of a despised minority,
without a past, tradition, and culture. He belongs, at least spiritually, to a vast humanity where people are "dark, proud, unapolo-
getic." But this identification is only partial and very often curiously
superficial. It is not perhaps as deeply rooted as an observer in-
ferred after a brief meeting with a New York Muslim:

> Call it escapism, call it self-delusion, give it any name you like. Laugh
> at it. But it is real. Emotionally, psychologically, this woman has been
> transformed from an American Negro and all that this means, to an Arab
> and all that that means. As I listened to her it became clear to me that
> there was absolutely no room for doubt in her own mind. *She was an Arab*
> (emphasis added).[74]

This lady must represent an extreme and unusual case. It is quite
possible for a casual observer to be misled by the symbolic and
verbal behavior of the Muslims. Culturally, the Muslims are Americans, restrained in many respects, unique in others, but only roman-
tically and superficially attracted to Arabic culture about which
they have little or no knowledge.

It was not clear from our study that the Muslims would support
an Arab government or any other against the United States in time
of war. The writer's study of this problem was limited. It seems,
however, that although the Muslims do not associate themselves
actively with the established authority in the United States, they do
not necessarily look to a foreign power — Arab, African, or other
— for the "deliverance" of American Negroes. Asked whether it
would have been a good thing if the Japanese had won the last war,
the majority of thirty Muslims interviewed said "No." Generally
they said: "Emphatically no. It would not have been the will of
Allah. Allah alone has the power to deliver us from our oppressors."

74. Peter Abrahams, "The Meaning of Harlem," *Holiday*, June, 1960, p. 142.

A few, however, felt that Japanese victory would have been a "glorious" thing. The reason given was that the Japanese would have "treated or understood" Negroes better. One respondent said: "I think so. I don't think that it could have been worse than it is now. I certainly think that it would have been better for us, although the Japanese in the United States are trying to be like whites."

There are probably many more who hold ambivalent attitudes on this subject. Respondents who felt that a Japanese victory would not have been in accord with the will of Allah expressed attitudes consistent with the logic of the Nation's ideology. Those who responded affirmatively are deviants from the ideological norm. The writer felt that these tried to make an impression demonstrating their "fearlessness" and devotion to the "cause." Their superficiality was immediately contradicted when the writer followed up the first question with another. They were asked: Which is worst: rape, murder, or being a traitor to one's country? Both those who responded affirmatively and negatively to the first question agreed generally that being a traitor to one's country was the worst of the three offenses. Only one respondent thought that murder was the worst; he implied that treason might be permissible in the case of American Negroes:

Murder is worst. Being a traitor depends on the country or nation concerned. . . . If it is in the United States for the Original man (Negro), there is no use talking about treachery to the country.

With this exception all others considered treason unpardonable. There appears to be a considerable difference between the Muslims' disassociation of themselves from the "normal" society and their loyalty to the existing institutions of the society.

The Muslims are likely to continue to resist induction into the United States military forces. In time of war, provided they have not changed their present ideological orientation, most will probably not enlist in these forces. They are not likely to engage in activities which might impair the military interest of their country. Before the outbreak of the second World War, the "Islamites," it was speculated, "would be likely to gravitate toward any nation of

colored people engaged in combat with the Caucasian devil."[75] This
was not the case. In fact, Benyon reported in 1938:

The solidarity and cultural isolation of the Moslems have rendered in-
effectual the various attempts made by interested parties to redirect the
activities of the cult in order to further their own particular purposes. The
first of these efforts was made by the Communists in 1932, but the cult members rebuffed their appeal. Then came major Takahashi, a reserve Japanese
officer, who sought to lead the Moslems to swear allegiance to the Mikado.
Only a small minority of the members followed him into the new movement
he organized — The Development of Our Own. With his deportation, this
schismatic movement came to naught. An Ethiopian, Wyxzewixard S. J.
Challaoueliziczese, sought in June, 1934, to reorganize the movement as a
means of sending financial support to Ethiopia. This too, was unsuccessful.[76]

The Muslims have not so far departed from their traditional
position — their desire to remain independent of other groups:
American or foreign. In September, 1959, a group of Negroes from
Harlem, Philadelphia, and Boston picketed the United Nations in
protest against French atomic-test plans in the Sahara. When the
Muslims in New York did not participate, they were denounced by
other black nationalists and charged with "sitting on their hands
seemingly indifferent to the plight of their African brothers."[77] Mu-

75. Bontemps and Conroy, *op. cit.*, p. 182.

76. Benyon, *op. cit.*, p. 904. Also see Padmore, *op. cit.*, chap. xvi, in which he discusses at great length the traditional opposition of the black nationalist movement to the
communists. Nearly all of the present-day black nationalists groups are anti-communist.
Recently, Mr. Carlos Cooks (African Nationalist Pioneering Movement) in a 4th of
July speech in Harlem self-righteously explained how in the thirties they (the nationalists) were having street fights with the communists and, unlike some Negroes, they do
not welcome "the communist regime of Dr. Fidel Castro's Cuba." Instead, Mr. Cooks
expressed some admiration for ex-President Batista. He said that under Batista Negroes
had a "fair deal" in Cuba and that Premier Castro's regime was a return to "white
supremacy." However, Minister Malcolm X, as a member of the "Welcoming Committee"
of Harlem's 28th Precinct Community Council together with two Negro reporters, had a
conference with Dr. Castro during his United Nations' visit. He later resigned from the
"Welcoming Committee" because the local press had attributed "sinister" political
motives to his meeting. In an "Open Letter" to the Editor of the *Amsterdam News*
Minister Malcolm complained: ". . . because you, your paper, the police, and the 28th
Precinct Community Council have failed to refute what you know to be lies in the
daily press, it is best that I resign from the 'Welcoming Committee.'" At a public debate
under the auspices of the Harvard Law School Forum, Cambridge, Massachusetts (March
24, 1961), Malcolm told the audience that "a libel suit for $3 million damages is pending
in court against the newspaper which spread these false rumors and lies." See *Mr.
Muhammad Speaks* (New York), December, 1960, p. 21; also *The Citizen-Call* (New
York), September 24, 1960, pp. 1 and 5.

77. *The New Crusader* (Chicago), September 19, 1959, pp. 1–2. This incident seems
to cast doubt on the allegation that his followers participated in the demonstration
against Prime Minister Ben-Gurion's visit to Washington, D.C., along with the Arab

hammad's view is that "Negroes cannot save Africa before they are able to save themselves."[78]

Much can be said for the view that Muhammad's movement is "organized, directed and used by some Arab groups" simply by pointing to his relationship with the *Moslem World and the U.S.A.*, which was avowedly pro-Nasser and pro-Arab. The conclusion does not follow, even though its editor might conceivably have thought of using the Muslims and other black nationalists for his or Arab propaganda. What the editor of the magazine did not know, perhaps, was that he had given some authenticity to Muhammad's brand of Islam. He lost Muhammad's support either because of his explicitly pro-Arab and pro-Nasser propaganda or because Muhammad had exhausted his usefulness.

Similarly, critics find sinister influences stemming from Arab students (and perhaps African students also) who visit the Temple of Islam and possibly speak before the Muslim audiences. This may well be the case. During the entire period of this study, however, the writer did not encounter a single Arab or Asian student at any of the activities or meetings at the Chicago Temple. As we have seen already, Arab students and other Asians who attempted to attend Temple meetings at Chicago were barred from doing so. A few might have attended one or both annual conventions the writer observed, but they did not receive any special recognition. It is possible that Arab students are allowed at meetings of the New York Temple. A few African students visited the Chicago Temple during the period of this study. Out of curiosity a group of three known to the writer visited after the "hue and cry" of the press in the summer of 1959. Their presence was recognized by the minister, who, after the formal aspect of the meeting, asked if they had anything to say. One student, speaking on behalf of the others, told the Mus-

League members. See Eleanor Roosevelt, *op. cit.* There are other less-publicized Negro Moslems, especially those belonging to the Moslem Brotherhood of America, who are more likely to have participated in the demonstration. These other groups are particularly concerned with seeking the "approval" of Arab countries. Muhammad would not be hurt by friendly relations with Moslem religious leaders abroad; such would help legitimize his leadership as a "true" Islamic religious leader. Muhammad's followers are said to have been conspicuously absent from the United Nation's demonstrations and rioting on February 15, 1961 during the Security Council meeting following the murder of M. Patrice E. Lumumba, then Prime Minister of the Republic of the Congo.

78. Speech, 1960 Convention. Writer's notes.

lims that they had heard so much about their activities that they "had come to witness for themselves whether they (the Muslims) were in fact planning to overthrow the United States government — an impression we got from the newspapers." Continuing, this student said: "We are satisfied that the impression given by the press was wrong. We were surprised when we were searched coming into the Temple and also to learn that the Muslims do not carry weapons."

Many groups invite foreign students to their meetings. It is rather curious that Negroes (and the Muslims who feel some identity with Africans) should be expected to respond differently to the interest which informed Americans of all races now appear to express toward Africa. The writer was rather surprised that no foreign student or visitor was invited to speak to the Muslims in Chicago, an excellent opportunity for them to learn about those countries which they believe to be their "homeland." Visits of African or Arab students or visitors to Muslim activities (when this happens) are especially gratifying to the Muslims who feel that they are being recognized by their kinsmen. The presence of these "brothers from home" authenticates some of their beliefs. The Muslims derive gratifications from the presence of such visitors. The net political significance is nil.

We found no evidence that Minister Malcolm X visited the Middle East as a guest of the Egyptian government. He denied that he was a guest of the Egyptian government in an interview with the writer, adding: "Both Mr. Muhammad and I would be a rare breed of so-called Negroes received by a head of state and did not make the most from it." Humorously, he said: "These newspaper people don't think we are Negroes born here in America." The writer watched motion pictures which Malcolm had made during the tour and there was no indication of his meeting with officials of the Egyptian government. If this had been the case, it seems probable, he would maximize on the propaganda value of such reception — for the consumption of the Muslims. We take the same view about Mr. Muhammad's visit. In fact, it was widely reported in the Negro press that Malcolm X was virtually "kicked out" of Mecca; and Muhammad is said to have been "kicked out" of Egypt by Mr.

Nasser's government which was angered because he had visited Israel before his Egyptian visit.[79] Motion pictures and photographs of Muhammad's tour showed his meeting with religious leaders in Egypt and the Sudan; but there is no evidence of official reception by either government.

Although we do not wish to explain away other possibilities, or endorse unsupported statements made by the critics of the movement, it seems to us that Mr. Muhammad is not interested in turning over his "bailiwick" for purposes other than those which enhance the interests of his followers as he sees it.[80] We do not attach undue political significance to the messages sent or received by him. First, we should bear in mind that messages sent by both Presidents Nasser and Tubman of Liberia were obtained by a public relations businessman, Mr. James Lawson, whose African tour was financed partly by Muhammad. The messages were delivered in time at the 1959 Annual Convention by "our brother who has just returned from the East." These cannot be adduced as evidence of any political influence.

One of the most significant evidences of Muhammad's resistance to outside influences on his movement involved Mr. Mohammad Bisar, a Moslem leader from Egypt. Mr. Bisar visited the United States purportedly to try to unite the various Moslem sects in this country. He established contact with lesser officers at the Chicago Temple and told them about his "mission." Muhammad was informed about him and his interest. His decision was quite simple: he would not see Mr. Bisar. For two years, reported Mr. Bisar, he tried to get an appointment with him and could not.

79. Both deny these allegations. Malcolm X explained that he was not barred from Mecca; rather, he fell ill and decided to return to the United States immediately. Muhammad, denying that he was kicked out of Egypt, states that he spent nearly thirteen days there.

80. Far more revealing is perhaps the embarrassment felt and expressed by Brother John 11X, the National Secretary, that the *National Guardian* had printed favorable comments about the movement. Brother John 11X erroneously believed that the *National Guardian* is an organ of the U. S. Communist party. Brother John asked the author if he had suspected any communist in the Nation. The author's answer was, No. Brother John then vowed an all-out attack on any one found in the movement who may have any sympathy with the Communists. But it would be difficult for the communists to infiltrate the movement. "We have a way," he said, "of checking intruders." Actually a leading Negro communist functionary has repudiated the Muslim movement. See Claude Lightfoot, "The Negro Question Today," *Political Affairs* (New York), February, 1960, pp. 84, 90.

The writer does not know whether the Afro-Asian Solidarity Conference has any ties with the Muslim movement. We do not know if the Conference or the government of Ghana ever acknowledged Muhammad's greetings to them.[81] Our hunch is that neither body has any ties with the movement. Muhammad's interest in them is peripheral. He feels some kinship with them and he is impressed by their efforts toward independence from colonialism. Attainment of politicial independence by these countries are examples of what black Americans might be able to do for themselves if only they had enough sense to unite, pooling their resources for self and community improvements.

There is no question, though, that his greetings to these bodies (widely publicized as advertisements in Negro newspapers) reinforce his own image of himself as well as the image the followers have of him. The messages which he received from the two heads of states give some degree of authenticity to his claims and to some extent legitimize his leadership even if these leaders did not intend it. The messages are also important for maintaining enthusiasm and morale among his followers. The Muslims are assured and gratified that their leader is not a "phony Muslim" as his critics claim. They are gratified because the messages assure them of their acceptance and recognition by "important" persons — the sort of recognition which they remotely expect to receive in their own society or even from the Negro middle class. That much of these are meant for the consumption of the Muslims, for the enhancement of their personal esteem, for maintenance of solidarity and morale as they face their daily activities seems quite clear.

We should, perhaps, repeat that Mr. Muhammad and his followers feel strongly about the emergence of what they consider "black power" in Africa and their feeling may well be much the same as the feeling expressed by Mr. Paul Robeson in a statement quoted in an earlier chapter. Mr. Muhammad speaks about the "untapped" natural resources in Africa but his primary concern is with the "solution" to the "Negro's dilemma" in America.

81. However, the *Pittsburgh Courier* (April 15, 1958) published a reply allegedly sent Mr. Muhammad by President Nasser in behalf of the Afro-Asian Solidarity Conference.

XI. Pressures and Constraints

THE NATION OF ISLAM exists and functions in a sociopolitical milieu over which it has no control whatsoever. We have shown already that separate institutions, imposed on Negroes almost entirely by the racial conditions in the United States, have enabled them to strike out for themselves in those areas of activities in which the resistance of the white society is marginal. Unlike the Nation, however, Negro separate institutions have generally conformed to the prevailing cultural patterns and ideology of the dominant society. Consequently, the pressures exerted on them by the sociopolitical environment have been minimal.* This is not the case with the Nation of Islam.

The movement is shackled and limited by colorful, gadfly pronouncements concerning black togetherness and the potential of such unity for action. This colorful publicity frightens, if only mildly, those in authority and others responsible for maintenance of law and order. It has the same impact, as we shall see, on Negroes

* To this we should add this profound limitation on the Muslim movement: the fact that Negroes are culturally trapped in the American mainstream in spite of how inadequately they have been assimilated into it. They share all the normal desires and aspirations of Americans, especially material aspirations and social approbation through conformity.

298

and some whites who otherwise might sympathize with Muhammad's practical-reform programs.

CONFLICT WITH FEDERAL AUTHORITIES

Aside from difficulties which arose during the second World War, there has been no open conflict (except cases arising from the Selective Service Act) between Muhammad and the federal government. Agents of the Federal Bureau of Investigation, however, keep a close watch on the movement's activities. There is little or no overt pressure, so far as the writer could discern, from state or federal political leaders, excepting Senator Keating's demand (noted previously) that the United States Congress investigate its leaders for possible subversive activities. No constitutional issue has yet arisen with regard to the legitimacy of the Nation's existence. It seems entirely possible that it may not arise so long as the Nation's activities are within the legal limits of freedom of association and are not regarded as a danger to the national security of the United States. In any event, the United States government, if it wished to limit the activities of the movement, could do so by sequestration of its property, just as it sequestered the property of the Mormons over the question of polygamy. The political community is thus a real limitation on the potential of the movement for "disruptive" political action and on its continued existence. The scope of activities and the limits of the movement are determined in considerable measure by factors and forces which lie outside of Muhammad's black community.

Of course, as Muhammad has complained, pressures on movements are not always open and direct. He has complained about "harassments" of the Bureau of Internal Revenues, "maltreatment" of his potential followers in federal penitentiaries,[1] and "intimidation" of the Muslims by agents of the Federal Bureau of Investigation. We could not ascertain the validity of these allegations. Minister Malcolm X claimed, however, that the Muslims are

1. *New Crusader*, September 10, 1960, p. 14. For an account of these difficulties in the state of New York, see "Muslim Negroes Suing the State" by Lawrence O'Kane, *New York Times*, March 19, 1961, pp. 1, 46.

not permitted by federal prison officers to practice Islam or to circulate the Los Angeles *Herald-Dispatch* and the *Chicago New Crusader* (both carry Muhammad's "Message") among Negro prisoners. They added that "only Uncle-Tom papers are allowed."

We suppose that Muhammad will strive to confine his activities to those areas within his constitutional rights so long as he is willing to yield to professional advice.[2] The movement faces, and will continue to face, pressures from local law enforcement agencies as well as from a hostile press and competing local "interest" and leadership groups.

There have been few and insignificant open conflicts between local law enforcement agencies and Muhammad's followers. The only serious encounter between his followers and the police occurred in Detroit on July 7, 1957, when several Negroes at a Muslim-sponsored street meeting attacked white passers-by. When the police came to disperse the crowd, a sergeant was struck and knocked to the ground; nineteen persons, including eight policemen, were injured. An "open warfare," says James L. Hicks, editor of The *Amsterdam News,* between the New York Muslims and the Police department was averted in 1957 because of his (Hick's) intervention.[3] There has been little or no violent conflict between the Muslims and the police since 1957. Local authorities, nevertheless, express concern about the growth of the movement.

In 1959, the Muslims were barred from holding a mass meeting in Indianapolis, Indiana, by a police inspector on the ground that a

2. Mr. W. R. Ming, Jr., a former teacher at the University of Chicago Law School, is a highly regarded attorney in Chicago. Mr. Muhammad consults his firm frequently. He is not a member of the movement. He is not formally retained by Mr. Muhammad, although according to Mr. Ming, the latter would think so.

3. "Sick of It All" by James L. Hicks, *Amsterdam News* (New York), July 2, 1960, p. 10. Mr. Hicks revealed how he had arranged peaceful settlement of differences between the Police Department and Minister Malcolm X. According to him, there were nearly 2,000 Muslims assembled and waiting for "action" orders from their leader. The police inspector knew it. After the meeting, Minister Malcolm X is said to have made a signal with his hand and his force of 2,000 followers "dispersed into the night as if by magic." A Deputy Police Inspector who witnessed their dispersion was astonished, saying, "Mr. Hicks that's too much power for one man to have!" The incident was provoked when police officers brutally assaulted (case was later decided in favor of the Muslims by the court) some Muslims. What Mr. Hicks fails to appreciate, however, is that the Muslims deliberately employ such peaceful demonstrations as a psychological weapon for obtaining a hearing.

statute of the Indiana law makes it unlawful "to create, advocate, spread or disseminate hatred for or against any person . . . by reason of race, color or religion."[4] The meeting was to be held in a Negro Methodist church, but its board of trustees, presumably pressured by the local authority, in an eleventh-hour decision, denied the Muslims the use of the church. The Muslims protested that they had not suffered "such indignities" in New York or elsewhere. The police inspector claimed that he had received letters from Indianapolis Negro citizens who had asked him to watch the meeting. The meeting was called off.

During their advertising campaign for the 1960 Annual Convention, the Muslims ran into difficulty with the Chicago Car Advertising Company and the Chicago Transit Authority. The advertising company refused to run posters for the convention after negotiations were contractually completed. The Muslims brought a suit in the Cook County Superior Court claiming $10,000 in damages and asking a temporary injunction to enjoin the companies from wrongfully discriminating against Muhammad's Temple of Islam because of race or religion.

Attorney Chauncey Eskridge, who represented the Muslims, said that signs announcing the Convention were due to be posted on February 2, but on that date a call was received from the advertising company cancelling the contract.[5] Judge Neimeyer denied the application for an injunction on the ground that the CTA was acting as a private group when it refused to sell advertising space because the group was "controversial." The Judge denied this argument as a basis for refusing them space, saying "this country was founded on controversy."[6]

On March 5, 1961, a police captain and several police officers in Monroe, Louisiana forcibly entered a Muslim Temple during their regular meeting. They are alleged to have beaten the Muslim Min-

4. Quoted in the *Chicago Sun-Times*, August 10, 1959, p. 11.

5. *The Daily Defender* (Chicago), February 22, 1960, p. 2. Furthermore, Queen's College, New York, refused to permit Minister Malcolm X to address a Campus organization although he was permitted to speak at Hunter College, Bronx. See the *New York Times*, October 27, 1961, p. 4.

6. *The Herald-Dispatch*, April 1, 1961, pp. 1 and 3; also "Mr. Muhammad Speaks," *The New Crusader*, April 1, 1961, pp. 5 and 9.

ister, Troy X, with blackjacks, arrested all members and non-members and put them in jail. The Muslims have sued the police, charging them with illegal entry and violation of their constitutional rights to practice the religion of their choice.[7]

NEGRO PRESSURES ON THE NATION

The Nation of Islam is seriously limited in its appeal for membership by the raw struggle for power and control over the Black Belt by other Negro leaders and their collaborators. Nationalism, religion, integration, and class differences mask this struggle for power. Divisions among the Negro nationalists are matched only by the endless and meaningless struggles among a multitude of religious leaders, preachers, crackpots, and by Negro politicians, all seeking control over the same ignorant masses.[8] Perhaps this is to be expected because Negroes cannot compete successfully for power in the larger society, and thus they concentrate their effort in the Black Belt. The result is that they help, more than they realize, in deepening and multiplying the existing irrational divisions among the Negroes, weakening their ability to cope with issues far more far-reaching and important than can be justified by the continued existence of these leadership groups. This incredible struggle for power is a limitation not only on Muhammad's movement, but also on other Negro leadership groups. A few of these groups are described to indicate more concretely the struggle for power and recognition in the Black Belt.

MIDDLE-CLASS OPPOSITION

Conflict between Negro middle-class leadership and Muhammad's movement has roots in the widening and deepening of class

7. The *Chicago Daily Defender*, February 29, 1960, p. 21. The suit for damage is still pending.

8. This American version of African "tribalism" (without the solidarity benefits of the kinship system) strikes one as the major African "survival" among American Negroes! The recent struggle for the presidency of the Negro Baptist Convention is a case in point. Twice in recent years, the matter had to be taken to court. See Dan Burley, "The Baptist and Lumumba," *New York Citizen —Call*, September 24, 1960, p. 19. See a more bizarre consequence of the struggle for power in the Baptist National Convention in *The Courier* (New York), September 23, 1961, Sec. 2, p. 2; September 16, 1961, Sec. 2, p. 3.

differences in the Negro community. The conflict involves the Negroes' identity and conceptions of community responsibility. It is over the "correct" path to Negro liberation. The path proposed by the middle class, symbolized by the NAACP and the Urban League, was stated unequivocally by Frederick Douglass several decades before both organizations were founded:

> I will not listen, myself, and I would not have you listen to the nonsense, that no people can succeed in life among a people by whom they have been despised and oppressed.[9]

The path represented by Muhammad has a long but weak tradition represented by Douglass' opponent, Richard T. Greener (reputedly the first Negro to earn a law degree from Harvard College), who urged Negroes to develop nationalism, seek for themselves a homeland in Africa, or strive to build a strong, self-sufficient all-Negro community wherever possible. Both men lived at a time when Negro rights were few and a Negro middle class still unborn. Since then Negroes have gained improvements in a significant number of areas, especially in the North. A Negro middle class has emerged and, it may be said now, is entrenched. The entrenchment of the Negro middle class has meant a widening of "social and psychological distance" between it and the Negro masses. It has meant the widening of opportunities for the middle class, and while the same may be said for the Negro masses, the fact remains that their lot is incomparably worse than that of the middle class. The result is that the Negro middle class (like the middle classes everywhere) is tending more and more to be concerned with advancing and consolidating its class interest. Their attitudes and style of life approximate roughly that of the white middle class (but largely without the sense of community concern and responsibility characteristic of the latter).

In general, there is an "exodus" (if not in fact, then in spirit) of middle-class Negroes, whenever and wherever they can, from the Black Belt into the white society of the northern cities. Psychologically, they have abandoned the Negro communities, and so far as the masses are concerned, the Negro communities are leaderless.

9. *Life and Times of Frederick Douglass*, p. 551.

Their level of community involvement is minimal; communication between them and the masses is highly impersonal. They, too, look upon the Negro masses with contempt and shame. A crisis is beginning to develop between the two classes, which deepens with each "new" success in the struggle for integration. It is a crisis of confidence. Most Northern lower-class Negroes do not share in any significant way the opportunities which integration "victories" are supposed to bring them. Northern Negroes have the right to vote where they please; yet this has not brought them nearer to the "promised land." They are conscious of the inequality of fortunes between them and the Negro middle class and whites in general. A great many Negroes know (and are discouraged by this awareness) that they will live and die in the Black Belt. They are beginning to resent the Negro middle-class leadership. They even feel elation when a middle-class Negro is humiliated, harassed, or actually prevented by whites in his effort to enter the white society. They are indignant and humiliated when the "exceptional" Negro marries a white person. It is true that such a reaction is defensive, but it is also indicative of the growing tension between the two classes. If one cared to be a prophet, and most prophets are more often wrong than right, the "impending" struggle in the Negro community may shift from one between whites and Negroes to a class struggle within the caste, i.e., between a semisatisfied Negro middle class and the Negro masses.[10]

The Negro revolt against the traditional middle-class Negro leadership takes many forms: in southern United States, the "sit-in movement" is an unmistakable evidence; in the North, the conflict involves the Negro's identity and conceptions of community responsibility. The "stay home" Negroes yearn for leadership that identifies with them and which is concerned with their inequality of conditions, that is, with their socioeconomic and cultural problems. The northern Negro proletarian, like the poor among the ancient Greeks and Romans, has had "equality of rights; but assuredly his

10. It should be noted, however, that the middle-class leadership, supported in the main by white liberals, has both the financial resources and professional personnel for stifling any real challenge from the unorganized masses. Nevertheless, this does not deny the possibility of displaced hostility against another social class which appears to them more vulnerable than the whites.

daily sufferings led him to think equality of fortunes far preferable."[11]

What differentiates Muhammad's path to Negro liberation from that of the middle-class leadership?[12] Muhammad pondered in an interview:

What is the nature of interpersonal relationships among Negroes? How do the Negroes relate themselves to one another? How do they relate themselves to their community? The Negro's relationship with one another is utterly deplorable. The Negro wants to be everything else but himself. He wants to be a white man. He processes his hair. Acts like the white man. He wants to integrate with the white man, but he cannot integrate with himself or with his own kind. The Negro wants to lose his identity because he does not know his identity. He lives in the black belt because the white man says he cannot move. He takes no interest in his community. As far as it is possible, the Negro does not wish to be identified with other Negroes. How can he integrate with the white man when he has not learned how to integrate with himself or with other Negroes? Why can't he take pride in improving the black belt? Why can't he put his money with another Negro for the improvement of the black belt? Why can't he own businesses in the black belt? No, the Negro is satisfied with being a front man for the whites and Jews in stores in the black belt. The Negro distrusts his brother and has no love or concern for him. They shudder if anyone tells them that businesses can be improved and that businesses can be established in the black belt by Negroes. Compare the complacency of the Negroes in America with the rapid tempo with which events are taking place in Africa. The recent Accra Conference is an example of how black people in Asia and Africa are trying to part company with the white man. In America the Negro wants to integrate. If the efforts and money spent in the cause of integration were put in uniting the Negroes for their own ends, the solution of the Negro problem would be closer in sight than any solution now offered by the integrationists. Negroes must go for themselves and be free to make their own mistakes.

11. Fustel de Coulanges, *The Ancient City* (Garden City, New York: Doubleday, 1956), p. 337. The remaining portion of Coulanges' observation is worth noting: "Nor was he (the poor) long in perceiving that the equality which he had might serve him to acquire that which he had not, and that, master of the votes, he might become master of the wealth of the city.

He began by undertaking to live upon his right of voting. . . . He sold his vote, and, as the occasions for voting were frequent, he could live. . . . All this did not relieve the poor man from his misery, and reduced him to a state of degradation." pp. 337–338.

12. For recent treatment of the leadership of the Negro middle class in the urban North see Wilson, *Negro Politics*; see also E. Franklin Frazier, *Black Bourgeoisie*, which is mainly an analysis of the middle-class style of life. However, neither author has taken notice of this developing class consciousness among the Negro masses and no observer has seriously analysed the long-run implications for the future of race relations in the United States.

Although the conflict ostensibly appears to be between "integrationists" and "separationists," Muhammad is not opposed to integration *per se*.[13] He is concerned with the destiny of Negroes as an identifiable entity in America, the state of their cultural development, their involvement and responsibility to society, and the "transitory" outlook of the middle-class Negro leaders on these questions. For the present, the masses of Negroes tend to respond emotionally to Mr. Muhammad's direction, thus challenging, if only symbolically, the short-run outlook of the middle class.[14] The latter, conscious of this trend, does everything to check it. We have already seen that the NAACP's leadership, represented by Roy Wilkins and Thurgood Marshall, unqualifiedly denounced the movement; it also tried to adopt a condemnation resolution against "black nationalism" during its 51st Annual Convention. The NAACP and allied groups consider the movement "anti-American and anti-Semitic." Although Muhammad has consistently refrained from personal attacks on other Negro leaders, he was compelled to answer Marshall's charges:

These charges are completely false . . . and will prove that Mr. Thurgood Marshall is the most *unfit*, and worse enemy of all to the real cause of freedom, justice, and equality for the so-called Negro thugs. . . . Thurgood Marshall cares not for the recognition of his kind (the Black Nation). He is in love with the white race. He hates the preaching of the uplifting of the Black Nation, unless it is approved by the white race, and is totally against his brother Negro ever thinking of being the supreme. . . . I am by no means interested in what the white race is doing, for their people. It is my people that I am interested in.

I think the white man is right in trying to preserve his civilization, and all Nations should do the same. I want the same for my people. . . .[15]

As for the NAACP, Muhammad said:

We have not been opposed to the N.A.A.C.P.'s cause for the National Advancement of the so-called Negroes. Only we feel that the N.A.A.C.P. should have as its head a Black Man, and not a white man, and that the organization should not at this late date seek integration of the Negroes and whites, but rather, separation from this people — which is the only solution to this

13. Mr. Muhammad's son (Minister Wallace) has actually supported Mrs. Daisy Bates of Little Rock, an avowed integrationist and a member of the NAACP.

14. Cf. "The Negro Revolt Against 'The Negro Leaders'" by Louis E. Lomax, *Harpers Magazine*, June 1960, pp. 41–48.

15. "Mr. Muhammad Speaks," *Herald-Dispatch*, November 21, 1959, p. 2.

400 year old problem. . . . Seeking love and equal recognition among this people is the most foolish and ignorant thing that a Negro leader could do in this late date, and it would eventually prove the total destruction of us, as a people.[16]

The editor of a nationalist organ, the *Herald-Dispatch*, described Mr. Marshall as a "competent attorney, who has consciously or unconsciously accepted Zionism as his philosophy." He was also pictured as an "Uncle Tom," "the ugliest American . . . dedicated to serving his white master."[17] The *Chicago New Crusader*, long before it collaborated with Muhammad, answered Rev. King, saying "We NEED BLACK SUPREMACY to get Negroes OFF THEIR KNEES in churches that preach a WHITE HEAVEN, a WHITE GOD and a WHITE UNIVERSE."[18]

THE NEGRO PRESS

The Negro press plays a vital role in this struggle for leadership. Most Negro newspapers have acted with duplicity and opportunism regarding Muhammad's movement. So long as Muhammad had not become a nationally controversial figure, the Negro press supported implicitly a growing opinion which Muhammad represented in his "Messages." They denied, however, any responsibility for opinions expressed by Muhammad; acting from the "highest of motives," they hoped nevertheless to increase circulation of their papers by "going along" with him. The *Pittsburgh Courier*, which has consistently opposed the "Buy Black" campaign in New York, went along with Muhammad for nearly four years, and it was not until the white press "exposed" him, that it severed the relationship. There is no question that it was actually pressured into doing so.[19]

Similarly, the New York *Amsterdam News* carried Mr. Muhammad's "Message," "White Man's Heaven Is Black Man's Hell," for quite some time. Recently, its editor has claimed that Mr. Muhammad's "Message" was discontinued because he found that it did not

16. "Mr. Muhammad Speaks," *Herald-Dispatch*, November 21, 1959, p. 2.

17. *Ibid.*, January 30, 1960, pp. 1, 3, also November 21, 1959, pp. 1, 2, November 7, 1959, pp. 1, 3.

18. *Ibid.*, August 29, 1959, p. 4.

19. Cf. Derrick Bell, Executive Secretary, Pittsburgh NAACP The *Pittsburgh Courier*, September 5, 1959.

represent Negro opinion! The Chicago *Defender* denounced Muhammad unequivocally only after the "expose." Our view that the
Negro press has acted with duplicity and opportunism toward the
Nation of Islam would hold for a few others.[20] After the tide had
turned against Muhammad, many Negro reporters for white newspapers and magazines found it profitable to write about the Muslims. Their attitude, generally, was condemnatory. Most, writing for
the white newspapers, became "experts" on the movement overnight
(precisely because most whites had no direct access). Negro reporters for these papers competed to surpass one another in the
viciousness of their attacks, which were largely sensational and
alarmist.[21] One wonders where they were before *Time* magazine
"got out" the news.

The writer detected the same element of duplicity or ambivalence
among "leading" Negro middle-class spokesmen before the white
press took the lead in "exposing" Muhammad. During his study and
long before the Muslim movement became a subject of nation-wide
controversy, the writer wrote to several middle-class Negro leaders,
asking whether they knew anything about the movement, and if
so, what they thought of it. The letter was sent to Negro leaders in
politics or otherwise. One, a congressman, wrote to say he would
meet and discuss the movement with the writer. The writer went to
see him at an appointed time. The congressman said he had no time.
That was the end of it. A Negro editor replied.[22] The rest did not.
But some of these same persons, naturally, "spoke out" after whites
had laid down the "line." Malcolm X has suggested, in effect, that
"they are afraid to talk to Negroes but will vaunt their disagreement

20. *Daily Defender* (Chicago), August 13, 1959, p. 13; also *U.S. Daily News and
World Report*, November 9, 1959, p. 114. The present collaboration between the Chicago *New Crusader* is a case in point. Cf. Harry S. Ashmore, "Muslims Seek Negro
Segregation Here," *Chicago Sun-Times*, May 12, 1960, p. 4. "It is interesting," says
Malcolm, ". . . that while the *Courier* carried a column by Mr. Muhammad, the circulation went up. When we discontinued the column the circulation went down." We
may add, the price went up. Mr. Ashmore observes "Whatever the reason, the Negro
press now generally treats the Muslim movement seriously, and in its usual sensational
way probably gives it a certain added impetus."

21. One Negro reporter for a Chicago daily told the writer that after investigating
the movement upon instruction from its editor, he found nothing "sensational" to
report. The editor did not publish his story.

22. The writer is grateful to Mr. George S. Schuyler.

with the other Negroes only before white audiences, where there may be no Negroes to challenge their claims."[23]

This account indicates in general terms the antagonism which exists between the Negro masses and the middle-class Negroes, which deepens as the middle-class position becomes more secure, while that of the masses is increasingly insecure. Class antagonism among Negroes was demonstrated clearly by middle class Negroes in Chicago who attempted to deprive Muhammad of a parcel of land he had purchased for the proposed Islamic Center.

THE CHATHAM-AVALON PARK COMMUNITY

Until a few years ago this Chicago South Side community was a preserve "for whites only." Negroes moved into the area against fierce white opposition marked by minor violence. As Negroes moved in, whites moved out. At present, Negroes constitute about 90 per cent of the total population of the community. Negro residents of the area are often heard saying that "it has the largest concentration of educated Negroes in the country!" In other words, it is a Negro middle-class community.

In 1958 the Chicago Park District and the City Planning Department were said to have earmarked the land bounded by East 85th and 86th Streets, South Park and South Prairie Avenues, as a park site. Residents of the community apparently opposed the use of the land for a park. The Park District is said to have offered the residents the site for a park twice later; and twice the residents turned down the offer. Consequently, the site was sold to Muhammad's Temple of Islam, which paid cash. Early in 1960, the residents of the Chatham-Avalon Community learned about the proposed $20,-000,000 Muhammad's Center in their community. They decided to block it.

Negro and white leaders of the community called several meetings of the residents to protest the sale of land to the Muslims. They also asked that the site be used for a park, an offer they had turned down previously. The writer attended two of these meetings, and to

23. Radio interview in New York, "Editors Report," on station WLIB with a panel of Negro reporters and radio commentators, July, 1960.

his amazement, discovered that Negroes in this community opposed the Muslims' project strictly along class lines. They did not want "those elements" — lower class persons — in their community. Several speakers voiced this class sentiment. The white leaders, some of whom had previously opposed these same Negroes, found a common cause with the black bourgeoisie. The Park District held public hearings to determine the claims of both parties and revoked its previous sale, thus depriving the Muslims of their property.[24]

The Muslims and their attorney charged that the Park District's decision was the result of religious intolerance. Religious intolerance, perhaps, but this was not a significant issue in the minds of the residents. They opposed the Muslims strictly on the basis of class interest — the common bond between the Negro and white middle class. It is frequently alleged that middle-class Negroes have opposed, though not openly, public housing projects in their neighborhoods for the low-income class.[25] Quite often, they advance dubious reasons for their opposition: One frequently voiced, as in the case of the much-needed Cook County branch hospital on the South Side, is that such projects perpetuate segregation! The attitude of the residents of the Chatham-Avalon Community toward the Muslim project provides evidence, perhaps not sufficient, of the social and psychological distance which exists between the two classes.

THE "HOLY WAR" IN THE BLACK BELT

Self-styled Negro "Imams" (Moslem religious leaders) and foreign Moslem missions seek converts among American Negroes. All seek membership from the same class of Negroes — lower-class, disillusioned, and gullible. Each group claims that it represents the "true" Islam. Claims of sectarian purity naturally bring conflict

24. The Chicago City Authority instituted condemnation proceedings and the court upheld the decision of the Park District Commission.

25. For attitudes of Negro politicians in Chicago toward the proposal for the enactment of an "Open Occupancy Ordinance" (aimed at breaking-up of the ghettos) see Wilson, *op. cit.* pp. 205–207. It is exceedingly difficult to fathom why six Chicago Negro aldermen in the City Council recently failed to raise their voice in support of the Open Occupancy Ordinance when it came up for debate. The proposal was defeated without one of them raising a voice. See Robert C. Nelson, *The Christian Science Monitor*, October 2, 1961, p. 4.

as each leader seeks to maintain leadership among his followers, gain status in the community, and recognition from foreign Moslems. The conflict among the Moslem leaders is dwarfed by their united opposition to Muhammad, whose movement has practically eclipsed their efforts. The pressure which they exert on Muhammad's movement figuratively resembles a Holy War in the Black Belt. Their disagreement with Muhammad is ostensibly doctrinal, but in fact it is also inspired by their desire to maintain and build their organizations.

The Ahmadiyyat movement[26] has been active in Chicago since 1921; the city was its headquarters until 1950 when it was moved to 2141 Leroy Place, N.W., Washington, D.C. The membership in Chicago is exclusively Negro. It has a "Mosque" — actually a small building, occupied by a family, with a room or two set aside for religious activities — on Chicago's South Side. The membership is less than two dozen. The group was led by a German missionary, Mr. Kunzy, until two years ago. The membership appeared to be very devoted to the Caliph (Hazrat Mirza Bashiruddin Mahmud, Second Successor of the Promised Messiah) in Pakistan. Nur al-Islam (Negro) is the President of the Chicago Mosque. Abdul Rahman, who lives with his wife and five children at the Mosque, is the teacher, and his wife is the secretary. The members abstain from drinking and pork, but some smoke. Their children attend public schools, and they believe generally in voting. They, like Muhammad's followers, trace their origins to Abraham. They frown upon such things as going to nightclubs and dances. A man may dance, however, with his wife on such special occasions as New Year's Day. He may not dance with another Moslem's wife or any other person's wife.

The writer asked Nur al-Islam, the president, what the major differences were between Muhammad and his group. This is his reply:

Muhammad is a self-appointed Messenger of Allah. He teaches nationalism. Places emphasis upon economic, political and social independence. Religion for him is the last thing. It is a tool for these goals. His move-

26. The Ahmadiyyat sect was founded in 1889. It had its headquarters in Qadin, a small town in the Punjab Province, India. Its headquarters is now in Pakistan. This group believes that its founder was the "Promised Messiah and Mahdi."

ment is gaining a lot of followers among Negroes. Ours is strictly a religious group. Mr. Muhammad's teaching is reactionary. It is a Jim-crow organization. How long he can last in the United States is anybody's guess. However, because of the way Negroes are treated in the United States, someone armed with nationalism is bound to arise. He is doing a lot of good work for the goals he seeks. Elijah has done a lot for his followers particularly by making them become self-respecting and proud of themselves — something the Negro people just don't have. He has at least made many aware of the fact that there is such a religion as Islam. He has lifted the moral character and also the social well-being of his followers. He has aroused a lot of interest among Negroes. . . .[27]

In a public statement, one of the leaders of this group, Adib E. Nuriddin, charged that Muhammad is a "race-hating, scheming, cynical and power hungry fanatic whose sole purpose is to monopolize power and profit":

Under the disguise of religion, Mr. Muhammad has perpetrated a most dangerous cult among the American Negroes. . . . using hatred to amass money and power. . . . In spreading his corrupted and mutilated teachings of Islam. . . . In addition to his vile hatred, he has given them a doctrine which is vague, unintelligible, unverifiable, contrary to nature and to common sense. . . . Mr. Muhammad's ravings are not only a serious danger to the solidarity of Islam, but a serious danger to the internal security of the United States.[28]

Although Mr. Muhammad did not react publicly to these charges, they became the subject of a lecture by the minister at the Chicago Temple. The writer's observations on his reaction are contained in his notes of January 7, 1959:

For the first time at Temple Meetings, James discussed passionately and at length a letter to the editor of the *Pittsburgh Courier* which attacked the Messenger. He discussed it with such clarity and feeling that this writer was impressed by his sincerity. The said article was written by Adib E. Nuriddin, a member of the Ahmadiyyat Moslem sect in Chicago . . . James spent nearly forty minutes replying to the attack and of course, this was meant for both the followers and the visitors. Since nearly all Muslims read the *Courier*, the Messenger could have sent out a directive to all Ministers to reply. James asked movingly, "Can it be said that the Messenger is preaching hatred when he is telling the Ne-

27. Interview.
28. "What Courier Readers Think," *Pittsburgh Courier*, January 10, 1959, Magazine Section, p. 7. Nurriddin came from the South at the age of 16. He has lived in Chicago ever since. He completed the fourth grade in school and works for a steel mill. He is the "inspirational" leader of the group.

groes to stand on their feet as men everywhere? To act like civilized people everywhere. Not to turn their cheek when the other is struck? Not to submit to humiliations and indignities? Not to remain "boys" until their death? To stop acting Uncle Toms? To build their communities into respectable communities? To do things for themselves and their people and not always to beg? To aspire to living a good moral and material life on this Planet Earth rather than wait for a heaven somewhere after death? Is the writer an advocate of the enemy? [29]

Such attacks serve especially to confuse initiates and frighten away others. However, it seemed to the writer that it had little negative effect on the Muslims. In fact, it would appear that external pressures tend to give cohesion to the movement and to inspire the enthusiasm of those who may doubt that the "enemy" of the Nation of Islam is only white people.

THE NEW CRUSADER-DAWUD ALLIANCE

The most sustained pressure on the Nation and Muhammad came from an "alliance" between the *Chicago New Crusader* (which now is in Muhammad's camp) and a self-styled Imam, Alhajji Talib Ahmad Dawud, 37 years old, a dark, bearded Negro who was born in Antigua, West Indies. Dawud's father was a carpenter by trade. He left Antigua when he was 10 years old. Before he became a Moslem in 1940, he worked with various jazz bands. He is married to a Negro jazz singer, Miss Dakota Staton, who also became a Moslem. Dawud established his first Temple in Philadelphia, his second in Harlem. Newspaper reporters, Negro and white, credit him with leading nearly 100,000 "true" Moslems.[30] He helped form the Moslem Brotherhood of America, Inc., in 1950. He owns two business enterprises in Harlem and Philadelphia. Most of the items in the Harlem shop are leather goods and handicrafts imported from

29. The remainder of Minister James' defense of the Messenger appears in Appendix C, "Notes from a Temple Meeting."

30. In fact Dawud's following is very small. The Moslem Brotherhood, Inc., of which Dawud's group is one of the constituent members, is a very loose alliance. Apparently, the press has been interested in "building him up" in opposition to Mr. Muhammad's larger and better organized group. His stature is consequently exaggerated. In fact, Dawud himself is alleged to have been expelled in 1958 from the Ahmadiyyat sect because he opposed the appointment of a white person as secretary of the national group. He has since formed his own group.

Africa and the Middle East. The Harlem shop, which the writer has visited, is well stocked with these items. He has made the pilgrimage to Mecca, and it is reported that he was guest of the Islamic Congress of the World held recently in Cairo. He is said to have been entertained at a royal dinner by the King of Saudi Arabia.

Dawud's attack on Muhammad began shortly after the white press had unleashed its "exposé" of the Muslim movement. He literally bought over the *Chicago New Crusader* and used it for spreading "facts" about the Muslim leader. He enlisted the aid of his wife, a popular jazz singer among Negroes, and Ahmad Jamal, another popular jazz musician, in his crusade against Mr. Muhammad. The alliance between Dawud and the *New Crusader*, which began in August, 1959, lasted five months. It ended in March, 1960, when the *New Crusader* began to collaborate with Muhammad. In a front-page news item, August 1, 1959, Dawud charged that Mr. Muhammad "does not believe in an unseen God" and "in life after death." He charged that Muhammad's followers do not make the required five prayers a day as required of all true Moslems and hence do not qualify as bona fide believers. He claimed that neither Muhammad nor his followers can go into Mecca because they "are forbidden by the Saudi-Arabian Government and the Hajj Committee" from making a pilgrimage. He said that this was why Minister Malcolm X was denied entry into Mecca during his tour of Africa and the Middle East.[31] His wife, Dakota Staton, said that Muhammad's movement "is an aberration. . . . Our religion does not preach hatred. It is for all mankind and favors no particular race." Ahmad Jamal joined in denouncing Muhammad.[32]

Muhammad, we have noted already, has tried consistently not to get into controversies with Negro leaders. Minister Malcolm X has explained:

> We black men are having a hard enough time in our struggles for justice, and already have enough enemies as it is, to make the drastic mistake of attacking each other and adding only more weight to an already unbearable load.[33]

31. Pp. 1 and 2; also August 29, 1959, pp. 1 and 2; September 5, 1959, pp. 1 and 2.
32. Quoted in the *Pittsburgh Courier*, August 15, 1959, p. 24.
33. Quoted in Los Angeles *Herald-Dispatch*, March 26, 1960, p. 33.

Muhammad's tactic has been to attack Negroes in general terms and to avoid mentioning names. However, he broke his reticence twice, once by naming Dawud and the Roy Wilkins-Thurgood Marshall team. He spoke of Dawud as a "West Indian, born in Antigua," suggesting the antagonism between American Negroes and West Indians, who is envious of his (Muhammad's) success. "Jealousy is about to run [Dawud] insane." He said that the *New Crusader* had erroneously called him an "Imam" and that Mr. Dawud and his wife "should have been ashamed of trying to make fun of me and my followers while publicly serving the devil in the theatrical world." Contrasting the "virtues" of his followers with Mr. Dawud and his wife, he said that Miss Staton is a singer of "dirty blues and love songs" and that she is an "immodestly dressed" television performer:

I do not allow my followers to visit such, nor do I allow my wife to go before the public partly dressed. If they would, never would I claim them to be mine any more.

Mr. Dawud has been trying for some time to do me and my followers harm in the Islamic world through the Muslim Embassy in this country and abroad, but he is only hurting himself.[34]

Mr. Dawud continued his crusade against Muhammad some months after this exchange. On August 15, 1959, the *New Crusader* published what was perhaps the most embarrassing expose of the Nation of Islam. Printed in bold red letters across the front page was this headline: "White Man Is God For Cult Of Islam." A picture of Master Wallace F. Muhammad, which until then had not been made public, was printed along with the headline. We have noted already that Master Muhammad is by all standards a white person. The article alleged that "Eli Muhammad's 'Allah' Is a Turkish Ex-Agent For Hitler" whom Muhammad had met in jail during the second World War.[35]

Mr. Muhammad and his followers were extremely embarrassed and enraged by this particular issue of the *New Crusader*. The writer was at Muhammad's home the morning this paper came out.

34. "Mr. Muhammad Speaks," *Pittsburgh Courier*, August 15, 1959, p. 24.
35. It is not correct that Muhammad met Master W. F. Muhammad in jail during the war.

No reference was made to these allegations in his conversations. He has not tried to refute them since. The writer noted that there was much activity around the Temple that day, Muhammad receiving many phone calls. The writer felt that something was wrong. Later he discovered that he and his followers were disturbed by the news story which Mr. Muhammad believed was inspired by Dawud. He said that he could stop it, but "let him waste his money." In Chicago, the Muslims were directed to buy every available copy of the *New Crusader* from the newsstands. They did so and publicly burned them both there and in New York. It is reported 250 copies sent to New York were burnt.[36] The writer went to several newsstands in Chicago seeking to buy a copy but none was available. Later, he found a few copies at the House of Knowledge on Michigan Avenue where the Director of the House had saved a few. A friend reported that a woman sold her a copy stealthily, warning she should not say where it was bought.

Mr. Dawud continued his attack, charging that Muhammad and his sons were ordered out of the Middle East [37] and that he did not actually make a pilgrimage to Mecca. He has called Muhammad a "liar, a phony prophet." [38] Upon his return from the Middle East, Muhammad declared that he had made a pilgrimage to Mecca and that anyone who cared might inspect his passport to the Holy City. At one time, it appeared as though the "Holy War" in the Black Belt might lead to bloodshed.[39] Mr. Dawud, meanwhile, had joined forces with Mr. James R. Lawson (United African Nationalists Movement) against Mr. Muhammad. At a reception organized by both for President Sekou Touré of the Republic of Guinea, Mu-

36. *The New Crusader*, August 22, 1959.

37. *Ibid.*, December 12, 1959, pp. 1–2. George S. Schuyler, New York editor of the *Pittsburgh Courier*, commenting on Mr. Muhammad's alleged expulsion from the Middle East wrote: "Egyptians asked Elijah Poole, alias Mr. Muhammad, to leave Cairo because he was posing as a Muslim and wanted to go to (sic) sacred cities of Mecca and Medina. Najj Talib Ammed Dawud (N.Y. Moslem) blew the whistle on him because he first went to Israel." See "The World Today," December 19, 1959, p. 20.

38. *The New Crusader*, August 29, 1959, pp. 1–2; also February 20, 1960, pp. 1 and 5.

39. Sectarian controversy among the nationalists recently led to an open conflict in Harlem between the Quedo group and the African Nationalists Pioneering Movement. Shot-guns and matchets were used by the Quedo Nationalists and in the fracas four African Pioneering Nationalist members were allegedly wounded.

hummad's followers were excluded. Both camps denounced each other, and acid was thrown at both Muslim leaders in Harlem. Mr. Lawson, who has alternated his support between Mr. Muhammad and Mr. Dawud, has since denounced the latter and has publicly disassociated himself from his group.

The antagonism between Mr. Dawud and Muhammad is ostensibly on differences as to the "true" doctrine of Islam. It is obvious that Mr. Dawud is also concerned with building an organization, gaining status in the community (from both whites and Negroes), and with recognition from Arab and African Moslems and leaders. The competition between the various nationalist and Moslem religious leaders has become very keen because they are seeking recognition from the same group of Arab and African leaders. There is a tendency among these contending leaders to present themselves to Africans and Moslems as being a "purer" African or Moslem than their competitors. There appears, from what the writer has read, to be little difference of opinion on a number of issues between Dawud and Muhammad. A non-integrationist, Dawud believes that the so-called leaders of people of African descent are leading "their people down the dead-end street of oblivion and extinction." His attitude toward the Negro church is as harsh as Muhammad's. He has stated that a huge portion of the black man's money goes into building numerous churches "for the purpose of worshipping a white God that the oppressor has created for him, so as to keep him mentally enslaved."

FOREIGN MOSLEMS

Besides the qualified recognition given Muhammad by Mr. Naeem of the Pakistani sect previously discussed, most foreign Moslems dispute the contention that Muhammad is a legitimate teacher of Islam. They say that despite the use of a few prayers and occasional quotations from the Koran, he relies mainly on the Bible and that his doctrines are directly opposed to Moslem doctrines and purely a personal matter. This attitude was expressed quite frequently by Middle Eastern Moslems in Chicago. Most said that this is why Mr. Muhammad does not allow them to attend Temple meetings: "he knows that he is not teaching Islam." Many Moslem groups have publicly disassociated themselves from Muhammad's movement. The Working Moslem Mission in Surrey, England, wrote in 1959:

In the February 1959 issue of the *Islamic Review* we published a letter from a certain Negro leader of Chicago (U.S.A.) Mr. Elijah Muhammad, under the impression that he was a bona-fide worker in the cause of Islam. We have since received from the Islamic Center, Washington the true story of this man, and some of his literature, which shows that he is preaching in the name of Islam (sic) is the most fantastic, to say the least — indeed a caricature of Islam. . . .[40]

This group denied that it has anything to do with Muhammad's views or his activities.

Locally, the opposition to Mr. Muhammad is led by Jamil Diab, a self-styled Imam who organized the Islamic Center on 1002 East 75th Street in Chicago a few years ago. Mr. Diab, we shall recall, is a Palestinian Arab who came to the United States in 1948. Mr. Diab collaborated with Muhammad for some time and was the principal of Muhammad's University of Islam. He was never a member of the movement, although he enjoyed an income estimated at $100 per week while he was employed. It is said that he was fired because he tried to teach the "true" Islam at the school. He claims to have 3,000 followers in Chicago, a figure which is, to say the least, exaggerated. His members are Negroes and Arabs in Chicago. However, in a public statement, Mr. Diab has said that Muhammad's "cult is totally lacking in the requisites which constitutes any Muslim group."

They have different religious books, prayers, their fasts, in fact the criteria by which Muslims and non-Muslims judge an organization or group to be an Islamic one — cannot be applied to this group.

. . . They propagate their views in the name of Islam. They start controversies everywhere, carry on . . . propaganda in an aggressive manner and continuously try to swell their numbers at the expense of Islam.

The vey cornerstone of Islam, universal brotherhood of man, black as well as white, has been turned into hatred by them . . . [His group] is not now, nor has it ever been a part of [of our faith].[41]

40. Quoted in the *New Crusader*, August 15, 1959, p. 2.
41. Quoted in the *Chicago Defender*, December 5, 1959, pp. 1–2. Furthermore, the Islamic Center (supported by Arab governments) in Washington, D.C., has not failed

Mr. Diab disagreed, however, that Muhammad is supported by Nasser, as Mr. Thurgood Marshall had alleged.

We do not know what effect these and other charges may have on Muhammad and his followers. He has not, as far as can be known, changed his doctrines to suit the wishes of these "foreign Moslems." In any case, he believes that they do not understand "the problems I am trying to deal with." It is possible that a few of his initiates may turn to other Moslem groups, but it is doubtful that any registered Muslims defect to Mr. Diab's group.

Mr. Nur al-Islam told the writer that a few of his members (the Ahmadiyyat) joined Mr. Diab's group. One of these "defectors" told Mr. Islam that he "feels happier with the Diab's group because it is a mixed group of Negroes and whites," suggesting that such an association of blacks and whites is prestigious. Another said he "is proud because through Diab's group he is living with whites — Arabs." One wonders if Mr. Diab is not also exploiting the gullibility of the Negro lower class, who run from place to place seeking to escape from being black! Such was the opinion of another Negro real estate agent who thinks that Diab is making inroads into the Negro housing market.

AFRICAN FUNDAMENTALISM

Disagreement among black nationalists on a "central idea" capable of uniting the Negro masses in purposeful action is as violent in the Black Belt as the doctrinal "warfare" between Mr. Muhammad and the "true" Negro Moslems. We have seen that the "true" nationalists insist that the "future of American Negroes is inextricably bound to the future of Africa." These are the African fundamentalists who belong to various sects of the moribund Garvey movement. Although most of these sects continue to think in terms of the "liberation of Africa" by American Negroes, a great many believe in establishing closer contacts and co-operation between "Africans at home and abroad" through cultural and economic ties. There are a few who feel that Negro emigration to Africa, pref-

to stab the Muslims whenever it can. A prominent African Mayor visiting this country, himself a Moslem, reported to the writer how painstakingly offices of the Islamic Center warned him not to see or even talk with any member of Muhammad's movement.

erably south of the Sahara, remains the "ultimate" solution to their problems. These groups are too small and disorganized to exert much pressure on Muhammad. However, they too regard Muhammad's nationalism as a "fraud." They embarrass him in terms of his own ideological claims, but not in fact. Mr. James R. Lawson of the United African Nationalists Movement and Mr. Carlos Cooks (African Nationalists Pioneering Movement) have been Mr. Muhammad's foremost critics.

Mr. Lawson has no organization deserving of its high-sounding name. It is doubtful that he has a dozen members in his outfit. He appears, nevertheless, to be highly regarded in certain African quarters, both among the African delegates at the United Nations and in a few African capitals. He appears to be a capable public relations man who by sheer personal exertion has vigorously supported and sought sympathy among American Negroes for African independence movements for many years. He is a member of the Ethiopian Orthodox (Coptic) Church. In 1954 Mr. Lawson was awarded a medal by the Emperor of Ethiopia. He was one of the American Negro spokesmen at the All-African Peoples Conferences, both at Accra and Tunis, and recently he was alleged to have been a guest of the Egyptian government. A newspaper published by him, *African News & Views: The Voice of Africa in America*, credits him with helping "unsnarl the affair 'Cleopatra.' "[42] It said that he was "hailed in Egypt" for his support. Because Mr. Lawson seems to have considerable contacts in Africa, his views about Muhammad can be important for the latter's desire to be given credit for what he is trying to do.

The United African Nationalists Movement operates mainly in New York. Mr. Lawson spoke regularly during the summer of 1960 at 125th Street and 7th Avenue. His headquarters are in the Hotel Theresa. At the weekly Saturday meeting (3 p.m.) styled "Report to Harlem," Lawson comments on events affecting Negroes in the United States as well as those taking place in Africa. We shall recall that he had collaborated with Muhammad for some time. He

42. *African News & Views* (New York), May 26, 1960, pp. 1, 3. "Cleopatra" was the Egyptian ship which a New York dock-workers union refused to unload because the U.A.R. discriminates against its members by barring Israeli ships from using the Suez Canal.

broke away to join Mr. Dawud and has since withdrawn his support of the latter. There are really few differences between Lawson and Muhammad. Lawson is violently opposed to integration. He insists that integration "is not a road to freedom," and that American Negroes should "think black, act black, buy black, and not trust the white man."

Mr. Cooks' opposition to Muhammad represents the "African Fundamentalist" position. He disparages Mr. Muhammad for his emphasis on religion and also for his "lack of understanding that the so-called Negroes are Africans and not Muslim, Asiatic or Arabs." He has a small organization, and except for placing Muhammad in the ambiguous position of being and not being a nationalist, he exerts no real pressure on the Muslims.

Characteristically, neither Muhammad nor his followers (at least those in New York) engages in these sectarian recriminations. He chides them along with other Negroes "willing to help restore [freedom for] all except your own self here in America":

> Millions of pennies are given in churches every week throughout the so-called Negroes' churches for foreign mission work in Africa. How do you know that these pennies are going for foreign mission work in Africa? There are some now giving their money to help Ghana's independence. Is the Government of Ghana sending you a receipt by the secretary of that state saying "Thanks" to you, that they received your gift; or do those whom you give it to here receive one from over there? *Has Africa ever sent you any help for the past 400 years?* The Prime Minister of Ghana was here visiting a few days ago, and we have not heard him asking private people for anything (Emphasis added).
>
> It would be a shame on the part of any independent nation's government to come here begging for help from the so-called Negroes whose status is that of *free slaves.* . . . If you have extra money to send abroad, why not use it on SELF and your people here in America. . . . *First,* help yourself and then if you are able, help others if you want to.[43]

There is a growing sentiment among Negroes in the northern cities for re-identification with Africa but Muhammad does not seem to fully comprehend it. His lack of comprehension severely inhibits his ability to recruit persons whose interests in Africa are broader. In the last few years a significant number of groups have cropped up among Negroes representing the interest of those who

43. "Mr. Muhammad Speaks," *Pittsburgh Courier*, September 13, 1958.

seek a re-identification.[44] Such interest should be expected in view of the wind of change blowing across Africa. Negro leaders cannot ignore it, however inarticulate this interest may now be.

These pressures appear to be of lesser consequence for Muhammad's movement than the constraints inherent in the character of the Negro subculture in general and in the ideology of the movement itself. Religious sentimentalism among Negroes is a powerful obstacle to the development of a secular mass movement among them. Insofar as his movement appears to be anti-Christian, it runs counter to the Negroes' deep-seated religious inclinations. One Negro summed up what perhaps is a representative religious feeling and preference when she said: "I'm a Baptist born, and a Baptist bred, and when I die, I'll be a Baptist dead." American Negroes are a Christian people and they are terribly conscious that they live in a Christian country. Some Negroes felt that Islam, especially Muhammad's brand, "will not work in this country." One said:

This is a white man's country. It is a Christian country. Make no mistake about that. I want you to understand that I do not think much of black nationalism. This is a Christian country and you must play the tune. I think that it is dangerous for the Negro to add to his problems the fact of being a religious minority. I am an American. I am not a nationalist and I do not think that nationalism is going to help us any way.[45]

In any case, most Negroes still turn to Jesus for spiritual and psychological needs when everything else fails them. In fact, Negroes appeal to Jesus not only for comfort of the soul but also for their worldly aspirations. Thus Negroes appeal to the "conscience" of white Americans as fellow-believers in the Judaeo-Christian tradition in their quest for integration and equal treatment. The appeal to the brotherhood of believers is a vital weapon to which Negroes resort in their struggle for citizenship rights, believing that their white brethren understand this language better.

The Negro masses are not clamoring for a return to Africa or any other country. They are not interested in the establishment of

44. For a listing of the more militant African-oriented groups in New York City, see "Negro Extremists Groups Here Step Up Drive for Nationalism" by Peter Kihss, The *New York Times*, March 1, 1961, pp. 1 and 25; also March 2, 1961, pp. 1 and 17 "Negroes Say Conditions in U.S. Explain Nationalists' Militancy," by Robert L. Teague.

45. Interview with a twenty-four-year-old Negro woman. Her father is a physician, and the mother a school teacher.

a Negro state. They want to improve their conditions here in America. Muhammad's rhetoric about a Negro state does not have an appeal for the masses, who think of themselves as an "American people" and seek to enjoy the benefits which American civilization proffers and to eliminate the disabilities which their present status entails.

Their quest for complete identification with America and their acquiescence in the ideals which America claims to represent are most important for understanding the Negroes' attitude toward black nationalism; it also explains their utter lack of interest in the social and political ideologies which have exercised the imagination of people everywhere in the contemporary world. They identify themselves with the goals which America seeks and hopefully look forward to acceptance by white Americans as first-class citizens. Negroes believe that their present aspirations are comprehended in America's profession of freedom, justice, and equality for all men without regard to color, race, religion or creed. For most Negroes, a different ideological orientation is superfluous. The movement's apparent concern with Negro exodus (voluntary or not) runs against the Negro's staunchest prejudice.[46] An attitude expressed by a Negro woman seems representative of the Negroes' feeling toward emigration:

Back when the Garvey movement was going strong, I used to tell Mom that if they ever decided to send the Negroes back to Africa, I'd go knock on some white woman's door and beg her to let me work for the rest of my life for nothing just so I could stay here.[47]

Although many Negroes respond emotionally to Muhammad's appeal, they point to the built-in limitations of the Nation. Its offensive against whites and Christianity and its proselytizing rhetoric alienate many potential members. Several Negroes expressed distrust of "cult-type organizations because they tend to be run for

46. "American Negroes have always feared with perfect fear their eventual expulsion from America. They have been willing to submit to caste rather than face this. The reasons have been varied but today they are clear: Negroes have no Zion. . . ." DuBois, *Dusk of Dawn*, pp. 305–6. DuBois argued in 1940 that the reason for this impasse was because "There is no place where they can go today and not be subject to worse caste and greater disabilities from the dominant white imperialistic world than they suffer here today."

47. Reported to the writer by Miss Alice M. Windom.

the benefit of the leaders." One said: "we have had enough experience with such movements." Others said: "we are waiting to see; Mr. Muhammad's movement appears to be different." Others expressed distrust about the internal organization of the movement. They felt that Muhammad's demand for loyalty was too exacting and the discipline too rigid for the masses of Negroes. As a mass organization, the movement fails to provide for different degrees of membership participation, namely, by distributing burdens between an inner core of disciplined and loyal workers and semiactive, dues-paying members.

The appeal of black nationalism is very special and it is not actively supported by the Negro masses. Black nationalism dramatizes, however, the problems of the Negro community and to some extent articulates some of the tensions and emotional concerns of the Negro masses. It does not, however, comprehend the issues and ideas which actively involve them. It is an atypical Negro orientation. It fails to take into account the long history of Negroes' quest for complete identification with, and even absorption into, the white society. Whether or not the pursuit of this end is articulate, active, or passive, Negroes have evolved a patient mood which implicitly assumes that in time the American creed will extend to them also. Black nationalism is a challenge to this mood. It denies the assumption of Negroes in general. It is reactionary from the point of view of Negro leaders. Its goal — a Negro Zion — is unrealistic. Many Negroes do not consider black nationalism relevant to their problems. Most felt that "things were getting better every day." The question was often heard: "Is Mr. Muhammad or white people giving us jobs?" These realities limit the potential appeal of the Nation of Islam.

XII. Conclusions and Trends

In the preceding chapters, those themes were singled out that seemed important for understanding the character of black nationalism in the United States. It would be foolish, however, to suppose that explanations have been exhausted concerning the behavior of the black nationalists. There is risk involved in any explanation of the behavior of human beings and, especially, of social groups. This caution applies equally to the subject of this study — a controversial, vocal, but numerically an insignificant minority of American Negroes, looking for a saving identity with which to transcend the social, psychological, and spiritual barriers of the "invisible ghetto."

Broadly, the study of black nationalism is a case study of the social and psychological consequences of what Gunnar Myrdal aptly summed up as "An American Dilemma" on the personal and group life of American Negroes. The sum total of these consequences — psychological constraints, institutional weaknesses, contradictory "value systems" of the subculture, and the absence of an ethos — is what we described as the Negro dilemma, dramatized in the doctrines of black nationalism. These constraints are deeply rooted in the subculture although they depend on and are supported by the white society. The Negro dilemma, in a subtle and profound way, exercises a constraint, which is by no means easy to specify, on the social advancement of the masses of Negroes, especially in northern United States. Although the study points to a possible relationship between these constraints and the obstacles imposed on Negroes by the white society, it does not, however, tell us much about the relative weight to be attached to one or the other on the advancement of the masses of Negroes. Common sense suggests, however, that the attitudes and actions of the white society are more decisive. Nevertheless, both are inextricably interwoven, and analytically, they are difficult to disentangle. The uneasy co-existence between them is not adequately understood or appreciated. Black nationalism, especially the Muslim movement, is an attempt to "break through" the vicious circle which emerges from this relationship.

Furthermore, the study underscores the Negroes' ambivalence toward assimilation, i.e., the loss of their identity, cultural traits, and history. Black nationalism, the Muslim movement in particular, raises such questions: Can the majority of Negroes be assimilated into American society? Do they really want to be assimilated? What "price" will they have to pay for assimilation or non-assimilation? If they want to be assimilated, what are they themselves doing to facilitate this process? If not, are there discernible attitudes among Negroes which impede this process? Were there a rational choice, can the Negro subculture successfully resist the pressure for conformity exerted upon it by the dominant culture? Can they (Negroes) revitalize and regenerate the subculture?

Negroes will argue, and often glibly, that they are not concerned with assimilation but with integration (i.e., total acceptance without discrimination) and that the prospects for the former are very remote. Hence, they dismiss the question as academic. Although the probability of assimilation is remote, the question is not psychologically insignificant for the Negroes. It is significant, in part, because one's attitude toward assimilation may or may not foster the feeling of separateness and will determine the intensity of one's effort to merge into the larger culture and society. However, the question is particularly important during this period of rapid improvement in the Negro's status and the trend toward integration. These changes, in themselves, are sources of anxiety to many Negroes.[1] Although Negroes do not express their concern publicly, the writer found that it was widely, but privately, voiced in and outside the Muslim movement. This concern and their ambivalent attitudes — be it at the level of conscious or unconscious awareness — explain, in part, why so many Negroes pay attention to black nationalism but do not actively support the Muslim movement, which is only a specific manifestation of their uncertainties. This question involves the "destiny" of the Negro people in America. We should seek to understand it; we should not explain it away. The price for assimilation is clear; the price for non-assimilation is not obvious. If, however, the sense of separateness and ethnic consciousness, now developing, were to dominate, society at large will have to pay a price for minority exclusiveness, especially for the kind now fostered by the Muslim movement.

Ideologically and culturally, however, the assimilationist strand has been stronger among Negroes. The dominance of this strand is already discernible and much stronger among the middle- and upper-class Negroes and intellectuals.[2] But this strand is somewhat weaker among the lower classes because the realities of their social situation do not support their assimilationist mentality. Consequently, the sense of separateness and ethnic consciousness actually dominate their lives. This feeling has always been present but they lacked positive articulation. The intensification of these feelings is one of the most important developments in the contemporary social situation of American Negroes.

1. It is interesting to note that a report of a two-year study of Negro and white attitudes toward integration, prepared for the State Commission on Civil Rights in Connecticut by Elmo Roper, revealed that although 90 per cent of Negroes questioned hoped for integration and favored it (in most phases of activities), 37 per cent voiced some misgivings for racial mixing in purely social affairs, especially, "parties", 46 per cent whites questioned objected to racial mixing in purely social affairs. "Connecticut Ends Study of Integration" by David Anderson, *New York Times*, April 14, 1961, p. 21.

2. Elmo Roper, the chairman of the Connecticut Civil Rights Commission report, referred to previously, explains that Negroes harboring racial prejudice against white people are either well-educated Negroes who have come up from the South and are resentful of their treatment there, or else are northern Negroes of poor education. *Christian Science Monitor*, April 14, 1961, p. 6.

Perhaps, the black nationalists' agitation is the loudest expression of a "manifesto of identity" — the Negroes' conscious, though slow, awakening to their heritage of abuse and degradation, and, especially, to their possible destiny as human beings. It may well signal the beginning of the end of the Negroes' aimless and vain desire to hide their dark skins behind a white mask. The manifesto of identity is a subjectivity: its voice reflects the past and the present and perhaps the future as well. It requires no real objects and relationships for its expression; yet in a significant way, the manifesto brings to public attention "voices from within the veil" and subtle and imperceptible changes which are occurring among the black masses. They are voices heralding perhaps the psychological and spiritual liberation of the black masses from the shackles of a past that still haunts the present. The manifesto announces their "presence" in America and their impatience and disaffection with the limitations imposed upon their "equality in opportunity." Their impatience and disaffection cannot be disassociated from the important changes (most contributing significantly to the general improvement of the Negroes) in the United States as a whole and in the Negro community or from the rising protest of millions in the non-white world against discrimination and exploitation based solely on racial or religious distinctions.

The "voices from within the veil" and the manifesto of identity do not deny the Negro's Americanism. Indeed, they affirm what is commonly known: that the Negro is American in heart, loyalties, and in everything else. In its mild forms the manifesto of identity is best expressed in the "Negro History Week" and by such organizations as the American Society of African Culture or the Afro-American Heritage Association. Its voice is a reaffirmation of the Negroes' faith in the possibilities offered by the pluralistic character of American society for their cultural, intellectual, and spiritual development. In its extreme form, the Muslim movement is the best example; it reveals how deeply the cancer of American racism has infected all its parts, making the oppressed and the oppressor mutually depraved.

The study of black nationalism illustrates the desperate character of the social situation of the lower-class Negroes in the large northern cities and the tensions which arise from this situation. We tried to show that their life is devoid of meaning and purpose. They are estranged from the larger society which they seek to enter, but which rejects them. Similarly, they are estranged from their own group which they despise. The result of this feeling of dual alienation is apathy, futility, and emptiness of purpose. In a psychological sense, many are lonesome within and outside their own group. They are rootless and restless. They are without an identity, i.e., a sense of belonging and membership in society. In this situation, there is neither hope nor optimism. In fact, most lower-class Negroes in these large cities see little or no "future" for themselves and posterity. This is partly because they have no faith in themselves or in their potential as black men in America and especially because important decisions which shape their lives appear entirely beyond their control. We should stress, however, that the sense of social estrangement and alienation is not limited to the Negroes. In fact, it is a problem common to urban dwellers. The consequence for a meaningful life is, in varying degrees, the same for Negroes as well as others in comparable social situations. The point, however, is that the impact of contemporary urban tensions and anxieties on an already marginal and despised group is dramatic and paralyzing. It corrupts the personality of its victims, depriving them of any sense of human worth and dignity.

Three more factors in the contemporary social situation of Negroes help to explain the growing sense of separateness and ethnic consciousness among the Negro masses: the bifurcation of the Negro caste, i.e., the emergence of a real Negro middle class and the Negro's re-definition of himself not only in terms of the whites but in relation to this "new" class; his re-definition of himself in relation to Africa; and his reactions to the traditional Negro institutions and leadership groups in terms of these new definitions.

The bifurcation of the caste, especially in the North, is an important development of which the implications are not generally recognized. Nevertheless, the emergence of a Negro middle-class may have serious consequences for the Negro masses, creating an

"imbalance" within the Negro community. One obvious consequence is that lower class Negroes are beginning to re-define themselves not only in relations to the white society but also to the
Negro middle- and upper-class "society." For this reason, they resent middle-class Negroes whose social situation is incomparably
better than theirs. This situation is important for understanding the
character of race relations in the North. First, the position of the
middle-class Negroes tends to obscure the problems of the lower-
class Negroes, in part because Negro "progress" (with some justification) is defined largely in middle-class terms; it is measured by
the conspicuous consumption of the middle- and upper-class Negroes, who, in fact, have found their identity with the white middle-
class. As individuals, they can escape the open contempt which
Northern whites have for the less fortunate of their race. They, too,
display haughtiness toward the lower-class Negroes. The "bonds of
solidarity in chains" which previously characterized the relationship between them is no longer apparent, i.e., the fact that in the
past middle- and upper-class Negroes were able to identify with
the struggles and aspirations of lower class Negroes. The interests
of the middle class are different and, in some measure, lower-class
Negroes are estranged from them. But, like middle classes everywhere, the essentially middle-class Negro leadership takes for
granted that its strivings represent unquestionably the interest of
the masses. This may well be, but the estrangement between the two
classes is incontestable. The important point is that precisely because lower-class Negroes are beginning to define themselves in relations to the Negro "image" portrayed by the middle-class and are
attracted to it, they are also repelled by it because their actual conditions do not permit genuine identification with the middle-class
Negroes. As it is in their relations with the white society, lower-
class Negroes tend to withdraw and disassociate themselves from
the middle and upper-class Negroes. This estrangement suggests the
beginning of class consciousness and conflict among the Negro
masses, directed not against whites, but against the Negro middle
and upper classes. This development aggravates tensions in the

Negro community and produces distrust of the middle-class leadership among the lower-class Negroes.

These Negroes feel powerless not only in relation to the white-power complex but also to what appears to them as the monopoly of power by Negro middle-class leadership. Black nationalism, especially the Muslim movement, reflects this sense of dual marginality and impotence in both power centers. But an important distinction should be made here: Although black nationalism is a general reaction against whites as "possessors" of vital social, economic, and political power, the nationalists do not question, except in utopian and religious terms, the legitimacy of the white power monopoly, nor have they sought to alter it. Instead, their sense of impotence produces a need for withdrawal and racial separation (a desire for a homeland) as the means by which Negroes might become masters of their destiny. However, the Muslim movement reflects the increasing class consciousness and conflict[3] among the lower-class Negroes and questions, specifically the legitimacy of the Negro middle-class leadership. In other words, the movement questions the "monopoly" of power by the middle-class leadership in defining both the "needs" and "destiny" of the Negro people in America. It questions the trend toward integration which its leaders see as a trend toward assimilation. Furthermore, its leaders question the "balance" between the ideal of integration and the definition of lower-class Negro "needs" in practical terms. The Muslim movement, in a real sense, is an attempt to alter the power relationship within the Negro community. The concerns now voiced by the black nationalists may well determine the character and style of future Negro leadership in their communities.

Another defect in the contemporary social situation of the urban Negro masses is the impotence of traditional Negro institutions in dealing with either the psychological or practical needs of their community. For a long time, these institutions and leadership groups have been the interpreters of the social scene for the masses of Negroes. Of these, the Negro church is the most important. There

---

3. That this conflict has not found widespread organized expression is not important for our analysis.

is evidence that the Negro church has lost its significance for the urban proletarian who seeks to define his situation in terms of the church. However, where its influence is still felt, the Negro church is particularly culpable for its general lack of concern for the moral and social problems of the community. Rather than face the problem of the degradation of its people and take positive action for moral, cultural, and economic reconstruction, it has been accommodatory. Fostering indulgence in religious sentimentality, and riveting the attention of the masses on the bounties of a hereafter, the Negro church remains a refuge, an escape from the cruel realities of the here and now. Furthermore, evidence abounds of the misuse of the pulpit for furthering personal ambitions at the expense of the already harshly exploited masses. The grim fact is that the pulpit, with exceptions spread far and wide, has become during the present century and especially in the large cities of the North, a route to social mobility for the charlatans in the Negro community. There is some evidence, however, of growing realization of their social responsibilities among many Negro church leaders. The most important evidence is the Southern Christian Leadership Conference, led by the Rev. Dr. Martin Luther King, Jr.[4] The same concern was shown by Dr. Joseph H. Jackson, President of the five-million-member National Baptist Convention, who recently announced the purchase of 600 acres of farmland for resettlement of Negro tenant and sharecropper families dispossessed of any means of livelihood by whites in Fayette and Haywood Counties as reprisals for their attempt to exercise the right to vote.[5] In large measure, however, both the Negro Church and other traditional leadership groups do not seem to appreciate how debased the life of the urban lower-class Negro is, nor the magnitude of effort in thought and action required for the reconstruction of the "Souls of Black Folk."

Lastly, the liberation movements and the emergence of the independent African states have had a significant impact on the Negro's total redefinition of himself, in relation to both his situation

4. See Martin Luther King, Jr. *Stride Toward Freedom: The Montgomery Story* (New York: Harper and Brothers, 1958).

5. *The New York Courier*, March 25, 1961, Sec. 2, p. 18. The *Courier* editorially described Dr. Jackson's action as "Statesmanship in the Pulpit."

in America and to Africa. These events have not only awakened an unprecedented interest in Africa but have led, in a limited way at least, to what may be called "an African orientation." This does not mean that their effort to re-define themselves in relation to Africa is an expression of their desire to emigrate there. The practical importance of their African orientation should not be exaggerated. It should be balanced against the strong integration and assimilationist trends. We may observe, however, that recent developments in Africa have led a great many Negroes to identify with the struggles and aspirations of the African people. This, together with the domestic developments and changes, appears to create a psychological situation fostering and intensifying the sense of separateness and ethnic consciousness among the masses. This psychological situation fosters among Negroes a new self-image, pride, and an impatient and urgent desire for equality, personal dignity and self-assertion. In some measure, the consequences of their "new" psychology are evident in the confidence shown by southern Negro student "sit-in" demonstrations. Similarly, the emotional appeal, though otherwise limited, of black nationalism to the Northern urban Negro masses suggests the same psychological changes.[6] We might add, qualifiedly, that the Negro's need for an identity and his desire for equality and dignity lead him increasingly to merge his aspirations with those of millions throughout the non-white world who are protesting against discrimination and exploitation. They, too, are caught in the "revolution of rising expectations!"

Elijah Muhammad, then, emerges against this background of tensions, change, and of neglect by the traditional Negro institutions and leaders; the failure of the white society to extend "equality in opportunity" to the Negro people, the Negro's dual sense of aliena-

6. It is interesting to note that Dr. Joseph H. Jackson announced recently that the National Baptist Convention has sent a three-man commission to Liberia with a view to arranging for purchase of 5,000 acres of land for young Negroes interested in resettling there. Although, Dr. Jackson stressed that his project was not a "back-to-Africa" movement, it is significant that this is the first commission of this nature sent to Africa since the abortive effort of Garvey in the twenties. *The Courier*, p. 18. For our analysis, what we describe as "an African Orientation" is important because for the first time in recent history, some Negroes are beginning to look to Africa as a possible alternative to the United States. Some are interested in business and cultural ties, but there are many who are interested in emigration.

tion and marginality; and the increasing sensitivity of the masses to their lowly material fortunes and the anxieties about their "destiny" in America. Keeping this background in mind, and disregarding but not condoning the excesses of Muhammad's ideological concoctions or racial mysticism, it is clear that his is a unique effort to reconstruct the Negro soul, by providing a "world" (a *mystique*) in which one could be black and unashamed, and by regenerating the Negro's moral and social values. So far as the writer knows, no Negro has ever dared to tackle the bewildering problems of the "Negro in the mud" with equal vigor and such obdurate determination as Mr. Muhammad. Seen in this light, and in the light of the limited alternatives open to these Negroes, the Nation of Islam, with its moral and economic reforms, provides a way out for these Negroes. The ideological and racialist excesses are more symptomatic and symbolic than crucial in themselves. They reflect the harsh cruelties, discontent, and the grave social malaise which afflicts millions of Negroes in America. Stated simply, the message of the Nation of Islam is this: Despite important, though slow, changes which have occurred in the Negro's formal status as citizens, the lot of the masses of Negroes in the North has not changed in substance. Evidence of pauperization, cultural disorientation, and moral degradation persist in spite of, and perhaps because of, the facade of public progress. These, Muhammad asserts, exist in spite of the fact that inequalities between blacks and whites are not legislated in the North; that the subordination of the masses of Negroes in the North reveals a few stubborn facts of social life which no amount of declarations of good intentions or wishful optimism can obviate. The first, he says, is the unequal distribution of political and economic power between blacks and whites. The possibility of an equalization of this distribution of vital social power is too remote to warrant speculation; but for a long time, there shall exist Negro communities, and the position of Negroes is likely to remain marginal. Thus, Negro striving for advancement, Mr. Muhammad says, is fundamentally circumscribed by their awareness of this fact. Their formal freedom is concomitantly limited by the substantive limitations as well as by their perception of the limitations. Yet within these restrictions, Negroes can give meaning to their freedom.

Formal freedom, insists Muhammad, without a substantive basis is, in effect, meaningless. Substantive freedom, a people's style of life — material, cultural, moral and a sense of human dignity — cannot be bestowed upon people who do not want it, and if they do, are not prepared to help themselves and make the sacrifice necessary for its attainment; they must help create the conditions for it. Thus, if the masses of Negroes are to rise in the social scale, if they are to gain respect from others, if they are to be regarded as human beings rather than social outcasts, they must become consciously aware of their predicament, their degradation which is the bond of their common identity. They must also become conscious of their opportunities, however limited, and must take advantage of them. It is pointless to indulge in the fantasy that through some biological miracle black Americans will be transformed into white Americans or that the Negro communities will disappear in the foreseeable future.

Muhammad is convinced that the chief obstacle to be overcome is the "mentality" of the masses of Negroes. This is the true enemy of their advancement and progress. The result of centuries of oppression, it has helped to produce the moral and material conditions in which the Negro masses now find themselves. The enemy of the Negro people, he maintains, is not simply white people, but also the "value system" of the subculture.

The writer is convinced that Muhammad's ideological pronouncements, which are popularly termed "black supremacy," are aimed at purging lower-class Negroes of their inferiority complex. The "real" rather than the "ostensible" enemy of the Nation of Islam or of the Negro masses in general, is not the white people *per se*, but the Negro himself — his subculture, his image of himself and of his "place" in society, his attitude toward white people, and his idealization of all that is white. From the point of view of all black nationalists, the Negro can never be really free until he has purged from his mind all notions of white superiority and Negro inferiority and thus ceases to despise himself and his group. In doing so, he may have to shed the outward appearances of white culture and, most importantly, the "old time" religion. Indeed, they insist that Negroes should proudly accept rather than deny any contrasts between them and whites. Thus, it seems, the mission of the Nation of Islam is to reverse the process toward assimilation by means of militant separatism.

The process by which whites have been able to create and sustain the Negro's image of his own inferiority is known in common parlance as "brainwashing." In Muhammad's teaching, this process is known as "tricknowledgy." It would appear to the observer that it takes another kind of "tricknowledgy" to undo the former. This, in the writer's view, is in part the significance of the racial doctrines, especially the eschatology emphasizing the eventual "supremacy" of the Black Nation. If, indeed, Muhammad is aware that whites used "tricks" to "fool" the Negro, then it is plausible that his eschatology or other doctrines of "racial supremacy" are gimmicks meant for the consumption of his followers and for combatting the "enemy within" — the Negro's "mentality." If this is correct, the frequent comparison of the Muslim movement with the Ku Klux Klan or with the White Citizen Council misses the point and has only a superficial relevance. Although alike in the crudity of their racial diatribes, they differ significantly in their objectives — for instance, the Muslims do not seek to deprive their fellow citizens of their political rights.

The Nation of Islam represents an esoteric, in-group struggle to provide standards by which the social, cultural, and moral life of the Negro masses can be raised to a meaningful community fabric. It seeks an outlet for Negro striving and performance. The movement combines the attractions of religion, nationalism, and political "pies in the sky" with a peculiar sense of belonging and achievement, and proposes the possibility of "greater" achievement for its members. The Nation assists its members to strive for traditional American middle-class values while maintaining their identity with the Negro community.

However, these values are interpreted for the members *via* the dogma of Islam, which in a direct and uncompromising way, assists them to overcome lower-class values which are held to impede the advancement of the Negro masses. Religious and nationalistic symbols, combined with a mutilated version of western eschatology, endow the practical and moral concerns of the members with meaning and a strong sense of purpose and destiny. However, these ideological strands seem to dominate the "community" fabric and conceal the socially relevant aspects of Mr. Muhammad's teachings, the primary concern of which is the "quality" of life of the urban lower-class Negroes. Although the ideological strands give the Nation of Islam an appearance of a wholly anti-white movement, properly conceived, it is uncompromisingly anti-lower-class Negro values, anti-Negro middle-class complacency and opportunism, and anti-white paternalism and injustice. Perhaps, more than the movement has been credited, it is far more opposed to the entire "way of life" of the lower-class Negro and the "dependence" mentality of their leaders than it appears.

The Nation of Islam is important not because it tells whites how bitterly Negroes feel about their present conditions, but for showing the Negro masses "why" they feel the way they do, "how" they may get out of their degradation, and "how" they may become self-respecting citizens. The Nation sets standards of achievement and excellence for its members and interprets for them standards of morality and economic norms generally cherished by middle-class Americans. (Of course there are some deviations.) The Nation recognizes the needs of Negroes, like other human beings, for membership and identity in some community. It insists that Negroes have the capacity to redeem themselves and recover their sense of human worth; that they must take the initiative in their struggle for human dignity. The alternative to these admonitions, says Muhammad, is continued complacency, moral deterioration, cultural degradation, crime, juvenile delinquency, and social and cultural stagnation.

Negro middle-class leadership being what it is and white attitudes being essentially unchanged in the vital areas of housing, equal opportunities in employment, etc., even in the Northern cities — what logical type of leadership can one envisage emerging from the deplorable conditions of the northern ghettos? What alternatives exist for meeting the urgent needs of the Negro communities except through an appeal to Negro initiative? It seems conceivable that if the masses of Negroes were in the *mood* for the Nation of Islam or for something akin to it, under the right kind of conditions and leadership, communal initiative (call it nationalism or what you will) not chauvinism, holds some promise as a way out for them. If this should happen, then it would be tragic if the white society did not understand it. The white society may even encourage it. In fact it promises to be for the good of society. In communal oriented activities, presently woefully lacking, Negroes would discover their identity and would best reflect what is good about America through self-assertion. It might enable them to develop their potential, a greater sense of the "public interest" and to participate more constructively in the society. The Negro is unquestionably an American, "reluctantly" at times, even as the deviant doctrines of Mr. Muhammad show; yet he is a member of a group with four centuries of unique experiences and traditions that cannot be easily wished away. Besides, the Negro, though removed by centuries from Africa, has never been, and cannot now be expected to be, indifferent to the land of his forebears. This remote heritage, no matter how insignificant its content may be, is part and parcel of the Negro's being. This too, like his Americanism, should be understood. In these circumstances, sentimentality toward assimilation or toward chauvinistic nationalism is blatantly wishful, unrealistic, and contrary to fact, in so far as the masses of Negroes are concerned.

American Negroes have contributed to American culture not by denying their identity (or contrasts) but by asserting it through music, folklore, etc., in spite of the harsh circumstances in which they found themselves. Indeed, they stand to contribute more to the culture and welfare of their society by recognizing and appreciating their own identity, rather than by despising themselves. Until most have been assimilated, the desire for ethnic self-assertion will continue to manifest itself in their social and cultural life, in private as well as in public matters, though taking various forms.

The Muslim movement is a grand reaction to the American scene and especially, the Negro's position in it; yet the scenery (the stage-set) shackles and delimits the drama—the potential for meaningful political or social action. Herein lie the factors which limit its social usefulness. It is handicapped by its very "style of life"—i.e., the mentality, the social and moral values and economic habits of the group which it seeks to redeem. Its separatist ideology is irreconcilably in conflict with the dominant assimilationist thinking of the vast majority of Negroes. On the other hand, it is limited by its anti-white ideology which strikes deep at the Negroes' fears as well as those of whites—their fear of a possibility of a "Black Revenge." The stark reality is that there can be no substantial or disruptive political action by the Nation of Islam other than that akin to the campus gadfly—a nuisance, mildly frightening, but actually not as deadly as the Tse-tse fly. Yet a frightened public or civic authorities, incensed by a sensationalist press, may well be led in such a way as to precipitate the fulfillment of alarmist prophecies.

A. Appendix

Interview Questions

1. What are the most important things you have learned from the Messenger?
2. Have you made new friends or lost old ones?
3. What does your wife (husband) think of Islam?
4. How has your life been changed as concerning:
   a) occupation or job;
   b) use of your leisure time;
   c) with friends;
   d) relations with wife and children;
   e) recreation;
   f) ambitions now as compared with the past.
5. Is there some respect in which you feel you are lacking, i.e., do you think that you are living up to your obligations?
6. When did you first come to understand that there is a difference between whites and blacks? How was it brought to your attention?
7. *a*) Have you ever known any white people well?
   b) What white people did you know best?
   c) What was the nature of your relationship?
8. What would you like your children to become?
9. How did you first learn of the Messenger?
10. How did you happen to come to the Temple the first time?
11. What were your first impressions?
12. What is your idea of a good man?
13. Aside from Abraham Lincoln, who do you think have been the greatest men in American history?

341

14. Do you think there are any men as great on the scene today?
15. Why do you suppose white people are so much against the black man?
16. What is it that the whites have against the blacks?
17. Do you think that the whites are at all justified in this view?
18. Do you think that the black man is better treated than he was fifteen years ago?
19. What do you think accounts for this change?
20. What would be an ideal solution to the race problem?
21. What can a person in your position do to help bring that about?
22. Would it have been a good thing for the black man if the Japanese had won the war?
23. What TV programs do you like best?
24. What newspapers, magazines, or books do you read?
25. What kind of people do you admire?
26. Which is worse:
    a) a grown-up son who gets drunk and hits his old father, but does not hurt him much, or
    b) a man driving while drunk who accidentally kills someone?
27. a) a husband who runs off with another woman, or
    b) a husband who is lazy and does not support his family?
28. a) a man who goes to church regularly but cheats on his income tax return, or
    b) a man who pays all his bills honestly but doesn't believe in God?
29. a) a woman who neglects her children for men, or
    b) a woman who steals?
30. a) murder or rape or being a traitor to one's country?
    b) why?
31. What was your experience when you first came to Chicago?

B. Appendix

Muhammad's Temples of Islam and Their Locations*

Muhammad's Temple of Islam No. 1
11529 Linwood, Detroit, Michigan

Muhammad's Temple of Islam No. 2
5335 Woodlawn Avenue,
Chicago 11, Illinois

Muhammad's Temple of Islam No. 3
1254 North 15th Street,
Milwaukee, Wisconsin

Muhammad's Temple of Islam No. 4
1325 Vermont Avenue, N.W.,
Washington, D. C.

Muhammad's Temple of Islam No. 5
3507 Reading Road,
Cincinnati 29, Ohio

Muhammad's Temple of Islam No. 6
514 Wilson, Baltimore, Maryland

Muhammad's Temple of Islam No. 7
102 West 116 Street,
New York City

Muhammad's Temple of Islam No. 8
2675 Imperial,
San Diego, California

Muhammad's Temple of Islam No. 9
625 Himrod Street,
Youngstown, Ohio

Muhammad's Temple of Islam
No. 10
419 Madison Avenue,
Atlantic City, New Jersey

Muhammad's Temple of Islam
No. 11
35 Intervale Street,
Roxbury, Massachusetts

Muhammad's Temple of Islam
No. 12
4218-20 Lancaster Avenue,
Philadelphia 4, Pennsylvania

Muhammad's Temple of Islam
No. 13
841 Dwight Street,
Springfield, Massachusetts

Muhammad's Temple of Islam
No. 14
1097 Main Street,
Hartford, Connecticut

* *Herald-Dispatch* (Los Angeles), December 19, 1959, p. 10. Smaller Muslim missions not included in this list.

Muhammad's Temple of Islam
No. 15
  377 Merrittes Avenue, N.E.,
  Atlanta, Georgia
Muhammad's Temple of Islam
No. 16
  408 South Butler Boulevard,
  Lansing, Michigan
Muhammad's Temple of Islam
No. 17
  119 Chicago Avenue,
  Joliet, Illinois
Muhammad's Temple of Islam
No. 18
  11005 Ashbury, Cleveland, Ohio
Muhammad's Temple of Islam
No. 19
  1147 Germantown Street,
  Dayton, Ohio
Muhammad's Temple of Islam
No. 20
  20 Camden Street,
  Camden, New Jersey
Muhammad's Temple of Islam
No. 21
  80 Clinton,
  Jersey City, New Jersey
Muhammad's Temple of Islam
No. 22
  7609 Baxter Street,
  Pittsburgh, Pennsylvania
Muhammad's Temple of Islam
No. 23
  1412½ Jefferson Avenue,
  Buffalo 8, New York
Muhammad's Temple of Islam
No. 24
  2116 North Avenue,
  Richmond, Virginia
Muhammad's Temple of Islam
No. 25
  80 Clinton, Newark, New Jersey
Muhammad's Temple of Islam
No. 26
  1563 7th Street,
  Oakland, California

Muhammad's Temple of Islam
No. 27
  1480 West Jefferson Boulevard,
  Los Angeles, California
Muhammad's Temple of Islam
No. 28
  4610 McMillian Avenue,
  St. Louis, Missouri
Muhammad's Temple of Islam
No. 29
  615 N.W. 2nd Avenue,
  Miami 42, Florida
Muhammad's Temple of Islam
No. 30
  1210 East 12th Street,
  Kansas City, Missouri
Muhammad's Eastside Temple
  7601 South San Pedro,
  Los Angeles 11, California
Muhammad's Temple of Islam
  687 Hoyt Street, Warren, Ohio
Muhammad's Temple of Islam
  329 State Street,
  Jacksonville, Florida
Muhammad's Temple of Islam
  1145 Emerson Avenue North,
  Minneapolis 11, Minnesota
Muhammad's Temple of Islam
  1456 East 11th Street,
  Winston Salem, North Carolina
Muhammad's Temple of Islam
  2931 12th Street, Masonic Temple,
  Riverside, California
Muhammad's Temple of Islam
  Odd Fellows Hall,
  12th and Orange Streets,
  Wilmington, Delaware
Muhammad's Temple of Islam
  525 East End Avenue,
  Durham, North Carolina
Muhammad's Temple of Islam
  1208 East 12th Street,
  Kansas City, Missouri
Muhammad's Temple of Islam
  2526 Flora Street,
  Dallas, Texas

Muhammad's Temple of Islam
579 East Spring Street,
Columbus 3, Ohio

Muhammad's Temple of Islam
2163 East 55th Street, at Cedar,
Cleveland, Ohio

Muhammad's Temple of Islam
708 Gulf Avenue, Orangeburg,
South Carolina

Muhammad's Temple of Islam
1805 Divisadero Street,
San Francisco, California

Muhammad's Temple of Islam
2815 Industrial,
Flint, Michigan

Muhammad's Temple of Islam
1228 Bailey Street,
Harrisburg, Pennsylvania

Muhammad's Temple of Islam
147 North Wellington Street,
South Bend 19, Indiana

Muhammad's Temple of Islam
1805 Divisadero Street,
San Francisco, California

Muhammad's Temple of Islam
2815 Industrial Street,
Flint, Michigan

Appendix

C.

Notes from a Temple Meeting

Assistant Minister to the Messenger, Brother James, presiding. Malcolm X, Minister in charge of Temple No. 7 in New York City, visiting. The date is January 7, 1959.

James began the teaching tonight by discussing three Negro personalities who in the past had attempted to organize the "so-called Negroes" into a dynamic mass or nationalist movement. The efforts of all had failed. Noble Drew Ali, founder of the Moorish Science Temples of America, A. Phillip Randolph, leader and organizer of the Brotherhood of Sleeping Car Porters, and Marcus Garvey were discussed. The technique was to build all of these persons up, to point to some degree of success, to show how difficult the task of organizing Negroes is, to show how they had failed, and of course, to point to the difficulties which the Messenger is having, but still to give reasons for believing that he will succeed where others have failed.

James said that Noble Drew Ali is said to have visited Morocco and to have met the King of Morocco, who commissioned him to teach Islam to the people of North America. When Noble Drew returned to the United States, he went to the President in order to obtain a charter for his Islamic movement. The President, according to James, is said to have told Noble Drew Ali that it would be as difficult getting Negroes to accept Islam as trying to "fit a horse with a pair of trousers." Here James noted that, according to the Messenger's statement, Allah had told him that He would only be able to re-convert 144,000 so-called Negroes into Islam. This was about the maximum Allah had promised. However, the Messenger believes that he can convert the nearly seventeen million members of the Black Nation or the Nation of Islam in North America. The Messenger, James said, knows this to be a very arduous and difficult task, but this has been the case with all the past

346

prophets. He urged, therefore, all Moslems to help the Messenger in this great mission. Continuing his description of Noble Drew Ali's efforts, James indicated that he had an initial success and rounded up a large number of followers, but shortly found himself in trouble with Uncle Toms who worked to destroy the movement from within. Drew Ali is said to have been killed by his foes or by his own followers. In any case, his death remains mysterious. He died without having been able to complete his task. James claimed that today the movement Drew Ali started amounts to nothing, although followers continue to have temples here and there.

Speaking of A. Phillip Randolph, James pointed out that as a radical he had tried to rally the Negroes together into a mass movement and had hoped to stage a march on Washington, D. C. Randolph did everything possible to organize them, but he also failed and now is no more than an Uncle Tom.

Marcus Garvey was highly exalted by James. He was well spoken of, as the Messenger himself has acknowledged. James had known about Garvey when he was a young man in the Southland, he told the audience. He was very impressed by Garvey's program for the so-called Negroes. Garvey, he said, was a West Indian who was sincere and had a very deep concern for his own people in America. He had a real desire to provide a solution to the so-called Negro problem in North America through an economic emancipation of the blacks. Garvey, he said, is perhaps the most important Negro in history, and the first to have been able to awaken a large number of the mass of Negroes to want to do things for their own kind. But Garvey, like Drew Ali, was beset by difficulties. His movement was destroyed by enemies from within as well as from without — the real Uncle Toms who had been planted to cause dissension and finally to lead to Garvey's trial on a trumped-up charge of using the mails to defraud. In this way they were able to destroy the movement, while Garvey was jailed in the penitentiary, and later deported to Jamaica. Garvey, he said, later died from remorse for failure to liberate his people. James stated that Garvey had said that the next man after him who would try to carry out his program, would succeed; this is supposed to refer to the work that the Messenger is now doing. At one point, Garvey had "prophesied" the coming of the Messenger, but later changed it to "predicted," which is probably the word he meant to use at first. In the end Garvey failed, his movement was destroyed, but his spirit remains.

Throughout his talk James impressed upon the audience the difficulty of organizing the Negroes into a really effective mass movement. He gave a real sense of the difficulty of the work of the Messenger. James stressed the problem of dissension from within. It appears that he is cautioning members against such dissension if the "utopia" is to be realized. This was one meeting devoted to the defense of the Messenger against troubles from within as well as attacks from without. The teachings included a stress on the injustices which the Negroes have suffered. An effort is made to keep constantly before the minds of the followers and visitors the injustices of the past and those they are experiencing at the present. For the future there is a deep feeling that no progress can be made so long as the devil is in power and the Negroes can only play second fiddle. Not only this; for as long as Negroes accept their present "nationality," they can never conceive of reaching out for themselves and therefore the problem will not be solved or even frontally attacked.

For the first time at a Temple Meeting, James discussed at length a letter to the editor of the *Pittsburgh Courier*, which attacked the Messenger. He discussed it with such clarity and feeling that this writer was impressed by his sincerity. The said article was written by Adib E. Nuriddin, a member of the Ahmadiyya Moslem sect in Chicago. (The letter is reproduced in the text of this paper). James spent nearly forty minutes replying to the attack and of course, this was meant for both the followers and the visitors. Since nearly all Moslems read the *Courier*, the Messenger could have sent out an earlier directive to all ministers advising them to reply. James asked movingly, "Can it be said that the Messenger is preaching hatred when he is telling the Negroes to stand on their feet as men everywhere? To act like civilized people everywhere? Not to turn their cheek when the other is struck? Not to submit to humiliations and indignities? Not to remain 'boys' until death? To stop acting as Uncle Toms? To build their communities into respectable communities? To do things for themselves and their people and not always to beg? To aspire to living a good moral and material life on this planet rather than waiting for a heaven which is somewhere after death? Is the writer an advocate of the enemy?" James noted that Nuriddin considers himself a Negro and that speaks for itself, for it implies that he has no "nationality" and cares nothing for the plight of his people.

James deplored the fact that in every war Negroes have fought whatever people are considered their "enemies," and yet these same Negroes refuse to admit that there can be "enemies of a people." He has fought against people who have done him no harm and yet he would not recognize or be willing to fight against his own enemy — the white man. Today, James said, the Negroes would be first to fight against their own people if Uncle Sam said they must, but never would the Negro fight for himself. James quoted from the Bible and the Koran to justify the idea that it is even in the nature of God to hate his enemies or the "devil." Everyone hates his enemy but the so-called Negro. That hate is as natural as any other experience. As an example, even the body, if fed with disagreeable food, would guard against it. The Messenger says that the white man is the Negroes' most deadly enemy. And the instrument for practicing his enmity against the Negro is Christianity, a fact which is common knowledge to all so-called Negroes. Every people knows its enemies. White America considers the Russians and the Chinese communist their enemies. It is publicly admitted and no one raves about it. The whites hate these people and their way of life. They do so in the interest of their own Nation, and yet followers of Elijah Muhammad are supposed to love their enemies. Who has treated the so-called Negroes as Hitler treated the Jews? He said that the analogy to Hitler is false, and that it would have been closer to the truth if he had said that the Negroes are treated as the Jews were treated by Hitler. "If the Messenger were teaching the hatred of the enemy of the Black Nation," said James, "it is about time." "Is the Messenger seeking power?" James asked, and replied: "No. How could he be seeking power in this devil's civilization and still attack the devil and refuse participation in the political life of the country? To get power in this country, one has to get into the service of the devil and that is what every Negro leader is doing. The Messenger doesn't want any part of his power.

As for money, the Messenger could get more money if he were willing to toe the line. What he is doing is telling the Negroes that if they were to drop certain ways of life, frivolous living, and the like, and to pool their resources together as a well-organized group, they would be able to do more for themselves. Hence, he picks up the masses of Negroes from the streets, cleans them, teaches them how to live a civilized life, how to balance their pocket books, and how through a common fund they can do things for themselves and hence elevate their conditions and those of his people. The Messenger is not seeking economic power. On the contrary, he wants Negroes as a whole to seek economic power for themselves. In this civilization, a seeker of economic power would be foolish to do so by attacking those who monopolize such power. Those who do always end up abandoning the struggle for Negro liberation in favor of enriching their own pockets." They live on economic hand-outs of the whites.

As to the question of the Nation of Islam being a threat to the internal security of the United States, James insisted that this was utter nonsense, for the Moslems in the United States are the most peaceful people in this North America. They carry no weapons and they are not seeking the destruction of this country. The Messenger merely teaches, like all previous prophets, that Allah told him that this civilization will be destroyed. Allah gave these people a certain number of years to rule and when their time is up, as it has already been, "Black Power" or the Nation of Islam would be restored. James went on to say that all followers are carefully taught to respect duly constituted authority and never to be the aggressors. However, this does not mean that they must not come to their self-defense if they are attacked. To attack, he said, is vicious and stems from lack of understanding of what the Messenger is trying to do. How could the Messenger be dangerous to the internal security of the most powerful government on this planet Earth? It is perhaps easier for Khrushchev to attack this government from Moscow, as well as Nasser in Egypt, but not someone who has neither arms nor sufficient numbers, and is right in the mouth of the enemy of his Nation. The Messenger is merely telling the world what Allah has told him. The last days of Sodom and Gomorrah were also forecast by a prophet.

Muhammad is aware that he is under the nose of the enemy. However, he will not be deterred from speaking for his people. James himself will not be frightened out of the Nation. Is the Messenger a fanatic? No. He doesn't appeal to emotion. One does not see his audiences yelling. On the contrary, he tells the people the causes of their troubles in the past, what the conditions now are, and what they should do to prepare for a better future for themselves and for their posterity. The Messenger is telling his people that they are a nationality by teaching them where they came from and where they may go from here, and how as a people the black nation can do things for themselves. The Nation is not an organization; it is a movement; it is a way of life. The

Messenger is trying to get the so-called Negroes to connect themselves with their own all over the world, a world-wide confraternity of all black, yellow, red and brown peoples of this earth through a common faith — Islam. In closing his remarks, he urged the people to patronize the Muslim businesses and the Courier, and to make free contributions to the building fund, for an Islamic center which will add to the cultural and aesthetic appearance of the black belt, besides providing a school and a two-thousand bed hospital. In concluding his remarks, James introduced Malcolm X.

Malcolm then came to the rostrum, greeted the people warmly, and received an enthusiastic response. He told of the activities of Muslims in other cities he had visited and expressed his pleasure at being in Chicago, the fountainhead of their movement. He assured them that wherever he goes, more and more Negroes are joining the faith and doing very well. In his effective and highly charged manner of speaking, he gave witness to the work of the Messenger. He pointed out that the Messenger's task is to restore freedom, justice, and equality to the so-called Negroes in America — to this lost-found nation, a people who had been roped and tied — and worked without pay for three hundred and ten years. Islam is here to restore their rights to the Negroes. To do this, a constructive economic program and a solid economic basis is necessary. Muslims can do it because they are disciplined and work hard, spend their money on items which produce concrete and useful benefits, cut out frivolous and conspicuous spending, and invest whatever is left after expenses in productive enterprises. He suggested that if it takes Christian so-called Negroes one hundred and forty dollars a week to live, it costs the Muslim only forty a week. The results are different because of the trimmings from smoking, drinking, and other useless living, which so many Negroes have taken to. The balance is freely put into the Nation for useful investment and as an insurance for members of the Nation in time of need. To build the Nation of Islam, he emphasized that money is needed and that members must continue keeping the Messenger happy, and for the next six weeks before the Annual Convention, should keep their problems away from the Messenger. They should pray for the Messenger's health, for what would they do without the Messenger? (Malcolm, like other ministers and followers in bearing witness to the Messenger, has a way of denying his own leadership and contribution to the Nation. Of course, it seems necessary that the secondary leaders must always re-emphasize that they themselves were "dead" people — blind, deaf, and dumb before they came to the Nation.) Malcolm concluded his remarks saying he was sorry he had to leave, but must hurry to catch his plane. Bidding the congregation goodbye, he walked swiftly up the aisle. He received a continuous ovation from the moment he left the platform until he was completely out of the building.

James resumed and asked Captain Sharrieff if he had any announcements. Raymond Sharrieff came forward and spoke briefly after saluting the minister in a formal manner. He urged the F.O.I. to show up on Thursday night after 6 p.m. to wash and clean the Temple. The order was given in a stern and serious voice. The meeting closed after the final prayer, which was led by Minister James, at approximately 11 p.m.

Bibliography

I. BOOKS

ALLPORT, G. W. *The Nature of Prejudice*. Cambridge, Mass.: Addison Wesley, 1954.

The American Negro in the Communist Party. Committee on Un-American Activities, U.S. House of Representatives. Washington, D.C., 1954.

The American Negro Writer and His Roots. New York: American Society of African Culture, 1960.

APTHEKER, H. *Negro Slave Revolts*. New York: Columbia University Press, 1943.

ASHMORE, HARRY S. *The Other Side of Jordan: Negroes Outside the South*. New York: W. W. Norton & Co., 1960.

AUSTIN, EDMUND O. *The Black Challenge*. New York: Vintage Press, 1958.

BALDWIN, JAMES. *Notes of a Native Son*. Boston: Beacon Press, 1955.

BANFIELD, EDWARD C. *The Moral Basis of a Backward Society*. Glencoe, Ill.: Free Press, 1958.

BARDOLPH, RICHARD. *The Negro Vanguard*. New York: Rinehart & Co., 1959.

BENEDICT, RUTH. "Continuities and Discontinuities in Cultural Conditioning," *A Study of Interpersonal Relations*. Edited by Patrick Mullahy. New York: Armitage Press, 1949.

BERNARD, J. *American Community Behavior*. New York: Dryden Press, 1949.

BIGELOW, K. W. *Cultural Groups and Human Relations*. New York: Bureau of Publications, Teachers College, Columbia University, 1951.

BIRD, C. *Social Psychology*. New York: Appleton-Century-Crofts, 1946.

BONTEMPS, ARNA, and CONROY, JACK. *They Seek a City*. Garden City, N.Y.: Doubleday, Doran, 1945.

351

BRADFORD, SARAH H. *Harriet, the Moses of Her People.* New York: George R. Lockwood & Sons, 1897.

BRODERICK, FRANCIS L. *W. E. B. DuBois: Negro Leader in a Time of Crisis.* Stanford, Calif.: Stanford University Press, 1959.

BROWN, WILLIAM WELLS. *The Rising Son: Or the Antecedents and Advancement of the Colored Race.* Boston: A. G. Brown & Co., 1876.

BUTCHER, MARGARET JUST. *The Negro in American Culture.* New York: New American Library of World Literature, 1957.

CARTWRIGHT, D., and ZANDER, A. *Group Dynamics: Research and Theory.* Evanston, Ill.: Row Peterson & Co., 1953.

CHICAGO COMMISSION on RACE RELATIONS. *The Negro in Chicago: A Study of Race Relations and a Race Riot.* Chicago, University of Chicago Press, 1922.

COHN, NORMAN. *The Pursuit of the Millenium.* London: Secker & Warburg, 1957.

COMAS, J. *Racial Myths.* Paris: UNESCO, 1952.

COULANGES, FUSTEL DE. *The Ancient City.* Garden City, N.Y.: Anchor Books, Doubleday & Co., 1956.

CRONON, EDMUND DAVID. *Black Moses: The Story of Marcus Garvey and the Universal Negro Improvement Association.* Madison: University of Wisconsin Press, 1957.

COX, OLIVER C. *Caste, Class and Race: A Study in Social Dynamics.* New York: Doubleday & Co., 1948.

CULVER, D. W. *Negro Segregation in the Methodist Church.* New Haven: Yale University Press, 1953.

DAHBERG, GUNNAR. *Race, Reason and Rubbish.* New York: Columbia University Press, 1942.

DAVIS, ALLISON; GARDNER, BURLEIGH B.; and GARDNER, MARY R. *Deep South.* Chicago: University of Chicago Press, 1941.

DELANY, MARTIN R. *The Niger Valley Exploration Party.* New York: Thomas Hamilton, 1861.

DEUTSCH, M., and COLLINS, M. *Interracial Housing: A Psychological Evaluation of a Social Experiment.* Minneapolis: University of Minnesota Press, 1951.

DEXTER, HARRIET H. *What's Right with Race Relations.* New York: Harper & Bros., 1958.

DOLLARD, JOHN. *Caste and Class in a Southern Town.* Garden City, N.Y.: Anchor Books, Doubleday & Co., 1957.

DOUGLASS, FREDERICK. *Life and Times of Frederick Douglass: Written by Himself.* Hartford, Conn.: Park Publishing Co., 1882.

DRAKE, ST. CLAIR, and CAYTON, HORACE. *Black Metropolis.* New York: Harcourt, Brace & Co., 1945.

DUBOIS, W. E. B. *Darkwater, Voices from within the Veil.* New York, 1920.

———. *Color and Democracy: Colonies and Peace.* New York: Harcourt, Brace & Co., 1945.

———. *The World and Africa.* New York, 1947.

———. *Black Folk, Then and Now.* New York, 1939.

———. *Dusk of Dawn: An Essay toward an Autobiography of a Race Concept.* New York: Harcourt, Brace & Co., 1940.

———. *The Souls of Black Folk.* 7th ed. Chicago: A. C. McClurg & Co., 1907.

———. *An Appeal to the World.* New York, 1947.

DUNCAN, OTIS DUDLEY, and DUNCAN, BEVERLY. *The Negro Population of Chicago.* Chicago: University of Chicago Press, 1957.

EDWARD, FRANKLIN G. *The Negro Professional Class.* Glencoe, Ill.: Free Press, 1959.

ELLISON, RALPH. *Invisible Man.* New York: Random House, 1947.

FAUSET, ARTHUR H. *Black Gods of the Metropolis.* Philadelphia: University of Pennsylvania Press, 1944.

FORD, THEODORE P. *God Wills the Negro.* Chicago: Geographical Institute Press, 1939.

FRANKLIN, JOHN HOPE. *From Slavery to Freedom.* New York: Alfred A. Knopf, 1956.

FRAZIER, E. FRANKLIN. *Black Bourgeoisie: The Rise of a New Middle Class in the United States.* Glencoe, Ill.: Free Press, 1957.

———. *The Negro in the United States.* Rev. ed. New York: Macmillan Co., 1957.

———. *The Negro Family in the United States.* Chicago: University of Chicago Press, 1939.

GARFINKEL, HERBERT. *When Negroes March.* Glencoe, Ill.: Free Press, 1959.

GARVEY, MARCUS. *Philosophy and Opinions.* Compiled by AMY JACQUES-GARVEY. 2 vols. New York: Universal Publishing House, 1925.

GINSBERG, ELI. *The Negro Potential.* New York: Columbia University Press, 1956.

GLASS, RUTH. *London Newcomers: The West Indian Migrants.* Cambridge, Mass.: Harvard University Press, 1961.

GOLDSTEIN, N. I. *The Roots of Prejudice against the Negro in the U.S.* Boston: Boston University Press, 1948.

GRODZINS, MORTON. *The Loyal and the Disloyal: Social Boundaries of Patriotism and Treason.* Chicago: University of Chicago Press, 1956.

———. *Americans Betrayed: Politics and the Japanese Evacuation.* Chicago: University of Chicago Press, 1949.

GOSNELL, HAROLD. *Negro Politicians.* Chicago: University of Chicago Press, 1935.

HANDLIN, OSCAR. *The Newcomers: Negroes and Puerto Ricans in a Changing Metropolis.* Cambridge, Mass.: Harvard University Press, 1959.

HARLIN, HOWARD H. *John Jasper: A Case History in Leadership.* Publications of the University of Virginia, Phelp-Stokes Fellowship Papers, No. 14, 1936.

HARRIS, SARAH. *Father Divine: Holy Husband.* New York: Permabooks, Doubleday & Co., 1954.

HAYWOOD, H. *Negro Liberation.* New York: International Publishers, 1948.

HOMAN, G. C. *The Human Group*. New York: Harcourt, Brace & Co., 1950.

HERSKOVITS, MELVILLE, J. *The Myth of the Negro's Past*. New York: Harper & Bros., 1942.

HUGHES, E. C., and HUGHES, H. M. *Where People Meet: Racial and Ethnic Frontiers*. Glencoe, Ill.: Free Press, 1952.

HUSZAR, G. B. *Anatomy of Racial Intolerance*. New York: H. W. Wilson Co., 1946.

JANHEINZ, JAHN. *Muntu*. Translated by MARJORIE GREENE. London: Faber & Faber, 1961.

JOHNSON, C. S. *Patterns of Negro Segregation*. New York: Harper & Bros., 1943.

JOHNSON, JAMES WELDON. *Black Manhattan*. New York: Columbia University Press, 1956.

KARDINER, A., and OVESEY, L. *The Mark of Oppression*. New York: W. W. Norton & Co., 1951.

KING, JR., MARTIN LUTHER. *Stride toward Freedom: The Montgomery Story*. New York: Harper & Bros., 1958.

KINZER, ROBERT H., and SAGARIN, EDWARD. *The Negro in American Business: Conflict between Separatism and Integration*. New York: Greenberg, 1950.

KOHN, HANS. *The Idea of Nationalism*. New York: Macmillan Co., 1944.

———. "Dostoevsky and Danilevsky: Nationalist Messianism," *Continuity and Change in Russian and Soviet Thought*. Edited by ERNEST J. SIMMONS. Cambridge, Mass.: Harvard University Press.

LISTON, POPE. *The Kingdom beyond the Caste*. New York: Friendship Press, 1957.

LOCKE, ALAIN (ed.). *The New Negro: An Interpretation*. New York: Albert and Charles Boni, 1925.

LOHMAN, J. D. *The Police and Minority Groups*. Chicago: Park District, 1947.

MAIER, N. R. *Frustration: The Study of Behavior without a Goal*. London: McGraw Hill, 1949.

MANNHEIM, KARL. *Ideology and Utopia*. Translated by LOUIS WIRTH and EDWARD SHILS. New York: Harcourt, Brace & Co., 1936.

MAYS, BENJAMIN E. *The Negro's God as Reflected in His Literature*. Boston: Chapman & Grimes, 1938.

MAYS, BENJAMIN E., and NICHOLSON, JOSEPH. *The Negro Church*. New York: Institute of Social and Religious Research, 1933.

McKAY, CLAUDE. *A Long Way from Home*. New York: L. Furnan, 1937.

MEAD, G. H. *Mind, Self, and Society*. Chicago: University of Chicago Press, 1953.

MONTAGU, M. F. A. *Man's Most Dangerous Myth: The Fallacy of Race*. New York, 1952.

MOORE, RICHARD B. *The Name "Negro": Its Origins and Evil Use*. New York: Afroamerican Publishers, 1960.

MYRDAL, GUNNAR. *An American Dilemma*. 2 vols. New York: Harper & Bros., 1944.

NIEBUHR, REINHOLD. *Moral Man and Immoral Society: A Study in Ethics and Politics.* New York: Charles Scribner's Sons, 1960.

NWOKEOJI, A. N. *Go East Young Man.* New York: African Nationalist Pioneer Movement, n.d.

OTTLEY, ROY. *The Lonely Warrior: The Life and Times of Robert S. Abbott.* Chicago: Henry Regnery Co., 1955.

——. *New World A'Coming.* Boston: Houghton Mifflin Co., 1943.

PADMORE, GEORGE. *Pan-Africanism or Communism?* New York: Roy Publishers, 1956.

RECORD, WILSON. *The Negro and the Communist Party.* Chapel Hill: University of North Carolina Press, 1951.

REDDING, J. SAUNDERS. *The Lonesome Road: The Story of the Negro's Past in America.* Edited by LEWIS GANNETT. New York: Doubleday & Co., 1959.

——. *They Came in Chains.* Philadelphia: J. B. Lippincott Co., 1950.

RIESMAN, DAVID. *Faces in the Crowd: Individual Studies in Character and Politics.* New Haven: Yale University Press, 1952.

ROGERS, J. A. *Africa's Gift to America.* New York: Futuro Press, 1959.

ROSE, ARNOLD M. *The Negro in America.* New York: Harper & Bros., 1948.

——. *The Negro's Morale: Group Identification and Protest.* Minneapolis: University of Minneapolis Press, 1949.

ROWAN, CARL T. *South of Freedom.* New York: Alfred A. Knopf, 1952.

RUCHAMES, L. *Race, Jobs and Politics: The Story of FEPC.* New York: Columbia University Press, 1953.

SCHUYLER, GEORGE S. "The Caucasian Problem," *What the Negro Wants.* Edited by RAYFORD W. LOGAN. Chapel Hill: University of North Carolina Press, 1944.

SEWARD, GEORGE, with case studies by Marmor, Judd, M.D. *Psychotherapy and Culture Conflict.* New York: Ronald Press Co., 1956.

SIMPSON, G. E. and YINGER, J. M. *Racial and Cultural Minorities: An Analysis of Prejudice and Discrimination.* New York: Harper & Bros., 1953.

STEIN, MAURICE R. *The Eclipse of Community.* Princeton, N. J.: Princeton University Press, 1960.

SUNDKLER, BENGT G. M. *Bantu Prophets in South Africa.* London: Luttenworth Press, 1948.

SUMNER, W. G. *Folkways.* Boston: Athenaeum Press, 1906.

THOMPSON, EDGAR. *Race: Individual and Collective Behavior.* Edited by EVERETT HUGHES. Glencoe, Ill.: Free Press, 1958.

TUMIN, MELVIN M. *Desegregation: Resistance and Readiness.* Princeton, N. J.: Princeton University Press, 1958.

VANDERCOOK, JOHN W. *Tom-Tom.* New York: Harper & Bros., 1926.

WASHINGTON, BOOKER T. *Up from Slavery.* New York: A. L. Burt Co., 1901.

WATCHTOWER BIBLE and TRACT SOCIETY, INC. *New Heavens and a New Earth.* Brooklyn, N.Y., 1952.

WEAVER, R. C. *Negro Labor: A National Problem.* New York: Harcourt, Brace & Co., 1945

WEBER, MAX. *The Protestant Ethic and the Spirit of Capitalism.* Translated by TALCOTT PARSONS. New York: Charles Scribner's Sons, 1958.

———. *Ancient Judaism.* Glencoe, Ill.: Free Press, 1952.

WEIL, SIMONE. *The Need for Roots.* Translated by ARTHUR WEIL. Boston: Beacon Press, 1950.

WESLAGER, C. A. *Delaware's Forgotten Folk: The Story of Moors and Nanticokes.* Philadelphia: University of Pennsylvania Press, 1943.

WILSON, JAMES Q. *Negro Politics: The Search for Leadership.* Glencoe, Ill.: Free Press, 1960.

YINGER, J. M. *Religion in the Struggle for Power: A Study in the Sociology of Religion.* Durham, N.C.: Duke University Press, 1946.

II. ARTICLES AND PERIODICALS

ABRAHAMS, PETER. "The Meaning of Harlem," *Holiday*, June, 1960.

African News & Views (New York), May 26, 1960.

Afro-American Heritage Association (Chicago). Undated.

ALEXANDER, C. "Antipathy and Social Behavior," *American Journal of Sociology*, LI (1946), 288–92.

Amsterdam News (New York), September 12, 1959, and June 2, 1960.

ANDERSON, DAVID. "Connecticut Ends Study of Integration," *New York Times*, April 14, 1961.

BALANDIER, GEORGE. "Messianismes et nationalismes en Afrique Noire," *Cahiers internationaux de sociologie*, XIV (1953), 41–65.

BALDWIN, JAMES. "A Negro Assays the Negro Mood," *New York Times Magazine*, March 12, 1961.

BARNES, E. W. "The Mixing of Races and Social Decay," *Eugenics Review*, XLI (1949).

BELL, HOWARD H. "The Negro Emigration Movement, 1849–1854: A Phase of Negro Nationalism," *Phylon*, XX, No. 2 (1959).

BENNETT, JR., LeRONE. "The Ghost of Marcus Garvey: Interviews with the Crusaders Two Wives," *Ebony*, March, 1960.

BENYON, ERDMANN. "The Voodoo Cult among Negro Migrants in Detroit," *American Journal of Sociology*, XL, No. 3 (May, 1938).

BERNARD, J. "The Conceptualization of Intergroup Relations with Special Reference to Conflict," *Social Forces*, XXIX, No. 3 (1951).

BRINTON, C. "Individual Therapy and Collective Reform: A Historian's View," *American Journal of Orthopsychiatry*, XX (1950).

BROWN, O. C. "What Chance Freedom," *Crisis*, May, 1935.

BROWNLEE, LESTRE. "Elijah's Theme — Hate Whites," *Chicago's American*, February 29, 1960.

Chicago American, February 23 and 29, 1960.

Chicago Daily News, February 8 and April 5, 1960.

Chicago Daily Tribune, March 6, 1935.

Chicago Defender, January 11, 1959, February 22, 1960, and February 29, 1960.

Chicago New Crusader, March–September, 1960, April 1, 1961.

Chicago Sun-Times, May 12, June 23, 1960.

Christian Science Monitor, April 14, 1961.

The Citizen-Call (New York), September 24, 1960.

CLARK, K. B. "Racial Prejudice among American Minorities," *International Social Science Bulletin*, II, No. 4 (1950).

CROMWELL, JOHN W. "The Early Convention Movement," *American Negro Academy*, Occasional Paper, No. 9 (1905).

DRAKE, ST. CLAIR. "Churches and Voluntary Associations in Chicago," WPA Project, 1940. Mimeographed.

DuBois, W. E. B. "A Negro Nation within a Nation," *Current History*, June, 1935.

———. "The Conservation of Race," *The American Negro Academy*, Occasional Paper, 1897.

———. "Three Centuries of Discrimination," *Crisis*, LIV (December, 1947).

———. "Keynote Speech," Seventh Annual Conference of the All-African Student Union of the Americas, Inc., Chicago, June 18–21, 1958. Mimeographed.

ERIKSON, ERIK HOMBURGER. "The Problem of Ego Identity," *Journal of the American Psychoanalytic Association*, IV, No. 1 (1956).

The Economist (London), February 25, 1961, pp. 749–50, 752.

Evening Star (Washington, D.C.), April 22, 1959.

FARBER, M. "The Armageddon Complex: Dynamics of Opinion," *Public Opinion Quarterly*, XIV, No. 2 (1951).

FLEMMING, WALTER L. "Pap Singleton, Moses of the Colored Exodus," *American Journal of Sociology*, XV (July, 1909).

FOOTE, NELSON N. "Identification as the Basis for a Theory of Motivation," *American Sociological Review*, XVI (February, 1951).

FRAZIER, E. FRANKLIN. "What Can the American Negro Contribute to the Social Development of Africa?" *Présence Africaine: Africa as Seen by American Negroes* (Paris), 1959.

FREEDMAN, M. "Race against Time," *Phylon*, 4th Quarter, 1953.

GRODZINS, MORTON. "Metropolitan Segregation," *Scientific American*, CXCVII, No. 4 (October, 1957).

HALEY, ALEX. "Mr. Muhammad Speaks," *Reader's Digest*, March, 1960.

HARRIS, A. L. "The Negro Problem as Viewed by Negro Leaders," *Current History*, June, 1923.

Harvard Crimson (Cambridge, Mass.), March 25, 1961, pp. 1 and 3.

Herald-Dispatch (Los Angeles, Calif.), 1957–60, April 1, 1961.

The Independent, CV, No. 3760 (February 26, 1921).

IRELAND, R. "An Exploratory Study of Minority Group Membership," *Journal of Negro Education*, No. 20 (1951), pp. 164–68.

ISSACS, HAROLD R. "The American Negro and Africa: Some Notes," *Phylon*, XX, No. 3 (1959).

IVY, JAMES W. "Le Fait d'être nègre dans les Amériques," *Présence Africaine*, Nos. 24–25 (February–May, 1959).

Jet (Chicago), August 27, 1959, November 5, 1959.

JOHNSON, GUY B. "The Development of Negro Social Institutions," *American Journal of Sociology*, XL, No. 3 (May, 1938).

KANE, LAWRENCE. "Muslim Negroes Suing the State," *New York Times*, March 19, 1961, pp. 1, 46.

KIHSS, PETER. "Negro Extremists Groups Here Step Up Drive for Nationalism," *New York Times*, March 1, 1961.

LEONARD, GEORGE B. "The Second Battle of Atlanta," *Look*, April 25, 1961, pp. 31–42.

LINDEMANN, E. "Individual Hostility and Group Integration," *Human Organization*, VIII, No. 1 (1949), 5–9.

LOMAX, LOUIS E. "The Negro Revolt against 'The Negro Leaders,'" *Harper's Magazine*, June, 1960.

———. "The Act and Art of Being a Negro," *The Urbanite: Images of American Negroes*, I, No. 2 (April, 1961).

MARTIN, KINGSLEY. "The Jamaican Volcano," *New Statesman*, April 4, 1961.

MATTHEWS, MARCIA M. "The Difference between Black and White," *Saturday Evening Post*, January 16, 1960, pp. 13–147, 56.

MORGAN, THOMAS B. "The Lure of Secret Societies," *Cosmopolitan*, January, 1960.

The Moslem World & the U.S.A. (New York), August, 1956–May, 1957.

"Mr. Muhammad and His Fanatic Moslems?" *Sepia*, November, 1959.

"The Negro Leadership and a Strategy for Integration," *Liberator*, May, 1960.

New York Courier, March 25, 1961, April 16, 1961.

New York Herald Tribune, April 4, 1961.

New York Times, June 26, 1960; March 1, 1961, pp. 1 and 25; March 2, 1961, pp. 1 and 17.

Northern Virginia Sun, March 23, 1959.

PALMER, E. N. "Negro Secret Societies," *Social Forces*, XXIII, No. 2 (December, 1944).

PIERIS, R. "Caste, Ethos and Social Equilibrium," *Social Forces*, XXX, No. 4 (1952), 409–15.

Pittsburgh Courier, June, 1956–August, 1960.

"Race: The Black Supremacists," *Time*, August 10, 1959.

ROWAN, CARL T. "Has Paul Robeson Betrayed the Negro?" *Ebony*, October, 1957.

SHEPPARD, H. L. "The Negro Merchant: A Study in Anti-Semitism," *American Journal of Sociology*, CLIII, No. 2 (1947), 96–99.

SHILS, EDWARD. "Metropolis and Province in the Intellectual Community," University of Chicago, n.d. Mimeographed.

SIMPSON, G. E. "Recent Political Development in Race Relations," *Phylon*, 2d Quarter, Summer, 1958, p. 209.

South East Economist (Chicago), March 27, 1960.

SOUTH, WESLEY. "Prophet Tosses Dud Bombshell," *Chicago American*, February 20, 1960, p. 3.

Stewart's Voice (Chicago), April, 1959.

STRONG, SAMUEL. "Social Types in the Negro Community of Chicago; An Example of the Social Type Method," Unpublished Ph.D. dissertation, University of Chicago, 1940.

TEAGUE, ROBERT L. "Negroes Say Conditions in U.S. Explain Nationalists' Militancy," *New York Times*, March 2, 1961.

TURNER, R. H. "The Relative Position of the Male Negro in the Labor Force of Large American Cities," *American Socological Review*, XVI, No. 4 (1951), 524–29.

The Urbanite: Images of the American Negro (New York), March and April, 1961.

U.S. News & World Report, November 9, 1959.

WALDRON, E. D. "The New Negro Faces America," *Current History*, February, 1933.

Washington Post, April 23, 1959.

WORTHY, WILLIAM. "The Angriest Negroes," *Esquire*, February, 1961, pp. 102–5.

YINGER, MILTON J. "Breaking the Vicious Circle," *Common Ground*, Autumn, 1946, pp. 3–8.

ZYGMUNT, JOSEPH F. "Social Estrangement and Recruitment Process in a Chiliastic Movement." Unpublished Master's thesis, University of Chicago, 1953.

III. PUBLISHED AND UNPUBLISHED MATERIALS OF THE NATION OF ISLAM

Islamic News (Chicago), July 6, 1959.

Messenger Magazine (New York), I, No. 1 (1959).

"Mr. Elijah Muhammad: Biographical Sketch." Published brochure. University of Islam, Chicago, n.d.

Mr. Muhammad Speaks (New York), Nos. 1, 2, 3 (May, 1960; December, 1960; March, 1961).

Mr. Muhammad Speaks to the Black Man. Chicago: Muhammad's Temple of Islam No. 2, 1960.

MUHAMMAD, ELIJAH. "Mr. Muhammad Speaks," *Herald Dispatch* (Los Angeles), 1957–60.

———. "Mr. Muhammad Speaks," *New Crusader* (Chicago), March–September, 1960.

———. "Mr. Muhammad Speaks," *Pittsburgh Courier*, June, 1956–July, 1959.

———. *Muslim Daily Prayers*. Chicago: University of Islam, 1957.

———. "Speech," Detroit, October 20, 1958. Typewritten.

———. "Speech," Milwaukee, January 18, 1959. Typewritten.

———. "Speech," Washington, D.C., May 31, 1959. Mimeographed.

————. "Speech," Muslim Annual Convention, Chicago, 1960. Typewritten.

————. "Speech," Muslim Annual Convention, Chicago, n.d. Typewritten.

————. *The Supreme Wisdom.* 2 vols. Chicago: University of Islam, n.d.

————. *White Christian Party Attacks the Negroes Equality, Purity, Beauty, and Religion — Mr. Muhammad Defends Islam and the Negro!* Chicago: Muhammad's Temple of Islam No. 2, n.d.

————. "What We Should and Should Not Eat." Unpublished brochure. Chicago: Muhammad's Temple of Islam No. 2, n.d.

MUHAMMAD, MASTER WALLACE FARD. "Lost-Found Lessons." Unpublished pamphlet. 1934.

MUHAMMAD, WALLACE DELANEY. "Condensed Outline: Order of Meeting," Chicago, 1958. Typewritten.

Salaam; "Peace." Philadelphia: Salaam Publishing Co., 1960.

Index

Abraham, 6, 129, 130, 311
Accra Conference of Independent African States, 62 n., 139, 305
Adrine, Sister Levinia X; see X, Sister Levinia
African Lodge, 26
African Mayor, 319 n.
African Nationalist Pioneer Movement; see Movements
African personality, 62 n.
Africanus, Leo, 133 n.
Afro-American Heritage Association, 95 n., 187 n., 328
Afro-Asian Solidarity Conference, 279, 279 n., 297, 297 n.
Ahmadiyyat, 80 n., 311, 311 n., 312, 313 n., 348
Akoni, Abdul Hamid, 205 n.
Akoni, Callie Cobb, 205 n.
Al-Azhar, Mosque—University of, 76, 203, 247
Ali, Duse Mohammed, 36
Ali, Maulana Muhammad, 156
Ali, Noble Drew, 18, 43 n., 45, 46 n., 48, 63, 66, 346; fate of enterprises, 35, 167; leader of the Moors, 33–36, 60–61; see also Movements, Moorish-American Science Temple
Ali, Verlene, 226
All African Peoples Conference, 139, 279 n., 320
Allah, Brother Karriem, 68 n., 69 n., 117, 204, 247

"Allah in the Person of Master Wallace Fard Muhammad"; see Muhammad, Master Wallace Fard
Allah Temple of Islam; see Muhammad's Temple of Islam
Alliance, New Crusader-Dawud, 313–14, 316
Allen, Richard, 24
American Economic League, 50–51
American Islamic Education Society, 278
American Party of the World Union of Free Enterprise Socialists, 51–52, 52 n.; see also Rockwell, Lincoln
American Society of African Culture, 31 n., 95 n., 328
Anderson, James 3X; see 3X, Minister James
Anthony, Brother John W., 90–91, 106, 118, 247, 249
Arm, Walter, 152
Armageddon, 7, 217
Armstrong, Louise, 245
Azikiwe, Nnamdi, 204 n., 232

Baker, A. B., 49
Banda, Hastings, 232
Bandung Conference, 139, 222
Barrow, Reginald G. (Bishop), 42
Bates, Daisy, 306 n.
Batista, Fulgencio, 293 n.
Bayen, Maluke E., 49
Becker, Carl, 240
Ben-Gurion, David, 293 n.

361